Praise for]

"Are we doomed to accept history, ins̶.̶.̶.̶.̶ ̶o̶f̶ ̶c̶r̶e̶a̶t̶i̶n̶g̶ ̶i̶t̶? Clone days, routines of pain, injustice as Destiny? [Daniel Singer's] *Whose Millennium?* helps us to believe that tomorrow is not another name for today."
—Eduardo Galeano

"Magisterial in its historical sweep, fiercely democratic in its vision, *Whose Millennium?* is the thinking person's 'bridge to the 21st Century.' There *is* an alternative to rampant inequality and the corruptions of power, and— ever so modestly and persuasively—Daniel Singer points the way."
—Barbara Ehrenreich

"No one could compare with Daniel Singer as an observer of developments in contemporary Europe, and especially Eastern Europe, Italy, and France."
—Frances Fox Piven

"Till the very end Daniel Singer—despite the ravages of the 'New Philosophers' and the havoc created by the 'Humanitarian War-Makers'— remained a clear-eyed champion of socialism and internationalism. His was a penetrating and inspired understanding of humanity. His intellectual labors were devoted to promoting the cause of the voiceless and the oppressed, both in the pages of the New York liberal weekly the *Nation* and in his essays for the leftwing *Monthly Review*. He was a fine journalist and his special gift was the art of the lucid statement—never repeating himself—which may explain the fact that despite living in Paris, he had no regular column in the French press."
—Tariq Ali

"As in few human beings, there was in Daniel a 'concrete utopia,' a wonderfully self-evident trust in the capacity of men and women to be better than themselves. His own relations to his intimates, to his readers, to those who disagreed with him, fully exemplified a robust optimism of heart and spirit. He found decency in others because he had so much of it to spare in himself! . . . He never concealed from himself or from those who looked to him the darkness of the age. But hope was to Daniel common sense and the indispensable instrument of intellectual and moral clarity. If hope is the affliction of the teacher, Daniel Singer was, and will be remembered as, a great teacher."
—George Steiner

DANIEL SINGER

DESERTER from DEATH

DISPATCHES FROM WESTERN EUROPE 1950–2000

Preface by Howard Zinn

NATION BOOKS
New York

DESERTER FROM DEATH:
Dispatches from Western Europe 1950–2000

Collection copyright © 2005 Jeanne Singer
Preface copyright © 2005 Howard Zinn

Published by
Nation Books
An Imprint of Avalon Publishing Group
245 West 17th St., 11th Floor
New York, NY 10011

AVALON
publishing group incorporated

Nation Books is a co-publishing venture of the
Nation Institute and Avalon Publishing Group Incorporated.

Library of Congress Cataloging-in-Publication Data is available.

ISBN 1-56025-642-7

9 8 7 6 5 4 3 2 1

Book design by India Amos

Printed in the United States of America
Distributed by Publishers Group West

Contents

1958: THE RETURN OF CHARLES DE GAULLE

THE BATTLE OVER ALGERIA

MAI 68

ITALIAN INTERLUDES

ON INTELLECTUALS

LETTERS FROM EUROPE

DAYS OF HOPE

Editor's Note

FOUR YEARS HAVE passed since the death of the *Nation*'s European correspondent Daniel Singer. We knew then in the immediate days and months after his death that we had lost a writer whose stylistic elegance and élan was inimitable, a journalist and historian who Gore Vidal lauded for his "Balzacian eye." But as his old friend George Steiner testified, we lost something more: "[Daniel] never concealed from himself or from those who looked to him the darkness of the age. But hope was to Daniel common sense and the indispensable instrument of intellectual and moral clarity. If hope is the affliction of the teacher, Daniel Singer was, and will be remembered as, a great teacher." The content of that loss was alluded to by another friend of Daniel's, Percy Brazil, in a lovely tribute published in *Monthly Review* and reprinted at the end of this book: "Daniel's luck and the old millennium ran out together; in December 2000 he died after a year-long battle with cancer. *We are going to have to find our way in the new millennium without him.*" [italics added]

As both Steiner and Brazil attest, in times of confusion and upheaval, Daniel's voice was one of extraordinary clarity and courage, and life without Daniel has been disorienting to many of us, especially in the wake of recent world events. The book you have in your hands is a small but, we hope, fitting memorial to one of our great correspondents and a reminder of what we lost when we lost Daniel Singer. But the spirit of this book goes beyond memorial and presents the reader with a resource of hope. As Steiner said, "So intense and essential a presence leaves us only partially. Today we are left numb and diminished. But Daniel would not want that of us. There is too much left to do; there are too many mornings ahead. And at each of these, Daniel will be with us."

Deserter from Death collects Daniel's writing, from when he was a young correspondent for the *Economist* in the fifties—he helped fill his mentor Isaac Deutscher's shoes initially and then was posted to Paris to become its Paris correspondent, where he was based for well over a decade until its support of the Vietnam War led him to resign in 1970—to his years at the *Nation*, where he had been its roving European correspondent since 1980. Much of the material will be new (and a revelation) to readers, including his coverage of the Algerian crisis in the late fifties and early sixties, and the effervescent events of May '68. And even though Daniel's pieces for the *Economist* were unsigned, his voice, even his political sympathies—witness his coverage of May '68—managed to come through, even though his work there was never as "engaged" as his later work.

This collection, however, is only really a tiny incision into Daniel's body of work. Daniel's widow, Jeanne, explored the archives of the *Economist*, the *New Statesman*, and *Tribune*, among others, to collect Daniel's work. His output was enormous and because of space, we have had to be extremely selective. We have deliberately excluded his work covering Eastern Europe and Russia (with the exception of "A Haunted Journey"); we hope these will be included in a subsequent volume. Also, Daniel's radio journalism—he was a frequent commentator on the BBC as well as Pacifica Radio—is thinly represented here though Jeanne discovered some transcripts of Daniel's reporting from the Portuguese revolution of 1974 and, though some of it is fragmentary, we have published it as it gives a strong sense of Daniel's journalistic immersion in this extraordinary moment.

Readers whose appetite is whetted by this book are urged to visit *www.danielsinger.org* for more examples of his work as both a writer and broadcaster; they will also find information about the trust and prize set up in Daniel's honor.

CARL BROMLEY
Nation Books
November 2004

Preface

DANIEL SINGER'S POLITICAL consciousness spans the half-century from the Second World War to the great demonstrations in Seattle against the World Trade Organization in 1999. In this collection, we observe that consciousness at work, bringing the perspectives of history and philosophy to events of the moment.

His boyhood was a time of tumultuous, indeed, astounding change: the swallowing up of his native Poland by both Soviet Russia and Nazi Germany and the annihilation of almost all the Jews of that country, while he miraculously escaped to France and Switzerland. And then the apparently invincible German armies being stopped at the gates of Moscow, Leningrad, and Stalingrad, and being destroyed in the East while a Western front opened up in France.

Studying in England after the war, watching the division of Europe into American and Soviet spheres of influence, he began to develop the political ideas that were to mark his writings. What stands out, in his essays over the years for the *Times Literary Supplement*, the *Economist*, the *International Socialist Review*, and the *Nation*, is his rock-like refusal, in the midst of the most bitter and even violent clashes, to declare loyalty to any ideology, any party, any country.

This independence of dogma did not mean that he held no solid positions in the social struggles happening all around him. On the contrary, what stands out as you read Daniel Singer's work is his unshakeable commitment to the idea of Socialism, but a Socialism uncorrupted either by Stalinist cruelties or by liberal timidity in the face of capitalist power.

He had no use for those who called themselves "Communists" but violated the spirit of a humanistic Communism by behaving like thugs. Khrushchev's startling revelation of Stalin's crimes at the 20th Party Congress in Moscow led Togliatti and the Italian Communist Party to break with the Soviet Union. And other Communists around the world were shaken. In the United States, many members of the Communist Party left as a result of Khrushchev's speech and the invasion of Hungary later that year.

The French Communist Party, however, remained Stalinist to the core and Daniel Singer, reporting on the Party Congress in Paris that year, was biting in his criticism of the French Communist leader Maurice Thorez and characterized the French party as "the crudest" of the Stalinist parties.

Six years before, in 1950, in the *Times Literary Supplement* he had reviewed a novel by the Communist Party stalwart Louis Aragon and found it "empty and stereotyped . . . not even good propaganda." He wrote wryly: "Some efficient and orthodox party maid seems to be watching that none of his puppets escape from the respective black and white pigeon holes."

Singer stood to the left of the French Communist Party, which he concluded was not truly a revolutionary movement. He found this illustrated powerfully in the events of May–June 1968. For him, that extraordinary moment in the history of France, when students went on a nationwide strike and then were joined by the workers in an exciting display of solidarity, presented a unique opportunity for radical change.

The student cry, "*Soyez réaliste, demandez l'impossible*" ("Be realistic, demand the impossible") was betrayed by the insistence of the Communists that realism demanded stopping short of radical transformation of the system. The major trade union confederation, the CGT, dominated by the Communist Party, channeled the enormous energy of the strike into demands for higher wages. This was more "practical," more realizable, but Daniel Singer felt it was a betrayal of the spirit of revolution that flowered in the universities and in the streets that spring.

The government had been overtaken by events, and the Communist Party was overtaken on its left, which it apparently could not tolerate. Ultimately, the Communists were seen by "the rebels of Nanterre" (where the first strikes arose) as "part of the Establishment." The events of May–June 1968 exposed the weakness of the capitalist state, but that weakness was not taken advantage of. History, Singer concluded, "has no soft spot for grandchildren who keep missing their opportunities."

Despite his persistent criticism of the Soviet Union and the Communists who followed the Stalinist line, Singer never allowed that to diminish his anger against colonialism and the capitalist system. He saw France's eight-year war (1954–1962), which attempted to crush the Algerian independence movement, as "a steady poison in the French body politic."

One learned to depend on Daniel Singer's thoughtful, complex evaluation of events and individuals. When de Gaulle died in 1970, he commented, "Nothing is more sickening than the outpouring of love on funeral occasions." He recognized de Gaulle's monumental contribution in extricating France from Algeria, but also saw that the general's exalted status was "only by contrast with surrounding dwarfs."

Singer was not naive about nationalist movements for independence. He understood that they were only a first step, often violent and corrupt, toward a decent society. The Algerian revolution, from the start, he pointed out, had been a revolution from above.

If there was one insistent note in his political analysis, it was that movements for independence, peace, and social justice must be based, if they are to fulfill their moral promise, on the mass mobilization of people, and not on the leadership of an individual or a party.

Daniel Singer was unswerving in his rejection of violence carried out in the name of revolution. The Red Brigades in Italy had kidnapped the Christian Democrat Aldo Moro in 1978, and executed him fifty-five days later when their demands were not met. Singer condemned "violence by a self-appointed vanguard . . . which substitutes itself for the people." He said, "The search for a historical shortcut, gun in hand, usually leads to a dead end, and often a bloody one at that."

Here, too, his repudiation of violence by a revolutionary elite did not lessen for a moment his rejection of capitalism and the way it connected with nationalism, both historically and conceptually.

He noted, in a 1967 appraisal of André Malraux's *Antimemoires*, the descent of Malraux—who had been a flier in the Spanish Civil War and had written the remarkable novel *Man's Fate*—from internationalist to nationalist.

Malraux, Singer said, with more sadness than anger, had made the journey from fellow traveler to anti-Communist. He had once been a "man of action." Now, he was a "voyeur."

This was only one instance of intellectuals whose thought processes were so dislodged by the revelations of Stalin's crimes that they became allies of the existing order. They either turned to the Right, or they pretended to neutrality. In an article in 1983 titled "The Rise of the Nouveaux Liberals," Singer remarked, "Nothing is louder than the silence of intellectuals."

An instance of Daniel Singer's nuanced appraisal of individuals was his reaction to Jean-Paul Sartre's death, in an article, one of his last, for the *Nation* in 2000. Sartre had once been reluctant to criticize the Soviet Union, but the Soviet invasion of Hungary in 1956 offended him. The subsequent crushing of the Czech "Socialism with a human face" in 1968 caused his final break with the French Communist Party, convincing him decisively that the party was not truly revolutionary.

Sartre was, Singer recognized, a rare figure of intellectual integrity, who refused the blandishments of the bourgeois West and also the dogmatism of the Soviet Union. He had turned down the Nobel Prize for Literature. He also said that Stalinism was "incompatible with the honest exercise of the literary profession."

Daniel Singer was by his own account a "non-Jewish Jew." He could never forget the fate of Jews in Poland, from which he had barely escaped. Yet, when long after the war, the French put on trial a Nazi collaborator named René Bousquet, Singer understood that "the punishment meted out to old men like Bousquet has been irrelevant for some time." This, and other trials of collaborators, he understood, substituted for a real examination of the institutions that fostered the collaboration. Liberation from the Nazis had come, but "a veil was discreetly spread over the awkward past."

Where the past was not veiled, it was turned into something useful for the established order. In 1989, the French government celebrated the bicentennial of the French Revolution, and Daniel Singer wrote about this with delicious irony: "But the climax will come, naturally, on July 14, when French President François Mitterand will be accompanied by such iconoclastic sansculottes as George Bush, Maggie Thatcher, and Helmut Kohl—a party that appears more suited to honor Marie Antoinette than commemorate the storming of the Bastille."

Living in Paris, Daniel Singer and his wife, Jeanne, an intrepid activist, observed the rise of the anti-immigrant, racist Jean-Marie Le Pen. Writing in 1992 in the *Nation*, Singer pointed out that it was the absence of a Socialist alternative that left a vacuum into which someone like Le Pen could flourish. Lacking such an alternative, Singer wrote (with remarkable prescience, we must say, looking at the world in 2004), "the dangerous mixture of race, religion, and ethnicity" becomes dominant.

Singer found the spirit of the "rebel sixties" challenging the consumer society and "the ruling religion of growth" rising once again in the great demonstrations in Seattle in 1999 against the World Trade Organization. In his article "Seattle from the Seine" (the *Nation*, January 2000), he pointed to the simultaneous demonstration in Paris and its insistence that "the world is not a commodity."

In the events of May–June 1968, he had been uplifted by "the vision of a radically different society." Thirty years later, he still held on to that vision and wrote about a "realistic utopia." As crucial elements of this vision, he suggested a drastic reduction in labor time, a true internationalism in defiance of globalization, an equalization of wealth worldwide, and democracy—self-management—in every aspect of social life.

His faith was always in people's movements, not in electoral politics, which he called "a trap for bloody fools." He was undaunted by the failed revolutions he saw around the globe. He would have agreed with the American farmer-philosopher Wendell Berry, who said, "Be joyous, even if you know all the facts." He could believe this because he knew all the facts had not yet played themselves out. The old order, as he liked to quote Rosa Luxemburg, was "built on sand." There were imponderable, unpredictable things to come.

HOWARD ZINN
November 2004

Overture

::

A Deserter from Death

JUNE 20, 1994
The Nation

ONE OF THE first signs of old age, I'm told, is when a young woman offers you her seat on a bus (and the next stage, presumably, is when you accept it). But there is a surer proof of the passing of time: when events from your adolescence are being commemorated as ancient history—as is now the case with the fiftieth anniversary of D-day. While giving you a jolt, it also puts you in a privileged position. At a time when neo-Fascist ministers are returning to government in Europe, when creeping revisionism is gaining ground, when items from Soviet archives are cleverly selected to blur the past and convince us that Communist and Nazi, resister and collaborator, victim and executioner were all the same, it is important both to say, "No, it wasn't so," and to ponder the purpose of such manipulations.

Let it be admitted from the start that this is not the neutral testimony of an objective historian but rather the committed one of a miraculous survivor of World War II who owes his life to sinus trouble. Before the war, in the Poland of my childhood, the gap between the haves and the have-nots was huge, as it was in the rest of Eastern Europe. Thus, my father, a very successful journalist, hearing that the Mediterranean climate would be good for his youngest child's sinusitis, could afford to send me, my mother, and my sister to the French Riviera. This happened in August 1939. After the war broke out we tried to rush back home, but—second stroke of fortune—it was too late.

Not that I was untouched by the bloody conflict. Far from it. My father was sent to the gulag in distant Siberia, my older brother was killed in the battle of Tobruk and my sister jumped from a second floor in Marseilles rather than face deportation. To escape the Nazis, I had illegally crossed the border into Switzerland and on the way I mistook in the dark the greenish uniform of the Swiss for the *Feldgrau* of the Germans. After such an experience, you grow up very fast indeed. At the time that Allied troops were landing in Normandy, I was attending Calvin's high school in Geneva and treating my classmates as kids. But in another sense, I was a youth like any other, reading Rimbaud, discovering not only the surrealists but also the "surprise parties," as they were called, at which we jitterbugged to Mezz Mezzrow and smooched to "Blues in the Night"—instead of providing fodder for the gas chambers as did my aunts, uncles, and innumerable cousins.

The reactions to D-day in occupied Europe were, naturally enough, contrasting. At one extreme, among the resisters and the victims, the Allied invasion buoyed hopes and strengthened the conviction that, whatever cruel damage the enemy might still inflict, it was the beginning of the end. At the other extreme, those who had linked their fate with the *Herrenvolk* were either getting ready for a last stand or wondering how best to climb on a new bandwagon.

But what about the mass of the people in between? By 1944, any illusions they had held about the occupiers and their collaborators had long vanished. The bulk of the population was yearning for change. True, because of the understandable obsession with food, most people's aspirations were down-to-earth. But there was also a growing revulsion against the prewar regimes that had made such a conflict possible. Only by grasping that feeling can one understand why, say, young British soldiers would vote in Labor and throw out wartime leader Winston Churchill; or why the French Resistance proclaimed that the moneyed interests would never again be allowed to dominate the press. How romantically unreal it all sounds today! Actually, on D-day the initial reaction, as a French writer reminded us, was to exclaim *"les Anglais!"* because in the popular imagination Britain was the first nation to be associated with the struggle against the Nazis. The Americans' turn (whatever their actual role in the invasion) would come later. As the G.I.s spread across the liberated continent they brought with them the myth of a distant cornucopia—the magic land of nylon stockings and Glenn Miller's "In the Mood." But it was the British who, at least to begin with, symbolized defiance of fascism. Or rather, the British and the Russians.

A personal aside: Nowadays, in these silly times, even when stating an obvious fact, one must first establish one's credentials. So, let me say that I have been an anti-Stalinist almost from childhood and that my antagonism toward the Georgian tyrant, because of crimes committed in the name of Socialism, has in no way diminished. Having said that, I find preposterous the current attempts to minimize either the role of Communists in the European resistance movements after 1941 or the part played by the Red Army in the Allied victory. Military experts will tell you that the landing in Western Europe would have been quite a different story if the bulk of crack German divisions had not been bogged down in the Soviet Union. Let me simply add that for someone who lived through those years of despair and contempt in France, the moments of hope were mostly connected with news from the Eastern Front. There was a joke at the time that ran, Which town is the biggest in the world? Answer: Stalingrad. Why? Because the Germans marched and marched and marched and never got to the railway station. This witticism, based on boastful Nazi communiqués claiming their troops were advancing toward the station, sounds quaint today. But at the time it was a flash of hope in a time of gloom, an optimistic message that the arrogant enemy might not be invincible.

Unique and Comparable

After the landing came the liberation of the occupied territories and then the invasion of Germany itself. Accompanying the hour of glory was the horrifying discovery of the concentration camps with their ossuaries and their waking skeletons. Even we who lived close to the camps and were supposed to know were completely shattered by those pictures from hell, defying the imagination of a Hieronymus Bosch, and will probably be haunted by those images for the rest of our lives.

Whenever I am asked, or ask myself, what it means to be a Jew—as one who does not think of Jews as a race, who is a nonbeliever, and was not brought up in Hebrew or Yiddish culture—I find the rudiments of an answer in my relationship to those corpses. I know and fully accept the proposition that we should share our sympathy and solidarity with the victims, the exploited, the downtrodden, and humiliated without distinction of nationality, religion, or skin color. Yet, I could have ended up in that charnel house myself. I almost wrote "should have ended up," assuming, with utter irrationality, that I am a deserter from the army of the dead.

Words should be handled with care. Not every reactionary and repressive regime is Fascist. Not every horror of our time can lie equated with the Holocaust. The organized, systematic, almost scientific extermination of a people on alleged racial grounds and on such a scale seems to me to be a unique event in human history. Unique but not incomparable; quite the contrary. We are living in a crazy and increasingly dangerous world. When Jews, even if a small proportion of the whole population, can rejoice, both in public and in private, over the mad massacre of praying Palestinians; when the death of one race-car driver in the Grand Prix takes five times more space in the media than that of two hundred thousand blacks in Rwanda; when "ethnic cleansing," which one thought had been discredited forever, becomes bloody purification in the former Yugoslavia and looks highly contagious; when blood ties, once again, seem to negate all other forms of solidarity across national frontiers—when all this happens it is important to recall the Holocaust as a reminder of what humans are capable of performing and as a warning that it can happen here, there, and everywhere if we don't tackle the deadly disease from its earliest symptoms.

For historians, the past has an attraction in its own right. They wish to study events in their proper context, understand their causes and consequences. For the rest of us, the main value of history lies in the lessons it provides for our own times.

Past and Present

"We don't know yet what our past is going to be" goes the old Eastern European jest, underscoring the fact that mastery of the past is often an instrument of current struggle. Stalin was a champion at the rewriting of history, but he was not alone in this nefarious trade. Indeed, we are now witnessing in Russia (though it is probably being prompted from abroad) a vast operation involving the doctoring of documents and the manipulation of memoirs for purposes that go well beyond commercial exploitation.

Let there be no mistake: We leftists are for open diplomacy. We are in favor of the declassification of secret documents both in general and in this particular case. Although the Soviet Union should never have been a model, we can learn from its bitter experiment with Socialism—and the more we know the better. Nor should we be hostile to stern judgments on that experiment, provided they are made in a historical context (taking into account, say, foreign intervention and the White as well as the Red terror). Actually, it is only in such a historical framework that a judgment can make sense. This, incidentally, is also true of studies, fashionable in recent years, of the infatuation of Western, particularly French, intellectuals with the Soviet Union. A fascinating subject, if the authors had painted in the background: the Great Depression before the war, with millions of unemployed; the anticolonial struggle in Algeria, Vietnam, and elsewhere after the war. Otherwise it is, at best, merely a more sophisticated form of propaganda.

In other words, we are for truth, but the whole truth; for the systematic publication of documents (and not just in Russia) under the supervision of serious historians. Otherwise, you never know whether the text was tailored to suit a purchaser who wants to prove that the

Rosenbergs were guilty, that Alger Hiss was a spy. Actually, this whole campaign seems to be aiming beyond such individual targets and probably beyond the objectives of some of the participants. If we were to accept its basic premise, namely that Hitler was merely a disciple, that the real trouble started with Stalin, nay, with the Bolshevik Revolution, we would have to reappraise our whole conception of modern history.

Revisionism itself is being revised. Its cleverest practitioners have realized they could not wipe out the Holocaust; those dead millions will not vanish into thin air. But you can make light of its importance and shift the blame for it. The revisionist historians in Germany no longer deny that Martin Heidegger was a Nazi. Instead, they argue that, faced with the choice of two evils—Communism and National Socialism—he wisely chose the lesser, i.e., Nazism. In France you can't yet go as far. Nevertheless, even there a brazen attempt was made last year—with a book, a television show, a press campaign, and, naturally, a "Russian document"—to describe the leader of the Resistance on French soil, Jean Moulin, as a Soviet agent. The whole fraudulent construction was rapidly destroyed by prominent resisters and principled historians. The purpose, however, was obvious: If even the hero Moulin was a spy, Soviet or Nazi, what does it matter, *ma chère?* Whom can we trust and whom should we blame? The next stage came in Italy, where the neo-Fascist Gianfranco Fini, the chief ally of the new Prime Minister Silvio Berlusconi, proclaimed that Fascism was no longer a relevant problem and that Benito Mussolini "was the greatest statesman of the century."

History's image is growing faint not only because of the passage of time and because many of the actors are gone. It is being distorted because the political climate has changed and conscious efforts are being made to change it still further. In the circumstances, anything that refreshes the memory—books, films, trials or celebrations, and particularly anything that transmits the true image to the younger generation—is very precious. Earlier this year, the French tried seventy-nine-year-old Paul Touvier who, during the war, was chief of intelligence and operations of the Vichy militia in Lyons. What is important is not that this former executioner and still unrepentant Jew-hater was sentenced to life. What matters is that many people learned about the past from his trial and that a Frenchman was, for the first time, condemned for his participation in "crimes against humanity"; they also learned about the role of a section of the Catholic Church in hiding and protecting the culprit. Touvier, however, was a mere thug, a flunky with blood on his hands. If, as may be hoped, Maurice Papon, a more important figure, is finally brought to trial later in the year, the complicity of the French administration will be illustrated and the impact will be greater.

But aren't D-day celebrations the best opportunity of all to teach about the past, with the beaches as the stage, the television cameras focused, and the entire world as an audience? And are we not lucky to have rulers able to rise to the occasion and proclaim in our name from Normandy our revulsion from Fascist tyranny and Nazi crimes? We would be luckier still if the same honorable men were not to embrace, next month in Naples, the newcomer Berlusconi, who whitewashes Fini, who thinks that Mussolini, etc. And they do all that because our masters believe that the new regime, with its businessman boss and its Thatcherite ministers, will keep Italy safe for capitalism. The French have a good expression for their empty talk: *des paroles verbales,* "verbal words." If we say much more on the subject, we could be sued for insulting our heads of state.

But we owe it to the Americans, the Canadians, and the British who risked and in many cases lost their lives to free us from the Nazis; we owe it to all the victims and to those who fought on other fronts, particularly in Eastern Europe; I owe it to the twenty-three-year-old kid whose head was blasted by a German bullet in Tobruk and who, by a quirk, will remain my big brother forever, to say what was the true nature of their struggle. Undoubtedly, they fought to break the barbarian rule of Hitler and his thugs. They also fought so that this world war would be the last. Yet in doing so, each one in his fashion and with varying degrees of consciousness, they also battled for a different world. It is this struggle that we must carry on, or rather resume. This is our heritage on D-day as dark clouds are, once again, gathering over Europe.

In Europe,
Hope Amid the Ruins

MAY 15, 1995
The Nation

"BLISS WAS IT in that dawn to be alive, / But to be young was very heaven!" The words of Wordsworth do not fully fit, because with so much bloodshed, the stench of corpses, and skeletons, dead or alive, just discovered as Allied troops entered the concentration camps, there was hardly scope for pure joy. The reference to youth, in turn, is a warning that when one tries, half a century later, not just to reconstruct events but to revive a mood, the past may be prettified through nostalgia for one's adolescence. Yet dawn seems appropriate. We clearly did feel at the start of a new era. The very horror of the conflict may account for the revulsion and explain why the "Never more!" was even louder than in 1918. Millions of people across Europe were rejecting an old world capable of producing such pestilence. If today the fashion is to stress the end of history, at the time it was to talk of its new beginning.

This yearning for a different society prevailed throughout the continent, including Eastern Europe, which I had miraculously left on the eve of the war and where German atrocities proved even more abominable than in the West. The neighbors of the Soviet Union were in such a mood even though the soldiers of the Red Army were being greeted there as liberators cum conquerors. The intellectual conception of revolution from above—the idea that Stalin's tanks, like Napoleon's armies, brought a more advanced social order—was still to come. The relatively high spirits right after the war rested on the rather optimistic assumption that Hungary and Poland, Bulgaria and Czechoslovakia would be somehow allowed to follow their "own roads to Socialism." Such hopes were soon to be dashed by the advent of the cold war and the closing of the Iron Curtain. Today, it is common to describe the Red Army as an invader. Things were much more complex at the time. With the corruption, inefficiency, and injustice of their prewar governments still fresh in their minds and their natural hatred for the Nazis, the new deal, though imposed by the Red Army, had originally a significant degree of support among both workers and intellectuals.

But it was in Western Europe that the quest for a new social order was most perceptible. The role played by the battle of Stalingrad in our imagination or the part performed by the Communists in the Resistance did not, by themselves, explain the big jump in the Communist vote in both France and Italy. To grasp the reason for that, or for the victory of the British Labor Party in the first parliamentary poll after the conflict, which ousted the war hero Winston Churchill, it is necessary to recapture the climate of public opinion during the period, with its wholesale rejection of greed, exploitation, and inequality. On the continent, fighters emerging from the underground were preaching that property could no longer stand in the way of social justice and that money should no longer be allowed to dominate the press. In Britain, if my memory is correct, *The Economist*, the voice of the capitalist gospel, was advocating a zero rate of interest. How distant and strange it all sounds now, and how revealing about the unsuspected flexibility and resilience of capitalism.

Why was that system not pushed off the stage? Propagandists who now tell the story should, paradoxically, pay some tribute to the Soviet leader, then known not as a tyrant but as good old "Uncle Joe." The German surrender took place three months after the conference at Yalta, where the division of Europe was confirmed. The deal meant that within a few years Stalinism would extend to the Elbe. But it also guaranteed stability for the other half of Europe and Stalin stuck strictly to his side of the bargain: Greek Communists facing the British were left to their own devices, while the large Italian and French party battalions were ordered to consolidate their positions without threatening the established order.

Naturally, it was not Stalin alone. The real reason for the system's survival was the American presence in its dual capacity as a provider of force and as a force of attraction. The G.I.s were staying behind as insurance against the temptation for any Western partisans to follow in Tito's footsteps and seize power. But America, with its skyscrapers and its Ford cars, was also a mythical country. The way we eyed your cigarettes and chewing gum, your nylon stockings and Parker 51 pens, was a portent, foreshadowing Europe's rush toward an acquisitive consumer society.

What happened need not necessarily have happened, and it may be rather harsh to call us fools because we dreamt in that dawn of a different future. We may have been starry-eyed and rather naive if we thought that somebody would build that society for us, that it was enough to give a mandate or, even worse, a free hand to our new masters. Inevitably obsessed with Nazism, we may have been too one-track-minded. Thus absorbed by the little flags on the map showing the movement of armies, we may have failed to discern the social forces that would shape fate beyond the battlefield. Personally, I must confess that three months after the German surrender I completely missed the historical significance of the atom bomb dropped on Hiroshima. I just did not understand at the time the momentous step taken by humankind on the road toward potential suicide. I, probably, did not even see that the dropping of the bomb was already a move connected with the coming cold war. Indeed, the mood of 1945 is so difficult to assess accurately because it was a year of transition, with the people still inspired by the wartime alliance against Germany and the politicians already preparing for the new East-West confrontation.

We don't know yet what our past is going to be, says the wit, reminding us that history is rewritten to suit the current predicament. Since the collapse of the post-Stalinist empire, the victors are dictating the line. With texts strangely filtered from the Soviet archives, they are trying to invent a new tale of wartime Europe, in which those who helped the Anglo-Saxons are heroes and those who helped the Russians are fools or knaves. Nothing, except the insidious poison of propaganda, compels us to swallow such a distortion.

Indeed, on this anniversary occasion, I would be tempted to draw only two lessons. The first is that revolutions—meaning the radical transformation of society, not the seizure of the Winter Palace—cannot be carried out from above; if they are, they spell nothing good for the people. Or, to put it differently, they cannot be carried out by proxy. A deal at the top, like the one at Yalta, hampered the social movements on both sides of the great divide. Our rulers yield only to pressure from below and no genuine long-term progress can be conceived without the active participation of the people.

The second lesson concerns history. If it is ridiculous to proclaim its end today, it was childish for us to think we were starting almost from scratch; we underestimated the weight of the past, the power of inertia and the resistance of the mighty. True, there are moments when history quickens, and if you miss them you may have to wait a long time for the next opportunity. Yet it is in the intervals that you must prepare so as to be ready for the climax. The struggle is, or rather should be, permanent.

Recalling the Europe of half a century ago, bled white, half-starving, with its towns torn apart and its factories blown to pieces, and setting it against our world with its computerized plants, its laser beams, its rockets to the moon and information highways, there is no denying the technological inventiveness of the human species. The more striking is the contrast with the lunacy of our social organization. Mass unemployment, the yawning gap between rich and poor, the explosive polarization, all show that, after a spell of progress, we are moving backward toward a dangerous past. Add to it wars spreading from Algeria to Chechnya and Tajikistan, "ethnic cleansing" from Europe to Africa, and the return of the earlier horror is no longer unthinkable. We have to wake up, and soon, if we don't want the millions who perished in the last world war, and who did so fighting fundamentally for a better world, to have died in vain.

POSTSCRIPT

I wrote earlier that we in Europe may have been too one-track-minded. Let this anecdote plead our case.

It was the autumn of 1942. A French train was nearing Switzerland, approaching Vallorcines, the last stop before the frontier, where we were to contact a priest who knew the way through the mountains. We were two in the empty carriage: My companion, old enough to attend university, had a foreign accent and had to keep quiet, but I, still a schoolboy, fortunately spoke French like a native. In fact, there was a third person, the conductor, who came close, looked me in the eyes and asked bluntly: "Are you going over?" I had a few seconds to decide how to gamble our lives. "Yes," I answered. "Fine. I'll tell the driver to stop the train before the station so that you can get off in the field. The station today is packed with policemen."

No wonder that now I am rather allergic to the increasingly fashionable versions of history, which, conjuring up the "Red peril" and the "Bolshevik menace," do not whitewash Nazism, but find all sorts of excuses for various shades of collaboration. If the conductor and engineer of that train had not been on the side of the Resistance—who knows, maybe Communists—I would not be here to tell the story.

On Nationalism

JULY 15 AND 22, 1991
The Nation

BORN IN ONE country, brought up in another, living and working in a third, I am what used to be known as a "rootless and passportless cosmopolitan," except that I have a British passport. Since I am also, unfashionably, a great admirer of Rosa Luxemburg, anything that is nationalist should be alien to me and I should be the last person to preach on the subject.

If I nevertheless had to proclaim a patriotic objective, I would define it as follows: to turn one's country into such a society of freedom, equality, and social justice that it would influence others by its example. The inevitable transcending of frontiers would thus not be the result of a "world order" imposed from above and abroad but a gradual construction by the associate producers first on the national and then on the international scale. Two points must be mentioned. The nation-state may be historically doomed, yet it still provides the first stage for the radical transformation of society. Second, the universal, toward which we tend and which corresponds to the economic and ecological needs of our planet, should in no way clash with differences in language, culture, and civilization. Instead of suppressing them, it must thrive on differences. But for the time being, as patriotism stands for the negation of the other, for oppression and for military parades, I can only repeat Rimbaud's words: *"Ma patrie se lève, j'aime mieux la voir assise"* or, roughly, "My country stands tall, I prefer it seated."

A Haunted Journey

SEPTEMBER 27, 1999
The Nation

*After the war life will begin to stir once again, but we won't
be here, we will have vanished just as the Aztecs have
vanished.*

—Vasily Grossman, *Life and Fate*

NALEWKI, NOWOLIPIE, NOWOLIPKI—the names are the
same, but the streets are not. It is like visiting a haunted city. Here
once stood the bustling, overcrowded, colorful Jewish district of Warsaw,
the heart of *Yiddishkeit*, the world center of Jewish intellectual and political life. Now it is a plain, unexceptional, reconstructed part of the Polish capital. The Jews have vanished in Poland, but anti-Semitism has not.

Is this contemporary anti-Semitism just a remnant of the past? Or
does this search for scapegoats reflect a deeper sickness? And does the
fact that a whole community—one-tenth of the total Polish population—was exterminated here, amid what some call outside indifference, weigh on the Polish conscience? Anti-Semitism is a Polish
problem. How serious it is remains to be seen, though the outside
world would not pay so much attention if it had not survived here in
the shadow of the Shoah.

There is a personal aspect to my trip. I was born in Warsaw. If it had
not been for a stroke of luck—a doctor recommended the Mediterranean climate for my sinus trouble and my father, a successful journalist, was able to send me, my sister, and my mother to the French
Riviera in the summer of 1939—I probably would have followed the
bulk of both my parents' families to the gas chambers of Treblinka. I

nearly wrote *"should* have followed," since I quite often see myself as a deserter from death. Thus, what started as an inquiry into anti-Semitism without Jews turned, inevitably, into a journey back into childhood and a pilgrimage from the Warsaw ghetto through Krakow's Kazimierz to Auschwitz in search of a vanished people.

REMNANTS OF A PEOPLE

One of the first things you learn as a child and that sticks in your mind is your address. Nowolipie 3, Apartment 3. I had no difficulty finding the place, even though it bore no resemblance to the original. I was not surprised. In 1947, as a student in England, I did go back. Warsaw was badly battered, its Old Town in ruins, but the ghetto was reduced to rubble, literally razed, with only the skeleton of a Catholic church left standing, a sinister and unforgettable sight. It is on top of that rubble that they put up new houses—at first, big gray slabs, blocks of flats hastily built to absorb the homeless; then, more comfortable accommodations. This new section of the town was built with the ruins of the ghetto as its foundation.

Although we moved away from the ghetto when I was a child, I used to go back there on Sundays with my father to buy herring, pickles, and various kinds of kosher charcuterie. My most striking memory is of a multitude of people. More than three hundred fifty thousand Jews lived in Warsaw, roughly one-third of the city's population, and most of them were packed into that district. There were tailors, cobblers, and watchmakers. There were shops galore, some with windows displaying luxuries, many of them mere stalls. There were a few wealthy financiers and lots of *luftmenschen* tossed about by the Depression. There were Hasidim in their religious garb and atheists; Zionists dreaming of a homeland in Palestine and Bundists determined to build a national future with the proletariat from crafts and light industry; Stalinists and Trotskyists. Yiddish was the dominant tongue. Two daily papers were published in that language and one in Polish. There was a famous theater, with Ida Kaminska as its star. There was politics and philosophy, poetry and passion. All this was wiped out in less than four years.

The figures speak for themselves: Jews represented about one-tenth of Poland's prewar population of some thirty-five million (and well over a quarter of town dwellers). After the Holocaust, even if we include among them those who survived in the Soviet Union, only about three hundred thousand were left. More than nine-tenths of Polish Jews had perished, and most of the survivors did not stay in Poland. A first wave left the country, amid the insecurity of a virtual civil war, after a pogrom in Kielce on July 4, 1946. A second wave followed in 1968, when Wladyslaw Gomulka, the Communist leader, allowed General Mieczyslaw Moczar to turn the "anti-Zionist" campaign into a purge of the Jews. ("This," I heard several times, was "the moral end of Communism.")

How many Jews are left today? Stan Krajewski, co-chairman of the Polish Council of Christians and Jews, puts the number registered at a maximum of six thousand. Even if you add those who hid under an assumed non-Jewish name during the war and kept the new identity, you're still left with twenty-five thousand to thirty thousand at most, an insignificant figure when set against a total population of forty million.

Among those born after the war, the consciousness of being Jewish has often come only recently. Krajewski, who at the end of a sophisticated argument puts on a yarmulke and says a prayer in Hebrew, is the great-grandson of Adolf Warski, Rosa Luxemburg's companion, that is to say, a fourth-generation atheist. Konstanty Gebert, who under the pen name Warszawski was a prominent writer for Solidarity, now devotes most of his time to editing *Midrasz*, a Jewish monthly published in Polish. Gebert's father was co-founder of the American Communist Party. Disliking the term "born-again Jews," they prefer the neologism "disassimilated." On the other hand, Bella Szwarcman, a *Midrasz* editor, had a Jewish upbringing; her world collapsed in 1968, when most of her Jewish friends emigrated. Jakob Gutelman, a respected scientist, is president of Children of the Holocaust, those who survived in the camps or in hiding. There are seven hundred members, including a Catholic priest. As we talk, those from a younger generation, grandchildren of the Holocaust, come into his office with their problems.

All these people are not asking for much. They want to live as Polish citizens with their own religion and culture and, possibly, the recognition that difference is an asset, not a threat. Their efforts to preserve their Jewishness against the odds are moving. They should be helped. A new law requiring the restitution of prewar property to religious and ethnic communities may provide some funds to restore the Jewish heritage, notably the badly neglected cemeteries (the one in Warsaw has improved somewhat, thanks to the efforts of American Jews of Polish origin, though there is still plenty to be done). But the survivors, for all their laudable efforts, can be no more than keepers of a shrine. The lively community that once irrigated and inspired Jewish life the world over is dead and will not be resurrected.

THE VIRGIN MARY IS POLISH

Its object having disappeared, the resentment remains. You can read it scribbled on the walls. Next to the cemetery, on a monument to Jewish and Polish victims, one sees the weirdly bilingual phrase *Juif Raus* ("Jews Get Out"). Elsewhere, an insult for a soccer team someone dislikes: *Legia=Zydy* (best rendered as "Knicks=Kikes"). You can find it, less crudely stated, in the press of the extreme Right. Seeking an anti-Semite ready to talk, I visited the weekly *Mysl Polska,* which in one of its stories had described the removal of the crosses outside Auschwitz before the Pope's visit as "a shame imposed on the Polish nation, on God's people." When we met, the editor did not come up to expectations. He spoke of foreign Jewish pressure in most diplomatic tones.

There are more subtle symptoms, like the reluctance of the Catholic hierarchy to disown Father Henryk Jankowski, a Gdansk priest, after he proclaimed that "the Jewish minority should not be accepted in our government," and the fact, mentioned by many, that anti-Semitic remarks do not make you the odd man out in polite society. There is also the more worrisome success of Radio Maryja, with an audience of three to four million, which allows its talk-show participants to preach that Poland is being endangered by a Jewish-inspired international plot.

Xenophobia, although never justified, may have its reason. Historically, to the Polish peasants the Jew was the representative of money in the countryside and, quite often, the servant of the exploiting landlord. In the towns, Jewish dominance of trade could be, and was, utilized as a bait to mobilize the Polish middle class. But what reason can one find for passionate attacks on a remnant representing less than a tenth of 1 percent of the population?

Let us dismiss at once the argument most often heard: that anti-Semitism survived because of the large number of Jews in the Communist leadership. It is not at all surprising that oppressed Jews, seeking equality, were attracted by a universalist doctrine stressing class as opposed to race or nation, and that their proportion in the C.P. was higher than in the general population. Since the leadership after the war was brought back from Moscow, it reflected this prewar proportion. But one should not confuse cause and pretext. I recall, while touring the United States in 1982 for Solidarity, speaking at a meeting in Amherst, Massachusetts. Some Jewish students there argued, Why bother about Poles, who are all anti-Semites? One of a group of Polish farmers protested, No, we simply hate Reds, and he rolled off the names Berman, Minc, and other Jews in the leadership. With the mike at my disposal, it was easy to answer, "You may hate Reds or capitalists, but in the latter case, if you always mention the Rothschilds and never the Rockefellers, there is a sneaking suspicion that you are anti-Semitic."

Before the war, a key source of anti-Semitism was a reactionary Catholic Church dominating a backward, predominantly rural country. I remember discovering from my friends in the countryside that Jesus was a Pole, because you were either Jewish or Polish, and Christ clearly could not be a Jew. I now hear, from a progressive priest, a more up-to-date version: The Poles have resigned themselves to the idea that Jesus was a Jew, but not the Virgin Mary. What role does the church play now?

I arrived in Warsaw on the day of the Pope's departure, just in time to see the celebration of his cult: a huge cross dominating Warsaw's main square (now renamed after Marshal Joseph Pilsudski), with banners everywhere. The one next to my hotel claimed, "Without Jesus you can't understand either this nation or this town." The church is stronger than I thought, though the hierarchy is perturbed by modern cultural trends threatening its hold, particularly on the young. On the Jewish question, I am assured, things have somewhat improved since the declaration by John Paul II that "anti-Semitism, like all forms of racism, is a sin against God and humankind." The tolerant wing of the hierarchy has gained some ground, though, judging by its conduct in the unending confrontation over the Auschwitz crosses and in the Jankowski case, there are still plenty of sinners within the Polish church from the lowest clergy to the cardinal at the very top.

According to sociological studies and polls, the church's traditional anti-Semitism, based on the teaching that "the Jews murdered Christ," is declining and survives mainly in rural areas and among the old and uneducated. In the cities the prevailing prejudice is against Jews as masters of finance, plotting to dominate the world. The Jew is a scapegoat—in the famous words of August Bebel, anti-Semitism is the "Socialism of fools." The industrial workers, who rightly feel that as members of Solidarity they were the prime movers in the country's political transformation, have discovered that they are the main victims of the transition to capitalism. The peasants fear that Poland's entry into the European Union, with its more efficient farming methods, will mean their elimination. Since the blame for such bitter disappointments cannot be put on "our own people," it is attributed to outsiders, and the Jew is still the symbol of the alien, the foreign exploiter. During my brief stay in Poland, twenty thousand striking nurses paralyzed Warsaw, and fired workers from Radom fought a bloody battle with the police in the capital. These samples of discontent were a counterpoint to the fashionable stories about a splendid, painless transition.

In fact, the target is an imaginary figure. According to Adam Michnik (a leader of Solidarity in the eighties, now editor of the daily *Gazeta Wyborcza*), the classic anti-Semite argued that if you are a Jew, you must be a villain. The new anti-Semite says: Because you are a villain, you must be a Jew. Thus, the scope for invention is unlimited. Indeed, if you took at their face value the slimy leaflets pretending to "reveal" the alleged real Jewish names of people pretending to be "true Poles," you would conclude that anybody who mattered in Poland—President Aleksander Kwasniewski, Lech Walesa, even the Pope—was a Jew. It's no wonder that when they are asked by pollsters to estimate the number of Jews in Poland, over a fifth of all Poles say more than half a million, and quite a few say five million.

Many more explanations of the survival of anti-Semitism have been offered. One is that since there was no collaboration with the Germans in Poland, the anti-Semites were not as discredited as in Western Europe, and soon after the war it became patriotic to resist "Jewish Communism." Poles complain that, singling out the Shoah, Jews have played down other victims, among them three million Poles. Poland used to be known as "the Christ of nations," and you hear the refrain about the difficulty of having two martyred nations, two chosen people. Clearly, more than half a century after the war, the Poles will finally have to face the fact that, whatever their own sufferings, a deeper tragedy was enacted under their eyes.

While traveling, I devoured in one night a small book titled *Ghastly Decade 1939–1948* by Jan Tomasz Gross, who now teaches at New York University. What shook me were extracts from the diary of a decent Polish doctor describing terrible days in a small town called Szczebrzeszyn. The diary reveals that in the shtetl there, as in so many others, most of the Jews were not killed after deportation or behind walls; they were massacred in full view of their Polish neighbors. Some denounced Jews trying to escape; others grabbed the spoils.

Let there be no mistake: The extermination of the Jews was the work of the Germans, or rather the Nazis; to come to the rescue of Jews in Poland was to risk the death penalty for your whole family, and you cannot expect a nation to be made up of heroes. But there is a difference between heroism, indifference, and open hostility, illustrated by such despicable comments as "Hitler is a bastard, but he is solving our

Jewish problem." Since amnesia is a disease for nations as well as individuals, Gross is right in arguing that the Poles must dig into their past to understand why the coexistence of the two communities ended in such a horrible fashion.

Everyone examines the world through his own prism. I emerged from the ghetto as a child and moved to the district of Zoliborz, with its progressive school and socialist environment. Most of my friends were not Jewish, and I had no problems, though I knew about anti-Semitism, about shops displaying a sign saying "Christian" (i.e., not owned by Jews), about Jewish students forced to sit on separate benches at the university or being beaten up by Fascist thugs. But I thought at the time that the Right was anti-Semitic and that the Left, on the whole, was not; despite General Moczar's 1968 purge, I still think I was fundamentally correct. It was a question of Left and Right. I know too many Poles who are beyond reproach on this issue to indulge in generalizations, and whenever I feel that I am beginning to oversimplify, I recall a personal episode showing the full complexity of the issue.

The families of both my parents, as I said, were wiped out—with one major exception. A wealthy uncle managed to immigrate early on, through Japan to Palestine. He took his sons and sons-in-law with him, leaving the wives and children behind on the naive assumption that even the Nazis would not harm women and children. When it became obvious that the ghetto was doomed, two of his grandchildren were handed over to the black-market partner of my uncle's Gentile chauffeur. The man, an adventurer who belonged to an anti-Semitic group, thought he was making a good investment: The gratitude of the man of wealth would, after the war, insure his future. What started as a calculation turned into a splendid tale of love. He came to cherish his two new children like the two he already had. But to keep them permanently concealed was a perilous, nerve-racking business. At one stage, one of the boys needed an operation. How do you take a legally nonexistent patient to the hospital? Money can work wonders, and our adventurer sold his apartment to perform the miracle.

Unique and Comparable

I am reminded of wartime relations as I drink coffee in Krakow's beautiful central square with Jan Blonski, professor of literature at the local university, whose comments on Polish attitudes toward murdered Jews provoked a nationalist backlash in 1986. He was brought up, like myself, in Zoliborz. It was there that, as a ten-year-old, he saw emerging from the sewers two Jewish boys, one his age, one younger, looking bewildered at the bright world outside. He knew he couldn't really help them and felt relieved that somehow he was not responsible; now he is ashamed of that feeling and has tears in his eyes as he recalls that scene.

Blonski is rather optimistic. In time, he thinks, prejudice may disappear. His students are not at all anti-Semitic and are genuinely interested in their country's Jewish past. This last point is confirmed by my subsequent appointment with Janina Rogozik, who has just completed a six-hundred-page doctoral thesis on my father, who wrote in both Polish and Yiddish. Rogozik, fascinated by this Jewish writer, proves so devoutly Catholic that, on a Friday, we must search for a place where she can find a meatless meal.

Krakow has not been destroyed like the Polish capital, and the Jewish district, Kazimierz, is also standing. Indeed, its most attractive square, with its four synagogues and cemetery, is beginning to look too commercial. One sign offers "*Schindler's List* Tours." I have fewer recollections from childhood here and am glad to be taken around by Raphael Scharf, who left the city for London on the eve of the war but comes back regularly to help the enterprising Center for Jewish Culture. He shows me where the more than sixty thousand Jews, accounting for a quarter of the town's population, used to live. He confirms that Remuh Cemetery is the place where Trotsky's biographer, my friend Isaac Deutscher, ate a pork sausage as a youngster on the Day of Atonement atop the tomb of a famous *tzaddik* and, having thus tremblingly defied Jehovah, emerged an atheist. As priests and rabbis clash over the heritage, this is a useful reminder that among the victims very many were not religious and quite a few, to use the term Deutscher coined, were "non-Jewish Jews."

The district is there, but there are almost no Jews. I probably saw most of them attending a concert at the center and, on another day, a painful exhibition of photographs and films at the former Isaac's Synagogue. The exhibit's purpose was to contrast the life of the Jews before the war with their subsequent agony, drawing on material found in SS and Gestapo archives. Notably, there were two poorly edited films, on the Warsaw ghetto and on deportations, which were at once nearly incomprehensible and awe-inspiring. You saw an unending stream of Jews running from the doorway of an unidentified building. Then, helpless and hopeless, they climbed into trucks and apparently paid a fee for their ultimate journey. There was also a scene showing their arrival in a camp and a Nazi officer with a gesture of his thumb deciding their fate: to the gas chamber or to work, that is to say, provisional survival. That evening, I crossed the Vistula to Harmony Square, now renamed the Heroes of the Ghetto. It had been the starting point for deportations to Plaszczow camp, which is within walking distance. All this was appropriate preparation for the inevitable final stage of this trip: Oswiecim.

Saturday was sunny and the bus comfortable (they hadn't traveled like this). On the way we glimpsed Monowice, a camp providing slave labor for the German chemical concern IG Farben; it was an important element of this concentration complex. Auschwitz is both familiar, with the notorious sign proclaiming *Arbeit Macht Frei* on its gate, and puzzling: The expected train platform and the wooden barracks are not here but a couple of miles away at Birkenau, or Auschwitz II. In Auschwitz I the buildings are of solid brick; originally they were Polish Army barracks. At first, the camp was for political prisoners, mainly Poles. You can see pictures of these early victims, with dates of entry and death recorded with German precision; some lasted ten months, most only a couple. It was only after 1942, when the decision was made to exterminate all Jews, that the camp was expanded, Birkenau built up, and the death factory began to function at full capacity.

Today, Auschwitz I is a museum for our memory, which each one perceives through his own sensibility. I was less affected by such horrors as the punishment cells, where prisoners often died of suffocation, and the execution ground, with its death wall. Even in the gas chamber, in which two thousand people could be put to death in less than half an hour, my imagination was not quite up to it. But I was shattered when I looked at those terrible masterpieces of twentieth-century art, the showcases with the remnant possessions of the dead. Not the hair for textiles or the gold from teeth for ingots, but everyday objects: brushes, spectacles, suitcases, shoes for kids and adults, and, to crown it all, because the victims believed or fooled themselves that they were being "resettled," a *humanité morte,* an extraordinary bric-a-brac of kitchen utensils, saucepans, washbowls. My eye was irresistibly drawn to a small child's chamber pot.

When you exit Auschwitz I, the skirmishes over crosses pale into insignificance (while I was in Warsaw there was a storm in a teapot because the outgoing chief rabbi had, in rather broken Polish, asked "Mister Pope" to remove the crosses from Auschwitz). Indeed, it took some time in neighboring Birkenau to realize that this really was the main terrain of mass extermination. Then you become aware of the space—about 425 square acres, in which some one hundred thousand people would be crammed at one time. There are the wooden barracks, copies of German stables, each with eight hundred humans instead of fifty-two horses; there are the latrines, which were fantastic carriers of germs. Disease, exhaustion, and starvation competed for victims with the gas chambers and the four crematoriums. The Germans, unusually, did not leave precise accounts of the manner of death. For Auschwitz as a whole, the dead are estimated at more than eighty thousand Poles, twenty-one thousand Gypsies (killed, like the Jews, because they were Gypsies), twelve thousand Soviet prisoners of war, and more than a million Jews from all over Europe. In my mind, one child's chamber pot captured the horror, the rational madness of the twentieth century, far better than these bare figures.

The point has been reached to draw conclusions. Polish anti-Semitism may be revived for a while if the law requiring restitution of prewar property, which has not yet been passed, is carried out on a wide scale and if wealthy American Jews then give the impression through their pressure that they are powerful enough to bully anybody into obedience. But, in any case, it is now a passion without object and a symptom rather than the disease. For Poland, as for the other countries of Eastern Europe, the politicians must decide whether they will provide progressive, rational solutions for the bulk of their population, and not only for the wealthy few; or, failing that, whether they will try to channel popular discontent against scapegoats.

For me, this pilgrimage has provided an answer to the difficult question: What does it mean today to be a Jew when you are not religious, do not believe Jews are a race, and do not have, as my parents did, real roots in a Jewish language and culture (a culture that, incidentally, is dying out together with its Polish source)? My deep links are with the dead whose ashes are interred here. But this should not be interpreted in any nationalistic fashion. The heritage I claim is that of standing on the side of the victims, of the downtrodden, of the exploited, whatever their color or passport, black, white, or yellow, Palestinian or Jew. The only difference is that I might have—should have?—died in the Warsaw ghetto or in Treblinka.

From the personal to the political. It is good that analytical light is now being applied to the Shoah business and to the political manipulation of the Holocaust. Take just the latest example: However much sympathy the uprooted Kosovars deserved, to compare them to the Jews and liken that minor scoundrel Milosevic to Hitler was simply a way to blackmail the critics of the "just war" into silence. Viewed from Auschwitz it was, to put it mildly, indecent. This does not mean that the Holocaust should be treated in splendid isolation. I always thought that it was at once unique and comparable. It is unique in its scientific organization, in its ruthless, systematic, and successful annihilation of a people, a "race." But it is also a warning, a call for comparison. We must now look at every situation with the permanent knowledge at the back of our minds that, if we are not careful, humankind can descend to unbelievable depths. Racism, xenophobia, anti-Semitism, are the curses, the maledictions, of our age. When you cast somebody out because he is other, different, alien, when you raise ethnicity to a political religion, you start on a slippery road that, we now know, can lead to hell on earth.

Passersby, if you stop in Warsaw, take time to proceed along what is called the Memory Lane, where the last Jewish fighters perished along with a dying world. They entrusted us with the task unfinished, nay, scarcely begun, of building a different world, in which such atrocities will be genuinely unthinkable.

From Our Paris Correspondent

::

France's Worker-Priests

MARCH 13, 1954

The Economist

THE DISPUTE BETWEEN the Catholic Church and its eldest daughter over the worker-priests has evoked a strong echo even outside the family circle. It is a tribute to the importance of the Roman Catholic Church that any dispute within it is likely to be scrutinized almost as intensely as a quarrel in the Kremlin. The affair of the French worker-priests, however, may have been over-dramatized since the Vatican's interference has provoked the resentment of the most articulate group among the French Catholics, the intellectuals and writers. It is exciting but rash to represent these differences as a revival of the old tug of war between the Vatican and the Gallican Church and to speak of an impending schism. On the other hand, the problem of the worker-priests undoubtedly goes to the heart of the most vital issue that the Church must face in the twentieth century—its relationship with the laboring masses which find themselves outside the pale of Christianity.

The French experiment, which the Vatican now tries to limit within defined narrow frontiers, began some twelve years ago when two young *abbés* published a book describing France as a land in need of missionaries to penetrate the eight-million-strong "heathen-world" of the factories. With Cardinal Suhard's backing, a *Mission de France* was founded at Lisieux, soon to be followed by a *Mission de Paris*. Both seminars prepared priests to work and live with the laboring classes. The idea behind this venture was the simple one that, in order to recover the lost souls of the forgotten men, it was necessary to get on terms with them as individuals; the missionary must contrive to become accepted as an equal by the dechristianised masses whom he was trying to convert; he must cease to be a part of a different order, cease to be one of "them."

The venture had its risks and among the priests laboring and living with the workers, many have joined in the political struggle of their brethren and a few have defected to Communism. This unfortunate example was given publicity on the occasion of the anti-Ridgway riots in Paris two years ago, when among the arrested there were some worker-priests. During last year's strikes, too, in several regions priests expressed their solidarity with the strikers. For some time warnings have been pouring into the Vatican that the Communist Manifesto was becoming the new gospel of the worker-priests; as early as 1951 French bishops were ordered not to increase their numbers.

BARRIER OF MISTRUST

The Vatican's remedy, now obediently if not wholeheartedly endorsed by the French hierarchy, was to insist that worker-priests must fish for souls with a shorter line; they must work no more than a given number of hours a day and no longer be so far removed from their religious communities and spiritual supervisors. The accent is to be on the priest rather than on the worker. The Church authorities maintain that this is no more than a matter of adjustment in an admittedly difficult situation. On the other hand the opponents of the Vatican's policy argue that the new regulations strike at the root of the whole experiment since "visiting" priests will not be able to break the barrier of mistrust among the often anticlerical masses, and without "naturalization" they will not even get a hearing. Indeed, it is hinted that in forbidding full-time participation in the workers' life the Vatican implicitly accepts the Marxist premise that one's outlook is really determined by the conditions of life and labor.

The anxious protests to which the new course has given rise in many Catholic quarters are both sincere and moving, but a breach within the Church is unlikely. It is not yet known how many worker-priests will defy the ultimatum to accept their new status, but for the Roman Catholics, there is no salvation outside the Church and a splinter group has little chance of survival. It is on the political stage that the present quarrel may have grave repercussions. In the inter-war period the threat of Gallicanism came from the nationalist right-wing connection with *l'Action Française*. This time the outburst against the Vatican was strongest among left-wing Catholic circles. True, Dominican intellectuals have expressed their sympathy and M. François Mauriac has written beautiful pages of restrained indignation in the undoubtedly respectable *Le Figaro*, but the main backing for the worker-priests came from the very same groups which are protesting against the swing to the right of the Catholic political party, the MRP. Both the MRP and the worker-priest movement were born out of the Resistance at a time when many thought that the Catholic movement would prove the vanguard of social progress. They now accuse the Church and its political party of betraying its mission.

Clearly the Roman Catholic Church, like most bodies, has its conservative and its liberal wings and it looks as though the conservative traditionalists have gained a point or two at the expense of their more progressive and adventurous colleagues. Meanwhile, the problem which gave rise to all this remains: the problem of offering the very poor something more attractive than Communism. While it is for the Church to decide the best possible way for it to proceed, outsiders have a stake in its success or failure. The Abbé Godin, one of the founders of the worker-priest movement, proclaimed: "They [the Vatican] are at the brakes. We are the engine. The two are needed . . ." It remains to be seen whether the machine can still move forward with the newly tightened brakes.

M. Poujade Goes to Town

March 26, 1955
The Economist

LAST WEEK THE world saw the sad spectacle of a French Chamber of Deputies most of whose members seemed to be mesmerized by an uncouth demagogue sitting with his acolytes in the public gallery. The incident gave a striking illustration of French parliamentary weakness. Frenchmen know well that on many other occasions powerful lobbies and pressure groups have dictated the course of voting. Never, however, has the pressure been so undisguised as last week, when many right-wing deputies seemed to owe no other allegiance than to M. Poujade, the provincial bookseller turned leader of the shopkeepers' anti-tax rebellion. True, the government finally managed to survive and to post-pone the fiscal battle to another day, but this delay was gained only after numerous and after many deputies had "groveled"—to use his own expression—before M. Poujade. When the leader of a mass movement can command parliamentary operations from the public gallery, order deputies about, and then pour violent abuse on those guilty of "dis-obedience," he ceases to be an amusing example of French individual-ism. He becomes a menace to democracy.

It is no accident that Poujadism sprang up in central and south-western France and was, for a time, limited to those areas. These are France's underprivileged regions. In the southwest, for example, less than one-fifth of the working population is employed in industry and about three-fifths in agriculture, which is less efficient and profitable there than in most other parts of the country. This backward sector of France cannot help but feel acutely the growing pains of any period of competitive modernization. Its poorer farmers, shopkeepers, and artisans are those "marginal units" which in economic textbooks disappear for the good of the community. In French practice they have clung desperately to their jobs, helped partly by a protection and partly by tax evasion, and often at a bare subsistence level. But today they can read the signs of doom. The good harvests of the last two years have done little to benefit the small, inefficient farmers, and for the shopkeepers the end of inflation has meant that they can no longer pass the burden of taxes on to the consumers. When the government decided last year to tighten its fiscal regulations, the showdown was near.

For many artisans and shopkeepers tax evasion was the only chance of survival. The government offensive left them with the alternative of bankruptcy or rebellion; to exploit these grievances was the chance of a Poujade. When the young bookseller from Saint-Ceré realized that tax inspectors could be resisted and that such resistance would receive widespread tacit support, Poujadism was born. It spread like a bush-fire through France's impoverished regions. Its success attracted mean wealthier men, who until then had stood skeptically aloof. Could not resistance to tax inspection be used to conceal the profits of the rich as well as the meager incomes of the inefficient? They climbed on the bandwagon alongside the poor people with real grievances. The Loire, that traditional frontier between poorer and wealthier France, was crossed, and circumstances were propitious for further advances. M. Poujade could rely on the sympathy of the peasants who were discontented with falling agricultural prices. The anti-alcoholic laws of M. Mendès-France gave the movement the support of the influential beet-root growers. The funds grew, although their source was sometimes obscure. Committees were established throughout the country and at the close of last year M. Poujade claimed a million adherents. Critics granted him less than half that number—but this was still as many as the membership of the Communist Party.

*

M. Poujade now felt confident enough to march on Paris. When the shopkeepers flocked to the capital earlier this year, outsiders were still amused. But when the *chef* packed the Vélodrome d'Hiver—the Paris Harringay—with a bigger crowd than any political party could readily mobilize, they watched with greater concern. The technique was reminiscent of Germany in the 1930s. The leader climbed onto the rostrum only when the audience had been warmed up by his lieutenants. He offered no constructive remedies, no alternative sources of revenue. He merely appealed for lower taxes and the abolition of the hated controls and penalties. He called for a tax-strike and, in vaguer terms, for the non-payment of debts: "We shall close the taps until the government gives in." His language was as vulgar as it was colorful.

In spite of these insults, the *Palais Bourbon* was now within the scope of the provincial bookseller. With France on the eve of elections—for the local councils next month, for the Council of the Republic in the summer, and for the National Assembly next year—parliament was now very sensitive to pressure. The Left was worried by M. Poujade's success in the traditionally radical regions, and the Right discovered how attractive his slogans had become too middle-class and peasant voters. So when M. Poujade presented the deputies with a questionnaire there was a rush to sign on the dotted line. The conservatives, Gaullists, and a large number of Radicals became the parliamentary representatives of Poujadism. The Communists adopted an equivocal attitude. At least some of them, unable to learn from their bitter experience, thought that grievances could be usefully exploited and Poujadism transformed into an antechamber to the Communist Party. Only the Socialist and Christian Democrat deputies have, on the whole, resisted his pressure.

Thus, the stage was set for last week's performance. At the head of a government dependent on the backing of M. Poujade's conservative supporters, M. Faure was forced to seek survival in compromise. He won a respite by promising to abolish the law authorizing the closer inspection of books and the imposition of heavier penalties for fraud. Apparently, the government now intends to launch a counterattack. M. Poujade may have overreached himself and last week's antics may well have been the climax of his brief career. There is already talk of a counteroffensive by the urban taxpayers—the wage and salary earners—against the tax-evaders. But even if M. Poujade himself falls, the consolation will be small if the price of his defeat is capitulation to Poujadism.

Admittedly the French fiscal system is inequitable, but Poujadism is not an attempt to distribute the burden more fairly. Indeed, if that were done, the poorer supporters of M. Poujade would be crushed and the richer would lose their windfall profits. In fact, Poujadism is a reaction to the government's attempt—a timid enough attempt—to let economic forces take effect, that is, to prevent tax evasion from being a shield to the inefficient. Growth and adaptation are always painful processes and the present unrest has shown that any attempt to disturb what has been called "the paradise of the inefficient" will meet with violent opposition from those who are affected. For a feeble executive there is therefore a strong temptation to let things slide.

On the face of it, there has been a remarkable French economic recovery in the last two years. Superficial recovery, however, ought not to conceal the deep-seated causes of economic stagnation. The latest report of the Economic Commission for Europe gives a timely reminder of the slowness of French economic progress in the last half century. It shows that in the economic race France has failed to keep pace not merely with the two giants—the United States and the Soviet Union— but also with its two natural competitors, Britain and Germany. Sir Winston Churchill's reference to the "empty seat" in Europe, Mr. Attlee's unexpected criticisms in the House of Commons and the revelations of what was said about France at Yalta have all rubbed salt into the wounds of French national pride. In their resentment some Frenchmen have even argued that France can restore its prestige only by brandishing the H-bomb. But if France is to regain its proper place on the international stage, its chief problem is not one of acquiring new weapons but of rapidly adapting its economy to the real conditions of the mid-twentieth century. And now above all this has to be done in the face of a resistance of the Poujadist type. It is one thing to crush a Poujade, quite another to dig out the roots of Poujadism. It has been judged politically impossible and socially unjust to let the French economy be modernized solely by the ruthless forces of the market. Only if the modernization of agriculture in the backward parts of France is accompanied by a program of industrial decentralization, to create jobs for surplus labor, can the causes of Poujadism gradually be eliminated.

The French government is thus faced with the gigantic task of effecting a painless transition—or at least as painless a transition as possible—to a modern economy. Last week's tragic-comic performance leaves little hope that it will find the funds and authority necessary for the work. The eyes of the world have been fixed this week on the Council of the Republic to see whether France will accept German rearmament and keep its place in the West European Union. Yet in the long run France's position in the world may depend even more on its handling of the problem of Poujadism.

M. Thorez Survives

JULY 28, 1956
The Economist

LE HAVRE WAS an appropriate setting for the French Communist congress. Not only has the municipality lately passed into Communist hands, but the town itself has acquired an eastern European look. The new town on the ruins of the devastated port had to be built on a cheap budget, and the result is more impressive in size than in beauty. "Stalin-Allee," said the wits of the avenue leading to the unfinished *mairie*, where the first Communist congress in western Europe since Khrushchev's denunciation of Stalin was being held. At the end of an interminable hall the presidium sat under a map of France covered with a hammer and sickle. On the right, above the fraternal delegates' boxes, the portraits against red cloth of Marx, Lenin, Jules Guesde, and Jaures dominated the hall. As the only concession to the new spirit Maurice Thorez lost his place in this gallery of immortals, but the "son of the people" lost no time in dissipating any illusions which might have resulted, proving himself still capable of staging his own show in the orthodox Stalinist fashion.

Even his health seemed to have improved for the occasion. He took the rostrum on the very first morning and spoke for hours. Jacket off, interrupted by rhythmic applause, with the familiar stentorian voice he hammered at the now familiar subjects: the contrast between socialist growth and capitalist stagnation; the new perspectives opened by the

SWH

spread of Soviet forms of socialism outside Russia; peaceful coexistence; the need for Algerian independence; the categorical imperative, unity of action with the Socialists. After a break, he came to the sore subject. The latest statement by the Soviet central committee provided, in his opinion, the "Marxist explanation" of Stalin's crimes demanded by western Communists. Besides, Soviet self-criticism should not be transplanted "mechanically" to France. To judge by M. Thorez, the French leaders have little on their conscience. After a guarded apology to Yugoslavia, he applied the established principle that attack is the best form of defense and lashed out at the dissidents who want to transform the "vanguard of the working class into a debating society."

A SHOW STALIN WOULD LOVE

M. Thorez invoked the Leninist principles of "democratic centralism," but he showed that he can apply them in practice only in their Stalinist version. There followed a performance Stalin would have loved, as one speaker after another climbed the rostrum, expressed his approval for the general secretary's report, and proceeded to paraphrase or elaborate some selected passages from it. M. Servin, who took the place in the secretariat of the excommunicated Lecoeur (a French substitute for Beria as scapegoat for past mistakes), and M. Kanapa, the primitive keeper of intellectual orthodoxy, reiterated stern warnings for recalcitrants who had dared to question the "law of absolute impoverishment" or to demand the proportional representation of various trends within the party. The decisions of the congress, it was declared, must be obeyed and not discussed; no thought was given to the premise implicit in such a proposition, that the decisions should be reached through discussion in congress. Here, instead, was a gigantic parade, impressive by the careful preparation of every slightest detail. The floor took its cues from the cheerleaders on the platform and distributed ovations discriminately: ordinary applause; locomotive-like clapping; a full-throated *International*. Mr. Mikhail Suslov, the first Moscow leader ever to attend this French function, was judged worthy of the whole gamut. His message was a cheering one for the orthodox; he, too, brought a special blessing for M. Thorez. Delegates, who for weeks had watched the French party seemingly at odds with the world communist movement, now found comfort in the thought that "everyone had been out of step except our Maurice."

And so the discussion ended before it had even begun. M. Duclos, looking like Pickwick, brought the proceedings to a more parochial level with a lengthy report on the municipal achievements of the Communists and their plans for local councils. Like model pupils, the delegates took copious notes. In the intervals they flocked downstairs, under a Lurcat tapestry, to the bookstall. (At no other meeting is the written word in such demand.)

On the fourth and last day came the moment of relaxation. Communist versions of the Boy Scouts, representatives of Paris women and youth strolled on amid confetti and paper planes to the accompaniment of revolutionary songs. So that the essential moral of this congress should not be lost in the rejoicing, it was finally driven home in the election of the new guiding bodies: Self-criticism might be good for others, but everything was apparently almost for the best in the best possible French party. All the members of the central committee and politbureau were duly reelected, a few newcomers being added as alternate members. (M. Joliot-Curie was the exception, his prestige giving him direct access to a full seat on the central committee.) The only sign of the new times was the official subordination of the secretariat—the key body in the Stalinist party system—to the other leading organs. M. Thorez did not trouble to climb the rostrum to receive a final homage. This was his hour of triumph; the storm was weathered.

Cultured, individualist France, of all places, has produced the crudest and most anachronistic of all Stalinist party performances. A combination of favorable circumstances helped M. Thorez to a success which may be temporary. The ferment provoked by the Khrushchev revelations had not had time to get the better of the well-oiled party machine. The existence of ferment and unrest could be gathered from the violent attacks on "petty-bourgeois deviationists." But there was also a natural reaction after the first agonies of destalinization; the conditioned reflexes of the faithful were at work—the dread of liberty, the fear of crumbling discipline. ("I hoped they would be less tough in handling the opposition," commented a well-wisher at Le Havre. "I feared it," replied the orthodox cardholder.)

The Russians, worried by the stir caused by the Khrushchev speech, by Togliatti's outburst, and by the Poznan riots, have evidently set themselves to slow down the pace to that of the slowest soldier; this is to the advantage of M. Thorez. And no alternative political magnet competes in France for the allegiance of the Communists. The Socialist party, burdened with office, saddled with the Algerian War, raising taxes, and refusing wage increases, cannot be considered as a rival for the affections of the discontented masses. Despite all their difficulties, M. Thorez and his colleagues could proudly point to five and a half million votes in the last elections.

And yet the triumph is likely to be short-lived. It was not difficult to discern uneasy feelings even among the hand-picked, disciplined delegates. The shock has been administered and its effects are at work, although the ranks were briefly closed. *Ex Oriente Lux* still seems a valid maxim for the Communist world and no party machine, however tight, will be able to resist the disturbing impulses from Moscow. Did not the same Mr. Suslov, only recently, take a message of comfort to Mr. Rakosi—a comfort which did not help for long. The Grand Guignol at Le Havre was superbly staged, but it marks the twilight of an era. M. Thorez and his managers may not be able to produce another one like it.

The French Army

January 30 and February 6, 1960
The Economist

THE ARMY'S WISHES and the army's intentions are the question marks that have seemed this week to govern France's immediate future. In a way, the political problem is now much more circumscribed than during the crisis of May 1958, which brought about the end of the previous regime. Then, it was relevant to wonder about the attitude of parliament, the parties, or the trade unions. Only when M. Pflimlin—the head of the government at the time—renounced any attempt to bring popular forces into play was he compelled to surrender to the army and accept the conditions of its commanders. In the Fifth Republic the political and institutional void surrounding the monarch is such that the whole affair is, from the start, reduced to a secret dialogue between General de Gaulle and the army commanders controlling the situation in Algeria.

In fairness, it must be stated that the army's importance in politics is by no means a new phenomenon. At the turn of the century, after the Dreyfus case, a bitter struggle was necessary to curb the political ambitions of the General Staff. After the Second World War the army's part in politics grew as successive governments of the Fourth Republic abdicated their responsibility and allowed commanding officers to run the country's colonial policy. A trial of strength became inevitable. It came in May 1958, when the army command in effect vetoed parliament's choice of government. After a parody of resistance, government and deputies gave in and France changed regimes. To grasp the ambiguous relationship between the army and the president of its choice—a choice since endorsed by a massive popular vote—it is necessary to glance back at the events which have helped to shape the attitudes of the military cadres.

Many French officers are haunted by memories of defeat. The army's last real victory is over forty years old; and even at Port Said in 1956, when victory of a kind came within its grasp, it was snatched away. The feeling is the more bitter since the French forces have been fighting, in colonial conflicts, almost uninterruptedly ever since the end of the Second World War. The Indo-Chinese war culminating, in 1954, in the disaster of Dien Bien Phu left a deep mark. Officers emerged from this traumatic shock with three fixed ideas: resentment against the civilian government in Paris "which has let them down"; a crude conception of a world in permanent struggle between the Christian good and the Communist evil; finally, an admiration for Communist techniques coupled with hate for Communist ideology. Mao Tse-tung's writings on revolutionary strategy were translated into French. They did more than provide military writers with quotations about the nature of revolutionary war; they became the bedside reading of many officers serving in Algeria.

One war was, in fact, succeeded by another. Algeria provided a fertile ground for the seeds brought from Indo-China. A glance at French military publications or conversations with French officers shows that many are still convinced that colonial wars form a vital part of the anti-Communist crusade. Communists, according to this version, are trying to bring western Christendom down by striking at its soft underbelly in the Middle East, in Africa, even in Latin America. In Algeria, faced with the nationalist rebellion of the FLN, the French command could use its new arsenal of counter-revolutionary weapons: strict control of the Muslim population, indoctrination, brainwashing—the task of the psychological warfare specialists was made easier by a huge resettlement of the Muslim population (involving more than a million people). In vain was it objected that Mao's methods succeeded because his was a national program and a program of social revolution. The soldiers came to believe that if their policy did not bring the expected results, the blame must be put on the civilian government in Paris, perverted by "defeatist" influences. No blame could be put on lack of men. In 1956 M. Mollet's government decided to send national servicemen and reservists across the Mediterranean; ever since, the military command in Algeria has had close to half a million men at its disposal. Since only a tenth were actually involved in fighting at any one time, the rest could be spared for other tasks. Such a wealth of manpower enabled the French army to extend its administrative control to remote villages and at the same time to embark on social work on a massive scale. The army supplied teachers, doctors, nurses, builders, engineers, and many more specialists besides.

Two important consequences have resulted. The army is now in full control of the country. No economic program—the Constantine plan, for example—can be carried out without its consent. Secondly, social work among the Muslim population has given the soldiers a sense of mission which renders them proof against liberal humanitarian agitation about the torture and other horrors which mark the war. Often contemptuous of the French settlers and their obsession with privilege, many of the soldiers firmly believe that they are working for the good of the Muslim population exclusively. Everywhere the officers have assured their Muslim collaborators that France has come to stay and will never abandon them. ("We shall not let our friends be punished as traitors, as in Tunisia or Morocco. We shall not allow them to be massacred by the FLN" is a refrain often heard in conversations with officers about the future of Algeria.)

Service in Algeria thus gives the army a sense of power and a sense of mission. By now this mood marks the French officer corps as a whole, and it is more relevant to General de Gaulle's decisions than any "threats" from politically minded colonels. Many officers who had close links with extremist settlers' organizations have been gradually removed from their posts through promotions and transfers. But their successors have been rapidly infected with the general mood. The war has its logic and the colonial atmosphere of Algiers is insidious. Twenty months ago the army had a striking confirmation of its political power. The Fifth Republic did not produce any political forces to restore the balance. General de Gaulle has implicitly admitted that in the crucial Algerian questions the mood in officers' messes is more important to him than that prevailing in the lobbies of the Palais Bourbon. Before revealing his policy of "self-determination" for Algeria on September 16th, the general did not consult parliament; but he made a special trip to Algeria in order to consult commanders of all ranks. Those officers who accepted the general's new plan (reluctantly, since it conflicted with the magic slogan of integration) did so on the assumption that it was prompted by international considerations and really designed for a distant future. Then came the rumors of a deal with the Muslim rebels (FLN), and the inevitable inference that the army's days in Algeria might be numbered. The mood was radically altered by such talk. In the last three months comment hostile to General de Gaulle's Algerian policy—on the lines of General Massu's now historic interview—was the rule, not the exception, in the officers' messes.

The attitude of the officers towards General de Gaulle is not the same as it had been towards M. Pflimlin. The general is a man of their choice. The army cannot stage a putsch every year. It does not want now to change regimes, simply to put a check on the Algerian policy of the present one. The riots in Algiers gave it an excellent opportunity to show who is master there. The immediate question is: What guarantees about policy will the army insist upon before it will agree to carry out the president's orders? Assuming that a compromise will be reached in the present crisis, the wider issue will remain whether General de Gaulle can ever offer the professional soldiers a sufficiently dazzling prospect in France, and Europe, to attract them away from the Algerian mission which has brought upon them the power and prestige that they have.

*

"Ours is the army best prepared for subversive wars." True or not, this claim, often repeated by French officers, hides the other side of the picture: that it is prepared for virtually nothing else. Five years of concentration on the Algerian War have distorted the French military machine and turned it into the army of the *djebels,* trained for fighting a guerrilla enemy, for controlling the population, and for psychological warfare. Many officers consider that this is all France will ever need, because atomic weapons are so destructive as to be unusable. But this is not the official French view. General de Gaulle plainly wants to have at his disposal diversified armed forces, with up-to-date conventional weapons, the nuclear deterrent, and all.

Some of the general's closest military advisers try to justify his well-known distaste for military integration within NATO by the psychological needs of the French army in its particular predicament. A nationalist force obsessed with colonial warfare and convinced of its patriotic mission across the Mediterranean cannot, they argue, simply be brought back and turned into a "stateless" army. The argument sounds far-fetched, since NATO integration is at the top, and the forces remain national forces. Admittedly, among French officers serving in Algeria there are strong anti-American feelings, because, in their opinion, the United States has failed to grasp the importance of subversive war and pays too much deference to Arab nationalism. It is also true that Frenchmen often complain that they are treated as junior partners in SHAPE (the stock complaint concerns documents marked AEO—for American Eyes Only). But they stop short of suggesting that French standing does not correspond to the French military contribution. General Jean Valluy is commander-in-chief of allied forces in the central (the most important) sector; his appointment could not be justified by the strength of the depleted French divisions stationed in Germany.

French opposition to integration may well be essentially tactical. It may be a means of pressure to obtain atomic secrets and allied help in the ballistic field. General de Gaulle is convinced that a nuclear deterrent is now an indispensable requirement for an independent foreign policy; once in possession of it, he holds, France would automatically gain the place in an Atlantic triumvirate, and greater say in allied decisions in the world outside Europe, that he demanded in his memorandum of September 1958. It is argued in Paris that France would then be able to agree to integrate the rest of its air forces and to accept American nuclear bombs on its soil under dual control. Until then, it will continue to be awkward, trying to trade the advantages of geography against American technical knowledge.

General de Gaulle's demands on the alliance are based not so much on existing strength as on his vision of a future army, still mostly at the paper stage. The atomic device to be exploded next month is usually reported as weighing around five tons. To slim it down will take years. The Mirage IV-01, the means of delivery now being prepared, is a light bomber with insufficient range to fly to Moscow and back at full speed. The project of a heavier and longer-range version of the Mirage was dropped in August partly to save money and partly because, by the time the French bomb is ready, nothing short of a missile will do. Several French firms have joined together to form a company for ballistic research (SEREB). Sceptics in Paris, however, suggest that without foreign aid, it will take at least a decade to fit French nuclear warheads to French missiles.

Thus the French deterrent is still in its infancy, while modern conventional French divisions, capable of waging war in Europe, are almost nonexistent. In 1954 France had a nucleus of modern divisions and plans for expansion. All this was disrupted by the Algerian War. Troops moved from Germany to North Africa left their heavy equipment behind: by now it is obsolete. In this year's defense budget of 16,530 million new francs, about half goes for the pay and upkeep of the overgrown forces. The army in Algeria is a great consumer of equipment, particularly of means of transport. Conventional forces in Europe have, therefore, become the Cinderella of the budget. Talking of up-to-date weapons for conventional divisions, M. Guillaumat, the minister of the armed forces, had to admit that, "for the army, our effort in this field had to be merely symbolic because of the necessities of the Algerian War."

France may not have the means at present. General de Gaulle and his advisers know their military ends. France should have a nuclear striking force capable of hitting "any point on earth." It must also have several divisions on European soil—the number is still undecided—strong enough and well enough equipped to make France once again a major military power in western Europe. France must have air transport and mobile troops which can be sent overseas at short notice, particularly to Africa, where the army is to serve as a vital link in a fast-evolving community. Finally, the army must be able to put down subversion at home.

The shape of the French army to come thus corresponds to General de Gaulle's design of twenty-five years ago, set out in his book *Vers l'Armée de Métier*, naturally with variations imposed by changes in technology. The mobile units of the future and the increasingly complex weapons will require professional soldiers for preference. They will be supplemented by national servicemen with a technical background or bent, who would serve a longer stretch even than they do now. The rest of the population could serve an initial short term with subsequent periods of training. A decree of January 1959, which set out the framework of the future organization of defense, provided for this development.

The mainly professional army is also thought to be more reliable for anti-subversion action at home than a big conscript force. A political ferment can spread to national servicemen. Professional soldiers, aloof and rootless, are more immune to such contagions—or so it is obstinately supposed. The January decree already mentioned put yet another weapon in the constitutional arsenal of emergency measures. The *mise en garde* can be proclaimed for all sorts of reasons (threat to a part of the territory, to a sector of national life, to a fraction of the population) and gives the authorities discretionary powers such as the power to requisition manpower, goods, and services.

General de Gaulle's relationship with the army can now be seen in its complexity. When last week he talked of his love for the army, it was not a mere figure of speech. He sees the armed forces not only as the pillar and guardian of the regime, but as the instrument of greatness and stability. But it must be obedient; while many of the commanders who brought him to power have a categorical imperative of their own—the permanence of the French army's mission in Algeria. As has been seen, the relationship contains the seeds of misunderstanding and even of conflict.

It is no accident that among the "loyal" commanders pushed forward in recent months, airmen, tank specialists and technicians predominate. They are the men who can contemplate a modernization of the armed forces with equanimity. Among infantry officers, who have most reason to fear the bowler hat, and paratroop commanders—the knights of guerrilla warfare—are to be found the men willing to enter into an alliance with semi-fascist settlers and extremists at home in order to impose on France any sort of regime that will put Algeria first. Last week the French army saved its unity by coupling *Vive de Gaulle* with *Algérie Française*. But the general must now know that this state of things will not allow him to shape the armed forces into an obedient tool or into a modern force with international standing. The simultaneous development of a deterrent and of conventional forces is likely to prove too much for a country with the national income of France (or, for that matter, of Britain). Coupled with a major colonial war, the idea cannot even be seriously contemplated. General de Gaulle remains faced with the task of transforming the French army from an Algerian force into a Gaullist instrument of power. Unless he is permitted to put an end to the Algerian War, he can hardly begin.

The Thorez Succession

MAY 20, 1961
The Economist

THE STAGE-MANAGERS of the French Communist congress at Saint-Denis, last weekend, could not conceal the fact that the real drama was being played behind the scenes. Yet they put on quite a show in the soberly decorated hall where they staged the official proclamation of the heir-apparent. For the first time in his thirty years' reign M. Thorez, though present, did not deliver the official report. The task was entrusted to fifty-six-year-old M. Waldeck Rochet. By Sunday, this faithful, though rather dull, follower of M. Thorez was nominated assistant secretary-general, a new post designed to accommodate the official *dauphin*.

But the real drama took place on the eve of the congress during the lengthy secret session of the political commission. There two former ex-members of the party's politbureau refused categorically to recant publicly their heretical views. M. Marcel Servin, who as party secretary was responsible for organization, and M. Laurent Casanova, who was in charge of the intellectuals, declined to pay this classic price for political survival. As a result, they and most of their allies were duly removed from the party's central committee and other responsible posts.

As usual, the views of the opposition have to be read between the lines of the indictment. The open attack against M. Servin and his colleagues was launched only last January, after the referendum on Algeria had revealed the weakness of the fascist fringe in France. The timing was clever, since the main charge against the group was that, by overestimating the threat of the extreme right-wing, it forgot that Gaullism in power was the chief enemy. This alleged softness about Gaullism has given rise to interesting speculation. Since M. Casanova received a Lenin prize only last year, it has been suggested that the opposition may have had some Russian backing. After all, hardly more than a year ago Mr. Khrushchev was flirting with General de Gaulle and, apparently, hoping that the general's schemes would put a spanner in the NATO machine. It is not utterly absurd to surmise that some French Communists thought, at the time, that they ought to revise their policy to bring it into line with the Russian attitude. The indictment, however, is full of contradictions. The opposition is accused at one and the same time of hesitation in the anti-Gaullist struggle and of attempts to strike bargains with other left-wing groups with a view to organizing activities that were obviously anti-Gaullist. What makes any assessment particularly difficult is the way in which most of the discussion centers round an analysis of the nature of the Gaullist regime worded in pseudo-Marxist jargon.

Beneath the crude ideological quarrels, however, the controversy is really about the methods and tactics of the leadership. Indeed, the third of the chief heretics, M. Kriegel-Valrimont, has been openly accused of criticizing the party line for the last five years. The date is significant, since it goes back to the famous 20th congress of the Soviet party. The secret indictment of Stalin that Mr. Khrushchev then made must have shaken the French Communist Party, reputed to be the most Stalinist of the western world. Two years later, although the French Communists regularly collected a quarter of the popular vote, they proved utterly unable to offer any real resistance to the Gaullist coup. After such setbacks, men like M. Servin, who were in charge of the party machine, may well have concluded that it needed a thorough overhaul.

But any condemnation of the past and any attempt to change the existing structure would obviously be blows against the man who for over thirty years has had control of the party machine. The counter-offensive which M. Thorez was bound to mount has now been successfully concluded. It did, however, meet with resistance. The opposition had sympathizers, and not only among the students, economists, and other intellectuals linked with M. Casanova. M. Servin for his part was, apparently, liked by many of his subordinates in the party apparatus. Yet although all this support proved of no avail, M. Thorez was forced to call a congress and most of the heretics refused to recant.

The opposition has been dealt with, but the question of the party line remains. The Communist leaders watch the Gaullist regime with a mixture of fear and hope. They fear that the general will use his vast powers to damage the Communist Party and its trade unions. They hope that the absence of political life and of any other effective opposition will benefit them when the Gaullist tide finally recedes. Last month's abortive coup gave some idea of what rewards they might hope for. The Communist-dominated CGT now finds it easier to stage strikes in cooperation with other unions. The party is reported to have improved its position among the young, particularly in the armed forces. Even the recruiting of new members has looked up. These favorable after-effects of last month's events are unlikely to last, but they increase Communist hopes for the future.

Thus the evolution of the French Communist Party is intimately linked with that of the regime. The immediate question is whether M. Thorez will try to exclude his defeated opponents from the party. If they are allowed to stay in, the party will for the first time have alternative leaders within its ranks. This would be useful, should the French Communists prove unable to emerge from their isolation without a radical break with their Stalinist past. This is certainly not M. Thorez's view; he seems convinced that no change is necessary and that the anti-Gaullist wave will send the Communist ship on its way to new successes. Although only sixty-one, he has a long political past behind him; he is, moreover, troubled with ill-health. In M. Waldeck Rochet he has chosen a successor who could take over the helm without changing course.

Faces of France

FEBRUARY 10, 1962
The Economist

MUCH OF THE image is in the eye of the beholder, who has two completely contradictory pictures of France to choose from. One picture shows a prosperous nation of holidaymakers with no greater cares than the twist-versus-jive struggle or the height of the waistline in the spring collections. Sun-tanned thousands stream back from winter sports. Production is booming, business is good. At the ministry of finance, M. Baumgartner has bequeathed will-filled coffers to his youthful successor. All this seems to justify General de Gaulle's message that everything is for the best.

If the spotlight is switched to other scenes—to policemen directing traffic in Paris with submachine guns in their hands, to the armored units of gendarmes that wait on the alert in the suburbs—it picks out quite a different picture. Both are true, within their limits; each is incomplete. The following notes try to illustrate some of the symptoms and causes of the disquiet that certainly exists despite the absence of any major social discontent.

HOAX OR HYDRA?

Last week the police forces in Paris were strengthened to 25,000 men and the government was able to claim the capture of some important henchmen of the OAS (Organisation de l'Armée Secrète). It is too early to say what will be the effect of this new police offensive. On previous occasions, notably after the abortive attempt on General de Gaulle's life, the claims that the OAS in France had been beheaded proved premature. Indeed, one of the psychologically most disturbing factors was the contrast between official assertion and reality. Last month, each government declaration of confidence and resolution was echoed by the daily explosion of *plastique* in provincial towns and in various parts of Paris, including the Quai d'Orsay. Communists were no longer the main targets; the flats of liberal and even conservative editors were attacked as well.

This is psychological warfare. Casualties are few, the damage mainly material, but an impression is created that the underground is omnipresent and the authorities impotent. Officials found two excuses for the government's initial lack of results: These handy bombs are easily hidden; and specialists, coming from Algeria, are able to enlist recruits among the disgruntled Poujadists or fascist youth. The ease of this recruiting raises the question of the deterrent.

ALL, ALL, HONORABLE

The French courts have shown remarkable indulgence toward offenders who justify their crimes through their attachment to *Algérie Française*. Many men who vanished while under suspended sentence are now on the general staff of the Secret Army. This caution on the part of the judiciary, combined with the government's appearance of indecision, had its inevitable consequence. On January 26th, three men who had been threatened by the Secret Army refused jury service at Nîmes, and the trial had to be put off. The government reacted swiftly. Several cases were transferred to a special military tribunal and, last week, a *plastiqueur* was actually sentenced to six years in jail.

It should not be concluded that military justice is always swift and severe. On January 16th, another Parisian military tribunal gave its verdict in the case of three officers accused of torturing a Muslim woman to death. The gruesome indictment was public; the trial was heard *in* camera; the three men were acquitted. It is enough to add that these three officers could not even plead superior orders or invoke the complicity of higher ranking officers. Such complicity has prevented all other cases of torture from being brought to trial.

POLICEMEN'S LOT

It used to be fashionable to say that the army was suffering from a bad conscience. Now the fashionable malaise concerns the conscience of the police. For years the police have been fighting against the Arabs; now they have to turn against the Secret Army as well. For an even longer time they have been told that the chief enemy was on the left; since 1947, anti-Communism has been a main qualification for recruits. Now the police are told that the opponent is on the right. To complicate matters still further, they are ordered not to forget that the struggle is on two fronts. Communism is the permanent danger; the Secret Army is a transient one. To the ordinary policeman it must all seem rather confusing.

There are, however, deeper reasons for the uneasiness and hesitation among magistrates, officers, and policemen. Occupation, resistance, and liberation undermined the simple rules of discipline. For years afterwards efforts were made to explain that wartime sanctions were the exception. Then came the change of regime in 1958 and many may have concluded that it is most comfortable to sit on the fence. With many of its former fellow plotters now on the other side, the regime provides a precedent against itself.

Suspicions about the government's ability, or willingness, to cope with the situation, increasing terrorism, and rumors of a putsch to come have led political and union leaders to meet and talk about filling the void, about self-defense, even about the succession.

OLD DILEMMA

"Without the Communists, the Left is nothing; with the Communists . . . the army will never tolerate it." This sentence, attributed to General de Gaulle, sums up a great deal in the French situation. It explains the ambiguous relationship between General de Gaulle and his armed forces. It reveals one of the reasons for the impotence of the French Left. M. Mollet, the socialist, who shares the view that the threat of a Popular Front could provoke the army into action, has recently been busy regrouping. He has met M. Pinay, the conservative, as well as Radical, Catholic, and trade union leaders, to see whether, if a vacuum arose, a coalition could be formed to fill it. At the same time, he has been trying to form a more active alliance of the non-Communist Left against the Secret Army; without, so far, much success.

M. Pinay, whom many tip for the succession, has no special reason to broadcast his views on Algeria from his retirement. General de Gaulle's illustrious precedent demonstrated the political efficacy of ambiguous silence.

Recent demonstrations against the Secret Army have confirmed two things: that the Communists can no longer bring as many people into the streets as they used to be able to do; and that no mass demonstration can be staged without them. The combination of these two lessons with the activity of the OAS has somewhat decreased the reluctance to work with Communists. The Left still stands divided, but whether the Communists will continue to be kept in isolation may now depend on events.

Waiting for What?

Stories of an impending peace or an impending revolt are plentiful. The Secret Army, which dominates the life of the European population in Algeria, has no real roots in France. The fight against the Secret Army, for what it is worth, is waged by the police forces, mainly the cloak and dagger men. Meanwhile the French army carries on the Algerian War, and each fortnight brings reports of, say, six hundred Algerian casualties. The wiser among the Secret Army strategists want to delay major action until the exiled Algerian leaders return to Algiers to take it over; they would then try to get the armed forces to join them in the struggle against the "common enemy."

In prosperous France there is no scope for a massive fascist movement. All the question marks, however, lead on back to the problem of the army. The questions are not new. The government's present display of precautions suggests that the next few weeks may provide the answers. It is then that the true face of modern France may be seen.

The Importance of Being Swiss

APRIL 24, 1965
The Economist

IS WESTERN EUROPE, in its postwar economic expansion, becoming a melting pot of nationalities, almost in the American way? Britain has its West Indians, and its (east) Indians. France, as well as its North Africans and Senegalese, now recruits Spaniards and Portuguese. Germany now looks not only to Italy and Spain but also to Yugoslavia, Greece, and Turkey for its new labor force. This mass migration in search of work and higher wages poses long-term questions as well as immediate problems. Is the new prosperity of western Europe to be marked by the birth of a new sub-proletariat of foreign workers who take on the nastier and worse-paid jobs, while the natives of each prosperous country occupy the higher rungs on the social ladder? Are we reverting to the pattern of ancient Greece or Rome, with an increasing part of the population having a share in production but not in political life? If the "outsiders" are not effectively absorbed, what tensions will develop between them and the older established local populations?

Why should one choose Switzerland as the place where some of these questions should be studied? For one thing, when xenophobia spreads to the land of direct democracy, to a country in which four different linguistic groups have become a single nation, the event is significant in itself. When the people of cosmopolitan Geneva are sharply divided by a referendum on the question of allotting more land for international institutions; when television reporters in Zürich ask passersby what they think of foreigners and get answers so abusive that nine-tenths of the tape cannot be used; when an association of *jeunes patrons* sends out a questionnaire that includes "Would you like your daughter to share a hospital room with a Sicilian? Would you like your daughter . . . ?" and other too familiar items, something has clearly gone wrong.

Yet the main reason for taking Switzerland as an example is simply that the substituting of foreign for home labor at the lower end of the wage scale has gone much further than anywhere else in Europe. At the seasonal peak last autumn, more than 800,000 foreigners were working in Switzerland. This means that no less than one out of every three person employed in the Swiss economy was a foreigner. To attain the same proportion Britain, or Germany, would need to bring in more than eight million foreign workers.

Reducing by Numbers

Britain, it is said, acquired its colonial empire in a state of absence of mind. Switzerland, it is now being said (but perhaps less facetiously), acquired its million foreigners in the same state of mind. To this, government supporters reply, with reason, that the "open door" policy was the basis of the Swiss miracle, that it led to a long period of expansion and that, as soon as the policy ceased to be wholly beneficial, attempts were made to shut the door. They do admit, however, that official policy was based on the assumption that the influx of foreigners was provisional and therefore did not justify any serious social investment. But even when the foreign workers come in without their families, the sheer weight of numbers begins to tell.

The strains began to be felt in the early 1960s at a time when the Swiss boom reached its "overheated" phase and when the shadow of the European common market made the Swiss wonder whether their economy was able to meet the common market's competition. It was probably the Italian-Swiss agreement, negotiated last year and ratified last month, that excited flights of unpleasing fancy among the Swiss. A clause in the agreement, shortening the period a non-seasonal worker has to wait before bringing in his family, was wrongly interpreted as opening the way to a foreign invasion. The conclusion was drawn that the foreign third of the labor force would soon be turned into a foreign third of the population—and since this third would consist of young southern Catholics, Swiss minds boggled at what would follow.

The Swiss now tend to blame the foreign workers for most social evils, from the housing shortage to the lack of teachers and the overcrowding in hospitals. Italians are charged with all sort of absurd and often contradictory sins. They have increased the crime rate—though statistics prove that they have not; they intrude on the familiar Swiss scene, yet stick to their ghettos. Prejudice, it seems, is international.

It is not the employers who are behind this silly campaign. It was their associations which, for obvious reasons, had inspired the open-door policy. When things began to get out of hand, they advised their members to exercise self-restraint, but in vain. The associations have now agreed to a five percent reduction of foreign labor by each firm this year on condition that the whole policy is revised in the light of economic developments.

The trade unions have asked the Federal Council to reduce the foreign labor force to 500,000 by 1972, a very drastic cut indeed. When trade union officials, who admit that they have very few foreign members, are asked whether they are perturbed by their position as leaders of privileged workers, they reply that their conscience is clear since foreigners are welcome and free to join. Critics point out, however, that there is little encouragement for foreign workers to join an organization that wants to kick them out of the country. The impression is that trade union leaders, having done little in the first place to educate their members, must now go along with their mood which, to put it at its mildest, is hardly internationalist.

A rapid contraction of foreign labor would put a strain on Swiss manpower. Automation would gradually relieve some of this strain, but not all. Even if wages for unskilled jobs were raised, as they would have to be, this would not be enough to tempt Swiss workers back to such jobs. One striking change since the war has been the social promotion of the Swiss workers. Between 1950 and 1964, total employment in factories went up by 152,000, but the number of Swiss factory workers went down by 21,800. And if the Swiss worker stays in industry he has a good chance of doing a white-collar job.

This helps to explain why the measures taken in the last three years have slowed down but not stopped the inflow of foreign labor. Individual firms were allowed to take on foreign workers on condition that their total staff (Swiss and foreign) would not then exceed a fixed level. But as Swiss workers moved up the ladder, foreign workers stepped in to fill the vacancies. This is why the new regulation, introduced in February, compels all firms employing more than ten people to reduce their foreign contingent by 5 percent.

Economists agree that Switzerland's gain in prosperity since the war owes much to borrowed labor (and something to borrowed money). The rapid inflow of foreign workers enabled Swiss firms to meet export orders. It kept wages down, increased profit margins, and stimulated investment. But it is equally agreed that the availability of foreign labor has affected the structure of the Swiss economy. The selective admission of tied labor has enabled marginal firms to survive. The low cost of labor has channeled investment away from technological development. For a country as dependent on foreign trade as Switzerland, a country lacking raw materials and relying on specialization and skill, such a trend could be dangerous in the long run. In Bern and Zürich the emphasis is now on the need for automation, for labor-saving schemes, for qualitative rather than quantitative progress.

The compulsory reduction of foreign labor was introduced together with two deflationary measures—a limit on credit and on construction. The new economic policy seems contradictory. A switch from labor-intensive to capital-intensive investment will not be encouraged by an unselective policy of credit restriction. The federal government has neither the power nor the will to reshape the economy by planning. The reshaping will have to be done by market pressures—and the freezing of the labor force is not a means to this end.

All this is admitted in Bern, where the present anti-inflationary phase is described as the prelude to a policy of greater mobility which will mean that marginal firms will have to suffer. But emphasis is put on the need for a gradual transformation. This also applies to the reduction of the foreign labor force. The number of foreign workers is expected to be only fractionally lower in the 1965 August census than it was the previous year. A fresh cut may then be decided on, but it will probably be hedged with exceptions for day and seasonal workers. A slight decline in the number of foreign workers is likely to be balanced by a slight increase in the number of families. Indeed, there are already those in Bern who think that, in time, the real difficulty will be at the supply end. As wages rise within the common market, Italians may be tempted to keep inside the community. But this is for the future.

The General's Secretary

(or, Caligula's Horse)

August 1965
Previously Unpublished

JOAN OF ARC naturally had no heirs; with General de Gaulle it is more complicated. In his system of personal rule there is no room for a genuine dauphin. He requires obedient officers and skilful servants. He can tolerate courtiers, but not a strong personality, a potential competitor. Yet he needs a successor, or Gaullism would come to be seen as merely an interlude in postwar French history. Who?

The official pretender is the Comte de Paris. The idea of a royal succession might flatter General de Gaulle, who had a royalist upbringing. He is too much of a realist not to grasp the difficulties. The ideal heir would be another military figure with a legend. But General Leclerc is dead. The French officers' corps is recovering from its traumatic Algerian experience. The French forces have still to be reshaped. None of the commanders seems, so far, to have the necessary stature.

The man tipped in Paris as most likely to be the next president of France has none of the expected ingredients. He has no royal blood in his veins, no brilliant resistance record, no military legend. He could be described as a self-made man were it not that he is so much the product of President de Gaulle's patronage. When M. Georges Pompidou was appointed prime minister in April 1962 and his dark face with bushy eyebrows and sly peasant smile was splashed on the front pages, most Frenchmen asked who he was. "Caligula's horse," retorted the experts, rather unfairly.

Statistically, a French workman's son has just over one chance in a hundred to get to university; a farmer's son has fewer than four in a hundred. But if a peasant's bright son rises to postman or schoolteacher, his son might in turn move into the liberal professions and thus into the establishment. M. Pompidou is a spectacular example. His paternal grandfather was a farmer. His gifted father was sent to a teachers' training college, finishing his career as *professeur* in a Parisian lycée. His mother was a teacher, too, though she came from a wealthier family of merchants and had quite a dowry. For such parents, the natural dream was to send their son to the highly competitive École Normale Supérieure, the classical gateway to a brillant academic career. M. Georges Pompidou, born in 1911 in his mother's home village of Montboudif in Cantal, was destined for that celebrated school in the rue d'Ulm.

Naturally, he had to be good at passing examinations. He proved to be a champion. Brought up with books around the house, he collected prizes with apparently effortless ease. This impression of leisure still puzzles people who meet him now that he is the prime minister. Some have concluded that he is an easygoing, unambitious man carried along by fortune. Those who know him better reply that the leisurely air has always concealed a great capacity for swift and concentrated hard work. In France, as in England, the privileged have succeeded in spreading the myth that culture is a gift from heaven. The young Pompidou paid a price for succumbing to this fashion. He did not get a distinction in philosophy and failed at his first attempt to get into the rue d'Ulm. Yet these were minor blemishes in an otherwise triumphant record. He not only got into the École Normale but emerged from there, at twenty-three, as first in the *concours d'agrégation* of French, Latin, and Greek. The young provincial was on his way.

There were other signs that he would get on. The young men who through scholarly brilliance emerge from the lower middle classes can be roughly divided into two groups: those who do not see in their own distinction a justification of the society in which they live, and those who cannot see anything basically wrong with a society which has given them an opportunity to rise. He seemed from the start to be willing to be absorbed by the establishment. True, his father had been an admirer of Jaurès and a Socialist. But he could hardly have been militant; he apparently allowed young Georges to have a good Catholic education. Again, the youthful Pompidou had a somewhat leftish reputation at the École Normale. Yet he was known there as a gifted dandy keen on enjoying life rather than as a politically minded student. Socialist principles were not to stand in the way of the future servant of France, the Rothschilds, and de Gaulle.

He took his first job as a classics master in a school at Marseilles. Having married Claude Cahours, the daughter of a doctor from a well-to-do Breton family, he was for a time, more concerned with the pleasure of life in Provence than with his career. To rise in the academic world he required a doctorate. He did pick a subject for a thesis, but did not go far beyond that. Yet, by 1938, at the age of twenty-seven, he managed to get a post in a Parisian lycée. But war broke out before the leisurely Rastignac had time to settle down in the capital.

Lieutenant Pompidou served in the front line. It is not his war but his resistance record that worries the hagiographer. He did not collaborate with the Germans or play up to the Vichy government. But he seems to have done nothing at all. His semi-official biographer[1] argues that this was because the general staff of the underground movement was in the so-called "free zone" and he hated the Germans so much that he would not stoop to asking them for an *ausweis,* a "permit" to cross the demarcation line. Yet the future prime minister had principles. In occupied Paris he would not attend the Comédie Française in any seats lower than the second balcony since below that there was the risk of mixing with the *Feldgrau* uniforms of German officers.[2] Such sacrifices by themselves were not enough for Gaullist promotion. The school tie was. In the exalted atmosphere of liberated Paris, the brilliant schoolmaster was not likely to stick to teaching. One of his fellow *normaliens* (M. René Brouillet, now ambassador to the Vatican) was on de Gaulle's staff. He brought M. Pompidou along. It was the chance of his lifetime. The newcomer proved a most valuable assistant. He was obedient, swift, shrewd, and had a special talent for precise writing.

But there was little time. In January 1946, General de Gaulle resigned as prime minister, convinced that he would soon be recalled and granted greater powers. The republic, to his surprise, went on without him. M. Georges Pompidou did not go back to teaching. He quickly moved to the Conseil d'État, the special institution watching over the legality of administrative measures and dealing with conflicts involving the state. A seat in this council is one of the top prizes for ambitious young French civil servants and competition is stiff. But the government has the right to appoint some members. Pompidou was put up by the Gaullist government.

The new job required, essentially, a legal background. He was good at it, and quick. In his spare time, he was able to show his gratitude and devotion to the master. He became the benevolent and efficient treasurer of the foundation for backward children named after Anne de Gaulle (the general's late abnormal daughter), thus gaining the goodwill of Madame de Gaulle. He also kept in touch with General de Gaulle, helping him to keep abreast of political changes. Progressively, he became the head of the Gaullist private secretariat of the ruler-in-exile at Colombey.

But the Fourth Republic refused to surrender. It had to be taken by storm. The chosen instrument was the Gaullist Rally or the Rassemblement du Peuple Français. The general himself led the offensive. Among his chief lieutenants the best known at the time were men like M. Jacques Soustelle, the ethnologist who was to become the champion of French Algeria; M. André Malraux, the former fellow traveller and former novelist; M. Michel Debré, the future prime minister. Significantly, M. Georges Pompidou was not thrown into the battle. He was kept in the background, at the general's headquarters, performing his tasks of coordination. But the tottering republic showed an unexpected capacity for passive resistance. The parliamentary elections of 1951 were to have marked its doom. Gaullist electoral successes were not sufficient to precipitate its collapse. The general—according to a saying attributed to André Malraux—had brought his troops to the Rubicon only to leave them there fishing in its water. By 1954, General de Gaulle had to admit defeat and retire to Colombey to wait for another occasion.

Once again, the master's retreat led to a change of profession for his faithful secretary. The Gaullist rallies had cost a lot of money. The electoral campaign left heavy debts behind. In the financial committees tackling these difficulties, M. Pompidou worked with a director of Rothschilds who thought that the skills of such a discreet and efficient manager might be an asset to the house.

In France, the name of Rothschild has a symbolic significance well beyond the present financial power of that house. M. Pompidou's friends strongly resent all the allusions to the "man of the Rothschilds." He was neither a big shareholder nor a partner, they argue; simply a very high official. He served the Rothschilds with the same detachment and leisurely zeal as he had served the state. But the Rothschild tag remains a drawback when the prime minister preaches the virtues of self-sacrifice to the workers. It is an asset with the business community which trusts him not to betray its vital interests.

He found banking no more insuperable than the law. Between board meetings and trips to Africa, Pompidou the financier found plenty of time to enjoy fashionable life. It is from this period—with its holidays at St. Trop and snapshots between a starlet and a crooner—that his reputation as a man of the world, and a rather gay one at that, has come. But could the teacher turned law-councillor turned banker imagine that he would soon be prime minister?

When the actions of the plotters of May 1958, who perpetrated an Algerian putsch, brought General de Gaulle back to power, the faithful servant came, too. For seven months, as *directeur de cabinet* of de Gaulle, the omnipotent prime minister, M. Pompidou took an active part in shaping the Gaullist republic. The following January, General de Gaulle was elected president. But M. Pompidou's moment had not yet arrived. M. Michel Debré, also an obedient Gaullist but a senator and the most vociferous defender of Algérie Française, got the job; M. Pompidou preferred to go back to the Rothschilds rather than to stay as a mere minister.

Once again, he found time for leisure; he even produced an anthology of French poetry.[3] Once again, he kept in regular contact with General de Gaulle. When, at the beginning of 1961, the general realized that he would have to negotiate with the Algerian rebels, he chose M. Pompidou to sound them out. In April 1962, the Evian Agreements, putting an end to the Algerian War, were sweepingly approved by the French people in a referendum. M. Michel Debré, having served his purpose, was discarded. M. Georges Pompidou was asked to form a new government.

From the government of the Rothschilds to that of France—so thundered the Left, missing the main point. The links between Gaullism and big business are more complex. The striking feature of the new appointment was that General de Gaulle had put his private secretary at the head of the government. M. Pompidou was never elected to any office. He has not belonged to any party, not even the Gaullist UNR. The president was the master and the prime minister his humble assistant. When a few months later Pompidou was defeated in parliament, it was parliament that was sent home. The government carried on, staging first a referendum and then a general election. This produced the desired Gaullist majority.

Yet the secretary, as could be expected, proved a quick learner. On his first performance in parliament, he addressed deputies as if they were directors at a board meeting and he was an obvious flop. Now he has learned to vituperate against the opposition with apparent passion, to the delight of Gaullist deputies. He has also quickly grasped how to govern under General de Gaulle's command and to his satisfaction. In economic matters, he has steered a middle course between the two Gaullist temptations of dirigisme and liberal orthodoxy, with a leaning toward the latter. Above all, he has kept a close eye on the president's cherished nuclear force. To General de Gaulle "the sword is the world's axis" and the army a pillar of the state. Despite the end of the Algerian War, and the resulting halving of the army, the French defense budget has been growing substantially from year to year. This is the prime minister's major service to the president and to his army.

"*L'appétit,*" say the French, "*vient en mangeant.*" Behind the easygoing Pompidou manner there is an iron will; behind the leisurely detachment, a great deal of ambition. The man is intelligent enough to know that he will not inherit the Gaullist legend. He may have the master's blessing but he can win only as leader of a conservative coalition. His appeal must be based on the slogan of law, order, and the stable franc.

Yet, will General de Gaulle lift his secretary to the very top? Can Bonapartism be dressed up in civvies and Gaullism, so dependent on myth and legend, perpetuate its attraction in plain prose? The shrewd and adaptable assistant has gained all his laurels as second-in-command. Can he be entrusted with the awkward succession? Will he be able to rule during the interregnum while France goes on being molded into Gaullist shape until it produces its own new commander? If only the adroit and leisurely climber wore a uniform and had at least three stars on his *képi*. Pondering over the future, the aging general, who hears voices, must sometimes wonder whether he has not another point in common with St. Joan—the inability to provide an heir.

1. Bromberger, Merry. *Le Destin Secret de Georges Pompidou.* Fayard, Paris, 1965.
2. Bromberger, Merry. Op.cit, pp. 86 and 89.
3. His taste is as eclectic in literature as it is in modern art, which he has introduced into the staid surroundings of the prime minister's office. He collects paintings of Max Ernst or Nicolas de Stael but also of the fashionable Bernard Buffet. His admirers see in this the sign of an open mind; his critics, the symptoms of the acquisitive instincts of a parvenu.

French Communists

Pathfinders or Renegades?

JANUARY 14, 1967
The Economist

SYMBOLICALLY, THE FRENCH Communist Party did not hold its 18th congress, which opened on January 4th, in one of its strongholds in the "Red Belt" of Paris. It held it in Levallois-Perret, a suburban municipality which it won in 1965 as partner in a left-wing coalition. This was a pre-election congress with "unity of the left" as its chief slogan. Inside the modern sports hall, the French tricolor merged with the red banner stamped with hammer and sickle. There were more than seven hundred delegates from all parts of France. They looked on the young side and many were obviously workers. They were a keen, studious, and disciplined audience who took notes, applauded in the right places, clapped thunderously when required and duly reelected the outgoing leadership headed by the rather ponderous successor of Maurice Thorez, Comrade Waldeck Rochet.

To anyone who a year previously had watched the congress of the Italian Communist Party, and who was aware of the debate that had taken place throughout France before the congress met, the Levallois performance looked remarkably like a Stalinist show. Paradoxically, the more flexible Italian Communists are now in almost total political isolation, while the more rigid Frenchmen have just signed an electoral pact with the rest of the French Left, and can seriously contemplate forming part of a Popular Front government some time in the future.

The French Communist Party has gained a little ground since the birth of the Fifth Republic. Last year 425,000 membership cards were apparently sent to all the local federations; allowing for wastage, this suggests a membership of about 350,000. It is claimed that since 1961 total membership has gone up by 50,000, and the number of party cells has climbed by 2,600 to 19,000. The first serious study of the social makeup of the membership reveals that out of every hundred party members, sixty are wage earners (including three farm laborers), eighteen are shop or office workers, seven are farmers, and six are shopkeepers or craftsmen. The remaining nine are in professional jobs, with teachers and researchers more numerous than engineers and technicians. About 40 percent of party members are under forty, and roughly the same percentage have joined the party during the eight years since General de Gaulle came to power. Thus it still seems as if the party has a greater power to attract than to hold.

In their search for a united front with the Socialists, the French Communists have made a number of concessions. M. Waldeck Rochet summed them up last week while insisting on the difference between Russia in 1917 and France fifty years later. Socialism, he argued, can now be established by peaceful means; the concept of single-party rule was a Stalinist deviation. But the true obstacles to unity are usually concealed by the verbiage of such ideological debate. Western socialists, in Britain, Scandinavia, Italy, Germany, and France itself, have formed or joined governments to manage, some would say to improve, existing societies. Can the Communists participate as the left wing of such governments? In principle, their ultimate purpose is still the revolutionary transformation of society. This is why they argue that, once in power, they ought to establish "socialist legality" in order to prevent the dispossessed from striking back. But people are beginning to wonder whether the Communists have not started to follow the socialist example of proclaiming revolutionary slogans while in practice settling for gradual reforms.

It may seem pointless to speculate about ideological and tactical retreats when one remembers that more than thirty years ago the French Communists made even bigger concessions in their drive for a Popular Front. The great difference between then and now is that then they made these concessions on Moscow's orders with the aim of implementing Stalin's world strategy. This is no longer the case. The only discordance in last week's congress came from the visitors' benches. Whenever, amid general applause, a speaker argued in favor of an international Communist conference, the Vietnamese, Italians, and Rumanians did not join in the clapping.

Gone are the days when Moscow's wishes were orders. Individual parties have their own problems to take into account. If Signor Longo refuses to support an international conference it is because he knows that his left wing would oppose him publicly if he did. If the French side with the Russians on this issue, it is largely because the Russian conception of "peaceful coexistence" suits their Popular Front tactics. However, on Gaullism and on electoral policy they do not see eye to eye with Moscow. Because of Moscow's sympathy for de Gaulle's foreign policy, it would suit the Russians better if the French Communists were to strengthen the general's position by facing the forthcoming election intransigently alone.

Times are changing and the modern paintings at Levallois were not the only symptom of change. The debates among the rank and file at the pre-congress regional conferences were apparently more lively than one would suppose after being told that 15,000 delegates assembled in all the regional conferences only managed to produce one "no" and 13 abstentions. "Some comrades," it is admitted, were bothered about the support promised to M. Mitterrand and the concessions made to his Socialist-Democrat federation. Many more are puzzled by the Sino-Soviet conflict and by events in Vietnam. The violence of the official attacks at the congress against the small pro-Chinese groups in the party was significant. So many disputatious students have had to be expelled that most Communist students in Paris are now outside the party. When, as happened last November, a meeting of protest against the war in Vietnam, which had been boycotted by the party, more than filled the biggest hall in the Latin Quarter, the party leaders began to get worried. They are afraid of being overtaken on their left.

Though they are still less articulate about it than the Italians, some French Communists are also pondering over the nature and direction of their movement. The party discipline achieved by the Bolsheviks was partly due to their revolutionary objectives, partly the result of the special conditions inside Russia. Stalin turned the foreign parties into battalions marching to order with military precision. Now, while still propelled by conditioned reflexes, they are beginning to wonder how to march and where to. Can they take the social democratic road? Will they split into revolutionary and reformist factions? How long can they remain both monolithic and reformist, as the French party is still managing to do? M. Waldeck Rochet must be glad that he can evade such questions for the time being by throwing his troops into the election. The immediate task, as the veteran M. Duclos put it in his closing speech, is to get people to vote Communist in the first round. If the party gets more than a fifth of the votes cast in the first ballot on March 5th, it will demonstrate that the Communists, far from slipping, remain the principal force on the French left. But the questions will not vanish, whatever the election results.

Death of a Salesman?

JULY 22, 1967
The Economist

TOMMY SIMPSON WAS probably better known in France than Harold Wilson. The twenty-nine-year-old draughtsman from Yorkshire, who moved his home from Brittany to Paris to Ghent, was the only Englishman among that select band of continentals, the cycling champions. When he collapsed and died last week during the Tour de France, climbing Mont Ventoux in the scorching sun on the way from Marseilles to Carpentras, the shock here was greater than a matador's death in a Spanish bullring.

The inquest that was immediately ordered raised the issue of "stimulants" or, to put it plainly, drugs. Mr. Simpson's death also started people thinking about the whole question of commercial competition. For the two things are connected with one another. These cyclists are professionals and it is for money that they drive their bodies beyond endurance.

For three weeks, throughout the Tour de France, the cyclists are accompanied by a caravan of commercial sponsors who each night provide a kind of public show or fair. Towns actually pay to be included in the itinerary. But the people who pack the stadium or watch the race along the roads of France are a tiny proportion of the Frenchmen—and Belgians, Italians, and Spaniards—who through Eurovision, radio and the newspapers passionately follow the struggle for the Yellow Jersey—the award for the competitor with the best overall record.

The tour exercises a fascination comparable to a test match series with Australia or a cup final. And it is the highlight only of a season that includes similar tours in Italy and Spain, a series of one-day races, particularly popular in Belgium, competitions on the track, and so on. Advertisers realized that professional cycling could provide a splendid opportunity for reaching a mass public. There was a time when cyclists were sponsored only by cycle manufacturers. Now they wear on their jerseys the name of an aperitif or of a make of refrigerator, television set, or ball-point pen. Commercial sponsors support a team, including riders from different countries, throughout the year.

But since people are still nationalist in their sporting loyalties, the organizers of the French tour reverted this year to the principle of national teams competing against each other. This is why Simpson came to take part in the race as leader of a rather weak British team. But the commercial sponsors did not want to be deprived of their standard bearers in such a popular and closely watched race. A compromise was reached. The riders were divided into national teams but were also allowed to carry advertisements on their jerseys. This, presumably, is the cycling equivalent of a compromise between *l'Europe des patries* and supranationalism.

Champion-class riders are few. The majority in each team is made up of what the French call *les porteurs d'eau,* the men who carry water for the top riders or stop to help them change a wheel. These services have to be paid for. The winner of the tour leaves the kitty for his teammates including all the prizes and bonuses. The leader himself makes his money from the prestige of winning; he secures a more attractive contract from his sponsor or he may arrange a series of well-paid exhibitions.

Tommy Simpson belonged to the small group of big money-spinners. A shrewd cyclist can buy a house, a farm, a business. But to earn that much money he must stay in the limelight, force himself to pedal even faster and to go on climbing those agonizing hills. These feats of endurance make the difference between affluence and merely getting by.

It is small wonder if a man becomes tempted to use artificial means to sustain his efforts. Whatever the truth in Simpson's case, it is well known that the anti-doping law introduced a couple of years ago has not prevented cyclists from taking drugs in order to keep the wares of their sponsors well to the front. Maybe the feeling aroused in France by Tommy Simpson's death will lead to a revulsion against the dangers that can turn the life of a sportsman into the death of a commercial traveller.

1958:
The Return of
Charles de Gaulle

::

France's Misdirected Fury

APRIL 19, 1958
The Economist

Is THE FOURTH Republic intrinsically incapable of coping with the Algerian conflict? Is it doomed to collapse, sapped by the physical and moral consequences of an unending war? These sombre questions spring to mind again as France is once more without a government. No doubt the parliament produced by the elections of January 1956, is no more unstable than its predecessors; but each successive government finds the Algerian problem politically more unmanageable. Far from vanishing—as French optimists prophesied in the early stages—it grows more intractable daily. M. Mollet, under whose rule the conflict was transformed into a kind of holy war, ended his record-breaking run when he asked the deputies to foot the bill. His successor, the no less bellicose M. Bourgès-Maunoury, fell when he introduced a bill of mild reforms. Now, on Tuesday, the Assembly turned down M. Gaillard's proposal to negotiate with President Bourguiba on the compromise achieved by the Anglo-American good offices. This Tunisian episode is just one more chapter in the gloomy Algerian story.

When M. Gaillard took office in November, his youth and his reputation led some to hope that he might somehow break the deadlock—that he might be the man to dictate terms to the right-wing members of his coalition, who reject any idea of compromise, instead of accepting theirs. His prospects were unproved in January, when the windfall of dollars brought home by M. Monnet from Washington insured France against a major payments crisis in the near future. But, scarcely a week later, French planes bombed the Tunisian village of Sakiet. Both the explosive nature of the North African situation and M. Gaillard's weakness were at once shown. Although his age had prompted comparisons with the youthful Bonaparte, M. Gaillard did not dare to sack guilty generals or responsible ministers. He was not master.

The Prime Minister showed skill in maneuver. He was greatly helped in his task by the Anglo-American good offices mission. In mid-February, France stood on the defensive before world opinion; by last week the positions were reversed. Now it was M. Bourguiba, rejecting international control of his country's frontier with Algeria, who was on the defensive. Under pressure from Mr. Murphy and Mr. Beeley he had agreed not only to talk to the French but also to accept reasonable terms on Bizerta, the airports, and the position of French nationals. The tragic incident, it seemed, could be closed, though not the tension, which has its roots in the Algerian War. But the French did not grasp this unexpected chance. M. Gaillard had promised his right-wing colleagues that he would insist on international supervision of the frontier. When he realized that a negotiated compromise was the best he could hope for—and was reminded by President Eisenhower of the risks France would run if it took the issue to the Security Council—it was too late. What two months ago would have looked like a heaven-sent solution was now greeted as a piece of American dictation. The deputies, recalled from vacation, came to Paris in xenophobic mood. After the most anti-American debate since the war, M. Gaillard's government was defeated by 321 votes to 255.

Once again a government has been brought down by a motley coalition with no alternative policy. Nearly half the adverse votes were cast by the Communists, who support the Algerian claim to independence. The bulk of the rest has come from right-wingers who share the ideas of MM. Soustelle, Bidault and Morice—the self-appointed leaders of the *ultras*. There is logic of a kind in the attitude of this group. They do not want to negotiate with Tunisia because they fear that compromise would be contagious. They still believe, against all experience, that the Algerian

War can be won by the force of arms; they would be willing to set the whole of North Africa ablaze in their quest for that unlikely victory.

The trouble with this formal logic is that it is quite divorced from reality. It ignores the real causes of the Algerian rebellion and the inevitable ties between North African neighbors. It neglects the political impetus of the Arab block, the mood of uncommitted countries, and the facts of competition between East and West. If these illusions, which belong to the nineteenth century and have been preserved in the twentieth only by incantation, still enjoy wide acceptance in France, the successive governments that have not dared to tell the people the plain political and economic facts about the Algerian War cannot escape blame. Such slogans as "Algeria is French" have acquired a hypnotic force. The French have been taught that any compromise will spell the end of France's greatness. Economic reports tell them that the war costs next to nothing. When prices go up, or when the clock fails to strike M. Lacoste's last quarter of an hour, the fault must lie with agents, foreigners, Americans, Jews, Reds, or parliamentary government.

And so miraculous saviors are once again in fashion. Only one of these—General de Gaulle—merits serious consideration. All the other would-be Bonapartes are too lightweight, and too openly committed to the extreme Right, to withstand the left-wing revulsion that would follow a coup from them. The general alone has the stature to make a national appeal and a past that makes him immune to charges of defeatism. His aloof silence in public, and his Delphic pronouncements in private, have created such confusion that people with exactly opposite views on Algeria claim the general as their man. He is also the only possible national leader who might count, in certain circumstances, on the neutrality, if not the support, of the French Left. But conditions are not ripe for him; neither the Communists nor the Socialists are ready to permit his return, and without their votes the constitution could not be amended to fit his requirements.

For the time being, President Coty will probably dispense another dose of the old medicine. After an attempt by M. Bidault or M. Soustelle—to prove that the *ultras* do not command a majority—this crisis is likely to end in a government headed by a man like M. Mollet,

M. Pleven or M. Pinay, with an unchanged policy. Whether they stay in the government or act by proxy, the Conservatives will continue to control France's Algerian policy. While the one hundred fifty Communist deputies remain untouchable, the Algerian lobby can block any compromise proposal. The present interregnum may not involve what the French call a crisis of the regime, but the road leads clearly that way.

To what conclusions does this sad analysis point? The Algerian War is acting as a steady poison in the French body politic. The growth in importance of the army at a time when its officer corps feels frustrated and cheated of victory contains a threat to political institutions. Unproductive expenditure on defense may jeopardize France's real economic achievements in other fields, and cannot fail to distort or dislocate the common market.

Is it too late for a French government to produce a plan which might be accepted, if not with enthusiasm, by both metropolitan Frenchmen and Algerian Muslims? Such a plan would have to promise independence to Algeria within the framework of a North African federation; it would have to safeguard certain essential rights for French settlers; it would have to be carried with, and not against, M. Bourguiba. To get parliament to accept such a proposal, the government would have to be ready, if need be, to accept the backing of Communists. Then the right wing, no longer enjoying the monopoly of blackmail, would probably rally again to the government's side. The risk, after years of procrastination, would seem worth taking.

For France's allies, and for the Americans in particular, the lesson is simpler. Washington long ago lost faith in the Lacoste policy of "pacification." But it has continued to treat France gently for fear of an upheaval within NATO. It now becomes plain that, the longer the conflict lasts, the less competent the Fourth Republic is to deal with it. As time passes, the chances increase of either a right-wing coup or a "Popular Front" which would admit the Communists to a share of power. The Americans have sown money and gathered abuse, without securing any progress towards a solution. What France needs is not gentle persuasion and dollar anaesthetics. It needs the dream to be broken.

The Challenge
from Algiers

MAY 17, 1958
The Economist

THE FRENCH REPUBLIC has come face to face with its long-awaited vital test; and, as is the way with such tests, what was long expected has come suddenly with the shock of surprise. On Tuesday night the Assembly was moving toward an orderly, indeed routine, conclusion to a conventional Paris government crisis, when the news from Algiers put the questions: Was the capital in Paris, or in Algiers? Did the republic, or its generals, rule? The alliance of settlers and paratroopers did not merely refuse obedience to Paris, it sought to tell the president of the republic and the National Assembly what sort of government they should choose.

M. Pflimlin's parliamentary day had begun quietly at three o'clock in the afternoon, when the fifty-one-year-old Alsatian leader of the MRP (Christian Democrats) climbed the rostrum to present the program of his prospective government and to ask for the vote of investiture. His program differed from the programs of his recent predecessors only in the suggestion that it contained a possible cautious shift in Algerian policy. Because the withdrawal of the socialists from the government meant the departure of M. Lacoste from his ministerial office in Algiers, such a change was in the air. M. Pflimlin's reputation as the supporter of a liberal solution pointed in the same direction; but he was measuring his words now so as not to give offense. While he did not exclude the use of the good offices of Morocco and Tunisia, he also proclaimed that France would fight until victory. In any case, the presence of the conservative ministers in his cabinet was a guarantee that there would be no abrupt change of direction, and so the debate at first proceeded in wholly conventional fashion, with a long list of orators and numerous breaks to enable the parties to make up their minds. When the Assembly suspended its session for dinner, all still seemed normal. Only the helmeted policemen massed outside the Palais Bourbon, and the lorries blocking the bridge from the Concorde, showed that trouble had been expected.

There had indeed been a little trouble in the Paris streets, but it was under control; in Algiers on the same afternoon it was out of hand. There the French settlers had felt the sense of power since the day in 1956 when M. Mollet gave way to their clamor in the streets of Algiers. Now seemed the time to use that power. Their conviction had never been shaken that a compromise in North Africa was intolerable and that, in resisting it, they had nothing to lose; and they could rely, they calculated, on the backing of frustrated and discontented troops. After they had stormed the building of the government-general, the news came that the troops had joined in, and that the paratrooper General Massu was head of a newly formed Committee of Public Safety.

This mixed body of soldiers and civilians at once sent a message to President Coty demanding that a similar "government of public safety" be formed in Paris. The pronunciamento had come. But the deputies in the Palais Bourbon went on for a time as if nothing had happened. To observe their procedure was like watching a ball through glass, without hearing the music. Then a Communist deputy broke the pretence and sounded the alarm. He urged, amid uproar, that all republicans should unite in face of a common danger. M. Pflimlin jumped up to reject the Communist offer; the Assembly, he said, would live up to its grave duties.

The make-believe over, the tension rose as the scene shifted between the seats of the Assembly, the government, and the presidency of the republic. Reports of numerous arrests of right-wing extremists in Paris showed that, in the government's belief, the rising was not entirely spontaneous. Parliament had reached the point where it must close its ranks, or disintegrate, and its reaction was to close its ranks. The parliamentary defense reflexes were set in motion; socialists, radicals and fellow-catholics assured M. Pflimlin of their support and urged him to persist in his bid for office. He did not hide the gravity of the situation; accusing some of the military leaders of insurrection, he said that France was on the brink of civil war. The Communists decided that, though they could not vote for a man determined to carry on the war in Algeria, in the circumstances they should abstain. This left the vote no longer in doubt; M. Pflimlin received the investiture by 274 votes to 129 with 137 abstentions; that is, he might have won even against Communist opposition. France had a government again, but the question to be answered was what authority it possessed. It has still to be answered.

Behind the uncertainties of the new government was ample ground for misgiving about the future of French policy in North Africa, and therefore of the western position in the Mediterranean. The settlers and the soldiers had chosen to precipitate the crisis on the mere ground that a prospective new government was suspected, without any very solid evidence, of a more flexible approach to North African problems. What, then, would happen if a French government were indeed to come to the point and make a real attempt at negotiation? Successive French governments for years past have been led by fear of just such an explosion to pass by any opportunities for peaceful settlement or any hope of capturing Muslim opinion. And the effects of these successive refusals reinforced the settlers' intransigence and burdened France with a discontented army of a dangerous size. If civilian authority were to capitulate in the face of the present open challenge—and there are many ways of giving in, with many nuances—then more juntas, more pronunciamentos, and more vetoes upon France's policies would have to be expected. The trial of strength may only have begun.

By Wednesday it seemed that a clear answer would be given to the question: Who governs France? President Coty's message to the troops and M. Pflimlin's to the population were being broadcast every hour to the tune of the Marseillaise. It all sounded solemn and serious. By evening there were signs that the insurgents, having over-reached themselves, were climbing down. General Massu, only a day after he had sent the president an ultimatum, was now declaring himself no more than a guardian of order. Reliable reports from Algiers indicated that the military and civilian members of the committee were at odds.

But with events appearing to come within its grasp, Paris may once again be drifting into a compromise solution which, while it wears the trimmings of success, may contain the seeds of defeat. M. Pflimlin took the decision to widen his government, offering one of the posts of deputy prime minister to M. Pinay, a conservative, and another to the socialist M. Mollet. This could be pretty close to the government of public safety that the insurgents had demanded. Their hostility to M. Pflimlin was due to fear that he would change French policy in Algeria. What is formed as a government of national union may be in effect no more than a wide coalition based on compromise from which no real change of policy can be expected. The other fear which roused the Algerian settlers had been that, once out of office, the socialists would rapidly drop the bankrupt policy of which M. Lacoste has been the symbol and upholder in Algiers. But now there were even rumors (since contradicted) that he might be given a seat in the government. No wonder the cynics are beginning to say that it will all end with another medal for Massu.

At the time this is written it is not yet clear what will emerge from it all, and it would be unfair to M. Pflimlin, who stood so stoutly firm during the night of crisis, to prejudge what he will do. All that can be said is that, if the government does not assert its authority now, it will have missed a historic opportunity. This week's events could even be made to serve a useful purpose: Is it to be woe to the republic that lets its generals cross the Rubicon, or woe to the generals who cross? Exemplary measures now might restore some discipline into the forces; but is the republic strong enough to take them? Certainly it cannot be wholly safe as long as the Algerian War continues to keep the army too big for its boots. But there, too, a chance waits to be seized. The rebellious settlers in Algeria have not received the support in France on which they evidently counted. In fact, the ostentation of their defiance has cost them a lot of sympathy. The new government could, therefore, be better placed than its predecessors to carry out the reforms in Algeria which have been prevented, or rendered ineffective, in the past by fear of Algiers. Resolute reforms, if they were sensibly supplemented by the good offices of Tunisia and Morocco, might even now lead to a peaceful solution. Some currents of opinion have been running in that direction.

The cost of hesitation and weakness, on the other hand, will be incalculable. Leniency will encourage more insubordination. More concessions to the Algerian settlers will substantiate their belief that they have the right, and the power, of veto on the composition and policy of the government. The authority of the state will be further undermined. The seeds of rebellion can cross the Mediterranean. It is no accident that the figure of General de Gaulle suddenly stands out again. On Thursday he broke his long silence with a terse declaration of his readiness to assume power. With the soldiers in Algiers now calling for De Gaulle, M. Pflimlin cannot but know that these days are decisive.

Steps to the Throne

JUNE 7, 1958
The Economist

NOW THAT GENERAL de Gaulle has cleared so quickly and successfully the parliamentary obstacles to his return and that telegrams of congratulation are pouring in from around the world, it is not in the fashion to scrutinize the last steps in his ascent to power. Yet these must be recorded, and not for the sake of historical accuracy alone. The manner of the climb to power is seldom without effect on the nature of the reign.

When autumn comes the general may, or may not, be confirmed in his position by a popular vote. He was not, however, called to office by the voice of the French people but rather by the government's cowardice, the relative indifference of bewildered Frenchmen in France, and the dictation of the Algerian settlers and soldiers. In Paris the only "Gaullist" voice was the cacophony that disturbed the peace of the night on Thursday and Friday of last week. The bright young things from the fashionable quarters—the *merveilleux* of 1958—drove through the streets sounding their horns to proclaim their attachment to the general and to "French Algeria." Yet the most ardent Gaullist would not claim this fashionable joyride by the excited few as a "popular" verdict—inviting, say, comparison with the republican mass march of the previous Wednesday. But the republican parties did not call the people of Paris out again. "We are no longer capable of three glorious days in succession," a Parisian remarked.

The epilogue was played out in the Palais Bourbon, where the votes of the Socialists were still needed for a legal performance. M. Mollet, chief inspirer of the Gaullist succession, was permanently rushing between Socialist meetings and the general's headquarters. M. Vincent Auriol, a former president of the republic, came to his rescue and their combined efforts succeeded in breaching the façade of hostility to de Gaulle in the party. The twin arguments of the general's liberalism and the threat of civil war gained ground. But when it came to the vote last Saturday, it turned out that the majority of Socialist deputies was still against the general. A compromise was reached by granting the deputies, on this occasion, a free vote, and freedom to join the new government if they chose.

Socialist resistance to threats and wooing had many causes. One reason was a reluctance to be a consenting victim and to lend a legal appearance to what some of the Socialists called a paratrooper investiture. Combined with this was a feeling of guilt that if things had come to such a pass it was largely through the Algerian policies sponsored by the secretary of their own party. The names of Mollet and Lacoste suddenly became anathema to many Socialists. But they were not only looking back. There are Socialists who think that the apparently aging general, for all his gifts, will prove another Hindenburg. The threat of civil war, to them, is simply postponed and they do not want to leave to the Communists the undisputed leadership of the popular forces. In the assembly the ghost of Vichy haunted the lobbies, producing the so-called "complex of the eighty" (the number of deputies who voted against the transfer of power to Pétain in 1940). An unkind critic summed up the attitude of many Socialists as a combined desire to be among the eighty and to see de Gaulle elected nevertheless.

The Communists have certainly acted on the assumption that the battle has only been delayed, though it is not clear whether they have not just made a virtue of necessity. Their moderation may have been dictated by the knowledge that in isolation they could not mobilize the strength to resist General de Gaulle and the forces of the law. Whatever the reason, they avoided a full-scale clash, acted as the faithful defenders of "republican legality" and wooed unceasingly their reluctant allies. They voted to the end against General de Gaulle's return. On the day of the investiture the militants were called out, but they were told to parade, not to fight. Several, nevertheless, were wounded in skirmishes with the police. But the party was still ostensibly avoiding a trial of strength.

The Communists' future strategy seems to be based on historical analogy. To them the next stage in France will be the "liberal empire." Only when the general gets lost in the Algerian maze (and, in their opinion, he cannot help it) will the regime become fully authoritarian, the general revealing his Bonapartist leanings or making way for others who will. Then will come the real battle and the Socialists will be left with the choice between unity with the Communists or mass desertion by the rank-and-file. In the meantime the Communists will prepare the ground by common action in the various vigilance and anti-fascist committees. Whatever the worth of this analysis, it has certainly influenced the stand of other anti-Gaullists who are frightened to leave the monopoly of resistance to the Communists.

Such, then, was the situation on the eve of the transfer of power. The Bourse was recovering its confidence. Gold was falling; the franc and French and Algerian shares were picking up. The Right, both extremist and orthodox, had rallied to the general. The MRP was following suit after some reassurances about foreign alignments and European policies (thrice M. Robert Schuman was told by an emissary that it was not the general's habit to go back on a signed treaty). Most Radicals were now favorable. But the question remained whether the general would agree to face parliament if the majority of Socialists refused to back him. M. Mollet, who had staked his political future on the Gaullist card, begged him to go on and the general agreed on condition that M. Mollet should lend him his name (for what it was now worth) as a sign of socialist approval.

And so to Sunday, June 1st. At three in the afternoon the general entered the packed chamber. For a moment he surveyed what were by now to him unfamiliar surroundings and faces. Then his tall figure towered above the rostrum as he read his brief speech of investiture. The government was asking for full powers for six months "to restore the unity of the nation." The general asked also for a mandate to rewrite the constitution and submit the result to a popular referendum. The relationship with the "associated states" would be redefined in the process. The assembly must vote the necessary laws rapidly and then depart until October. The speech lasted only a few minutes before the general was gone, giving no indication of his foreign policy nor of his plan for Algeria and only the vaguest hints about the constitution. All he did say was that it would be based on universal suffrage, the separation of powers and governmental responsibility to parliament.

The composition of the cabinet was not much help either. Admittedly, the colonialist *ultras* had been excluded. Indeed, the general was taking over the main figures of the dreaded "system." M. Mollet, who had dominated this sorry legislature, and M. Pflimlin, who had presided over its last abdication, were included among the four ministers of state; the conservative M. Pinay at the ministry of finance was a guarantee of orthodoxy. The newcomers were mainly civil servants. The choice of M. Couve de Murville, ambassador to Bonn, for the ministry of foreign affairs was interpreted as a reassurance for "Europeans"; that of M. Guillaumat, of the Atomic Energy Commission, to the ministry of defense as a sign of contemplated modernization. But will they be more than subordinates? More important is the fact that the whole cabinet is tentative, to be reshaped after General de Gaulle's return from Algiers.

Voting in the Dark

The deputies were thus asked to vote in the dark. The alternative to the general was civil war. They were to trust him, his past, and his spoken confidences to party leaders. In the circumstances, it is not astonishing that the best speeches were made for the opposition. M. Mendès-France balanced a severe criticism of the performance of the Fourth Republic with a declaration of faith in the republican parliamentary system. He concluded that this was not a free vote; and he could not give his consent under threat. M. Mitterrand proclaimed that the general "in law, will get his power from the representatives of the nation; in fact, he holds it already from the *coup de force.*" M. Duclos, significantly milder than on previous occasions, expressed his confidence in the opposition of the people as a whole. M. Cot, a *progressiste*, claimed that since it was carried under duress, the vote was null and void; he, too, appealed to the verdict of the people.

General de Gaulle was invested by 329 votes to 224. In addition to the 147 Communists and their allies, the votes against were cast by 49 Socialists (42 voted in favor), 18 Radicals, three followers of M. Mitterrand and three members of the MRP. The majority, though not impressive, was sufficient to get the vote on special powers through; it was not enough for the new clause on constitutional revision, which required approval by at least three-fifths of those voting. The commissions immediately set to work. For the next twenty-four hours one often had the impression of watching a congress of solicitors convinced that, even in these exceptional circumstances, democracy could be preserved by the clever drafting of a paragraph. The government agreed to some clarifying amendments, but it was sure of ultimate victory. Having come to the point of abdication, the assembly could not now turn back. The general made the submission easier, even, in the end, coming to the chamber to answer questions. The last night session was the setting for a remarkable performance.

It started, as expected, with an ultimatum: the final text submitted by the government must be approved or the government would insist on the inevitable consequence. The general's parliamentary skill was shown in the discussion of amendments. He was full of charm and indulgence. He made a graceful actor's bow to a Communist who suggested that sedition was now followed by seduction. He was full of republican fervour: the lower house was to be supreme; there was to be no presidential government; to be among the deputies was a pleasure and an honor. Was this the man who had been so scathing about the regime at his press conference two weeks before? The Socialist rebels decided to abstain, assuring a government majority. Even the journalists in the lobby started to talk of the general's conversion.

Only when it was over could one appreciate the quality of the performance. The general had not given in an inch. He had rejected the proposal that the constitution be submitted to parliament before the referendum on the ground that he would refuse to set the executive and the legislature at odds before the people. Yet, when M. Mitterrand asked him whether, on other occasions, he would decline to appeal to the electorate over the head of parliament—a manœuvre dreaded by republicans since Louis Napoleon—the general remained silent. M. Bidault made the apt parting comment: "Today chamber music, tomorrow *musique militaire*."

IN ALGERIA

On Wednesday the general began his Algerian pilgrimage. Algiers greeted the man it had imposed on France in a mood of delirious triumph, mingled with doubts. Addressing the huge crowd massed in the Forum, the general assured it of his sympathy and understanding. Then, taking at their face value the slogans of political equality launched recently by the settlers, he proclaimed that the Muslims of Algeria were now fully-fledged Frenchmen and as such would take part in the constitutional referendum (to be held in three months' time) and in parliamentary elections. Has the general opted for the policy of integration, which at best is a political gamble beyond France's economic possibilities? (This week, in an interview granted to *L'Express*, President Bourguiba stated that he would not insult the intelligence of the French authorities by suggesting that they might seriously think of basing a constructive policy on the so-called "fraternization"). The more left-wing of General de Gaulle's supporters in Paris, still convinced that he will grant Algeria a form of independence, stress the facts that he did not use the word integration and that he reserved the right to discuss the future with the Algerian representatives produced by the elections. But beyond the delphic passages in the text, one thing is clear. The general is banking on the soldiers, whom he is seeking to bring under his full control. "I rely on the army for today and tomorrow." In this crisis, the tragic weakness of the state's authority has enabled the army to discover its vocation as king-maker. And the army has proclaimed that it will not tolerate any other master than the general. This is a key factor for the future of French politics.

The Army's Choice

JUNE 14, 1958
The Economist

GENERAL DE GAULLE'S brief tour of Algeria has thrown a great deal of light on the balance of power in the new French situation. It has also shattered illusions that the Algerian conflict can be brought to a rapid conclusion. Before his visit, the general, though carried to power by the staunchest partisans of a policy of force, retained with many people the reputation of being the only man capable of bringing the war to an end by negotiation—promising Algeria a form of independence within a broader framework which would include Tunisia and Morocco. In other words, it was claimed that only a man of his stature could achieve what M. Mollet and his successors so patently failed to accomplish.

The general was not expected to proclaim Algeria's "right to independence" on his tour, but the partisans of a liberal solution expected him not to say anything that might jeopardize such a solution; and "liberal Gaullists" in Paris were encouraging this expectation. Even after his inaugural speech in Algiers, and in spite of his blessing for the settlers and soldiers in revolt, the advocates of a negotiated settlement clung to their hopes: there were some of the settlers' formulæ which the general had not repeated. Yet at each stage in his journey the liberal argument wore thinner. When he got to Oran the general stated that Algeria must show "that it is a French land today and forever." Finally, at Mostaganem he ended his last speech before he left for Paris with the cry:

"Long live French Algeria." For the settlers, the army, the FLN and President Bourguiba the doubts were over. The general, in their opinion, had chosen the path of integration, and rejected that of independence.

The previous illusions sprang from an initial misunderstanding. General de Gaulle's trip was described in Paris as a journey to reassert the authority of the state over a recalcitrant army and insubordinate settlers. The description would have been accurate if anyone else had been attempting to reassert this authority: M. Pflimlin, say, or M. Mitterrand, whom many had considered the most likely candidate to lead a resolute republican government, willing to stand up to the men of Algiers. But for General de Gaulle it was misleading. He was the army's choice; its spokesmen had stated plainly that they would accept no one else.

Admittedly, the French army (or rather its officer corps) was merely united in its refusal to obey the civilian authorities in Paris and in its determination to bring de Gaulle back. Within its ranks there was—and still is—a wing that wants to take things entirely in its own hands. The paratrooper officers, the colonels who after years of fighting against national revolutionary movements in Indo-China and Algeria have developed a thirst for direct political action, first set the pace. They found numerous allies in the committees of public safety, and together they urged that the first victory—the return of General de Gaulle—should be followed immediately by a wholesale purge of the politicians and the rapid establishment of a single-party, totalitarian regime. The risks of a considerable fascist movement in the home country are limited at this stage in the absence of unemployment and mass social unrest for it to feed on. Its only possible recruits on a considerable scale are the small men squeezed by the industrial revolution who had flocked to M. Poujade's banner. But changes in the economic situation might increase this threat.

The general has refused to become the leader of the extremist faction, but he has come to a compromise with it. The committees of public safety have been ordered to submit themselves to the public authorities, which, incidentally, are the military, since General Salan has been entrusted with civilian powers. But the committees were not dissolved. They were merely told that the aim of their revolution was achieved—the general being now in power—and that they should concentrate on the rather nebulous task of "integration of the souls."

Encouraged by this recognition, the Algerian committee has tried to force the general's hand. On Tuesday it sent a message, sounding like an ultimatum, urging him to hold no elections in Algeria before the referendum; to announce plainly his approval of integration; and to get rid of the party system in France. The committee has over-reached itself and General Salan received a rebuff from General de Gaulle for his part in this threatening message. The general, though banking on the army, does not want its most extreme elements to run his show.

When a provisional balance-sheet of the new Algerian policy is being drawn up, the deadweight of army investiture becomes apparent. Most of the recent moves point in the direction of integration. Algerian Muslims have been promised "equal rights and duties" (a term that still needs definition). They have been assured that they will vote on equal terms with Frenchmen in the referendum and in the elections for a legislature which are to follow. Since then it has been announced (though M. Malraux, as chief government spokesman, has already denied this) that municipal elections will be held in Algeria within a month and that the government will guarantee complete freedom of choice throughout the territory. It is difficult to see how either of these pledges can be kept. The elections may have to be delayed if only because, as the settlers claim, no machinery for them exists. More important, with the army committed to integration and the committees still in action, would the Arab nationalists favoring independence have a real chance of presenting their case? The FLN has answered not only by announcing a boycott but by launching a new military offensive. President Bourguiba, who had pinned some hopes on General de Gaulle, has expressed his disappointment that another opportunity has been missed. The war goes on and the armed forces are apparently asking for another £100 million.

Yet let us assume for a moment that the French would be willing to accept all the political sacrifices involved in genuine integration—the settlers agreeing to Muslim predominance in all the elected offices in Algeria; and metropolitan Frenchmen agreeing to a proportionate Muslim representation in the Paris parliament, whatever its future functions may be. The fact remains that to stand a chance of success the policy of integration would involve even greater economic burdens than those already carried by France in Algeria. Equal family allowances and other social benefits are only the beginning. To provide the population with a livelihood would require agrarian reforms and rapid industrial development, creating threats to many vested interests in Algeria and at home. Further tremendous investments would be required to keep pace with the soaring Muslim birthrate. The loans which M. Pinay proposes to raise cannot possibly pay for this; it will be surprising if the American taxpayer will pay for it, either.

The magnitude of this economic task leads French opinions to exactly opposite conclusions. The settlers think that the new plan will go the way of its stillborn predecessors. It is their hope that General de Gaulle has been as effectively stifled with laurels as M. Mollet was silenced with rotten tomatoes. Liberal Gaullists, on the other hand, claim that, in spite of appearances and concessions, the general will opt for a form of independence and will reveal his plans in his forthcoming constitutional project.

Could he carry the army with him? A few weeks ago it would have seemed strange to apply to sophisticated France a question that is usually asked in a Latin American context. But the details of General Ely's resignation, for instance (he has now returned to his post as chief of staff of the armed forces), show convincingly that military disobedience was not limited to the paratroopers or the troops in Algeria; it was general and systematic. The soldiers having won their political battle, what alternative source of political strength is available to the new prime minister? The government was enlarged on Monday. Of its twenty-one members, fourteen are parliamentarians. With parliament in recess, however, they are neither responsible to the assembly nor can they exert influence through the parliamentary support which they can muster for the government. They are the general's counsellors, whose advice he may follow or not, as he thinks fit. The constitutional projects will show how the general intends to fill the parliamentary vacuum. In Paris, in the meantime, a ten-year-old saying of M. Malraux, the minister of information, has once again become fashionable: "In France there are the Communists, ourselves [that is, the Gaullists] and nothing." Only, it is added, the Gaullists have changed; most of them are now in uniform.

Parisian Panorama

MAY 24, 1958
The Economist

WHAT MIGHT HAVE been the end proved to be only the beginning. General de Gaulle's statement on May 15th transformed a trial of
strength between Paris and Algiers—which was turning to Paris's
advantage—into a struggle for the life of the Fourth Republic; and the
outcome is still uncertain. The Algerian settlers, who on May 13th had
stormed the offices of the Government-General, put the paratrooper
General Massu at the head of their Committee of Public Safety and dictated terms to Paris, were still in angry mood, but the generals themselves were having second thoughts. Paris had not given in. M. Pflimlin
was invested as prime minister with a big majority. Generals, like
everyone else, have to consider their careers, and they were beginning
to think in terms of a compromise.

Then came the rumor that General de Gaulle would speak. This was
a godsend for the generals. Now they could look for Gaullist honors
instead of Republican sanctions. On the Thursday morning (May 15th)
the Algiers crowd, gathered in the Forum, responded enthusiastically
to General Salan's cry: "Long live de Gaulle." The general did not disappoint their hopes. At 5 P.M. in Paris journalists crowded into the
quiet Rue Solferino, outside the Gaullist headquarters. They pushed
inside and emerged with a simple sheet of paper which was nevertheless a political bomb. In his laconic statement the general had no

word of reproof for Algiers in revolt. He repeated his usual charges against the degradation of the state and ended with a challenge: "I am ready to assume the powers of the republic."

History, it has been said, repeats itself, first as a drama, then as a farce. General de Gaulle drew an analogy with his stand in 1940, but was his new message perhaps only a parody of its predecessor? In 1940, with his country trampled underfoot by the Nazis, he replied from London that France would regain its freedom. Now his voice came as an echo to the cries of Algerian settlers and their military accomplices who were defying the French Republic. "Powers of the Republic": this plural did not pass unnoticed in Montesquieu's country; it could cover legislative as well as executive powers, and to many it smacked (though the general, pointing to his past record, has disclaimed it) of dictatorship. What worried people even more was the sponsorship under which he was essaying to make his political comeback. He had been out of political life for six years; he had kept silent for three. Now he broke this silence— to lend support to the settlers and soldiers defying the government; and he worded his first statement not to give offense to the *ultras*.

It was difficult to maintain the pretense that all this was a misunderstanding. The general had restored the flagging confidence of the insubordinate soldiers and settlers in revolt. He now had only to wait until the government proved unable to cope with the situation and called him to take over. Algiers had no doubt about his message; it put out flags. The generals, their confidence revived, assumed power throughout Algeria and challenged the president of the republic to form a government headed by de Gaulle. Algiers was once again dictating terms to Paris.

On this side of the Mediterranean the threat first produced reactions likely to lead to a Popular Front. That night, in the lobbies of the Palais Bourbon, the sight of M. Duclos in friendly conversation with Radical deputies revived memories of the nineteen-thirties. From the country, too, came first reports of Committees of Republican Defence being formed, including both Communists and non-Communists. The government decided at once to stop this trend—intelligibly; some argued that an appeal to the people would result in a Communist victory; others, that cooperation of any sort with the Communists would act on the army, and others, as a red flag to a bull. In any case, for very many members of the government majority, anything was preferable to Communist embraces; no amount of caution, no reassurances from M. Duclos that the Communists were only interested in defensive action, could alter their minds.

GUNFIRE AT WINDMILLS

A democratic government faced with rebellious settlers and insubordinate generals derives its strength not only from its legal authority but also from its popular support. This government, however, had to debar itself from bringing popular support to bear in its deadly struggle. Parliament had to fight with its left hand tied behind its back, and was thus compelled to perform some strange shadow boxing. It had to bring the generals to heel by pretending that they were its most obedient servants. It had to face General de Gaulle's challenge while imploring his help. The government was refusing to be forced to choose between Gaullism and some sort of Popular Front. The question was whether it could avoid the choice.

On the Friday (May 16th) the dilemma of the government and its resulting contradictions were shown in the debate on the introduction of a state of emergency. Emergency laws provide the government with immense powers of arrest, deportation, censorship and other controls. Yet in asking for them M. Pflimlin could not frankly describe the situation in all its gravity. He admitted that General Salan had replaced some officials in Algiers without prior consultation with Paris and that this raised the issue of the part played by the army in the state. That was as far as he would go in indicting the army. Simultaneously, he admitted that M. Gaillard, as acting prime minister, had transferred all military and civilian powers in Algeria to General Salan and that the present government had endorsed this act. If the army was in control and had the government's confidence, why all the fuss? It was true that, in France, right-wing extremist leagues had been disbanded and more than a hundred people, both civilians and officers, had been arrested; and there was every indication that the Algerian rising had been staged to coincide with troubles in metropolitan France. The admission of such threats, however, did not justify the measures proposed. In its desire not to cut its contacts with the army, the government of the republic, in real danger, had to present its defense preparations as big guns directed at windmills.

Another contradiction sprang from the nature of M. Pflimlin's majority. In theory, only the Poujadists and the handful of Gaullists were against the government. The independents had four ministers in the cabinet, but most of their group was now going to vote against the emergency powers, while M. Mollet, the Socialist, had accepted a vice-premier's post. The independent leader, M. Pinay, refused a similar post when M. Pflimlin turned down his conditions, which included sending the discredited M. Lacoste back to Algeria. Since then, many independents have not missed the opportunity to tell M. Pflimlin that he should give way to a government of national union. M. Pflimlin received the solid backing of his fellow Christian Democrats and of the Radicals and Socialists. The biggest block of votes in his favor, however, he could not claim. He announced that he would not count the votes of the Communists, and added that the emergency powers would not be used only in one political direction.

But more than this was needed to discourage M. Duclos. Although the Communists had an awkward feeling that these powers might be turned against them, they still voted in favor. Their strategy is to work on parallel lines with the Socialists and Radicals and the non-Communist unions which still refuse formal unity of action. In a moment of real danger they expect that the parallel lines will be forced together, and that the leaders will have to accept common action under pressure from below. This rejection of a dangerous ally has compelled the government to be courteous to its open opponent. Instead of attacking General de Gaulle, M. Mollet, in the Assembly, and M. Pflimlin, in the Upper House, requested him to go on to, explain what he meant.

Questions to de Gaulle

Their questions can be summarized as follows: Does General de Gaulle recognise the government as the legitimate one? Does he disavow the Committee of Public Safety in Algiers? Would he feel responsible to the National Assembly if invested? And would he retire if he failed to get the investiture?

In the meantime, the parliamentary machinery, for once, worked smoothly and swiftly. The state of emergency was accepted in the Assembly by 462 votes to 112 and was passed by a large majority in the Council of the Republic that night. The government received its wide powers; in judging its strength, however, one should not be too impressed by parliamentary arithmetic.

While Paris was waiting for its answers, the "town meeting" of Algiers was once again summoned to the Forum. The novelty was that a third of the crowd now consisted, on the face of it, of Muslims proclaiming their allegiance to France. The total numbers gathered were originally estimated at 20,000, then 45,000, and later put even higher. Strict censorship in Algiers and the arrest of independent journalists there make it hard to check the reports. (The FLN has claimed that the Muslim participants were brought to the Forum under threat.) Experts in Paris explain that for months French authorities unable to protect friendly Muslims in the countryside had been moving them to the towns, and these may now have come out for the parade. The settlers go on to proclaim that Frenchmen and Arabs are equal, and that Algeria is an integral part of France. Does this mean that they are now willing to accept more than one hundred Algerian deputies in the Palais Bourbon? All this is uncertain and out of focus.

Tense Weekend

Paris had a weekend of spring. The crowds in the street were bigger than usual, but their mood was inscrutable; all demonstrations had been forbidden. Only hooting lorries carrying crack policemen from all over France were a sign of the times and a reminder that M. Jules Moch, the new minister of the interior, meant business. M. Pflimlin broadened his cabinet by admitting three new Socialist ministers. M. Moch is the best known of them outside France, his name being associated with international negotiations on disarmament. In France he has a reputation for toughness which he gained dealing with the strikes of 1947. The other reputedly strong man is M. de Chevigné, minister of defense. It was his actions that resulted in the final resignation on Saturday of General Ely, the chief of staff, who wanted to protest in this way against the removal of two close collaborators. The putting of two generals under house arrest indicates what are believed to be the ramifications of the plot in the armed forces.

In some cases the security services were not as vigilant. M. Soustelle, the former chief of de Gaulle's secret service and M. Lacoste's predecessor as resident minister in Algiers, was known as one of the colonialist leaders in the Assembly and as such was suspected to have close connections with the Algerian putsch. He was therefore placed under police protection under the pretext of FLN threats, but on the night of Friday to Saturday (May 16th–17th) he managed to slip from his house concealed in a friend's car and, via Geneva, flew to Algiers. There he was received with acclamation by the crowds; they felt that at last they had a politician of distinction with them. Nevertheless he did not take over the leadership of the Committee of Public Safety. The probable explanation is that General de Gaulle could scarcely pose as arbiter between France and Algeria if one of the protagonists in the dispute were his former faithful assistant. Algiers, too, was waiting for the general's press conference.

Just after lunch on Monday (May 19th) a few hundred journalists and guests of honor fought their way through the Hotel Palais d'Orsay to an old-fashioned hall with crystal chandeliers—a very Third Republican background. From behind the photographers' flashes emerged the aloof, grey-clad figure of the general. He spoke distinctly, in well-constructed sentences, with a touch of disdain. This air of haughtiness (evidence, some said, of his Joan of Arc complex) was strengthened by his occasional references to "de Gaulle" in the third person. There was little in what he said to console admirers from the Left. All the scorn was poured on the incapacity of the party system to solve the great problems facing France and the Algerian question in particular. Those who had in fact dictated that policy for years went unscathed. The rising in Algiers, the general thought, was natural; the army had done a good job. He had a word about "my friend" M. Lacoste, and a patronizing passage about M. Mollet. His one proffered guarantee for the future was to ask: "Does anyone believe that at sixty-seven I shall embark on the career of a dictator?" "Pétain was older," a journalist murmured. There was also a crucial passage:

> If exceptional powers were to be delegated to de Gaulle for an exceptional task at an exceptional moment one would have to adopt an exceptional procedure for the investiture by the National Assembly. In case of need I shall make it known to whoever is legally entitled which procedure would, in my opinion, be the best.

And so it was over. "I will go back to my village and remain there at the disposal of the country."

It was an adroit performance. Perhaps the only mistake was to make his blessing for Algiers too obvious. He did not demand power at once. This could have precipitated a general strike and civil war. But, by encouraging the generals in Algiers to resist the government, he could expect that parliament, finding itself at a loss, would soon call him to the rescue. In General de Gaulle's opinion Marianne need not be raped; conquest will come of its own accord to Colombey. M. Pinay has gone there already (May 22nd).

When the general began to speak the Métro stopped; so did most of the Paris buses. Elsewhere, the strike call by the Communist-led CGT was not so successful. M. Duclos subsequently proclaimed that this was only the first warning. Could the CGT precipitate a general strike? Probably not, in isolation. On Monday evening the Socialist and Radical parties, as well as the non-Communist unions, condemned the general; but they merely told their followers to remain vigilant.

MENDESIAN LOGIC

An outsider coming back to the Assembly on Tuesday (May 20th) after a week's interval, for the debate on the extension of the special powers in Algeria to the new government, might well have thought that he had lost his senses. A week before, Algiers had rioted and a general had taken the lead in a committee of public safety just because M. Pflimlin was suspected of liberal views on Algerian policy. Now the government and its conservative critics were outbidding one another in protestations of faith in the army. To make confusion worse confused, at the end of the debate the Communists, who openly disagree with the Algerian policy now foreshadowed, decided to vote for M. Pflimlin in order to defend the republic.

In between, M. Mendès-France delivered probably the most moving and honest speech of the entire crisis. He first tackled General de Gaulle, whose companion and minister he had been; he has also been one of those who had faith in the general's ability to solve France's African problems. Hence, he confessed, his terrible disappointment that General de Gaulle had kept quiet for so long, yet was so quick to fall in with rebellion. The general was lending his name to a cause that could lead to civil war. Coming from an avowed admirer, the condemnation was bitter. M. Mendès-France then turned to M. Pflimlin; he offered his support in order to defend democratic freedom. But he warned M. Pflimlin against ambiguities in his policy which the country could not be expected to understand, and urged him to act with greater resolution. Earlier republican leaders, he recalled, when faced with insubordination by generals, had known how to overcome it with the help of the people.

The government's dilemma stands out in sharp relief. To force the generals to obey, the government would need the active support of the population. But it does not appear to be willing to run the risk involved.

So, to prevent a breach with Algeria and to outlast and outwit General de Gaulle it must try to come to terms with the very generals in Algiers who demand its abdication. M. Pflimlin pushed through the transfer of the special powers in Algiers to General Salan himself. His hope must be that once the emergency is over, and the Gaullist danger has subsided, he will come into his own. The flaw in the calculation is that to placate the generals the government must swallow the Algerian policy dictated by the *ultras*. And even if the perpetuation of the war reduced Paris to a province of Algeria and made the government the prisoner of the generals, there would still be no guarantee against the return of General de Gaulle.

THE SHADOW LENGTHENS

Indeed, the shadow of de Gaulle is lengthening. He has the support of the colonialist lobby—illustrated by M. Bidault's open letter—and the sympathy of some Conservatives such as M. Pinay. Against them, as long as a parliamentary crisis may result in a call to de Gaulle, the Communists are determined to go on voting for the government. M. Pflimlin wants to use his outwardly massive majority to carry out constitutional reforms strengthening the prerogatives of government.

Power, however, is not acquired on paper. Its substance is progressively shifting to Algiers. The government clings desperately to General Salan, but it is the insurgents who are making the pace. On Wednesday (May 21st) General Salan replied to the Paris Assembly's message of confidence by telling the crowd: "We shall walk together up the Champs Elysées."

Paris is packed with policemen. Scaffolding outside the Palais Bourbon is evidence of the intention to redecorate the building in which the National Assembly sits. M. Pflimlin's government will have to reassert its authority in Algeria rapidly if this seat of the sovereign republic is to remain something more than a relic for tourists.

Cinderella and
the Prince-President

MAY 17, 1958
The Economist

CONSTITUTIONS ARE WHAT practice makes them. M. Pflimlin's surrender last May was not for lack of constitutional powers; it can be argued that what went wrong with the Fourth Republic lay not in the provisions of its constitution but in the manner in which they were applied. Still, the rule that a new regime should begin with a new constitution is traditional in France.

The draft of the new constitution has been submitted to the consultative committee. This purely advisory body is in no position to bring about any great changes. Courtesy, however, requires judgment on details to be suspended until this formality is over and the final project is launched for the referendum on September 28th. Another reason for postponing detailed study is the number of important gaps which the document leaves to be filled later by decree. The size of the lower House and its period of tenure, for instance, are still to be determined, while the provisions for the "federation" of overseas territories—a crucial subject—have been left purposely vague.

But the main lines of the project, obviously cut to measure for General de Gaulle, are clear. And it seems that the president—the prince of the new system—will not live happily ever after with its Cinderella, the National Assembly, unless Cinderella is content to be his obedient servant. Otherwise, the seeds of conflict are there in the text.

The new National Assembly is to be chosen by direct universal suffrage, though the electoral law remains to be decreed. The president, on the other hand, is to be elected indirectly by a large college of between forty thousand and one hundred thousand electors. This college will include parliamentarians—from the assembly and the senate—as well as overseas delegates. But the bulk of its membership will come from representatives of local councils. Now, in France the division of local districts favors conservative, rural areas; it has a strong anti-urban bias. (For comparisons with England it is not necessary to go back to rotten boroughs; it is enough to say that under such a system a farmer in Dorset would have a political weight equal to that of some dozens of Londoners or Mancunians.) The president will thus be the choice of the provincial *notables* and, as is shown by senatorial precedents, this indirect method will always give a more conservative result than will the direct elections for the lower chamber. The constitution thus postulates that the president will be to the right of the popular assembly.

The mode of presidential election did not matter greatly as long as the president was mainly a decorative figure. But he now becomes the pillar of the whole constitutional edifice. He chooses the prime minister and nominates his government. His is the right of appointment to government posts, civil and military. He does not merely sign international treaties; he negotiates them. He can insist that parliament reconsider any subject; he can dissolve a recalcitrant parliament, if necessary once a year. Finally, when in his judgment the institutions of the independence of the nation are threatened, when territorial integrity or the fulfilment of international obligations are in danger, the president can take all powers into his hands. He alone decides whether the country needs a dictator.

Faced with a head of state holding such powers, parliament can no longer be sovereign. It can legislate only within a limited field, leaving the rest to the government. True, it keeps a truncated right of veto. Following the form prescribed, it can bring down the government (but not the government's real master, the president) by a vote of censure. The position of the executive in this new setup is really curious. The government is responsible to parliament, but it exists by the president's grace. Those of its members who are parliamentarians must give up their seats on appointment. And should government and assembly together side against the president, he can, by dissolving parliament, dismiss them both.

The system may work so long as parliament remains a rubber stamp. A Gaullist chamber endorsing the decisions of a Gaullist cabinet will create no trouble. But what are the chances of an opposition, of a real alternative, which is the very basis of parliamentary democracy? In case of conflict, the struggle seems unequal. The president is there for seven years and—because of the method of election—is likely to succeed himself, or to be followed by a man of a similar political coloring. The life of parliament, on the other hand, is precarious.

The optimists claim that, faced with a repeated popular verdict, the president will have to submit as Marshal Macmahon had to give way to the parliament of the Third Republic. Yet will he, with the immense powers at his disposal and an army which now has a stake in politics? The French historical analogies that spring to mind—of Louis-Philippe, or of the prince-president, Louis-Napoleon—suggest that similar structures end in absolute rule or revolution. The constitution seems still incomplete. In the part devoted to the president, it should have a Roman provision for cases of conflict: *aut Caesar aut nihil*. It may not be too bold to prophesy that this constitution, born of an insurrection in Algiers, contains within itself the seeds of revolution, and will end one day with barricades in Paris.

Many French liberals who, from fear of civil war, had given their blessing to the Gaullist experiment, are now perturbed by the limitation of parliamentary prerogative and the vast powers attributed to the president. Some of them seek consolation in their faith that General de Gaulle is not a man to abuse his power. But does an adult nation shape its institutions to fit one man? Quite different men may fill the job after him.

Divided Opposition

SEPTEMBER 20, 1958

The Economist

"ONLY THE COMMUNISTS and their dupes will vote against the constitution"—thus runs the government's refrain. "We shall not leave to the Communists the monopoly of defending the republic"—answers the non-Communist opposition. The two contrasting statements have one point in common. They agree that the French Communist Party, despite its weak showing in May, remains an important factor in any political calculations about the future.

When Algiers launched its pronunciamento, the Communists did not reply by paralyzing the country with strikes or calling their troops to revolutionary action: the troops would not have obeyed it they had. There are many reasons for this apathy. The substantial increase in the real wages of French workers between 1953 and 1956 dampened the fighting spirit of the postwar years. A series of unprepared political strikes merely ended in disappointment. The personality of General de Gaulle neutralized many workers who might have fought against "the colonels." Finally, Communist isolation, and the passive attitude of other trade unions, reinforced the feeling that this was not yet the time for a fight.

It would be a mistake to assess the potential power of the Communists on the basis of their sporadic strike in May or even in terms of the militants still willing to brave the truncheons of the police. Economic difficulties might revive the fighting spirit of the industrial workers. In any case, although the Communists are in no mood for barricades, they have not apparently deserted their party. Most experts in Paris expect that they will still account for about a fifth of the poll at the next general election (they polled about a quarter last time).

The mood of their rank and file explains the behavior of the communist leaders. In May, the party clung desperately to M. Pflimlin's government, causing confusion among its more extremist elements. Since then, it has been talking in Republican and not revolutionary terms, offering an alliance to all the anti-Gaullists and promising guarantees for the future. The Communist leaders are convinced that a period of Gaullist rule will be one of persecution for their party. They are aware that France is not ripe for a Communist dictatorship and that a coup at this stage would involve the risk of world war. For the time being, they might be genuinely in favor of defensive action, which would naturally strengthen their position but not bring them to power.

This does not mean that the Communist Party has no alternative, should it be isolated and defeated in the "Republican" battle. The party can go underground. MM. Thorez and Duclos remember that the Communists emerged from the resistance as the biggest party in France. If the Gaullist hopes are disappointed, the Communists will face the country as the first champions of a new "resistance." In that case, they will not be content with the role of junior partner in any coalition.

Other groups in the opposition also contemplate seriously such a possibility. But it is now clear that no other established party will campaign against the constitution. Things have changed since that day in May when the Socialist deputies proclaimed their "never" to de Gaulle; their party congress at Issy-les-Moulineaux last week decided by nearly 70 percent of the votes to campaign for the Gaullist constitution. Once M. Defferre decided to vote "yes" in the hope of a liberal solution for Algeria, M. Mollet was certain of victory. For three days he could watch the progression of resigned delegates—including such well-known figures as MM. Pineau, Gazier, and Moch—who, having explained the dangers of the constitution, put party discipline above their conscience and said they would obey the decision of the congress. In the end, only the hard core of opposition, the members of the old "minority" (such as MM. Depreaux, Verdier, and Savary) who for years had opposed the Lacoste policy in Algeria, decided to walk out and form an independent Socialist Party.

The doggedness of M. Mendès-France made the battle more equal at the Radical congress in Lyons. There, the alliance of the *mendèsists* and of some deputies from the Southwest meant that over two-fifths of the party voted against the constitution. It is even claimed that the decision would have gone the other way but for some irregularities in the vote itself. The fact remains that no party except the Communists has gone into opposition.

This retreat by the established parties increases the importance of the Union de Forces Dèmocratiques. Sponsored by M. Daniel Mayer, chairman of the League of the Rights of Men and former head of the Socialist Party, the UFD is a loose alliance. It groups liberals, like M. Mèndes-France and his friends, M. Mitterrand, and many academic figures; Socialists from the minority mentioned above; and various small left-wing movements. Indeed, if the lunatic fringe on the Right is excluded, it covers the whole of the non-Communist opposition.

M. Mendès-France has, inevitably, become the chief spokesman of this movement. He has argued that the referendum will really be a plebiscite with confused issues, and that it is meant to provide a legal stamp for what was an insurrection. The constitution, in his opinion, is dangerously reactionary and will only increase the ills of French democracy. The performance of the government on the crucial Algerian question does not justify the swallowing of principles for the sake of a solution. On the contrary, giving in to successive blackmailing demands is not the way to defend the republic; it will merely encourage its foes in Algeria and elsewhere.

Should the "noes" carry the day, which nobody for a moment can expect, M. Mendès-France would support election in November for a constituent assembly which should produce a simple draft constitution within a month; an African congress to be called immediately, and freedom of expression to be restored in Algeria so that genuine spokesmen of the Algerian people could be found. M. Mendès-France and his colleagues are less explicit about the forces they could command, apart from the verdict of the French people, to make the army and its allies obey. One reproach against the opposition that is frequently heard in Paris is that it does not face squarely the issue of its relations with the Communists.

Only the leftish elements in the UFD are in favor of a provisional, but open, alliance with the Communists. The others, particularly the liberals, are still dreaming of a third force in which the political pendulum swings only between Center-Left and Center-Right. They know that they may be driven to the choice that they want to avoid. They say that the Gaullist referendum and the ensuing elections will divide the country and force the people to choose between extremes. They fear that the Gaullist experiment will ultimately leave Frenchmen with no alternative but Fascism or Communism.

The referendum will tend to divide these liberals from some of their natural allies. The consequences of this will be important. Should there be only, say, six million votes against the constitution in metropolitan France, the conclusion will be drawn, rightly or wrongly, that the bulk of them are Communist (the Communists polled 5.5 million votes in the last election). The opposition will have to poll much more heavily to convince public opinion that it can talk with the Communists on equal terms. The UFD intends to campaign throughout the country and can rely on the backing of intellectuals, professors, and teachers. But will many Socialists follow the minority? Can M. Mendès-France convince the middle classes? The tide is flowing the other way. It may seem strange that M. Mendès-France should be blamed for the vagaries of the Fourth Republic, while MM. Mollet and Pinay are the heralds of a new order. Still, the republic was defeated in May and things are awkward now for those who did not desert it then. After all, it was a Gaul who threw his sword on the Roman scales shouting *Vae Victis*.

The two oppositions are going to battle separately. The non-Communists give the impression of knowing that it is a losing battle. But they hope to act as a dam against the Gaullist tide that is now sweeping the country, so as to be able to act as a dam again when the tide recedes. On September 28th they will try chiefly to limit the damage.

Gaullist Landslide

OCTOBER 4, 1958
The Economist

IT WAS A landslide. The result exceeded the hopes of the victors.
They expected two-thirds of the French poll, hoped for three-quarters
and got nearly four-fifths. In all, 17,666,828 metropolitan Frenchmen
(that is to say 79.25 percent of those voting) said Yes on Sunday, while
only 4,624,475 said No. No French ruler since Napoleon III has
obtained such a massive popular vote.

The *nons* fall 830,000 short of the Communist poll at the last general election in 1956. Communist losses can be estimated at somewhat
over one million (or about one-fifth of the party's electoral strength), the
figure varying according to one's assessment of the rest of the opposition. The Communist decline is particularly striking in the traditionally
conservative and Catholic areas of eastern France; in Alsace and Lor-
raine the Communist positions have crumbled. But the decrease is general and the Communists suffered substantial losses in the industrial
areas of the Nord and Pas-de-Calais, in the Red Belt of Paris and Lyons
and in the ports of Marseilles, Toulon, and Le Havre.

Though greater than expected, the Communist defeat is no surprise. It was always known that some of their electoral support came
from people who merely voted against the regime. The Gaullist Rally
had already snapped up some of these votes on previous occasions (the
Communist figures in Paris, for instance, have now sunk roughly to

the 1951 level). This time the general feeling in the country was that to say *oui* was a vote against the past and against the "system." Many commentators suggest that, elections being a different matter, the Communists may recover the bulk of their losses in the November poll. This is dubious since, if nothing succeeds like success, nothing fails like failure. Much will depend on the electoral law itself.

More than by their own losses, the Communists must be alarmed by their isolation. The main victims of the referendum are probably those liberals and Socialists who dared to swim against the current. Well-known figures like MM. Mendès-France, Mitterrand, Baylet, and Daladier have carried only a few of their supporters into opposition. The votes of the non-Communist opposition can probably be counted in a few hundreds of thousands. It has even been suggested that the effect of its propaganda was only to alter the ranks of the abstainers. The poll was high on Sunday, but those who stayed at home were not necessarily the same as before. Intense propaganda has succeeded in bringing to the polls people who are traditionally outside politics. Part of the non-Communist left, on the other hand, apparently solved its problems by contracting out. In any case, the ghost of the Popular Front has been laid for the moment. It will return, as an avenging ghost, only if popular disappointment leads to a turn of the tide.

The swollen bag of the "ayes" defies analysis. The size of this vote shows how many Frenchmen, fed up with the Fourth Republic, wished *"que ça change."* Change, however, can have several meanings. For some, *oui* meant the reduction of the army to its proper place and a negotiated peace in Algeria. For others it spelt the end of the parliamentary regime and the beginning of strong rule, backed by armed force if necessary.

Ambiguity has paid handsome dividends. General de Gaulle not only got a massive vote. He has also been given almost unlimited dictatorial powers for the next four months. During that period he can fill the important gaps in the new constitution by decree. He can determine the new electoral law and, hence, to some extent, the coloring of the next assembly. On one issue the general may not be able to use his full powers—over Algeria, where he has flown after victory. Electoral success there has rather limited his scope for action. If the purpose of the referendum in Algeria was to prove that by day the army is stronger than the FLN and controls the country, the proof has been given. The French army succeeded in registering more than three-quarters of the Algerian population of voting age and then to bring about 80 percent of those registered to the polling stations. It is irrelevant that the army played the electoral game with all the democratic niceties. It is not irrelevant that, as has been reported, the Muslims feared reprisals. In Algeria, 97 percent voted *oui*.

It is useful for the military to be able to face the general with an "accomplished fact" at a time when a massive vote frees him from their past sponsorship. But he is unlikely to endorse their integration slogans; and he should now be able to negotiate with the other side without a clash with the army. If he fails to take that risk, it will not be for lack of support at home. Precedent shows that compromise with the civilian and military masters of Algeria means that the war goes on.

General de Gaulle can rightly point out that he got a blank check and not a clear mandate for a policy in Algeria. "The bride is too beautiful," the editor of *Le Monde* has written. In a divided country one cannot remain Mr. Eighty Percent for ever. The general now has immense power and prestige, but electors are fickle, and whichever way he uses his power he must disappoint some of his supporters. As the veil over the new Gaullism is lifted, who will be those who regret their contribution to the overwhelming majority of last Sunday?

The General's Plan
for Algeria

OCTOBER 11, 1958
The Economist

THE FOG HAS not lifted. General de Gaulle travelled to Algeria last week flushed with victory. His speech in Constantine was expected to be a revelation; he was finally going to choose between the contradictory views of his followers. Yet, when he had spoken, both sides were again satisfied. The "Left Gaullists" saw in the speech a confirmation of their liberal ideas. The colonialist wing greeted the Constantine program as "integration in deeds, if not in words." Instead of puzzling over this French logic, it seems preferable to stick to facts.

General de Gaulle did not offer the Algerian people the prospect of independence. Like M. Mollet before him, he argued that the first thing to do was to improve living conditions in the country, and he outlined a five-year plan designed for the purpose. In France, one-tenth of the jobs in the civil service will be reserved for Algerians. In Algeria, 250,000 hectares of land are to be divided among Muslims; wages are to be brought into line with the home country; new jobs are to be found for 400,000 people; new housing is to be provided for one million, and schools are to be expanded to accommodate two-thirds of Algeria's children.

The plan is still too general to assess its actual cost. The cost of a house in Algeria, for instance, varies from less than £200 for an Arab cabin to about £6,000 for a luxury flat in Algiers. A study published in

Le Monde, however, gives at least an idea of the burden involved. It shows that the new program is largely based on a ten-year plan drawn up by M. Lacoste's administration before the change of regime, except that it is now to be carried out at a much faster pace. In the original plan 4,710 billion francs (about £3,900 million) was to be invested over ten years, roughly half from state and half from private sources. Metropolitan France was to provide 2,510 billion francs, two-thirds of it coming from various budgetary sources, the rest from private investment. The annual state contribution was to be raised from 140 billion francs next year (in 1958 it amounts to 78 billion francs) to 200 billion francs in 1962; by that time it was to be supplemented by some 100 billion francs of private investment. Since the pace of development is to be speeded up, these figures must also be increased substantially.

Algeria has about one million unemployed and a poverty-stricken population growing at an astounding rate. The new plan will not solve its problems; it will only be the beginning of a solution. But France is asked to make the effort at a very awkward moment. The European common market will increase foreign competition. The rising birthrate will very soon make its impact on labor exchanges. Heavy investment at home is now imperative for France. All that and atom bombs, too— no wonder that once again there is talk in Paris of foreign loans. It should not be forgotten that civilian investment in Algeria is to come on top, and not instead, of the military effort, which absorbs more than twice the amount now envisaged. And if the war continues, the new plan will have to bear two additional strains: fighting will prevent the fulfilment of some projects; it will also discourage private investment. What prospects, then, does the Constantine speech offer of a peaceful solution?

General de Gaulle does not exclude any solutions for the distant future. Like M. Mollet before him, he spoke only of Algeria's "personality." Moreover, speaking of the next few years, he did not mention either independence or negotiations. If his economic plan is a speedier version of his predecessor's blueprints, the political program of

Constantine is rather a retreat from that of the previous regime. The *loi-cadre* of the Fourth Republic at least envisaged an Algerian assembly, that is to say a potential nucleus of autonomy, if not of independence. General de Gaulle promises Algeria increased representation in the French assembly and he tells Muslims that they will get two-thirds of the Algerian seats in Paris. Elections, however, are to be held within six weeks. They will, therefore, be held under army control and the Muslim candidates will have to have the army's blessing.

All this explains why the General's speech aroused anger only among a very few hotheads in Algeria. The settlers' real fear has always been that Paris would negotiate a settlement, which would inevitably end in the rule of the Arab majority. Short of this, they think that they can preserve their privileged position. The settlers easily converted the officers' corps to the idea that Algeria must remain French, and that idea was not undermined in Constantine. The general has slapped down the Algiers colonels who wished to meddle in French politics. But it would be a mistake to say that he has tamed the army as a whole; the trial of strength has not taken place. The fact that General Salan's removal, rumored for weeks, did not materialize is relatively unimportant. It is more significant that, in his letter to General Salan on leaving Algeria, General de Gaulle congratulated the army on its performance and asked it to go on with "pacification."

Has France changed regimes only to perpetuate M. Mollet's policy in Algeria? And, if so, can the general succeed where M. Lacoste failed? The new plan can work in two possible ways. One would be if it were supplemented by a political plan, offering Algeria self-government and the prospect of independence, which would serve as a basis for talks with the FLN. The general did not say that this was his intention.

The other possibility is connected with the weariness of the Algerian population. M. Ferhat Abbas has admitted that Muslim losses in the conflict reach the fantastic figure of 600,000. (A corresponding figure for Britain would be three million people.) It is, therefore, natural that this exhausted population should obey the stronger side. The referendum seems to have confirmed this weariness. If the French succeed in driving the FLN into a few remote areas and eliminate it elsewhere, they may be able to rule the country. This solution of "armed peace" could only be provisional and costly, but it might last for a time. If neither of these premises is fulfilled—if the general does not talk with the FLN and the army does not manage to crush it completely—the Constantine manifesto is likely to join the long list of paper plans for Algeria.

The Battle Over Algeria

::

Algeria's Communities

MARCH 4 AND 11, 1961
The Economist

THE LOST TRIBE

BLACK FEET ARE no Indian tribe, but the *pieds noirs*, the European settlers in North Africa. In Algeria they include Frenchmen, who have gone there during the past century, and a Mediterranean mixture—Maltese, Sicilians, Corsicans, Spaniards. If some 120,000 Jews—who have lived there for centuries but were rapidly assimilated by the French—are added, the European community is more than a million strong. To question the "Frenchness" of the *pieds noirs* by examining their grandparents' birth certificates would be invidious. Still it is important to realize that less than a tenth of the European residents of Algeria were actually born in France. France is the country where the wealthier among them go on holiday, where they buy luxury goods and invest their money. But the roots of the *pieds noirs* are in Algeria.

They are French in yet another sense—by contrast with the rest of the population. The difference between the two communities strikes vividly as soon as one arrives, and it is confirmed by the figures. Privileged Muslims—feudal landlords or richer merchants—are too few to change the pattern. The differences within each community, however important, do not alter the fact that the frontier between the haves and the have-nots runs roughly between the national groups. The two communities live side by side, with different birth and death rates, distinct dress and diet, housing conditions, and social habits, all reflecting a deep gap in living standards.

Statistically the differences are most striking in the countryside where modern, mechanized agriculture coexists with primitive native subsistence farming. Numerically, the Europeans in the rural area are few; perhaps 100,000 earn their living from agriculture. About 8,200 big European farmers own more than six million acres of land, or about a quarter of the total under cultivation; more than half of it lies in the coastal semi-coastal areas. They, together with a few thousand big Muslim landowners, are the obvious targets for any land reform—not that land redistribution, on its own, would solve Algeria's acute food problem. The political power of the big *colons*, however, has always been much better then their numerical strength. Many of them have resources in France; it is the white smallholders who are more likely to be desperate.

In the towns, too, the outlook varies for different European groups. According to a recent study published by the Club Jean Moulin, about a third of the Europeans in Algeria have an income well above the French average. Relatively few of them are in industry. Efforts are now being made to foster industrialization, but in the past the free entry of French goods has not encouraged this process. The upper third is thus recruited—apart from farming and industry—from trade and transport, finance and shipping, as well as from the higher grades of the vast civil service. Many members of this privileged group have either financial reserves with which to start afresh in France or qualifications to find a good job there. They might even keep a privileged position in an independent Algeria, if the transition were not too abrupt. Socially, the most dramatic problem is that of the "poor whites."

Two-thirds of the European population of Algeria are apparently living at a level well below the French average. Such comparisons are bound to be rough, but the statistics are borne out of the evidence of one's eyes. A walk through the European suburbs of Algiers or Oran reminds me more of the Red Belt of Paris than of its middle-class districts. Indeed the suburb of Algiers, like Bad-el-Oued, used to vote Communist, while Socialists and Communists competed for votes in the poor white quarters of Oran. This was at a time when politics appeared to be a game reserved for Europeans. But after the insurrection broke out, the same districts became the strongholds of the *ultras*, and their conversion cannot be explained purely in terms of racial solidarity.

Already by 1954—the year of the last census, and the year the rebellion broke out—nearly all the unskilled laborers in Algeria were Muslim. Muslims also predominated among the semi-skilled, and were timidly making their way into office employment and lower branches of the civil service. Their bid for political power caused the Europeans to panic. The poor whites looked at the overcrowded Casbah and beyond at the huge reserves of manpower living in a countryside where the means of subsistence cannot keep pace with the birthrate. The European foremen and postmen, the railwaymen and the small shopkeepers, were frightened that they would be swamped by the Muslim multitude. To defend their own relative privileges, mediocre as they were by European standards, they provided the big battalions for the *colons* and their allies.

Herein lay some of the strength of the Algerian lobby, which has played such a part in French politics. Not only did it have strong connections in Paris and important funds to distribute, it also had massive popular support with which it could affectively maneuver in Algeria whenever its interests were threatened. But after six years of war Paris shows signs of impatience. The patience of the Muslim town-dwellers seems exhausted, too. When these came out into the streets last December the Europeans had their biggest shock yet. They suddenly grasped the fact that they were outnumbered, even in the big towns, into which they have largely withdrawn. Only in Oran is the balance still slightly tilted in their favor. They are even beginning to doubt whether the military force can maintain the present social structure for long.

This traumatic shock is too fresh to judge its final impact. The reactions that your correspondent came across during a recent journey ranged from the racial hatred of an ambulance driver ready "to work overtime for nothing to carry Muslim corpses" to the hope of a liberal—a rare bird—that, after a swiftly negotiated settlement, the ex-insurgent government would prove strong enough to keep the Muslim masses in check. Yet the most typical were the comments full of contradictions; the same man would assure you that his best friends were Arabs and, in the same breath, "that it is useless to treat them like decent human beings." Threatened in what they believe to be the roots of their existence, the poor whites feel themselves a lost tribe.

This is the stuff of which fascists can be made. It is significant that people in Paris are beginning to think about the absorption of the poor whites of Algeria in France. The gist of the argument in the Jean Moulin study already mentioned is that France would be wiser to spend its money on providing full compensation at home for those of its citizens that have been squeezed out of Algeria than to go on wagging a costly war to save what it is no longer possible to save. The potential European migration back to France is conservatively estimated, over a period, at between 300,000 and 400,000. A real transfer of political power in Algeria would shake the economic and social foundations of the country.

THE MUSLIM MILLIONS

Shoeshine boys swarming around a reluctant customer are not a rare sight in the Arab world. In Algiers or Oran, this sometimes embarrassing performance reminds the western visitor of the two major social problems of the area: the pressure of population combined with acute unemployment, two factors that go a long way toward explaining why the insurrection has lasted more than six years. They have a bearing on the present search for a peaceful solution, and they will stay relevant whatever the outcome.

The relative youth of Algeria's Muslim population is striking. In 1954, when the insurrection broke out, 52 percent of the Muslims were under twenty years of age. The birthrate—at 432 per 10,000—was among the highest in the world and, if the trend had gone on unchecked, the Muslim population would have topped 36 million at the turn of the century. It is still too early to assess the losses of war and their impact. The latest figures put the Muslim population at 9.3 million and the birthrate still seems to be high.

Unemployment is less perceptible. It is visible in the overcrowded Arab quarters of the towns where able-bodied men sit idly waiting for Godot. But the real source of surplus manpower lies camouflaged in the countryside. There are several thousand fairly prosperous Muslim farmers and even a few big landowners. Yet the bulk of the 630,000 Muslim farms are small holdings, cultivated by ancient methods and barely adequate for mere subsistence. The average farm has too many mouths to feed and too many hands for the job. It has been estimated that if half the Muslim labor were removed from the countryside, output would remain unaffected; the remaining half would simply be fully employed.

Migration to the towns has been limited by tradition and lack of outlets. It went on, nevertheless, because throughout this century the means of subsistence, in good Malthusian fashion, could not keep place with the growth of the population. The move to the towns has been accelerated by civil war. It is expected to go on, and even accelerate in coming years, because the nearly two million Muslims "resettled" by the French army were not transplanted according to any economic plan; uprooted, many of them will now drift to the towns. There were some 300,000 Muslim town-dwellers at the turn of the century and nearly double that figure in 1930; now they are more than two million strong, accounting for about 22 percent of the total Muslim population, and still growing. Already the Muslims are more than twice as numerous as the Europeans in the towns.

When they come to town the Muslims enter the market economy. They acquire new needs, new wants, and the ability to compare. But more than a fifth of the Muslim town-dwellers are wholly unemployed. Nearly as many get only occasional work. The Arab quarters at the town are nearly bursting at the seams. Constantly swollen by new recruits from the countryside, the army of Muslim labor exerts ever-increasing pressure on the fully-employed Europeans.

French planning has taken several bites at the problem of mopping up this surplus manpower. The Constantine plan is only the latest and most ambitious attempt. It provides not only for employment but also for housing and education. The planners have a political end in view— to reconcile large Muslim groups to the French presence, and to produce an elite willing to collaborate. Many economists think that, even in conditions of peace and even if all its objectives were reached, the Constantine plan would fail to solve unemployment, let alone reconcile the two communities. These doubters believe that, short of radical rural improvement, the flow of population to the towns will be much larger than the planners have assumed.

Most people, however, agree that the plan cannot be fulfilled without peace. Its political assumptions have crumbled already. It is curious with what unanimity Muslims, when asked about the undoubted French achievements in housing or education, give credit for the change not to the French but to the insurrection. The "elite" is more reluctant than ever to collaborate. It is true that the middle class was always relatively weaker in Algeria than in the rest of French North Africa, because of the greater weight of the European population. The reasons for its present reluctance, however, are political. Moderate Muslims now say quite openly that they will play no part in any scheme directed against the leaders of the insurrection.

Since Muslim demonstrations in Algiers and Oran in December, liberal optimists in Paris and Algiers hope that General de Gaulle will act as a realist and change his course. This would amount to offering the insurgents political concessions in order to preserve economic and strategic positions. Once at the negotiating table the French will have many cards to play, besides the card of military control. There are 300,000 Muslims who work in France and who keep numerous families in Algeria out of their earnings. There is Algeria's foreign trade, geared completely to the French economy. The French could ask for a slow, gradual transition in exchange for economic and technical aid.

With peace, social differences would reappear in the Muslim community, and the French would no longer be faced with a united nationalist front.

Against this must be set the tensions built up through years of war. None of the moves tried by the French in recent years have worked out to their advantage. Even the spread of education has only intensified the conflict between the two communities by rendering the Muslims more competitive. Talks with youth and trade union leaders show that for many, independence has become synonymous with radical reforms. The guerrillas, recruited mainly among poor peasants, are also reported to be dreaming of drastic change. The Communist Party has little following in Algeria, but the idea of a shortcut from backwardness to economic power exercises a great attraction, particularly among the young. The insurgent government-in-exile cannot but take this mood into account,

Without entering the field of fiction, it is vain to divide individual rebel leaders into "toughs" and "moderates." It is enough to say that the leadership as a whole has to decide between evolution and revolution, between compromise and economic collaboration with France, and holding out for the maximum stakes. The kind of settlement Mr. Bourguiba is known to favor would include bargains over Sahara oil and a gradual political transition eased by French economic aid. The question is, Is it too late for such a settlement? The influence exerted on the leaders of the insurrection by the pressure of the Muslim masses provides only one part of the equation. The other, unknown, is the extent to which General de Gaulle, having as a realist revised his positions, is now willing to meet his opponents with political concessions. More than the immediate future of Algeria is at stake.

Charles and
the Kingmakers

APRIL 29, 1961
The Economist

IN MAY 1958, the French army tasted political power. The government and parliament submitted to the will of the insurgent commanders in Algeria and were relieved that the choice of the military men fell on General de Gaulle. The French people sighed with relief; they were spared a fight for their rights. The savior had once again come to their rescue. De Gaulle would come to terms with the officers in revolt and solve the Algerian problem. Thus one army coup was sanctified by a popular vote. The Fourth Republic was buried without tears. Its successor had a new institution, an assembly and a senate, parties old and new—all the trappings of a French Republic. The stature of the man at its helm, and the cult of his personality, concealed the fact that the president was surrounded by a political vacuum. But the first real test revealed that the dialogue that mattered in France was between the president and the army.

General de Gaulle was not burdened by gratitude toward the men who brought him back to power. He never shared their conviction that Algeria could remain French forever. Gradually, he removed those most committed to this myth from key positions in Algeria, loading them with honors and setting them aside. By September 1959, he felt strong enough to launch his policy of self-determination for Algeria. Four months later the barricades raised by the settlers in Algiers enabled the army commanders to show their strength during a few days of passive disobedience. General de Gaulle, assuming full power, exhorted them to obey. He even threatened to use popular backing to crush resistance. At the same time, General Ely, a recognized keeper of "army unity," was sent to Algeria to persuade his colleagues that it was in the army's interest to play the game.

General Challe, who was then commander-in-chief in Algeria, finally decided to carry out the president's orders. The barricades vanished immediately in Algiers. In France, public opinion, scarcely aroused, fell back into its sleep. In a tour of the officers' messes in Algeria General de Gaulle assured he army that it would stay there. The penalties for disobedience were virtually reserved for the civilian ringleaders, but again several officers were removed from Algeria.

The compromise was short-lived. The French president was aware that he needed peace in Algeria both to consolidate his position and to make his foreign policy work. After the failure of the talks with the Muslim rebel envoys at Melun in June he began groping again towards a negotiated settlement about the end of last year. In recent weeks it has been obvious that such a deal could only be struck with the Algerian government-in-exile and would necessarily lead to an independent Algeria. The question was, Would the French officers who for years had taken *Algerie Française* as their slogan accept such an evolution? Only last week M. Messmer, the minister of defense, dismissed this as an idle worry. Clearly he was not informed about the plans of General Challe and his fellow-plotters.

It is easy now for General de Gaulle's critics to point out that his policy of compromise with the army was wrong, and that to indulge the plotters merely encouraged them in their designs. Yet such charges beg the question, ignoring both the origins of the Gaullist regime and its structure. The officers in revolt accepted General de Gaulle as president because he was a general as well as a national figure. He, in turn, always had a high place for the army in his concept of the state. Naturally it was an obedient army he wanted, a disciplined instrument of Gaullist policy. He sought to fashion this tool circumspectly by persuasion and gradual maneuver, avoiding a clash. A nation situated as France is, with a military power traditionally self-sufficient and traditionally political, needs strong political forces if the civil power is to hold its own. General de Gaulle has never hidden his distaste for the "intermediaries"—the parties and political organizations—standing between the nation and its ruler.

The French paratroopers have been trained to believe in force, not in political communion. The coup of Saturday last was staged despite the confirmation by January's referendum that the overwhelming majority of the French nation was in favor of a negotiated settlement in Algeria, and that the *ultras* were a tiny minority in France. This did not prevent generals Salan, Challe, Jouhaud, and André Zeller and the colonels in league with them from staging a coup and coming very close to getting complete control of Algeria. So far the "unity of the army" was working in their favor. Even if it was true that only the shock troops—the paratroopers and the Foreign Legion—took an active part in the operation, they were helped by the passivity of the rest of the armed forces and the nation. To arouse "all Frenchmen and first and foremost every soldier" to a sense of their duty, was therefore the main purpose of General de Gaulle's televised speech on Sunday night. Armed with powers furnished by article 16 of the constitution (though it was less on constitutional than personal authority that he depended) he forbade all cooperation with the insurgents and called on the nation to use all means to block their path until they could be subdued. The issue then was whether the bulk of the officer corps was willing to abandon the extremists to their fate and follow this lead. There could now be no compromise between General Challe and the president. Both sides had burnt their boats. For the rebels, the seizure of government was now the only target.

Indeed, a few hours after the president's speech M. Debré, the prime minister, warned the public, and Parisians in particular, that there was reason to expect landings by paratroopers from Algeria that very night. There was something pathetic in his call to Parisians to go "on foot or by car, to convince these misled soldiers of their grave error," as soon as the sirens announced the landings. It was a tacit admission that, except for the Compagnies Républicaines de Sécurité, the armed forces could not be relied upon. Yet, as the night went by and there were no landings, the situation improved. The trade unions began to rally their members. Volunteers gathered at the ministry of the interior, where members of the neo-Gaullist UNR were given precedence in the hasty enrollment that went on.

The Sunday night alarm proved false. Rumor has since had it that an American warning in Algiers stopped the expedition; but there is no confirmation of this. While the alarm lasted there was talk of some thirty aircraft that were to have brought perhaps 1,500 paratroopers. For the second time in three years the fate of a modern nation seemed to depend on the actions of a tiny body of professional fighting men.

On the morning after the false alarm the government recovered its poise. There was no longer any question of distributing arms to volunteers. General de Gaulle developed his counteroffensive in masterly fashion. Unlike M. Pflimlin in 1958, he was determined to resist. Instead of pleading and imploring he ordered imperiously, as a commander. As soon as some units obeyed his orders, turning from passivity to action, the "unity of the army" began to work for instead of against him.

The turning point probably came late on Tuesday morning, when the navy fired some warning shots against a paratroop detachment trying the take over the base of Mers-el-Kébir. The tide ebbed at extraordinary speed. The paratroopers fell back everywhere, and by midnight they had lost even Algiers without, surprisingly enough, offering any serious resistance. The professional knights of *Algérie Française* did not even stage a heroic exit. General de Gaulle spoke about his opponents with real indignation. Yet, the heroes of May 1958, have once again rendered him a service, this time unwittingly. For three years he had tried to avoid a head-on clash with the army. They thrust it upon him and then lost so fast that the consequences he must have feared from such a clash did not have time to follow. The passivity and hesitations of the officers' corps did not prove so intractable that they must now compel General de Gaulle to discard the army as a pillar of his regime. They were sufficient, however, to enable him now, if he chooses, to eliminate his opponents, to purge and reshape the army and transform it into a disciplined Gaullist force.

Armed with full powers, the French president can do as he pleases in this hour of triumph. He can alter the constitution and get his mandate renewed. Above all, he can try now to reach rapidly a negotiated settlement in Algeria, while the defeated champions of *Algérie Française* can offer no resistance. It now remains to be seen to what advantage General de Gaulle will turn his undoubted victory.

Algerian Leaders

MAY 13, 1961
The Economist

THE FATE OF Algeria depends on the talks that will start at Evian on May 20th. Who are the leaders of the rebel FLN who will decide the limits of a compromise on its behalf?

Often supposedly divided into "tough" soldiers and "soft" politicians, they reflect in their different backgrounds the divisions in the nationalist movement before the insurrection broke out in November 1954. There were then two main nationalist parties. One, the Democratic Union of the Algerian Manifest (UDMA), was led by Ferhat Abbas, now head of the rebels' provisional government.

At sixty-two, the dignified and sad-eyed Ferhat Abbas is the elder statesmen of the revolution. A pharmacist by profession, he was involved in politics from his student days onward. Once he believed in assimilation to France. He doubted the very existence of an Algerian fatherland. "I have questioned history. I have questioned the living and the dead, I have visited cemeteries; nobody has spoken to me about it." These words of his have often been quoted by his French critics.

Even when he abandoned hope of winning equal rights for Muslims, he still aimed at Algerian self-government in association with France, to be attained peacefully. The French response was electoral fraud and legal obstruction. By 1955, disillusioned, he came to share the rebels' belief that only revolutionary violence would move the French. In 1956 he joined them in Cairo; in 1958 he became head of the first provisional government. His name became a symbol of the rebellion; it echoed through Algeria during last December's Muslim demonstrations. Although the leadership is really collective, he apparently has a casting vote in its councils, often held in his villa in Tunisia; but there is no evidence that he is any less sensitive to the mood of the fighting guerrillas than are his colleagues drawn from their ranks.

His brother-in-law, Ahmed Francis, twelve years younger, has followed closely in his footsteps. A doctor, he has become minister of finance and economic affairs—and thus knows where the FLN's funds (apart from its local levies) come from. He revisited Moscow at the end of March; his knowledge of the sources of further potential aid may affect his assessment of the situation.

To complete the ex-UDMA trio, a man must be mentioned who does not hold formal ministerial rank. The massive Ahmed Boumendjel has the stuff of which revolutionary heroes are made; the names of Mirabeau and Danton come naturally to mind. Eloquent and witty, he can coin the apt phrase and perceive the historical perspective. Now fifty-two, he was a lawyer who specialized in defending nationalists, and a political figure known in both Paris and Algiers. His younger brother was "made to commit suicide" during interrogation by paratroopers in Algiers. Ahmed headed the delegation to the abortive Melun conference last June. After that, he may have concluded that the light would come from the East—the Far East if need be. If the conflict were internationalized he might be forced to the front of the stage.

THE EX-MESSALISTS

The second group in the leadership has its origins in the other pre-1954 nationalist movement, that led by Messali Haj, whose dictatorial ways led to a split between him and the central committee of his Movement for the Triumph of Democratic Liberties (MTLD), and who now, as a leader of the Algerian National Movement (MNA), is the bitter enemy of the rebel FLN. His MTLD had both a legal and an underground element; it even had the nucleus of a fighting force, its Security Organization (OS). When it split, the picked men of the OS decided on direct action. Among them were the nine "historical leaders" who gave the signal for the insurrection in November 1954. three of these are now dead, and five are prisoners in French hands. The only one at large is Belkacem Krim.

Krim, born in 1922, is a small tough mountain man from Kabylia, with a reputation as a veteran guerrilla. A former corporal in the French army, he lived as an outlaw in Algeria from 1947 until he left it ten years later. In 1954 he took command of *Willaya* 3 (Kabylia). Now deputy prime minister, he has long been in general charge of military operations, and in January 1960 was also entrusted with foreign affairs— involving frequent visits to Cairo, which is still the seat of that ministry in the provisional government. He has now recovered from an operation undergone in March and the expectation has been that he will lead the delegation to Evian next week.

Small, thin, with slightly slanted eyes, Lakhdar Ben Tobbal is almost Asian in appearance and seems a controlled bundle of nerves. Over twenty of his thirty-seven years have been spent in political action. He joined the MTLD while still at school, and went underground in 1950. In 1954 he was among the twenty-two resistance chiefs who met to approve the future leadership. He was in command of the north Constantine *willaya* in 1957, when he left to become minister of the interior in the provisional government. In this post, his concern extends to Algerians throughout the Maghreb and in France. He is responsible for the political apparatus as well as for administration and policing. In his MTLD days he learned the weakness of a movement without contact with the masses. Having worked chiefly among peasants, he is convinced that the masses want land and better living standards as well as the symbols of independence.

Abdelhafid Boussouf, at thirty-four the youngest of the leaders, comes from the same village near Constantine as Ben Tobbal, and was likewise a follower of Messali Haj in his teens, an OS member, one of the twenty-two. He fought in the Constantine area at first, then commanded the Oran *willaya*. His organizing skill and intimate knowledge of the whole country made him a natural choice to be minister of communications. Contact, chiefly by radio, is vital for a scattered resistance movement, and the rebels are very proud of their system. Strong, shortsighted, with an enigmatic smile, he seems a man on his guard. In Tunis he retains the mental attitude of the resistance, and diplomacy is to him much like "war by other means."

Said Mohamedi, now a minister of state, is a fourth "ex-colonel" — he succeeded Krim as commander in Kabylia. But the direction of the fighting is done by the triumvirate of Belkacem Krim, Ben Tobbal, and Abdelhafid Boussouf.

THE PRISONERS

Of the five ministers held by the French, four were captured when the Moroccan aircraft taking them to Tunis in October 1956 was diverted by its French pilot. Best known among them is Ahmed ben Bella, now in his early forties, a former warrant officer in the French army with a fine war record, and a national leader of the OS. Condemned to forced labor for life, he escaped from Blida jail in 1952 and reached Cairo, whence he played a key part in staging the insurrection. He is a legendary figure in Algeria.

His companions are all "historical leaders" too. Mohammed Boudiaf was the link between the heads of the insurrection in Algeria and their supporters abroad. Mohammed Khider was in charge of the Cairo end, and was helped there by his youthful brother-in-law, Hocine Ait Ahmed, who has a leftish reputation. Rabah Bitat, caught by the French in 1955, was until then in charge of the Algiers region.

Five years behind bars is a long time. The international context of the insurrection has changed since 1956. The question is whether there has been a parallel evolution among the imprisoned leaders, who have been kept informed and have all spent much time in study. It has already been agreed that the Algerian delegation to talk with the French will be able to consult ben Bella and his companions. Which way will they throw their weight?

SPOKESMAN AND SCHOLAR

Two ministers are neither ex-guerrillas nor ex-Fabians from the UDMA. One is the tall, bespectacled M'hammed Yazid, minister of information, official spokesman, and a familiar figure in the United Nations lobbies. Married to an American, he conducts his briefings in an informal American way; but his easy manner could prove misleading. Born in 1923 into a family that had provided several officers for the French army, he has a long record of nationalist struggle, including a two-year sentence in Algeria and four years in hiding in France. He rallied Cairo in 1954 and has been the rebels' representative at many international gatherings.

The only Arabic scholar in the government is Abdelhamid Mehri, minister for social and cultural affairs, thirty-five years old. There is no Arabic university in Algeria, and for the others Arabic is a colloquial mother tongue; but Mehri, though from a poor family, was able to study in Tunisia. His literary polish often comes in useful at international Arab gatherings.

Outside the ministerial ranks, the most brilliant of the younger men in responsible positions is the frail Mohammed Ben Yahia. Not yet thirty, once president of the Muslim students of Algeria, a negotiator at Melun, he is now both secretary-general of the government and *chef de cabinet* to Ferhat Abbas. Though he never lived in France, he has all the qualities of a Left Bank intellectual. He has views about using the millions uprooted by war in modernizing Algeria, and has thought hard about the political implications of an economic deal with France.

The distinction between "tough" soldiers and "soft" politicians has been lost during the years in which former moderates have come to the top of a revolutionary movement, while men reared in guerrilla war and underground activity have taken on diplomatic and political responsibilities. Political divisions may reappear with peace; but it was a French illusion that "fighters" and "politicians" were likely to fall out within the leadership in time of war.

The FLN leaders do not seem as yet to know very precisely what sort of society tomorrow's Algeria will be. They tell you of the need for planning and land reform, and speak contemptuously of the reforms carried out by some newly independent states. But they give a general impression of being still uncommitted, "available," much as Castro's *barbudos* probably were in their first hour of triumph. Unlike a Communist movement, the Algerian leadership does not have a fixed enough conception of its ultimate aims to determine lightly what concessions it can afford to make in negotiation. But now, at Evian, it will have to decide whether the French price for independence can be paid without betraying the Algerian revolution.

Les Pieds au Grand Soleil

JANUARY 6, 1962

The Economist

NOWADAYS, IF A Frenchman were set to write an essay on the elephant, he would not write the elephant's love life as he was supposed to do in the old days; it would be "The elephant and the Algerian question." It is Algeria that is uppermost in French political minds nowadays, and the Algerian passages that were most attentively listened to when the president broadcast to the nation on December 29th. General de Gaulle's contrasts between the recent political and financial stability and the merry-go-round of the past were adroitly done, and effective as far as they went. But he could not announce, as some had hoped, any concrete steps leading to peace in Algeria. He did declare that "one way or another" France must put an end to this drain on its men and resources. He added that he "still" believed a mutually acceptable agreement to be the best possible solution. He concluded, however, that whatever happened, 1962 would witness the gradual withdrawal into Europe, and modernization, of the bulk of the French armed forces. Two more army divisions and several air force units will begin their evacuation this month.

The reduction of the French forces in Algeria is politically significant. The presence of the bulk of French forces on the other side of the Mediterranean has been a major factor in shaping French policy. In the forty-three months since General de Gaulle's return to power, his

Algerian policy has been determined by two contradictory aims: the desire to end the war, and thus consolidate his position at home and abroad, and his reluctance to provoke a major crisis between the state and the armed forces. What a distance separates the early declarations that all Algerians are "fully fledged Frenchmen" from the current talk of a "sovereign and independent" Algerian state. The road is marked by successive refusals of the Muslim insurgents to accept Gaullist terms and by French inability to impose such terms on the Algerian population. The Algerian leaders have changed in status from rebels to potential partners. Negotiations broke down at Evian and Lugrin last year on, apparently, the question of future sovereignty over the Sahara. In September, only a few weeks after the Lugrin breakdown, General de Gaulle suggested that this was not a major obstacle after all. Critics who claim that a bargain could have been struck at half the price now offered, if only concessions had been made in time, forget, however, that these unfortunate delays were not caused only by miscalculations about rebel strength. General de Gaulle's strange relationship with his army was equally a cause.

In May 1958, the armed forces converted a settlers' revolt into a successful insurrection, brought the Fourth Republic to its knees, and chose General de Gaulle for the succession: and all in the name of French Algeria. But, once their choice had been confirmed by a massive popular vote, the Algerian policy of the new ruler gradually departed from that of the kingmakers. Some officers rebelled, others chose passive resistance, others still resigned themselves to discipline. In order to avert a rebellion of the whole officers' corps, General de Gaulle decided that persuasion and ruse were a better method than surgery. He used promotions and reshuffles, promises and threats, ambiguous homilies uttered on tours of officers' messes, to cure the army of its Algerian fixation while avoiding an open clash. Last year, on November 23rd, officers and NCOs from France, Algeria, and Germany were summoned to Strasbourg to hear General de Gaulle's views on the world crisis and on France's need for a national strike force. The French parliament, a wit observed, had been replaced by the Strasbourg assembly. But it is easier to calculate the votes of parties at the Palais Bourbon than to forecast what the military officers will do.

Many of these officers are known to put their Algerian "vocation" well before any Berlin crisis, imaginary or real, in the scale of importance. Others are skeptical of France's ability to build and maintain its own independent deterrent. Others again see a danger to their profession in a modernized army, which would not require the present huge officers' corps swollen by the long years of uninterrupted colonial warfare. Nevertheless, during the Algiers mutiny last April, most of the professional soldiers simply waited to pick the winning side; and only a tiny minority have railed to General Salin's OAS (Organisation de l'Armée Secréte) since then. On the other hand, the OAS, even enjoying as it does the sympathy of the bulk of the European population, could not act with such impunity in Algeria without a good deal of complicity within the armed forces. Now that the OAS is trying, with some success, to extend its methods of intimidation into the home country, where its popular support is very thin indeed, the relative impunity that it seems to enjoy in France raises the question of complicity at all stages within the machine of state.

Wishing to show the OAS that a coup would be faced with popular resistance, trade-union and left-wing organizations called an anti-fascist demonstration in Paris on December 19th. A popular demonstration in France raises inevitably the problem of Communist participation. Yet the feeling that something had to be done to stop the rot was such that even the union to which the majority of the Paris police belong asked the minister of the interior to authorize the demonstration. The minister's reply was the mobilization of tremendous forces, including special squads, to break it up. Thousands of Parisians who were brave enough to get near the Bastille that evening learned that the police had been ordered to use their truncheons. About a hundred, treated in hospital, discovered by physical experience that the government's effectiveness is greater in breaking up a popular demonstration than in tracking agents of the OAS.

The brutality used on this occasion has stirred up much feeling. The liberal cause has been well put in *Le Monde* by M. Fauvet, who accused the authorities of "objectively assisting" the OAS. He reminded the government that the people on whom it was using its truncheons in December were the very same it had called upon for rescue in April, and whom it may very soon have to call upon again. His basic contention was that, in the exceptional circumstances created by the Algerian War, the government will not be able to crush the OAS and keep the army under control unless it can show that it has the articulate backing of the nation and the support of its "organized forces," whether parties or trade unions.

If it were to follow these precepts the government would be betraying the Gaullist conception of power. In the Gaullist pattern, the people are intended to approve, applaud, and express confidence in the ruler's wisdom. In a crisis their voice may be used as background music, for instance to help General de Gaulle in his exchanges with the recalcitrant military. But to let parties or unions influence policy would mean behaving like any other regime and might push more officers into the ranks of the OAS.

For such a design to work, the instruments of state power must be disciplined and obedient. It remains to be seen whether General de Gaulle can settle the military question *en famille*, while pulling the army out of Algeria. A couple of weeks ago, the official mood was one of euphoria. The president was then preparing to announce, in his New Year message, an imminent cease-fire resulting from a general agreement with the Algerian rebels, the details to be completed by further negotiations. While these proceeded, advantage would have been taken of popular satisfaction to alter the constitution, by an overwhelming vote, to strengthen the president's powers and fill the new assembly with neo-Gaullists on a platform of peace. Unhappily, no such auspicious disclosures could be made in the presidential message. It is now said that the secret negotiations with the insurgents are held up by three stumbling-blocks: military bases, which mean in effect Algeria's future international alignment; the status of the European minority, which involves the social structure of the new state; and sovereignty in the transitional stage, an issue that reflects the mutual mistrust accumulated by the seven years of war.

If and when these obstacles are overcome, the army's obedience will be put to its real test. Without an agreement, and assuming that the evacuation of the French troops from Algeria continues nevertheless, the government will drift toward a partition of Algeria; a large proportion of officers may decide not to treat the partial evacuation as a sufficient cause for revolt, and the relationship between state and army may remain for a while unresolved.

Battle for Peace

MARCH 24, 1962

The Economist

PEACE DID NOT descend on Algeria with the ceasefire on Monday. The illusion was kept up for a day as Paris, half-astonished, rejoiced over the news of quiet from Algeria. Yet even that silence had a double meaning. In the Arab quarters, nationalist (FLN) stewards kept the crowds quiet and prevented mass demonstrations of joy. In the European districts, it was the silence of a deserted city, paralyzed by strikes. By Tuesday afternoon, the OAS (Secret Army Organization) had broken the silence and the illusions. Mortar shells fell on a crowded square at the entrance of the Casbah in Algiers, killing and wounding dozens of Muslims. All reports agree that, but for the discipline and authority of the nationalist cadres, this horrible provocation could have precipitated a race riot.

The dangers threatening the precarious peace were thus immediately demonstrated by this and similar, if less spectacular, provocations. It was obvious from the start that General Salan's Secret Army would use methods such as these to sabotage the agreement. What is not certain is whether the nationalist cadres will always be able to keep their people in check. Nor is it certain that the Algerian government-in-exile, now reinforced by Mr. ben Bella and his companions, will be willing to accept responsibility for this state of things for long. Although its own guerrillas have not surrendered their arms, they are not at present using them. Its terrorists have stopped their activities in the towns. The French can no longer justify their weakness by the difficulties of a struggle "on two fronts." The battle for peace is now plainly the battle against the Secret Army.

Who is to carry on this struggle and how was not clearly defined in the Evian agreements. It is hoped in Paris that Algeria's provisional institutions will be set up next week. The provisional government should have at its disposal an Algerian police force of 40,000 men. Their recruiting is not a major problem. There are many more Algerians who can be transferred from the French army and police forces, though there will certainly be a shortage of officers. But, although this is not specified in the agreements, French sources suggest that the new Algerian police force will be used only in the countryside and kept out of the towns. Yet it is in Algiers and Oran, where he has the backing of the European population, that General Salan can operate most effectively. Paris may be reluctant to use Muslim troops against the European population, but does this mean that French forces will now seriously tackle the task for which, in the past, they have shown so little enthusiasm?

There are many possibilities in this ambiguous situation. The Secret Army may not prove capable of provoking a major upheaval. The Algerian nationalists may urge their troops to be patient for a few more months, promising that they themselves will crush the Secret Army after independence. Alternatively, the Evian agreements may be drowned in blood. The unknown in all these equations is the French army. For nearly four years now General de Gaulle has been striving toward a solution in Algeria acceptable to the bulk of his officers. He is now convinced of his officers' loyalty and obedience. The test has come, and on its outcome much will depend, not only in Algeria.

In the meantime, Paris is scanning anxiously the reports from Algeria and wondering about the future. This week the National Assembly held a special session, probably the last of the present parliament, to discuss the Evian agreements. It was a poor debate and understandably so. The opponents of the agreements spoke with passion of dictatorship and treason but did not press for a vote because they did not wish to reveal how few are General Salan's open sympathizers in the chamber. The advocates of the agreement, particularly the neo-Gaullist deputies, were half-hearted. They were not allowed to forget that they, too, had been elected on the platform of *Algérie Française*. And the prospect of dissolution added to the general sadness. Few people outside the Palais Bourbon will shed tears over this important and mediocre assembly.

The expectations of a general election spring from General de Gaulle's message to parliament on Tuesday. On April 8th Frenchmen will, once again, go to the polls to approve the Evian agreements and grant him full powers to carry them out. The general does not need this approval, and if he required exceptional powers he could assume them under article 16 of the constitution. Article 16, however, does not allow the dissolution of parliament and the general's choice suggests that he wants to keep that possibility open. Some Gaullist strategists are against an early election, arguing that no miracle will give them a chamber more obedient than the present one. Most of the general's advisers, however, consider that the undoubted triumph in the peace referendum must be used rapidly as political capital to give a new lease to the Gaullist regime. The choice will, naturally, be affected by events in Algeria. The battle for peace will also determine the next chapter in the Gaullist history.

The Death of a Legendary Hero

NOVEMBER 30, 1970
The Nation

THE VERDICT OF history is the one that really mattered to Charles de Gaulle, and we obviously shall not get it amid the current chorus of genuine and hypocritical praise. Had the general departed, say, three years ago, it would have been easier for his admirers to make of his second reign a saga of unmitigated success: the miracle worker switching his country from chaos to stability, from the brink of civil war to unity, from near bankruptcy to prosperity. And, having thus consolidated his base, successfully defying the American giant. But this image was shattered by the political crisis and social upheaval of May 1968, which showed the divisions and the depth of discontent hidden beneath the glittering surface. Indirectly, they also revealed the limited means of Gaullist foreign policy. Instinctively, the general must have felt that the days of grandeur were gone. His official exit—in April of last year, after a lost referendum—had all the elements of political suicide. Nevertheless, he managed to use even this retreat to boost his image: Cincinnatus was returning to the plough—in his case, to the writing table at Colombey.

Nothing is more sickening than the sudden outpouring of love on funeral occasions. With de Gaulle now closely following Nasser, we have had our ration. Let me, then, state quite bluntly that, whatever my occasional sneaking admiration for the general as a performer, I have never, as a Socialist, shared his nationalist outlook or his political conceptions. Even when in sympathy with some of his struggles—not just against the Nazis but also against French colonials in Algeria or the American war in Vietnam—I always remained suspicious of his motives. This openly admitted, I see only more reason to try to understand why it fell upon a conservative military man to extricate France from its colonial ventures; or why a man, who at home was a pillar of the capitalist establishment, was hailed abroad as a champion of the anti-imperialist struggle. One should not minimize de Gaulle's stature for polemical purposes. The only duty is to seek a proper balance and historical perspective; to disentangle, if one can, fact from fiction and reality from myth. But in the case of Gaullism, the task is difficult because the legend itself was vital for the general and he himself was its artful keeper. Mastery of the spoken and the written word were among his key weapons.

One of the legends will stand the test of time. It is the original one, presenting him as a symbol of French resistance, which was born on June 18, 1940, when, from a London studio, he urged the French people to carry on the fight. He was an acting brigadier and a junior minister, nearly fifty years old at the time. He found the courage to dissociate himself from his fellow officers, most of whom were rallying around Pétain, and to break with his class—the bulk of the French bourgeoisie having chosen collaboration with the Germans. The London episode, as recorded in his memoirs, hovers perilously between the sublime and the ridiculous. De Gaulle, in those first days in England, had few forces at this disposal and probably more conflicts with his allies than with the enemy. His very weakness dictated a policy of intransigeance and, for once, the man was really destined for his role. In the end, he achieved his objective: France was one of the victors and, officially, one of the big powers.

But however genuine, the original legend lies at the root of many subsequent troubles and misunderstandings. To present France as an ally, it was necessary to describe collaboration as an exception and resistance as the rule. Far from being a traitor to his class, de Gaulle proved its savior. He limited the scope of reforms to what was unavoidable and prevented a more radical transformation of society—a vision which had inspired many a fighter in the underground. Altogether, the fiction of national unity, transcending all class conflicts, suited General de Gaulle better than it did the French Left that dominated the resistance. Contemptuous of parties and "intermediaries," the general was not going to settle for less than his own concept of the divine right of elected monarchy. A clash seemed inevitable. De Gaulle's departure in 1946 was a miscalculation. He expected to be called back with enhanced powers. When that failed to happen, he had to form a party—the Gaullist Rally or RPF—and launch it against the regime. The Fourth Republic, however, showed an unexpected capacity for passive resistance. After the assault, Gaullism seemed a spent force and the general doomed to exile. He might have stayed at Colombey but for the inability of the French bourgeoisie to extricate itself from the colonial war and for the putsch of military commanders in Algeria.

That the general used the putsch seems undeniable. On one side, he was encouraging the rebels to step up their threats; on the other, he was pressing the regime to call him in as a savior. A couple of weeks was enough to force the cowardly rulers of the Fourth Republic to surrender. Despite the legal trappings, it was a shotgun transfer of power. *"Vae Victis,"* retorted the Gaullists, and besides the transition was legalized by an overwhelming vote. The argument sounds rather strange coming from men who are, by now, Agnew-like upholders of law and order. Still, it is wiser to assess the Fifth Republic on its record rather than on its original sin.

Like the general in his last book, one may best start with institutions. After years of merry-go-round, when the average government lasted about six months, the stability of the French Republic is impressive. Two governments in a decade and really only one ruler. But how much was it due to constitutional change? A system of "direct democracy," based on the master's "communion" with his subjects and occasional referenda, requires a charismatic figure at the top. De Gaulle himself was to discover that it yielded diminishing returns as his support dwindled from the initial 80 percent. A heavy price also had to be paid: Parliament was reduced to a rubber-stamp institution and the television to a government tool, while official propaganda and pressure reached unprecedented proportions. The absence of safety valves and warning signals may have had something to do with the May explosion.

Political stability was indispensable to economic recovery; so runs the Gaullist argument, and it has some validity when not overplayed. The empty vaults of the Bank of France were refilled with gold, trade expanded, and production grew. But Gaullist France carried out no major structural reforms; it merely widened the gap between rich and poor. The outcome was the biggest general strike the country had ever known.

The failure of France to introduce more radical reforms than did its neighbors should put an end to a once fashionable theory that Gaullism is a superior form of capitalist rule, liberal democracy being no longer able to cope with monopolistic competition. The theory was linked with the dream of French technocrats that the regime would allow them to speed up the process of economic concentration and rationalization. The dream did not come true. De Gaulle had to gather votes for his referenda from somewhere, and a great deal of his support came from the very people, such as small farmers and shopkeepers, who were supposed to be squeezed out. Gaullism was a response to a specific situation, in a country faced with colonial complications and a militant working class. Indeed, the French experiment confirms that parliamentary democracy is a more efficient defense mechanism, whenever capitalism can afford it. After de Gaulle comes a Guizot, with his slogan, "Enrich yourselves," though whether neo-Gaullism can provide the safety valves and avoid an explosion remains to be seen.

Are the external achievements more solid? The fact that Algeria, once a cancer on the French political body, can now be treated as an external matter must be cited as an achievement. Here, again, however, the critics have their points. It is true that the war lasted as long—four years—under each republic. It is equally true that the delay under the Fifth Republic was due not only to de Gaulle's need to come to terms with the French military commanders, with the barons who had made him king. For a time, he also clung to the illusion that he could force the FLN to accept his conditions. Yet, when all this is said, he did make peace in the end, unlike his allegedly Socialist predecessors, and his experience is relevant for America. France, after all, had half a million men in Algeria; it also had native troops and a better control of the military situation than Americans have in Vietnam. It took General de Gaulle quite a time to realize that this was not enough, that war against a determined liberation movement was pointless. His strictures against American policy in Vietnam were no less valid because they were the fruit of bitter experience.

Foreign policy proper was the general's favorite field and here the verdict is difficult. To dispel some ambiguity, one must recall that the now classical image of de Gaulle as the champion of détente with the Russians and the darling of the Third World really arises from the second half of his reign. In the first four or five years, admittedly handicapped by the Algerian War, he pursued quite a different policy. He was trying to gain the leadership of a continental coalition, based on the Paris-Bonn axis, which was to put him on a par with the superpowers. Konrad Adenauer, the cold warrior, was then his chief ally. The scheme had logic. The snag was its basic premise—the assumption that Germany could be forced into a junior partnership, particularly in an enterprise aimed at the United States. Yet, by about 1963, when his edifice was obviously in ruins, de Gaulle showed his extraordinary capacity for recovery and his skill in performance. Within a short period, he was opening lines to Eastern Europe and challenging "American hegemony," to applause echoing from Asia to Latin America.

Performance, nothing but performance, claimed the critics, but they were only half right. To take France out of NATO, to keep Britain, the "Trojan Horse," out of the Common Market, to slow down the process of European integration were themselves achievements of a negative kind. The strength and weakness of Gaullist foreign policy were connected with the role of the nation-state in our time. Having grasped how strong the state still was, the general defied the United States, putting to shame his European colleagues who had never dared say no to Washington. But the nation-state, particularly one of medium size, can no longer transcend the imperatives of internationalism. His was, thus, an anachronistic realism. To say that de Gaulle did not have the means to match his ends does not mean simply that France was too small. Internally, he did not have the instruments ready to resist the American invasion; externally, he could not turn to the people of Europe, offering them a different life, a society radically different from the American model. You cannot expect a general, however skillful and bold, to propose the foundation of the United Socialist States of Europe.

As heads of state filed into Notre Dame for a last tribute, many thoughts crossed one's mind. These included strange reflections on the role of the individual in history, remembering that de Gaulle, having so dominated his country for a decade, then vanished almost without a ripple. One recalled his stature, if only by contrast with surrounding dwarfs. His foreign policy, for what it was worth, showed up the failure of the European Left, the bankruptcy of social democracy. Finally, with the last of the old heroes gone, one also felt that the postwar period was at last over. The general's own reign had really come to an end in May 1968, when the master tactician seemed utterly bewildered for a while by new political and social forces. That was not yet a change of the guard, but for Europe, at least, it marked the beginning of a new age of conflict in which we shall need not the deceptive protection of a legend but the more potent weapon of political consciousness.

Algeria Slides into Civil War

FEBRUARY 21, 1994
The Nation

"*VOICI LE TEMPS des assassins,* the bilingual Algerians could exclaim, echoing Rimbaud, when nearly a year ago, their intellectuals began to be slaughtered by Islamic fundamentalists. Poets and psychiatrists, doctors and professors, writers and journalists had their throats cut or their brains blasted by a bullet. In France, where those who had opposed colonialism still have a feeling of responsibility, an international committee was set up, headed by the sociologist Pierre Bourdieu, to help those intellectuals in danger. But it deliberately denounced the violence of the state as well as that of the terrorists. A wise move, since in this bloody mess the educated classes are not the only target, and the so-called God's Party, the Islamic Front of Salvation (FIS), provides both the killers and many of the victims. Ever since the electoral process was dramatically suspended by the army in January 1992, when the Islamic Front was poised for victory, its members and sympathizers have been driven underground, arrested by the thousands, tortured, shot, or deported to the Sahara Desert.

The government's attempt to solve a political problem by repression predictably had the opposite effect. The so-called ninjas, the hooded special squads from the army that hunt down bearded Muslims in the poor districts of Algiers, serve as recruiting agents for the FIS Resistance is steadily growing. Last month, units of the Islamic underground attacked army barracks in the west of the country, and fatalities on both sides are now running between two hundred and three hundred a week. The country is drifting into a civil war in which the stakes are high, since a victory by the Islamic fundamentalists would have political consequences not just in neighboring Tunisia and Morocco but in Egypt and beyond. And the conflict is being waged amid a deepening economic crisis. The servicing of Algeria's foreign debt, which now amounts to 70 percent of the gross domestic product, absorbs the bulk of export revenues. Prices are up and investment and production are down, while unemployment is approaching a quarter of the labor force—a highly explosive factor in a country in which 70 percent of the population is under thirty-five.

Is it still possible to prevent a full-scale civil war, to gain time, and, thus, evolve alternative solutions? The "reconciliation conference," sponsored by the authorities at the end of January and boycotted by all key parties, was a total flop. The subsequent appointment of General Liamine Zeroual, hitherto defense minister, as president of the republic for a three-year term of "transition" was an admission of that failure. But tentative talks with the Islamists are apparently continuing behind the scenes.

To assess the chances of such efforts we must go back to the roots of the crisis. To the casual observer of the North African scene, the present Algerian predicament is particularly puzzling. After all, Algeria was one of the few countries that gained independence, thanks to a genuine resistance movement forcing out the colonial power, France. And, only twenty years ago, Algeria, with its "Islamic Socialism," was described as a model of independent development and one of the leaders of the Third World. Admittedly, the other leader was Yugoslavia. Things were not quite as simple, or as attractive, as they were being painted at the time.

The Algerians did win their independence, but they inherited a country bled white by eight years of war and ruined still further by the mass departure of the European settlers, the million or so *pieds noirs* who, in 1962, made up about a tenth of the population. Second, the people never seized power. It was usurped almost at once by the army—not by the resistance fighters but by the more regular army stationed on the Russian frontier under the command of Colonel Houari Boumedienne. For the first three years after the revolution the army shared power with President Ahmed ben Bella, one of the nine "historic leaders" who had launched the war of liberation. Then, after kicking ben Bella out, Boumedienne took over. When he died in 1976, another colonel, Chadli Benjedid, was picked to preside over the regime on its road to ruin. Yet, throughout this period, the army did not rule alone. It did it in conjunction with the National Liberation Front (FLN), the resistance movement turned instrument of authoritarian rule.

Thus, from the very start, power flowed from above. It was allegedly exercised for the people, though certainly not by the people. All the key jobs at all levels in politics, administration, and the economy went to handpicked members of the FLN Rapidly the privileged caste developed its vested interests. Nepotism grew, corruption spread, and the gap between the rulers and the ruled widened. When in 1990, after nearly three decades of one-party rule, the system was badly shaken by an electoral contest, the analogy that naturally came to mind was the crumbling regimes of Eastern Europe.

Actually, the Algerians started their perestroika at the beginning of the eighties. But the shift was not the result of a movement from below. As in the Russia of today, it was part of the struggle between clans and factions within the ruling party and the army over the best way to perpetuate their power and privilege—through state channels or through privatization? Where the two models differed was in the role attributed to religion. The Algerians, from the start, had emphasized the Arabic and Islamic nature of their regime, although it was only under President Benjedid that it acquired fundamentalist overtones. Even earlier, however, presumably to counter secular "Marxist" influences, the regime brought fundamentalist masters from the Middle East to teach literary Arabic in its schools, thus sowing the seeds of its own destruction.

The hour of reckoning was put off by profits from petroleum, Algeria's almost sole source of foreign exchange. The windfall gains from the second oil shock in the late seventies were used, however, to import consumer goods rather than to invest in future jobs. When the trend was reversed, as a result of the drop in the price of crude and the fall of the dollar, which reduced Algeria's petroleum revenues by 80 percent between 1985 and 1991, everything was ready for an explosion.

It happened in October 1988, when, driven to despair by rising prices and the absence of prospects, the angry young men from the overcrowded slums of Algiers took to the streets. It was, incidentally, during those riots that the future leaders of the Islamic Front, Abbasi Madani and Ali Benhadj—now serving twelve-year sentences each but possibly tomorrow's negotiators—first gained prominence. The army was called to the rescue and the riots were quelled in bloody fashion. The regime, however, did not alter its policy of liberalization, moving rapidly toward the legalization of opposition parties. In the local elections of June 1990, its popularity was put to the first real test. Since the Front of Socialist Forces (FFS), headed by Hocine Ait-Ahmed, another "historic leader," boycotted the poll, it was essentially a trial of strength between the FLN and the newly created FIS. With the Liberation Front now standing for privilege and corruption, the Islamists could parade as champions of the downtrodden, offering them dignity now and salvation in the hereafter. Their victory was undisputed. The FIS won 54 percent of the votes cast and conquered some 850 town halls throughout the country.

The authorities did nothing to refurbish their tarnished image. They acted as if they were sure of victory—or, more likely, as if President Benjedid had reached a deal with the fundamentalists. Whatever the case, the government's policy was suicidal. In preparation for a parliamentary poll the following year, it introduced an electoral system, modeled on France's and based on single-member constituencies. An absolute majority was needed to win in the first round and a simple one in the second. It was a system designed to amplify national trends and favor the strongest party.

And so the inevitable happened in December 1991. Although the Islamic Front's share of the vote dropped to 47 percent, this was enough to win 188 seats outright and to guarantee a landslide victory in the second round. The FLN, with 23 percent of the vote dispersed throughout the country, garnered only fifteen seats. The FFS, with its 7 percent of the vote concentrated in Ait-Ahmed's strongholds, took twenty-five seats.

The final outcome, however, was beyond doubt, and thus the FLN government was faced with a momentous choice. Should it give the benefits of democracy to its enemies, hand victory on a plate to a fundamentalist party, which made no secret of the fact that once it has imposed an Islamic state there would be no question of going back to a secular society? Should it give power to a party that would deprive half the electorate of a role in society, since its attitude toward women is an Islamic version of the Nazi ideal of *Kinder, Kirche, Küche,* hardly improved by the veil? But, on the other hand, can you accept the will of the people only when it suits you and ignore it when it goes against you?

The huge demonstration sponsored by the Front of Socialist Forces in Algiers right after the vote, with its message of opposition to both the police state and the religious one, pointed toward a solution. Could the alliance between the intelligentsia defending human rights and the people, a link still weak and full of contradictions, have grown into a major political force?

There was no time for such a movement to develop; the army intervened, put off elections till doomsday, banned the FIS and drove it underground, removed Benjedid from the presidency, and replaced him with a five-man High State Council. To prove it was in earnest, at the head of the council the army installed a political outsider, Mohammed Boudiaf, who, although a "historic leader," had spent the past twenty-eight years in Moroccan exile. Whether this solitary hero could have mobilized the people and smashed the ruling political mafia remains a question. Five months later he was shot dead. Whoever pulled the trigger, the negligence of the security services made it plain that powerful interests were keen on his disappearance.

And so things went back to normal. The members of the old *nomen-klatura* were again shifting among top jobs in the administration, The *trabendo* (the black market in smuggled goods) prospered. Discontent grew. Indeed, things became worse. No foreign capital would venture into such a climate of political uncertainty. Repression, as those who fought the French should have known, merely strengthened the resistance, whose counterblows have maddened the authorities. In reprisal, Islamic sympathizers are now being murdered by semiofficial death squads. The fundamentalists are not only fighting back against the troops; they have also targeted secular intellectuals in a policy not of blind terror but, as was rightly pointed out, of terror designed to render the people blind.

After two years of treatment that was supposed to cure the country, this is the predicament from which the rulers are now trying to extricate themselves. The military solution, which some people, notably the ex-Communists, still advocate, is obviously a blind alley. Five years ago, a political, though not democratic, case could be made that such drastic action could win time, which could be used to purge the establishment, carry out radical reforms so as to win over the people and isolate the fundamentalists. Clearly, the opposite has happened. The Islamic Front has consolidated its base and no one can now gain popular acceptance without a genuine electoral test. But the reverse prospect, a victory for the fundamentalists, known as the "Iranian Solution," is also ruled out by most experts, on the grounds that the Islamic fighters cannot defeat the army, that in the fight against fundamentalism the army could rely on a great deal of support in the country and, last but not least, that a sweeping victory for the FIS would provoke the mass exodus of the bilingual, French-speaking professionals and thus further cripple the economy.

It is between these two extremes that the scope for a bargain apparently lies. Most of my Algerian friends, with a perfect anticolonial record and an allergy to fundamentalism, nevertheless argue that, while a reconciliation conference should be held and attended by all parties, the crucial deal must be struck between those who are fighting, the

Islamic Front and the army. Both must make concessions. In order to resume the electoral process, from which it hopes to emerge victorious, the FIS must accept conditions insuring that its victory will not be irreversible, that it will not install a religious tyranny, that it will preserve scope for the development of secular forces. Once this is agreed, a parliamentary election could be held, preferably under a system of proportional representation, which would allow smaller secular parties to play a role. The army, for its part, must give up its rule, by proxy or otherwise and, through a long transitional period, act as guardian of the constitutional pact, protecting the country from dictatorial and fundamentalist temptations—a tall order and one raising a host of questions.

It is not certain that the FIS is still willing to compromise and, if it is, that it could count on the cooperation of the Islamic fighters. Should the army and the FIS reach an agreement, it does not have to be on a democratic platform. They could share power in an Islamic dictatorship and still win the blessings of the international financial establishment. After all, the FIS, linked to commercial capital, to the souk, is no enemy of private enterprise.

Finally, I must mention the mood of my Algerian friends, mostly women, who echo the anguished cry of one academic still teaching in Algeria: "If the *barbus* [bearded ones] get hold of power, there is no future for me in my country. I shall pack and go and and I won't be the only one. We shall be a legion."

The chances of heading off this collision seem slender. Yet the Algerian message, though strewn with corpses and written in blood, is not very different from the one the Left is now getting in various parts of the world. Its failure to provide progressive rational solutions and to mobilize people behind them has given dangerous opportunities to the forces of unreason. In the abstract, it is easy to say where the way out in Algeria lies: in an alliance between the progressive intelligentsia and the bulk of the working people, based on a democratic program with sufficient social content to attract the exploited now seeking solace in Islamic salvation. But we are not there. All over the world, the Left is fighting rear-guard actions, staging holding operations, trying to gain time to rally people around a new vision. That seems a defensive and not very exalted task. Yet, if they fail, we shall really find ourselves in *le temps des assassins.*

Battle of Algiers
on Paris Métro

NOVEMBER 6, 1995
The Nation

Paris

ON SEPTEMBER 29, French viewers watching the news were offered a bloody Hollywood thriller as an extra. It was the end of a long manhunt. The villain was finally cornered in a dark provincial street and, after a shootout, a cop kicked the body to check whether the man was really dead. It was gruesome but, we were assured, the police had acted in "legitimate self-defense." Doubts crept in when it was learned that the film had been edited to cut out the sound of an unknown voice yelling, "Finish him off! Finish him off!" In any case, Jean-Louis Debre, the bungling interior minister, at once proclaimed not only that it was all perfectly legal but also that the victim, the twenty-four-year-old Khaled Kelkal, brought to France from Algeria as a baby, had been a key figure in all the bombings that had shaken France in the preceding couple of months. The implication was that the French could now take the Métro in peace. Wiser commentators pondered whether the authorities were not building Kelkal—a bright student turned delinquent, converted to fundamentalism in jail, yet clearly no more than a cog in the terrorist machine—into an Islamic hero and role model for young rebels. Clearly, France did not get rid of its Algerian connection through an execution; a new gas canister filled with bolts and nails exploded in

Paris the day of Kelkal's funeral, and twenty-nine were injured by a similar device on the Métro on October 17. While this brought out soldiers on the street corners, the suggestion that French suburbs are swept by a fundamentalist wave is, to say the least, premature.

Algeria's undeclared civil war, with its forty thousand dead, is now well into its fourth year; it is certain that the country's November 16 presidential poll, which will be boycotted by the Islamists and the key opposition parties, will not bring it to a close. France was bound to be affected because of the links forged during 130 years of colonial rule, including the traumatic eight years of the war of national liberation; because it is Algeria's primary trading partner and, therefore, the chief backer of the ruling military junta; and last but not least, because of the large population of Algerian origin living here. Yet it wasn't until July 25 that the war crossed the Mediterranean, literally with a bang, when a bomb exploded in the heart of Paris—at a subway station in the Latin Quarter—killing seven and wounding nearly ninety. There followed a series of explosions with fewer casualties, the bombs fortunately misfiring, exploding not on time or not at all (like the one found on the railroad tracks near Lyons, which was actually linked to Kelkal by fingerprints). Those in the know claim that the Latin Quarter job was the work of professionals brought from abroad, whereas the other, more amateurish attempts were carried out by local squads. The Armed Islamic Group, the most ruthless opponent of the regime in Algeria, was reported in October to have claimed responsibility and made demands, though such is the ambiguity of this civil war that many people still see the hand of the Algerian secret services behind the whole operation. (They would do it, in this version, to provoke popular indignation in France and thus strengthen French backing for the military regime in Algeria. The Islamic Salvation Front, the more moderate antigovernment movement in Algeria, has made this accusation publicly.)

At least one casualty of this conflict is plain to see. Despite official proclamations that one should not confuse Islam and fundamentalism, Arabs and terror, the omnipresent police in their inevitable street checks are instinctively guided by skin color. Once again, as with the

Gulf War, a section of the population is under suspicion and must prove its allegiance. Behind these troubles loom two wider questions: Can Europe, torn by the current structural economic crisis, cope with immigrant workers, brought in under different circumstances as cheap temporary labor but who are now here to stay? Can France, for a century a champion of assimilation, now absorb such a large number of "Islamic" immigrants? Before we can answer these questions, we must look at the size and shape of this so-called Muslim community.

BEURS IN FRANCE

Strange nicknames abound in Franco-Algerian relations. The *pieds noirs*, you may recall, were not Indians; they were French (or European) settlers in North Africa, a tribe that went back to the home country where, alas, many of them joined the xenophobic battalions of National Front leader Jean-Marie Le Pen. The *beurs* are the opposite. In the reverse slang of the young (known as *Verlan* for *l'envers*), it means "Arabs" and refers to young people of North African origin living in France (the nicer-sounding feminine is *beurette*). The difficulty lies in calculating their number.

Islam is now described as France's second-largest religion; Muslims are estimated at between 3.5 million and 4 million, out of a total population of 57 million. The estimates are vague because ethnic and religious questions are forbidden in the French census. Thus the only firm figures from the last census (1990) refer to foreign nationals. If you add to the 616,000 Algerian nationals the 572,000 Moroccans, and also the Tunisians, Turks, and Muslims from black Africa who are now living in France, you will get altogether less than 1.8 million. Thus, there must be close to 2 million French citizens who are Muslims, most of them of Algerian origin (until they won their independence in 1962, Algerians on both sides of the sea were, at least nominally, fully fledged French citizens). The very concept of a Muslim community, however, is an invention. The Algerians themselves are split, the Turks differ from the North Africans and so on. The religious link, too, is artificial.

The young of Algerian origin are no more Muslim than their French equivalents are Catholic. The latest survey suggests that in both cases nearly 70 percent are not practicing. The number of Muslims is greatly inflated by Le Pen to frighten people with the specter of an "Islamic invasion." Here they are lumped together simply to examine whether French society is still capable of absorbing both a new immigrant population and an additional religion.

As assimilationists, the French are second to none. Their Jacobin centralism has its ridiculous side. The best-known example is of school textbooks imposed throughout the empire so that black children in Africa could learn that "our ancestors the Gauls had blue eyes and blond hair." The steamroller, however, was fairly efficient. My wife's Breton parents learned French at school; their children know no Breton. And what the French did to their inner minorities, they repeated with successive waves of Italians, Spaniards, and Poles. And these are now convinced of their Frenchness. Among Le Pen's followers you find many whose name makes it plain they would not be here if their party's policy against foreigners had been applied in the past.

"But the newcomers are not the same," object the reactionaries. They have a different religion; they don't mix or intermarry; they don't eat like us or live as we do. You let them develop their argument and then slyly reply, "The same used to be said about Jews in the thirties." It is a good blow because, while it is already widely acceptable to be anti-Arab, making anti-Jewish remarks still requires caution. Yet the point is valid and the only difference is one of numbers. There were about three hundred thousand predominantly Ashkenazi Jews in France before the war; now, with the arrival of Sephardic Jews from North Africa, there are slightly more than twice that figure. What the numbers suggest is that assimilation could take longer to add more color to French culture. But problems lie elsewhere: Even if France were still an efficient machine for absorbing outsiders—and it is now caught up in economic, social, and political crisis—cultural clashes are arising as Islam's tendency to move beyond the religious comes into conflict with French *laïcité*, the strong secular tradition based on the separation between church and state.

Veiled Contradictions

The most publicized confrontation first erupted in 1989, when the head of a provincial high school banned three pupils who insisted on wearing a veil, or *hedjab*, inside the building. Though conflicting legal decisions have since been given and the ministerial recommendation now is to ban only "ostentatious signs"(?!) of one's beliefs, the matter still arouses passion, as I discovered when raising the issue among friends of Algerian origin. Djamilla, who studied in France, taught in Algiers and left when she found life there unbearable, was against yielding an inch: You give them a finger, they take the whole arm; you allow them to wear a veil, they shoot you because you are not wearing one. Malika, a *beurette* who knows Algeria only through family and holidays, was less categorical. Though herself against allowing the veil, she noticed that school authorities were more lenient in permitting Catholic or Jewish signs of distinction. Above all, like many progressive schoolteachers, she felt that to kick the girls out was to hand them over to fanatics. But the opposite case was also argued with passion, particularly by feminists, since the *hedjab* is a symbol of women's subservience. I must confess I felt sympathy for a *beur* who, summoned to take sides in a public debate, simply hedged: I am against the veil and against the ban.

This debate, while dramatized by the media, also reflects the country's changing mood. The French Left, centralist by tradition and favoring an egalitarian uniformity, after 1968 discovered both roots and the right to be different. Then, with unemployment rising, Le Pen pushed this to a perverse conclusion: Immigrants are so different they should get out. The pendulum of leftist opinion then swung back toward equal rights and the struggle against discrimination. However, movements identified with that line, like SOS Racisme, did not manage to consolidate their position among immigrants because the Socialists, with whom they were connected, did not dare to face squarely the rising tide of jingoism. Conservative governments that followed actually swam with the current and pandered to xenophobia, insisting on their strong stand against immigration. If you add that immigrant workers, brought here mainly to perform unskilled jobs, were the main victims of restructuring, foreigners and their children have plenty of motives for discontent.

Yet it would be wrong to conclude that the social and cultural gap between communities is widening. Some *beurs* are entering the trades and teaching, the media and the arts. The number of mixed couples is increasing. A poll shows that more French (38 percent) are opposed to intermarriage than Muslims are (29 percent of Muslims are opposed if the Muslim is a woman, 18 percent if it is a man). With Algeria torn by civil war, the temptation to migrate there, never very strong among those born in France, has vanished altogether. The only "elsewhere" now is a mythical Islam. Quite a lot was also made here of Muslim quiescence during the Gulf War, though it would be unwise to read too much into this silence. One point Malika made did strike me: "I don't speak of such subjects in the office with my colleagues, *Français de souche*" (best translated as "French of old stock").

"ALLAH'S SUBURBS"?

What the inner cities are to America, the suburbs—to which the poor are driven from the heart of the town—are to Europe. By high-speed subway you can travel quickly from the center of Paris to La Courneuve, in what used to be the "Red Belt" and is still the last French department under Communist control. From there you go to the city of Four Thousand (the original number of apartments), a depressing combination of fifteen-story blocks of flats. The staircases look drab and the space for garbage cans is dirty, but there are TV satellite dishes all over the place (you can catch Arabic programs from overseas; the dishes apparently mushroomed after the Gulf War). There is a very nice public library with a good section for children, though otherwise the social amenities are few. The supermarket, with long lines dominated by *beurs* and blacks, is full of junk food. In the yard idle young men ask me, "You looking for somebody?" Clearly they don't want anyone snooping on their turf. It's all dreary and predictable.

The subsidized "accommodation with moderate rents," or HLM, is an important part of French postwar history. Between 1957 and 1975, the years of glorious expansion, about 2.9 million such apartments were built. Now France has to cope with these rabbit warrens. Experts say that to repaint, improve acoustics, and modernize would help but would not solve the problem. At stake is the very function of the institution. At one stage, the HLM was a place of social promotion—for immigrant workers moving from shantytowns and French on the way to owning their own houses. Since the economic crisis of the mid-seventies and the ban on immigration, foreign workers stay put, while the French left behind feel downgraded. Unemployment has risen steadily and is now around 12 percent. It is double that level for those under twenty-five and double again for the young from North Africa. An HLM is quite often a place of exclusion and despondency: no hope, no future, and a deep thirst for dignity.

Such fortresses of frustration are to be found around most industrial cities. The two terrorists who shot tourists in Morocco last year were recruited at the Four Thousand. Khaled Kelkal and his companions were brought up in a similar suburb outside Lyons. One can read the past thoughts of the dead youngster, since a German researcher interviewed Kelkal a couple of years ago and Le Monde published three pages of extracts. He is symptomatic in his almost cliché-like emphasis on the wall separating the suburb from the town, on the injustice called justice, on violence as the only accepted language, on the quest for acceptance and recognition, which in his case only the family and Islam provided. But he is also highly atypical—not every kid who feels like an outsider attends a posh high school and turns to robbery, and not every rebel reaches the point of planting bombs. It is important to stress that whereas during the war of independence the National Liberation Front was among Algerian workers in France like fish in water, neither the Armed Islamic Group nor the Islamic Salvation Front enjoys comparable support. The bombers are rejected by most Muslims in France for selfish as well as moral reasons—they spell trouble. Yet, will not circumstances breed a growing number of Kelkals?

My instinct tells me that, given time, the French will absorb yet another wave of immigrants. This hunch, however, rests on my refusal to accept that our future will be barbarian. The smoothness of the transition is less determined by the customs of the migrants than by the nature of the receiving society. Muslims do not have a monopoly on fundamentalism or irrationality. Le Pen's xenophobic National Front has spread faster in France than Islamic "fanatics." A genuine integration, allowing for cultural and religious freedoms, depends on Europe's capacity to emerge from the current crisis, on the ability of the Western Left to raise class solidarity above ethnic prejudices and to provide solutions that require no scapegoats. It depends, as was so often heard in this French debate, on our being able to avoid an "American future." We cannot get away by shifting the blame to the victims. Shakespeare, as so often, had something to say about it:

> *The fault, dear Brutus, is not in our stars,*
> *But in ourselves . . .*

Mai 68

::

Paris Burns

MAY 11, 1968
The Economist

THE CARCASS OF a car or something was burning on the corner of the Boulevard St. Michel and Boulevard Montparnasse. It was two o'clock on Wednesday morning. The fire brigade rushing to the spot met a long convoy of black lorries filled with helmeted police armed with shields and long riot truncheons. Moving toward the corner of Raspail, the convoy was overtaken by screaming ambulances. A major drama had just been avoided: The police had thrown tear gas bombs into a cafe that was then closed. The Red Cross had to break in to save people from asphyxiation.

Yet, this scene of night violence was not typical of Tuesday, which, compared with its bloody predecessor, was relatively quiet. Its main feature was a long march across Paris by some twenty-five thousand students. Prevented by vast numbers of police from entering their own district, the Latin Quarter, which looked like a besieged fortress, they trekked for hours through the capital, chanting slogans, marching up the Champs-Elysées and then back to the Left Bank. There seemed to be a tacit agreement between the organizers, the Union Nationale des Étudiants de France, and the police to avoid clashes. Only toward midnight, when the students tried to enter their district, did fights flare up and the atmosphere resemble that of the day before.

Bloody Monday, May 6, was quite a day. It witnessed the most violent demonstrations the Latin Quarter has known, at least since the war.

The government hoped to deal with a handful of extremists. It had to cope with ten thousand students, on this occasion determined not to yield. Though the police were out in impressive numbers and armed to the teeth, they did not have it all their own way. Some of the students had helmets and sticks. Cobblestones answered tear gas. From 3 P.M. to well into the night it was a permanent struggle with skirmishes, battles, and tactical retreats. Streets were unpaved to provide ammunition, cars overturned as improvised barricades. Boulevard St. Germain between the Deux Magots and Odéon was no place for strolling tourists. The figures speak for themselves. The police claimed 345 casualties in their ranks. At least 500 demonstrators were wounded and 422 arrested.

Demonstrations are usually much more violent in Paris than in London and, probably, than in any other west European town. The reason seems to be that violence breeds violence. France has shown once again that it has a domestic *force de frappe* of the first order.

With its Gardes Mobiles and its Compagnies Républicaines de Securité (the initials allow the demonstrators to chant the slogan CRS-SS) France has the troops needed for a civil war and its various regimes have often used them ruthlessly. The classical questions about who started the violence and who was within the law are in France only a part of it. The police did not enter the Sorbonne on May 3 until they were called for, and on Monday they were handling an unauthorized demonstration. But once French policemen get going, they are not particularly tender. The many eyewitness reports of passersby beaten, people sitting in cafés getting a taste of truncheons, and isolated demonstrators thumped to the ground testify to that.

The efficiency and ruthlessness of repression has as its counterpart, in the long run, an improvement in the techniques of street fighting. The angry young men who went out on Monday were spoiling for a fight.

But it was on the preceding Friday that the trouble had really started. For reasons that are still not quite clear the rector, M. Jean Roche, decided on the historically unprecedented step of calling the police into the Sorbonne. The government complied, probably very willingly, convinced as it was that unrest among students was limited to small groups, to the so-called *enragés* of Nanterre—the new faculty of arts built in a slum suburb of Paris.

It must have thought that a show of force would solve the problem amid the applause of the populace and the indifference of the rest of the student body. The calculation proved entirely wrong. The closing of the Sorbonne, the brutality of the repression, the stiff sentences passed against demonstrators had the opposite effect. The movement gathered momentum, it spread to the provinces, and attracted the support of a number of lecturers and professors.

It is easy to see why the government miscalculated. The revolutionaries of Nanterre are undoubtedly a minority. The various groups—the followers of Mao and of Che Guevara, the admirers of Trotsky and the less precise seekers after some kind of Socialist society—are deeply divided among themselves. But the government did not grasp that their mood of rebellion, their rejection of the established order, corresponded to the mood of a wider student community.

Swollen by the population bulge, the French universities are now undergoing a revolution of numbers. There are now some six hundred thousand students, more than twice as many as at the beginning of the sixties. But changes in methods, syllabuses, and approach have not kept pace with numbers. The harshest critics describe the universities as factories for misfits. Everybody agrees that they are no longer suited to the needs of the moment.

Many students fall by the wayside. Even those who get a degree are not sure of a job. Students do not worry only about being squeezed lemons at forty, they worry about their immediate prospects. It is not surprising that the movements of protest started among art students. It is not just that students in sociology or philosophy are more concerned with the meaning of society; it is among them that the future unemployed are more likely to be found.

Obviously, many of today's rebels will be absorbed tomorrow and be concerned only with climbing into the establishment or getting their slices of affluence. But they are still young enough to listen with sympathy to slogans about the overthrow of the established society. The truncheon did the rest.

The government was not alone in misjudging the situation. The Communist Party made the same mistake. It went on vituperating against tiny ultra-leftist "grouplets" when its own young supporters, or ex-supporters, were already flocking to mass demonstrations. It is here that the French case adds a twist to the international analysis of student unrest. It was generally assumed that whereas students in Prague or Warsaw fight against a political order—against the remnants of Stalinism—students in western Europe or America rebel against a society, that their revolt is the other side of the coin of political consensus. With a Republican indistinguishable from a Democrat in America—the argument ran—with one Harold resembling another in Britain, with Italy governed by the Center-Left (and the Communists tempted to join), with a coalition ruling in Bonn, the protesters have no alternative. But France was seen as the exception to this rule. Here, there was a Gaullist government and a hostile opposition, including the Communists.

It is significant that the rebels of Nanterre have treated the Communists as part of the establishment, part of the consensus; and the Communist Party did its best, at first, to justify this judgement. Like the government, it was overtaken by events and, to its discomfort, overtaken on its Left.

By midweek, after yet another peaceful march on Wednesday night, there were some signs of appeasement. The politicians had at last managed to grasp the importance of what had happened. General de Gaulle said something vague about the need for order and the need for change. The National Assembly discussed the subject in a special session. Naturally, students alone cannot change society. They cannot even reform the system of higher education. But they can act as a spur or an eye-opener. And Paris was awakened this week.

France's
Cultural Revolution

MAY 18, 1968
The Economist

THE WEATHER SMILED on the victors. Monday night was mild and gay as students directed traffic in the reconquered Latin Quarter. The Sorbonne, whence the police had vanished, was open to all. Soon everybody was going to start talking about France's "cultural revolution," but for the moment the atmosphere was more one of Kermesse Héroique, with overtones of the early days of the Cuban Revolution. In the courtyard of the Sorbonne, a band was playing jazz. In the university's entrance hall, covered with posters, a notice proclaimed, *"Il est défendu d'interdire"* (It is forbidden to forbid"). In the lecture rooms, earnest young men, exhausted and exhilarated, debated until dawn about relations between students and workers, about the place of the university in society, about culture and capitalism.

How many had they been in the streets of Paris on that extraordinary day? They were a human sea which invaded the capital from the Gare de l'Est, where schoolboys, students, and professors met at 1:30 P.M. Two hours later, at the Place de la République, this huge wave met another, led by the trade unions, and the combined procession marched through the heart of Paris, across the Seine, up the Boulevard St. Michel to the Place Denfert-Rochereau, the meeting site of this revolutionary fortnight. Long after the first marchers reached their destination, those at the tail of the procession had not yet started; they did not arrive until after one o'clock.

It was the biggest march Paris had seen since the war, the youngest, the most dynamic, and, outwardly at least, the most revolutionary. Red flags were flying, clenched fists were held high, the Internationale was a recurring refrain. The fierce slogans were not aimed only at ministers; President de Gaulle himself was denounced as a murderer and called upon to resign. The politicians, men like M. Mitterrand, M. Mendès-France, and M. Waldeck Rochet, were lost in the crowd. There were no police in sight. The difference of mood between the generations was most apparent toward the end of the march, when many students wanted to go on to the Elysée, while Communist stewards used loud-speakers to tell the crowd to disperse.

How had the face of Paris been changed so suddenly? To understand that, one must go back to Friday, May 10, and the storming of the barricades in the Latin Quarter. The thing really began that afternoon, when older schoolboys, wanting to express their solidarity with the students, gathered in the Place Denfert-Rochereau to listen to speakers who addressed them from the statue of the Lion of Belfort. In the evening, it was the students' and lecturers' turn; at first they marched rather aimlessly, but from time to time their Japanese-inspired rushes added speed to the procession, and there were moments of tension when all side streets were blocked by helmeted policemen ready for the fray. The demonstrators shouted "CRS-SS" at the Compagnies Républicaines de Securité and greeted them with the Nazi salute. But, once again, the student stewards showed that they had the situation under control; linking hands, they acted as barriers and prevented clashes.

When the demonstrators sought to cross the Seine, they found all the bridges blocked by strong police forces. The march was then channeled by way of the Boulevard St. Germain to the Boulevard St. Michel. The choice for the students at this stage was either to disperse or occupy and hold their own districts. Once they decided on the latter course in the face of the formidable array of police that had been brought against them, the building of barricades followed naturally. The barricades sprang up like mushrooms after rain, particularly in the area around the Luxemburg gardens and the Rue Gay-Lussac. Cars and all sorts of other materials were used.

Yet, as Friday night fell, the atmosphere, though tense, was not one of battle. People living in the area—and the Latin Quarter is not very leftish—were giving food to hungry students. (Later, they also poured out water to disperse gas and opened their doors to give refuge to hunted students.) Nobody could really believe that the police, if they were going to charge, would first have allowed the barricades to be erected. There were also unfinished negotiations with the authorities. On two points raised by the demonstrators—the withdrawal of troops and the reopening of the Sorbonne—there was no real difficulty. But the third demand was for the release of those arrested in earlier demonstrations. *"Libérez nos camarades"* had become the marchers' particular cry, a cry to which the government was to yield—but not until twenty-four hours later. For the time being, its answer was no. The ministers concerned were in uninterrupted conference. At 2 A.M. the decision was taken to storm the barricades.

A quarter of an hour later, the attack began with the kind of softening-up process that suggested a real battlefield. Gas grenades were fired at the barricades. *"De Gaulle assassin,"* yelled their defenders through the handkerchiefs protecting their faces. The air was so thick with gas that the police had to retreat when the wind changed direction (they suffered many casualties from burns or gas). But they went forward ruthlessly, taking one barricade after another. The Red Cross was not allowed to move in to evacuate the injured, despite a dramatic appeal by Professor Monod, the Nobel Prize winner. The official count of 367 hurt was certainly too low; many students preferred to lick their wounds quietly rather than invite police attention again. By five o'clock in the morning the main battle was over; but, amid the calcinated cars, the police were still pursuing individual leftists into courtyards or even into flats, and herding battered young men into black marias (466 were arrested).

By Saturday morning, order had been restored in the Latin Quarter. But, for the government, it was defeat in victory so obviously that M. Pompidou had to concede to virtually all the students' demands that very evening. It was too late. The outburst of popular indignation paved the way for Monday's improvised general strike and mass demonstration. By the middle of this week, the student movement had gathered extraordinary momentum. Not only the Sorbonne but most other faculties in Paris and the provinces were occupied by students, who were sitting together with their professors in groups discussing the future of the universities. Divergences have already appeared among them, between the less and the more politically minded, between reformers and revolutionaries, between those concerned more about jobs and those concerned more with the structure of society. What to do about examinations is the least divisive issue. These cleavages may grow. For the moment, however, they are united by a sense of victory and a mood of unprecedented elation.

A Revolution Set Alight by Students, Snuffed Out by Communists

MAY 25, 1968
The Economist

A MODERN REVOLUTION requires the coincidence of a revolutionary situation and a party or organization ready to seize power. As France comes virtually to a halt, the situation might look revolutionary. But the party which has always claimed the revolutionary role now shows no sign of fulfilling it. The Communists have climbed on the bandwagon, but only to put the brakes on. This is not basically because they want to preserve General de Gaulle's regime. It is because they are using a revolutionary weapon—general and unlimited strikes—in order to achieve a parliamentary aim, the formation of a Popular Front government.

FROM STUDENT TO UNION POWER

Students walked out of the Sorbonne, just as night was falling on May 16, with red flags flying and a banner proclaiming, "The workers will take up from the fragile hands of the students the flag of struggle against the unpopular regime." That evening marked a vital turning point in the story as strikes began spreading fast around the country.

The celebrating students were living in a dream world. Many of them had been inspired by Trotsky's history of the Russian Revolution. In the setting of the Paris commune they saw their own chance and felt entitled to believe that anything could come true. Hadn't they, an active minority, precipitated the students' revolt? Had they not forced the government to hit back and then to surrender? The country was now grinding to a stop. Their dream, it seemed, was coming true.

After the mass demonstrations on the previous Monday, young workers at Sud-Aviation in Nantes had taken over their factory. But the workers' movement did not really spread until Thursday, May 16, when the Renault works at Citroen and Flins were seized. This time, it was not a case of Paris being redder than the provinces. The strikes spread fastest in western France, where the discontent was most acute. The disparity was not geographical but between generations. The pattern was everywhere the same; younger workers took the lead and their elders followed.

Once again, the Communists had been overtaken by events. But this time, they reacted swiftly. The Communist-dominated CGT, the biggest French union, first got in touch with its Catholic partner, the CFDT. It then sent instructions to its militant members to endorse the movement, including the sit-in strikes, but to keep the demands to the traditional pattern of higher wages (a monthly minimum of 600 francs for all and a minimum of 1,000 francs in certain factories, such as Renault), shorter hours, and the abolition of the unpopular decrees on social security.

With the CGT in control, the leftist students from the Sorbonne could not expect a cordial welcome at the Renault works in the Paris suburb of Boulogne-Billancourt. The shutters were down on the understandable ground that provocation must be avoided. Still, students were cheered by workers standing on the roof and the two sides chatted near the gate well into the night. But when, on the following day, the students' union suggested a big march to the factory, the CGT did not conceal its displeasure. Nevertheless, a few thousand students came and the discussions in the square outside the plant were significant. The Communists, mobilized for the purpose, repeated the party line about the working class being adult enough not to need lessons from anybody. But they had no answer to student hints that they were scared of a real debate.

There are two reasons for Communist coolness. One is specific. Many of the students flocking to Billancourt belonged to Trotskyist or other opposition groups. Braving Communist shock tactics, they had been preaching to the workers that their Communist leaders were bureaucratic and reformist bosses. Indeed, the only posters as one approached the Renault works this week were warnings against distributors of ultra-left literature.

The second reason is deeper and provides a key to Communist behavior in this crisis. The CGT is frightened of pressure from below. Students dreaming of abolishing the capitalist order will not limit the debate to the pay packet. The Communists do want to limit the revolutionary ferment. They want to keep the movement under control.

Whenever one hears somebody on the French radio vituperating against "adventurers" one can be sure that M. Cohn-Bendit or some other leftist student is the target. But one cannot guess the political color of the speaker. It might be a Gaullist or it might be a Communist. On the other hand, if somebody talks about revolution, structural changes, or Socialist society, one is safe in assuming he is not a Communist. The CGT is angry with its CFDT partners not only because they are in favor of debates with the students, but also because they have raised the slogan of workers' control, autogestion.

Similarly, the Communists refute suggestions that the present strike is insurrectional. But it is here that the ambiguity begins. The CGT demands may not be concerned with the structure of society, but they are stiff all the same. The French Communist Party is using revolutionary means to achieve a parliamentary end. Its political objective seems to be the same as it was on the eve of the crisis: to consolidate its alliance with M. Mitterrand's Social Democratic Federation and, so, to form a Popular Front government. The dream is a repeat of 1936, when the Blum government presided over the Matignon Agreements in which employers, under pressure, made big concessions to their workers. But then the Popular Front had already won the election. Now, General de Gaulle holds power and shows no intention of yielding it. The contradiction between the Communists' means and their ends makes future action unpredictable. It also provides a smokescreen for their reformist action.

THE ASSEMBLY'S MISSED CHANCE

French parliamentarians this week showed no sign of grasping the importance of the situation their country is facing. Politicians have been issuing statements for some time with the Gaullists calling on the people to rally around the general and with opposition spokesmen echoing M. Mendès-France's solemn declaration that the only service the discredited regime can now render to the nation is to retire. But the neglected Cinderella of the Fifth Republic, the National Assembly, at last had its moment on Tuesday. For once it had the limelight on itself. It did not make much of its chance.

It was not only that there was no suspense. As soon as M. Giscard d'Estaing and his followers confirmed that they would not vote for the motion of censure and members of M. Duhamel's Center Party decided to divide, there was little question of the government being defeated— the motion fell eleven votes short of success. The real trouble was that deputies and ministers, arguing over facts and figures, did not sound as if they were on the same wavelength as the nation. Ten years as a rubber-stamp institution have not prepared the assembly to rise to the occasion. No wonder the demonstrating students bypassed it.

On Wednesday, things were somewhat brighter, with a speech by a former Gaullist minister, M. Edgar Pisani, announcing that he would vote for the motion of censure and resign his seat. But it was Prime Minister M. Pompidou who was waited for with interest. He said that the government was in favor of negotiations with both employers and the unions. At roughly the same time, the leaders of the two main unions, M. Séguy of the CGT and M. Descamps of the CFDT, proclaimed their own willingness to negotiate. The negotiating process has begun.

Trial of Strength

When General de Gaulle speaks to the country on Friday, he is understood to be going to announce a referendum to be held in June. It is assumed that he will ask for special powers so as to foster "participation" at all levels, including the factory level. But what matters is how the social conflict will have evolved between now and the middle of next month. When a government behaves as if it almost wanted a revolution, and the allegedly revolutionary party does not try to seize the occasion, virtually anything can happen.

It looks as if the general has opted for a strategy of attrition. He can rely on time to soften his opponents, and possibly to divide them through granting some concessions. He can rely on it to frighten the *patronat* (employers' associations) so that it will be ready to give something away. And above all, he can hope that, as alarm spreads, the bulk of the people will once again rally round him.

But time can work both ways. The country cannot go on for very long in this state of growing paralysis. And the state runs the risk of gradually losing its powers. One illustration of this is the rebellion of the staff of radio and television, the chosen instruments of Gaullist policy. The Communist CGT is trying to keep events under control. It is braking hard. But it has to compete with the students, the CFDT, and the small but active left-wing Socialist Party, the PSU. As tempers rise among the strikers, the CGT may have to keep up with the mood of its own troops. Thus, though the main official protagonists, General de Gaulle and the Communists, still act as if they wanted to reach a compromise, the trial of strength is gaining an explosive logic of its own.

The General
Charges into Battle

JUNE 1, 1968
The Economist

GENERAL DE GAULLE soldiers on. He went to Colombey-les-deux-Eglises on Wednesday not to resign but to prepare his plan of battle. On the way, he apparently held a secret conference with army and police chiefs. On Thursday, he ended the suspense by revealing his decision first to the cabinet and then later in the afternoon to the nation.

The general stays. So does the prime minister with a reshuffled government. The National Assembly was dissolved on Thursday. General de Gaulle hopes to hold both a referendum and a general election some time between June 19 and July 9. But he is aware that this will not be easy. He has hinted that the next stage might be a declaration of a state of siege. The immediate question is not how the French will vote—red, pink, or blue. That will come later. The immediate question is whether the Gaullists can hold any elections at all.

Is France drifting toward civil war? Is it going to be a violent struggle between soldiers and strikers, the armed forces against the army of labor? Not necessarily. True, both sides seem determined. The general has just shown his own determination. The Gaullists are mobilizing their powers. By Thursday evening it was their turn to organize a mass march in Paris. On the other side, the strikers are in no mood for yielding. The left-wing opposition has made up its mind to try to take over. For General de Gaulle, the problem is how to outstay the strikers; how to wear them out. But the country cannot live in utter paralysis for very much longer. Either side can still yield. If it does not, the trial of strength could turn into civil war.

The general's critics have already reacted strongly. M. Mitterrand has spoken of the "voice of dictatorship"; a trade unionist of a "declaration of war on the people." All the big trade unions have proclaimed that the strike goes on.

In a revolutionary situation conventional ideas are obsolete. Comments by outsiders, out of touch with the quickened pulse of Paris, read here like messages from outer space. Constitutional lawyers bother about niceties, politicians about electoral calculations, economists about percentage shifts in the gross national product. All this will be relevant soon. But at this very moment the one vital question in Paris is power—who holds it or who will seize it. It is more accurate to speak of a race for power, rather than a struggle for it, so important is the time factor. The Gaullists hope to cling to power till the elections. They bank on the hope that, once again, a frightened nation will vote for the general. The two traditional left-wing partners—the Communists and M. Mitterrand's Federation of the Left—jockey for position and hope somehow to form a Popular Front government. And the totally unorganized revolutionaries, who precipitated this upheaval, still hope to crown it with a revolution.

Three major points have already emerged from the turmoil. First, a revolutionary situation can occur in an industrially developed state—the social upheaval provoked by the strikes is already greater than it was in 1936. Second, the French Communist Party has shown that it is not yet ready or willing to exploit such a situation. Third, a significant revolutionary movement has appeared almost spontaneously to the left of the Communist Party. And this raises two new questions: Can the Communist hierarchy, which is losing much of its rank and file to the new movement, radically alter its original line? Can the new revolutionary Left improvise in the heat of battle an effective organization?

At dawn on Monday, May 25, all seemed fine in the elegant Hotel de Châtelet. After two sleepless nights and twenty-three hours of negotiations, the representatives of the trade unions, the employers' associations, and a government team headed by M. Pompidou had reached a draft agreement for settling the strikes in private industry. True the package was bound to be inflationary, but a bout of inflation did not seem too high a price to pay when the spread of the strike movement threatened both the regime and the capitalist structure. The Communist-dominated CGT, with a bigger membership than its Catholic and Socialist competitors combined, had its own reasons for trying to prevent the situation from getting out of hand. By Monday morning there simply remained the "formality" of getting the settlement endorsed by the workers.

But when Georges Séguy, the forty-one-year-old boss of the CGT, and Benoit Frachon, his veteran predecessor, rushed to the Renault works at Boulogne-Billancourt, they were greeted by a vociferous *non*, which was then echoed at Citroen, Berliet, Sud-Aviation, and all the big factories. It was an extraordinary miscalculation for such experienced trade union leaders. They may have been misled by a false historical analogy. Back in 1936, a similar working-class explosion had been checked by a tripartite agreement at l'Hotel Matignon, the prime minister's official residence. But the government then was the Popular Front government, headed by Léon Blum, and the workers saw it as their own. Besides some of the concessions they obtained at the time—such as the forty-hour week and the introduction of two weeks' holiday with pay—were a breakthrough for the period. Now what the workers were being offered was essentially a rise in their nominal wages, one likely to be swallowed by inflation. Feeling instinctively that the offered rewards did not correspond to the sweep of the social upheaval, the workers simply said no and asked for more.

The vagaries of the CGT reflect the bewilderment of the French Communist Party. Indeed, in its hesitations, changes, and successive mistakes, the Communist leaders closely resemble the Gaullist government. The party has repeated so often that it stands for the working class that it half believes this itself. It is so used to giving orders from above that it is lost now that the channels of transmission are jammed, despite the size of the apparatus and the number of devoted activists.

The French saw that it is not the cowl that makes the monk. But the French Communist Party, having carried the revolutionary mantle for fifty years, had attracted to itself the most militant radicals, particularly among the workers. These are now the men who are shaken in their convictions, while the intellectuals among them are further shocked by the party's attitude toward students. It is not only around the Sorbonne that members have had to be kicked out of the party for disobedience.

In party cells everywhere there are discussions bordering on revolt. The Communist leaders face their biggest crisis yet.

To some extent, the Communists have digested all this. Though still not talking about social reforms, they became, in the negotiations about a settlement for the nationalized industries, the hardest bargainers of all. By Wednesday, the marathon march organized by the CGT in Paris was clearly political. The Communists, by then, had the open objective of overthrowing the Gaullist regime. Nor were they alone in stepping up the offensive. M. Mitterrand, the leader of the Federation of the Left, had already proposed the formation of a provisional left-wing government. And M. Mendès-France had, in principle, accepted the job of leading it.

What of the New Left? Unlike its American counterpart, the French New Left does not depend on students alone: It has managed to attract a sizeable proportion of young trade union members. It is this alliance that allows the revolutionaries to hope for victory. Their revolutionary committees are seen as the Soviets of the new French revolution. Their aim is to spread them throughout the country—in factories, offices, and elsewhere—to coordinate them, and, finally, to crown them with a central committee of revolutionary action. The question is whether the inspirers of this improvised movement will have time to build their organization before the tide ebbs. The outcome depends largely on the length of the strike and the mood of the workers. But by now in Paris it is folly to rule out anything. As is written proudly on the walls of the Sorbonne: *Tout est possible.*

General de Gaulle is being paid back in his own coin and paid back with a vengeance. Ten years ago, he took over power by keeping in the background an army of paratroops. Now that he is struggling to stay in power, the paratroops are replaced by his opponents' army of ten million workers. The general has at his disposal 83,000 policemen (of whom 13,500 are members of the special security force, the CRS), 61,000 gendarmes and 261,000 members of the armed forces stationed in France and Germany. But most of the soldiers are national servicemen. Can the regime rely on this force to break so huge a strike? And will it really come to this?

From General Strike
to General Elections

JUNE 8, 1968
The Economist

ON TUESDAY, PARIS suffered one of its worst traffic jams. All
its car owners seemed to be out celebrating the resumed flow of petrol.
This did not quite mean a return to normal. One cause of the jam was
that there was still no public transport in the capital, just as there were
no trains running throughout France. All key sectors of the economy
were still strikebound. By Thursday, public transport was beginning to
seep back into action all over the country. The post office was starting
work again. But even earlier in the week tension had clearly been eased.
The trial of strength was shifting from the factories to the electoral
arena. Political leaders on both sides had agreed to carry their conflict
to the polling stations. The election campaign has in effect begun.
Frenchmen will vote on June 23 and 30 for a new National Assembly.
The parties are already busy preparing platforms, registering candidates, and making alliances.

To assess the chances of a Gaullist election success, one must consider how the other, more dramatic, crisis somehow fizzled out. Gratitude is probably not a political virtue, and certainly not one of General
de Gaulle's vices. In his fighting broadcast on May 30, he set the style
of the Gaullist election campaign by putting the blame for everything
on "totalitarian Communism"—although he owes his survival, to a
large extent, to the cautious conduct of the Communist Party.

The French Communists did everything in their power to contain the revolutionary wave and, once the general made it plain that he would not abdicate, to direct it back to electoral channels. On the night of May 30 there was a risk of confrontation between the armed forces and the army of labor. Next morning, the risk had vanished because the army of strikers had been dispersed. M. Séguy, the boss of the Communist-dominated CGT, could not demobilize his followers. But, followed by other trade union leaders, he divided his troops into separate battalions, each seeking additional gains, particularly in wages, from its employers. What had begun to look like a frontal attack against the state rapidly became a series of individual skirmishes. And L'Humanité, the Communist daily, started to use the language of an election campaign.

The part played by the Communists in this crisis has been crucial. Retrospectively, their role looks essentially negative, in the sense that the bewildered leadership seems to have been guided by no general plan, but by three dominant fears: the fear of being overtaken by a growing revolutionary Left; the associated fear of being overwhelmed or deserted by their own rank and file; finally, the fear of Gaullist repression. For a few days in late May that last fear almost vanished. The state itself gave the impression of vanishing. Even then the Communists opted for a semi-parliamentary solution, for a coalition with M. Mitterrand's Federation of the Left in a provisional government headed, if necessary, by M. Mendès-France. But when the general declared that the state was still there, the Communists appeared almost relieved.

Once bitten, twice shy. The union leaders dared not risk a second disavowal by their followers. Many of the workers, feeling vaguely frustrated of a bigger victory, have stepped up their demands. The government has been torn between its wish to see the strike end and its reluctance to make more concessions. The employers' association has somehow recovered from its state of panic. So, the bargaining has proved hard. There are still few signs of compromise in engineering, although police removed strike pickets from the Renault works at Flins on Wednesday night to allow a ballot to take place.

The Communist decision to call a retreat and the general's speech marked the turning point in the crisis. They were more decisive than the big Gaullist demonstration that followed the general's speech on May 30. Was that march through Paris as massive as the demonstration the Left had staged on May 13? The pro-Gaullist marchers were certainly more numerous than anybody expected; the organizers, fearing a fiasco, had brought coachloads of supporters from the provinces. The sight of red flags in the streets and on factories, the symbolic burning of the Bourse, the threat to the established order brought out the kind of people who would never normally demonstrate, and led to a reconciliation of the factions of the Right. Behind ministers and deputies, the old men of Vichy marched together with the former Free French. That night, triumphant car horns played the rhythm that stands for "Algérie Française." So much for the hero of the Third World.

When people take to the streets and to "civic action," there is apt to be an alarming side. This time there was the Fascist fringe with its unforgivable slogan *"Cohn-Bendit à Dachau"* (The students' internationalist slogan had been: "We are all German Jews.") But this was only a fringe. The real difference between the two demonstrations was not so much age (the Gaullists were, on the whole, much older) as class. On May 30 fashionable ladies, officers, and company directors appeared among the angry and frightened middle classes. When these ladies and gentlemen chanted "Open our factories," it was plain that not many among the thousands present would have been able to man them.

In electoral terms, the two big demonstrations carried almost equal weight. But at a time of social upheaval it was those who could paralyze the economy who carried the most. General de Gaulle had no illusions about this. He did not await a demonstration of popular support before making up his mind. We know that he went to Baden-Baden the day before his speech to get General Massu's blessing and a pledge of support from his troops. Whether that would have been enough for his purpose remains a moot point, since the Communists decided not to force the issue.

Against this background, it may be ungrateful of General de Gaulle to emphasize the Communist menace, but it is a shrewd move. With the franc in jeopardy and the economy in turmoil, with his international monetary policy frustrated and his European hand much weakened, he cannot urge the electorate to let him carry on in the name of grandeur and in recognition of his achievements. But he can exploit people's fear of the black flag of anarchy and the red flag of revolution. A general strike is a tactic for seizing power, not for persuading voters. If the Left had seized power, it would now be the new order itself; but it stopped halfway—after frightening many floating voters among the middle class. A few weeks ago, polls and by-elections indicated that the Gaullists could hardly face a parliamentary election. That was why the general wanted only to hold a referendum. Things may be very different now.

The other consequence of the crisis is a further polarization of the French into two antagonistic blocks, which correspond roughly to the two big Paris demonstrations. There will admittedly be many middle-of-the-road candidates in the elections, since M. Edgar Pisani's friends will now join the followers of M. Lecanuet and M. Duhamel in the center of the spectrum. The French electoral system, in which the voter can indicate his preferences on the first ballot, allows for that. But when it comes to the second ballot and the real choice, it will be a choice between Gaullism and the Popular Front. Many of the centrists are then likely to move to the Gaullist side. The prime minister, M. Pompidou, is in no mood to make concessions to his reluctant coalition partner, M. Giscard d'Estaing, whose followers want to put up their own separate candidates for seats now held by the opposition. M. Pompidou feels confident that in any such duels on the first ballot the orthodox Gaullists will prevail over the "Giscardiens."

The left wing will also face the first round divided. The Communists hope that their claim to be the main force of opposition to Gaullism will put them ahead of their partners in the first ballot. The Socialist and radical members of M. Mitterrand's federation are, once again, looking nostalgically toward the center. The Communists and the federation have not yet been able to produce a comprehensive joint program, any more than they were able to do so last year; but they have been thrown together by events. As to M. Mendès-France, he has not yet revealed whatever lesson he may have drawn from the recent events.

Should one not take account, in this election, of the revolutionaries who precipitated the crisis? Hardly at all. Many of the students do not have votes. Most of the others hold that they did not build barricades to help parties that are content to work within the present system. Only the small Parti Socialiste Unifié could benefit from their vote.

The election depends on two unknowns. One is the impact of the domestic bankruptcy of Gaullism. The other is the widespread fear of disorder. Most observers think the latter will prove stronger. They see the Gaullists returning with a majority, the workers discovering the lack of substance in nominal wage increases, and the same causes once more producing the same effects. Some prophets already talk of the May days as a dress rehearsal, the 1905 of a new French revolution.

End of a Phase

JUNE 22, 1968
The Economist

THE FIRST PART of France's crisis is drawing to an end. The crisis started on May 3 when the police entered the Sorbonne. Ten days later the students were back in their university and the cultural revolution was on. On Sunday, June 16, the circle was completed with the police once again occupying the place. Order has not yet been fully restored in the Latin Quarter, since other parts of the university are still occupied by students. But the Sorbonne was a symbol.

As such it had to be stormed. The government's scheme was pretty obvious. It began with a press campaign about the horrors of the Sorbonne: the drugs, the orgies, and the Katangais (supposedly mercenaries from the Congo). But the unkind students did not oblige. They themselves removed the Katangais and started cleaning the place in preparation for summer conferences. And, so, another reason was found—an investigation into the stabbing of a man outside the Sorbonne on Saturday. Ever since the first riots, the infirmary of the Sorbonne has been used as an emergency ward for the district. The stabbing on Saturday was not an exceptional case, but it provided an excuse for the police to go in. Once inside the Sorbonne, the prefect of police soon made it clear that he was less concerned with an investigation than with the evacuation of the Sorbonne. Some people left the place on their own accord. The occupation committee, consisting of both students and professors, had to be removed by force.

That night, the professors involved held a conference to explain what had happened and to announce that they would refuse to teach so long as the Latin Quarter was occupied by the police. Walking through the district afterwards, one saw what they disliked. The famous Boulevard St. Michel looked like an area just taken over by the army. There was no light. Police lorries and vans were all over the place. Helmeted policemen were massed at street corners. Men ready for combat stalked up and down the boulevard.

This show of strength may win additional votes for the Gaullists. But it will not solve the problem of what to do about the university. As M. Pompidou himself said, there is no question of turning the Sorbonne into a barracks for the police. Nobody has seriously suggested that it should become a school for the CRS. And when the police are removed, what will happen?

The strike is also drawing slowly to an end. The Renault works were not quite the first to strike but by May 16 all Renault factories were occupied by the workers. Exactly a month later, last Monday, the workers voted to return to work. Considering their weariness, the fact that the general strike had died down and the determination of the Communist-led CGT that the deal with the government must be accepted, the number voting against a return to work was high. It ranged from 22 percent at Boulogne Billancourt to 44 percent at Flins.

Despite the victorious headlines in *L'Humanité,* the mood of many returning workers was not exactly triumphant. They had discovered that they possessed power, but they felt that they had not yet learned how to use it. If the wage increases prove ephemeral they will plainly feel cheated. On the labor front, too, there could be trouble in the autumn.

To avoid galloping inflation, the government will be forced to make some changes in its budget. Several ministers have hinted that this may involve delays in the development of the nuclear strike force. But there is no question of drastic reductions in the military budget. The army commanders were able to remind General de Gaulle during the crisis that they are the defense against revolution. Any further cuts in the conventional forces would be resented. So the only possibility is a slow-down in the nuclear field. Projects for ground-to-ground missiles will probably remain in their files. The Mirages will have to go on flying for longer than planned and the delivery of Polaris-type submarines may be delayed. Some people believe that this slowdown foreshadows the end of an independent strike force. One reply is that what the general now needs is not a *force de frappe* abroad but at home.

The End of the First Act, Not the Final Curtain

JULY 6, 1968
The Economist

FINITA LA COMMEDIA? At first sight, France's two months' crisis has run full circle, with the Gaullists back in command of things—only very, very much more so. The barricades and the general strike of May begin to look distant. Communists seek to justify themselves, Gaullists, and outsiders to find comfort, in analyzing the May crisis through June's electoral prism. Psephologists have taken over from social analysts.

The main reason for the Gaullist triumph in the second ballot was that the floating voters of the Center rallied massively to the Right. The second reason was that the alliance between the Communists and the Federation of the Left, cemented last year by the prospect of victory, was shaken this time by the wind of defeat. The wastage of left-wing votes was small in Paris but high in areas of traditional competition between Communists and Socialists.

The two factors combined cost the Left more than half its seats. The main Communist leaders survived, as have the principal members of the Federation—MM. Mitterrand, Mollet, Defferre, and Billières scraped through. But M. Mendès-France did not and M. Mitterrand's young lieutenants, who last year won a series of marginal seats, were now thrown out by the swing. Yet, for the Left, loss even on this scale is less harmful than the loss of perspective. Here the political crisis has only begun.

In terms of seats, the Gaullist victory is as big as the Left's loss. Sweeping from their strongholds in western and eastern France, the Gaullists have reconquered a large part of Paris. They have recovered positions in the industrial north. They have made serious gains in the so-called "red south," in the apparently impregnable areas around Toulouse and Montpellier. As a result, the orthodox Gaullists have a comfortable majority on their own and, though the followers of M. Giscard d'Estaing did well, they are no longer indispensable.

Yet, this kind of statistics is for static minds. The parliamentary success is useful—not that parliamentary obstacles ever bothered the general—but the crisis has left residues that cannot be swept up as easily as the election could. Men like M. Pompidou, who understood the depth of the social upheaval, cannot simply forget. In his hour of triumph the prime minister soberly reminded his followers that their exceptional victory came at the close of a very serious crisis "of which we should not forget the causes, the features and the consequences."

The main financial consequence is the swelling of the wage bill. The minimum wage was raised by a third, while other wages should increase this year by roughly 13 percent, about twice as fast as usual. In general terms, the government has a choice of two methods. It can try to keep prices down and take the opportunity to accelerate industrial concentration. The snag is that this would add to unemployment, which is already approaching the half-million mark. The alternative is to let a rapid rise in prices absorb the nominal gains in wages. This would lead inexorably toward devaluation. It could also provoke a second explosion by workers now conscious of the power of the strike weapon.

The government will probably maneuver between the two policies. It may also try to counter-attack through its program of "participation." This pet Gaullist scheme, a still unspecified elaboration of the general's old corporatist plan of association *capital-travail*, may not solve much. It could nevertheless be used to create trouble for the trade unions at a time when many workers feel that their unions did not give them a proper lead during a strike which had started spontaneously. The Communist-led CGT has already begun to lose voters to the more militant CFDT.

Has anything been basically changed by the May crisis? The upheaval took almost everybody by surprise, both in France and abroad. The startling and significant thing was not that students dared to defy the government and put up barricades. It was that this precipitated the biggest general strike France has ever known, a strike that threatened the regime and sent General de Gaulle seeking reassurance from his army. The other key lesson is that the Communist Party did not seize this opportunity. It proved Stalinist in manner, but Fabian in action. Nobody really knows whether, if there were a second explosion, the Communists would once again act as the firemen of the regime.

This brings us to the basic division among observers about what happened in May. Some see in it a historical quirk, after which things resume their normal course. Others wonder whether this storm, apparently out of the blue, does not herald a change in the political and social climate of western Europe. For France, a first act is ended and General de Gaulle and M. Pompidou, his rising lieutenant, are seeking to consolidate their position by taking advantage of the interval—an interval that may merely have been extended by the size of their electoral victory.

Hope Was Reborn in May

JULY 1968
International Socialist Journal

> *To stand still, to mark time on one spot, to be contented with the first goal it happens to reach, is never possible in revolution. And he who tries to apply the homemade wisdom derived from parliamentary battles between frogs and mice to the field of revolutionary tactics only shows thereby that the very psychology and laws of existence of revolution are alien to him and that all historical experience is to him a book sealed with seven seals.*
>
> Rosa Luxemburg

CE N'EST . . . QU'UN début . . . continuons le . . . combat . . . once again the jerky rhythm of the slogan forever associated with the May movement echoed in the streets of Paris as the demonstration, red flags flying, left Montparnasse. The marchers were predominantly young and students were more numerous than workers. There were new slogans, too, like *"De Gaulle, Franco, Salazar"* or *"Nous sommes de plus en plus enragés."* At the Gare d'Austerlitz, at the close of the march, there were brief speeches and, as if to underline the internationalism of the crowd, an Italian delegate was loudly applauded, whenever his listeners could grasp such words as *polizia* or *borghese.* It was June 1 and, for the last time in this first act, the police had allowed a mass march to get together. The CGT had already called the strikers to an orderly retreat. The

NOTE: While writing for *The Economist,* as the unnamed "Paris correspondent," Daniel Singer contributed this piece to the *International Socialist Journal,* under the nom de plume of "Daniel Martin."

revolutionary wave was receding. Yet, this was not a funeral procession. The young students and workers had not come to mourn the past. They could proudly look toward the future. They have opened a new chapter in revolutionary history.

The main message of May is that a revolutionary situation can occur in an advanced capitalist country. Admittedly, this is a Marxist truism. Yet, this basic premise was not only dismissed by the bourgeois apologists of the so-called affluent society it was also set aside, explicitly or implicitly, by the Socialist Left. There is no denying that one of the big unanswered questions of Marxist theory is why Socialist revolutions did not take place in the countries for which they were designed. And doubts naturally spread as time went on.

Lenin and the Bolsheviks had rendered a historical service to mankind as pioneers showing that workers could seize and hold power. They themselves, however, expected the revolutionary movement to spread to the industrialized countries of western Europe. They knew that, without this help, isolated, backward Russia would have to pay the political price of what Preobrazhensky called "primitive Socialist accumulation." And it did. Since the war, the revolution has spread, from above and from below, to other countries, but once again to areas of relative industrial backwardness. Inevitably, the idea of a Socialist revolution (in the sense of a sudden and radical transformation of power, property, and other social relationships) in the West suffered the fate of a relic that many treat with signs of outward respect, but few really believe in. The choice offered to the proletariat and the Socialists of the Western world seemed to be limited to more or less radical reformism at home coupled with an auxiliary role in the revolutionary movement of the Third World.

This does not mean that in the anti-imperialist struggle, that the help for heroic Vietnam or Cuba should now lose in importance. Quite the contrary. But a Socialist revolution in an advanced country like France, with its own methods, its own ways, its own solutions, would have a contagious effect in western Europe, a bearing on what happens in the eastern part; it would affect the general balance of power in the world.

This is the dazzling prospect that the revolutionary students and workers have opened or rather reopened.

The French student revolt is part of a wider world movement. Its peculiarity was not so much that from the very start it pinned its hopes on the working class (*"Étudiants solidaires des ouvriers"* was among the early slogans). Its peculiarity was that it found an echo, a response among industrial workers. Barricades in the Latin Quarter and student courage, coupled with blunders from a government which alternated bloody repressions with temporary surrenders, acted as an inspiration and an example. The huge popular demonstration of May 13 served as a link. Revolutionary students had precipitated the biggest strike, the biggest social upheaval that France has known this century. This, in turn, revealed the true nature of bourgeois democracy, the nakedness of the police state and its relative fragility. It also provided another Marxist reminder, a reminder of the political strength and social power of attraction of the working class once it sets itself into motion.

At this stage comes the obvious objection that France did not have its revolution, that it all fizzled out, at least temporarily, in an electoral farce. History does not allow for experimental tests in a laboratory to check whether the situation was prerevolutionary, quasirevolutionary, or whatnot. In one sense, it could be argued that the situation could not be truly revolutionary because it lacked a leadership and organization to carry it through.[1] This, however, raises the problem of the part played in May and June by the party which claims as its birthright the role of the "vanguard of the proletariat," namely the French Communist Party (or PCF). Yesterday it was possible to ask the question whether "the leaders of the PCF are now ready publicly to assume their new role as potential reformers of capitalist society"?[2] The question has now been put to the test and Socialists all over the world must draw their own conclusions.

Criticism of the PCF centers for the moment on the moral aspect, on the alleged misunderstanding of the student movement and the ensuing unbelievable nature of Communist propaganda. Starting with the article of Georges Marchais in *L'Humanité* of May 3 (the day when

the police storming the Sorbonne precipitated the crisis), in which
Cohn-Bendit was described as "a German anarchist" and the members
of the Twenty-second of March Movement as predominantly "children
of grand bourgeois contemptuous of students of working-class origin," the performance has culminated, so far, with posters calling to
vote Communist because they have been the first (i.e. before the
Gaullists) to denounce the troublemakers. In the meantime, *L'Humanité* republished without a word of comment or disapproval the
vilest attacks against the students uttered by the Gaullist government
and its police. It concentrated its own wrath against "Geismar and his
gang." In hardly veiled terms, it urged the government to arrest all such
"provocateurs" and when all the revolutionary movements were
banned, *L'Humanité* did not utter a word of protest. Such extraordinary
behavior naturally shocked Communist intellectuals who were driven
to protest against the party line. Still, social-democratic precedents
show that such, to put it very mildly, unprincipled conduct is a reflection of something deeper, that it is a symptom of the malaise of a party
failing to fulfill its historical mission—which brings us to the heart of
the matter. Let us accept the premise of the PCF that the situation was
not revolutionary. It will be granted, nevertheless, that the strike, involving over nine million workers, was not a routine operation. It started
spontaneously, but was rapidly channeled by the CGT into its traditional, essentially wage-driven, demands. Not for a moment is it being
suggested that there is something wrong with wage demands or something wrong with using them, even in exceptional circumstances, in
order to move gradually from quantitative to qualitative objectives. A
"vanguard" which runs miles ahead will not be followed. But the crucial question is whether the CGT has tried, at any stage, to spur the
movement beyond its conventional limits? The plain answer is that it
has done exactly the opposite and one of the reasons for the conflict
with the students was the visible fear of any "ultra-leftist" ferment.

There is much talk now about May as a dress rehearsal and analogies
are drawn with Russia. It must be remembered, however, that in Pet-
rograd in 1905 everything had been done to exploit the potentialities of

the situation. The inevitable anarchy created by the general strike had been used to set up the organs of parallel power—the Soviets. In France, all effort to spread or regroup the revolutionary action and strike committees, to sponsor self-management by the strikers, to suggest the mildest forms of even self-defense met with the strongest rebuff from the CGT. The PCF had chosen to act within the established law and order. Any illusions on this score were dispelled on May 31, the day after General de Gaulle's challenge, when M. Séguy, the CGT leader, demobilized the army of labor, when he turned the general strike into a series of individual or branch bargains. The Communist leadership has too much experience to believe that a general strike, a weapon for seizure of power, could be magically transformed into an instrument of electoral propaganda. They must have known that Gaullism would emerge victorious from an electoral battle. The choice of a parliamentary road was not just a tactical mistake. It was the reflection of a long-term strategy.

In theory, during the ascending phase of a revolution, the initiative moves gradually to more and more radical groups. In France, on the left of the PCF there was no group sufficiently solid and coherent to take over and none could apparently be improvised. The elemental forces carried the movement as far as they could against the resistance of a powerful apparatus. The revolutionaries who tried to push it further were not helped by the limited political consciousness of the masses. It would be inaccurate and wrong to claim that the workers who loudly rejected the draft agreement reached rue de Grenelle, who opposed the return to work did so in the name of a conscious political alternative. Most of them had just rediscovered their collective power. They sensed that they could obtain more. They were dimly aware that their victory could not be preserved without the overthrow of the capitalist system. But this awareness of class interest was semisub-conscious and largely inarticulate. Superficially, this strengthens the case of PCF arguing that the situation was not revolutionary. It also raises some questions about the ideological work carried amid the masses by the allegedly revolutionary party. In the inevitable international discussion about the role of the PCF, not only its conduct in May and June, but also its groundwork over the last ten—some will say last fifty—years will have to be taken into account.

France has had no revolution. Yet even this first round, these few weeks of disintoxication have taught people more than years of relative calm. They confirmed some old truths, provided new insights, raised some serious problems for study. All such issues can only be mentioned here in shorthand.

The events revealed the real nature of the bourgeois state, based ultimately on the coercive power of its police and armed forces. It is to Baden-Baden that de Gaulle travelled to get his investiture from the army commanders (whether the army, at this stage, was capable of defeating the army of labor is doubtful; the question was not put to a test, since M. Séguy ordered a retreat). The bourgeois ideologists also threw off their masks. When it became apparent that this was no student rag, that vested interests were threatened, the alarm was sounded against "nihilism."[3] There was no longer much talk about the industrial society of freedom.[4]

The highly improvised movement of young students and workers blew a breath of fresh air throughout France. It also reminded us all that revolutionary Socialism is spelled with spontaneity, freedom of debate, and internationalism (symbolized here by the moving slogan, "We are all German Jews"). The posters spreading all over the Latin Quarter gave us some idea of China's cultural revolution. The discussions, not always productive, revealed the desperate need felt by millions in our society—and not only intellectuals—for communication, for a meaning in life. The changing direction of events showed the passive mobility of the lower-middle classes torn between their desire for, and their fear of, change.

Amid the questions requiring closer study, one can mention: the apparently strong popular reaction against bureaucratic centralism; the analysis of the growing student body (based not only social origin but on its suspended function in production); youth, not as a separate class, but as a dynamic element within its class; the revolutionary potentialities of the working class in its new structure with the growing proportion of technicians and salaried cadres (one of the main lessons seems to be that cadres can be attracted not by a middle class platform but by the prospect of a role in a different society). All such study is, naturally, connected with the search for a new party, or movement, which will not miss historical opportunities. Which brings us back to the old debate between those who still pin their hopes on pressure from without, considering that the party is by now at once too monopolithic and too reformist to offer scope—an old debate which must be resumed in a new light after the May crisis.

There is no time to waste. Revolution, national in its first phase, is international by nature. The next occasion may arise in Italy or it may repeat itself in France if, cheated of their gains, the workers are once again spurred to action. Now that the tide is receding, that the mood is depressed by the inevitable electoral defeat it may sound sanguine to proclaim that the Montparnasse marchers were no mourners, that they were pioneers of a new era. And yet a new ghost, or rather a revived one, is once again haunting Europe—it is the specter of Socialist revolution. This exhilarating prospect brings with it some dangers. Unlike an indulgent grandmother, history has no soft spot for grandchildren who keep missing their opportunities.

1. "Without a guiding organization the energy of the masses would dissipate like steam not enclosed in a piston box. But nevertheless what moves things is not the piston or the box, but the steam."—Trotsky, *History of the Russian Revolution.*
2. *International Socialist Journal,* Nr. 22, p. 609.
3. Beuve-Méry in *Le Monde.*
4. The refrain of Raymond Aron: "Do you expect a bourgeois state to provide a Cuban university?"

The Ghosts of May

MAY 31, 1993
The Nation

TODAY THE COBBLESTONES of Paris's Latin Quarter are covered with asphalt. Twenty-five years on, the memory of the French uprising—the only one in the spectacular 1968 series stretching from New York to Tokyo to have moved beyond the campus, paralyzing the country and threatening the political system—is so distant that it requires a refresher for the new generation. What happened in that jolly month of May? For once, faced with the police, the students did not sign a petition. They fought back. There followed a week of confrontation, often bloody, cobblestones versus truncheons and tear-gas grenades. The resistance of the students inspired the workers, who staged the biggest general strike in French history. As the factories stood idle, minds did not. People began to talk to one another. Surrealist scribblings flourished on the walls. For a brief spell, everything seemed possible and a slogan even suggested that imagination might seize power.

But it didn't and things, at least on their asphalted surface, went back to normal. Nostalgia no longer being what it used to be, it is not my purpose to bore the reader with the sentimental reminiscences of yet another lost generation. There are two connected reasons, however, to look back at the French May movement today. One is that the questions it raised (though never answered)—about the nature and purpose of growth, the deadly weight of a hierarchical society and of an unwithering state, about the inanity of frontiers—are more topical than ever in a depressed Europe with its millions of unemployed. The second reason is that the humiliating defeat of the French Socialist Party marks the close of a cycle, the end of an attempt to prove that the aspirations of 1968, admittedly watered down and integrated, could be realized by other, purely parliamentary, means.

In this strange period of transition, not just the French Socialists but the Left in general throughout Western Europe must answer a question that has historical significance: Is it still able to tackle such problems, to offer the vision of an alternative society and thus serve as an example to the world, or has it become so Americanized that it must sever all organic links with the Labor movement and drop altogether its Socialist pretenses? Finally, a glance at the past twenty-five years of French history leads to another message for both sides of the Atlantic: Progressive social change will not materialize magically as a gift from heaven for dutiful voters. Without permanent popular pressure, a reformist president is bound to succumb to the forces of social inertia, whatever his original intentions.

Seeds of surrender. May '68, in a sense, produced nothing. It raised problems without solving them, and the movement was defeated. It was just a breath of fresh air, an awakening. But because it challenged all the established institutions and denied that change must be marginal, it put the idea of a different society and, hence, of some form of revolution back on the agenda. Admittedly it did so in a country with a revolutionary tradition, yet one in which both Communists and Socialists—then nicknamed the *gauche respectueuse* (the respectful Left) had chosen the purely parliamentary road to office. The events of May had upset their advance on that road. It was now vital to put the revolutionary steam back into the institutional kettle.

The imperative was particularly categorical for the Communists, who claimed a revolutionary vocation as their birthright. It did not really matter whether the upheaval in the streets had been potentially revolutionary or not. What was clear was that the C.P., instead of pushing the movement as far as it would go, acted as a brake. Now the

Communists had to prove that they had an electoral solution. For this they needed an ally, the Socialists (and considering the weakness of today's C.P., it is ironic that it then helped the Socialists to recover from the disarray into which they had fallen), but also a project, the Common Program, which the two parties signed in 1972. That program contained all the elements of future drama in a nutshell. It did not propose to abolish capitalism in France, but it was radical enough to hurt the interests of big business at home and abroad. As such, it stood a chance of being applied only if parliamentary action were backed by a mass movement, by a real mobilization of the people, and that prospect both parties ruled out, fearing another May.

When the Socialists were resurrected, at Epinay in 1971, they were at once taken over by a newcomer, François Mitterrand, who simultaneously discovered that he was a Socialist. He was a quick learner, however, and was soon preaching against the "corrupting power of money" and promising "a break with capitalism." Above all, he was a clever politician who postulated that the Left could not win in France without the Communists and that its victory would be accepted only if the latter were the junior partner in the coalition. Add to this the assumption that in an alliance with a moderate program, the more moderate member tends to gain, and you get the secret of Mitterrand's 1981 presidential victory—granted that it took him twenty-three years to achieve it.

To see the seeds of defeat in that victory one must also take into account an ideological factor, best described as Operation New Philosophers. Nineteen sixty-eight revealed the depth of discontent pent up below the glittering surface at a time when the European economy was still growing at an unprecedented pace. By the mid-seventies, with a structural economic crisis coming on top of it all, the threat to the system looked real. Hence it was crucial for the establishment to convince the young rebels that any attempt at collective action to alter society radically was bound to lead to catastrophe, to the gulag. The task was entrusted to the children, or rather bastards, of May, to Maoist turncoats who fulfilled it with zeal. At the intellectual level, their dish was

tasteless: a rehash of *The God That Failed*, a good helping of Solzhenitsyn, a drop of von Hayek, and a zest of Popper, the French providing
no more than the salad dressing. But as an exercise in propaganda,
backed by the full power of the media, it was quite effective.

And, so, to May 1981 and the election of a Socialist president at a
time when pressure from below was at its lowest, contained as it had
been by the very victors, and when the ideological ascendancy had
shifted to the other side. The inevitable happened. The Left in office
began by keeping its pledges. It did so without mobilizing the people
and so when capital, domestic and foreign, launched its counteroffensive, the Left simply surrendered. From 1983 onward, the Socialists followed in the footsteps of their capitalist predecessors. As to Mitterrand,
he just changed parts. Originally he saw himself as a Socialist reformer
taking France beyond the Swedish model. Now, he was to win his laurels as the man who kept France safe for capitalism, as the normalizer,
the destroyer of dreams, of the belief that life can be changed by political action—in short, as the gravedigger of May. It is this chapter that
is now coming to a contemptible close.

Utopian realism. In a world fantastically changed within a quarter of
a century, the old questions, curiously enough, have gained rather than
lost in relevance. The striking novelty of the rebel sixties was the rejection of the so-called consumer society, the repudiation of the ruling religion of growth. Growth for whom? For what purpose? For whose
profit? Those questions have now been dramatically extended to include
our place and our survival in the universe. (Both the ecology movement
and women's liberation really developed in France after '68.)

The extension goes even deeper. When the gospel of growth was first
attacked, the gross national product was rising at an average annual rate
of some 5 percent in a Western Europe enjoying almost full employment. Today, such a pace is unthinkable and even if it were reached, the
long lines of jobless would not vanish. After the economic crisis began
some twenty years ago, we were assured that the cuts in manufacturing would be compensated for by the expansion of the service sector.
Now that "labor saving" has inevitably spread to the latter, there is no

easy way out. Our technological genius is matched by the coherent absurdity of our social organization. It still has to be proved whether our society can replace profitable arms manufacturing and heavy industry not with financial speculation but with the development of health, education, and culture. To cut working hours, the labor measured by time, it is necessary to tackle the social division of that labor, the frontier between work and leisure, to invent new forms of democracy both on the shop floor and in the political arena for the nation at large, to address a host of other fundamental issues that were put on the agenda in the sixties and then cast aside as inconvenient.

The May rising in France was probably the first of this century that had nothing to do with the Soviet model (and its references to the "cultural revolution" had little to do with China). But the young students and workers had neither the time nor the desire to move from a vague vision to a concrete project. Today, after so many hopes dashed and promises broken, no political movement bent on long-term action to reshape society can be set into motion without such a project, without outlining where it is heading and how it intends to get there. Because the floor is littered with shredded blueprints, it is indispensable to spell out what such a project can and cannot be.

It cannot be a fully fledged model imported from abroad or handed down from above; experience has confirmed the crucial function of democracy. Nor can it offer instant solutions—you seize the Winter Palace and everything inexorably follows. Even if this time the radical change were to start in one of the most advanced capitalist countries, say—stretching the imagination—in the United States, the transition would be long: the market, the state, the classes, the social division of labor, would not vanish overnight. Finally, it must be a project for our times, taking into account the deep transformation of the labor force, the extension of capitalism throughout the globe, the extraordinary spread in recent years of international finance. Yet, when all these reservations have been made, in order to advance, any movement must preserve throughout the journey the vision of a different world in which working people, the "associate producers," and not the forces of the market, would shape things and one day become the masters of their own fate. And this is where the sixties come to the rescue. To an establishment that no longer argues that altering society is undesirable, because it is convinced it has proved that such change is impossible, the echo from the past brings the seemingly surrealist and utopian answer: "Be realistic; ask for the impossible."

Not by ballot alone. In the heat of battle in May 1968, French students ran round the National Assembly with total contempt for the institution, and, at the end of the month, in the hour of defeat, described elections as a trap for bloody fools (the term was actually more anatomical). Afterward, the politics of the French Left was conducted as if nothing mattered except the ballot box. Both were exaggerations. Elections are affected by real conflicts in the country and vice versa. French history, a good laboratory for political scientists, provides an illustration of this link.

When the Left won its first big victory in the Popular Front election of 1936, the workers occupied factories on the assumption, We have won; it's ours. The capitalist establishment eagerly granted Léon Blum, the new Socialist prime minister, important concessions (a forty-hour week, two weeks' holiday with pay), begging him to get the workers out of the factories and then back to work. During the general strike of 1968, government and employers were equally ready for concessions; no price is too high for political survival. But in 1981, the first presidential victory of the Left was celebrated in a different fashion. Some two hundred thousand people flocked to the Bastille to dance and rejoice. Their most militant slogans, however, cursed the TV darlings of the previous regime. (The nearest translation would be "Down with Dan Rather and Barbara Walters!") This not only reflected the inflated importance of the media in political life; it also illustrated the abdication of the left-wing electorate. The good-humored crowd at the Bastille was proclaiming, We have won; St. François do it for us!

Any president or prime minister attempting to change the status quo, however moderately, is bound to meet stiff and growing resistance from the system itself, which yields only when it has to. When a reforming president is not pushed consistently by his own side, he is bound to surrender sooner rather than later. The volte-face of Mitterrand and the Socialists was not just a betrayal. It was a case of a party totally unprepared for battle. Admittedly, the situation varies from country to country, and in France, unlike in the United States, the system itself was, at least in theory, at stake. The outcome, however, is always dependent on the balance of forces. This should be pondered by those in the European Left who want to imitate Clinton and by the Americans who can draw on their own precedents from the New Deal. Even what Rosa Luxemburg called the "parliamentary battles between frogs and mice" do not take place in a vacuum.

Seen from the perspective of a quarter-century, an event tends to be stripped to its essentials. The most important feature of the French May movement was its link, however ambiguous, between students and workers. Beyond that, it projected a mood of defiance, the climax of a decade when young people suddenly ceased to take things for granted.

After the reactionary eighties we are going through a complicated period when the main actors have outplayed their parts yet can stay onstage, since there is nobody to push them off. How quickly Francis Fukuyama has vanished: History may have dangerous hiccups, but it certainly has not come to an end. The establishment, however, has succeeded in persuading the public that beyond the capitalist horizon there is nothing except the gulag, and it is this conviction that a revival of the old mood can destroy.

Hope was reborn for a time in May because a great number of French people rediscovered their belief in change beyond the confines of the system. More generally, the '68ers argued, and not just in France, that if a society cannot provide social justice, equality, a decent life, you don't just conclude, "So much the worse for the people." If life is unbearable, you don't try to fit in, you change society. We must now prepare for the advent of another generation bold and realistic enough to demand what is the purpose of our professors, the privilege of our pundits, and the paid duty of our propagandists to describe as impossible—namely, the vision of a radically different society.

Italian Interludes

::

A Sad Smile on the Far Left

FEBRUARY 5, 1966
The Economist

Rome

BEFORE LEAVING THE congress hall the delegates stood singing
and clapping. On the platform, against the background of a vast red
cloth, covered in one corner by slogans and portraits of Gramsci and
Togliatti, stood the leaders. It was Monday, January 31st, and the end of
a whole week's labors. Luigi Longo had just been reelected the party's
first secretary. All the unanimous motions had just been unanimously
approved by a show of hands. Outwardly, everything was perfectly in
keeping with the usual Communist routine. And yet the 11th congress
of the Italian Communist Party will mark a significant date in the
annals of Communism if only because it provided an echo, however
faint, of a real debate that had shaken the party in a whole series of local
meetings in the preceding weeks.

In the congress itself, at least in the sessions to which the public was
admitted, the debate was restrained and allusive, with the minority giving the impression that it did not dare to spell out what it really meant.
All the same, the divergences were never far below the surface. And
when on January 27th a man with a sad smile, who is the leader of the
unofficial opposition, declared openly that "I would not be sincere if I
said I was convinced" by the official line on the vexed question of "publicity of debate" within the leadership, he was really staking a claim for

the right to dissent publicly—which for Stalinists and Jesuits alike is a cardinal sin. The way in which the opposition was then defeated, or as some will say defeated itself, was a reminder of the past. The debate among the rank and file and the absence of recantation may have been significant pointers to the future.

With its 1.6 million members and its 7.8 million voters, the Italian Communist Party is the biggest in Western Europe. It has been gaining votes at every parliamentary election and in 1963 obtained more than a quarter of all the votes cast. The party has large-scale support throughout the country and is particularly powerful in the so-called Red Belt in the center of Italy. This is one side of the story. The other is that the Communists find it increasingly difficult to gain new members among the young or among the workers in the large factories of the industrial north. Above all, the party is becoming increasingly isolated. Once it had a pact with the Socialists. Now Signor Nenni, a former Stalin prize winner, is a pillar of the government and his Socialists are on the point of fusing with the Social Democrats. This will threaten the unity of the CGIL, Italy's biggest trade union federation and the last organization in which Communists and Socialists work together.

The Italian Communists were bound to ask questions about their own prospects. Was the "Italian way to Socialism" merely a slogan? Even Togliatti could not prevent a debate. It broke out into the open two months after his sudden death at Yalta in August 1964. Giorgio Amendola agued in public that since both Communists and Socialists had failed to achieve what they wanted they should start afresh and form together a sort of big Labour party. This proved too much for some of the rank and file, who insisted on the class struggle, the need for a radical transformation of society and the impossibility of carrying this out with partners who were barely pink. Pietro Ingrao, that man with the sad smile, who is a fifty-one-year-old former schoolteacher and leader of the parliamentary group, became chief spokesman of the intransigents. Throughout last summer, while the theses for this congress were being drafted, the battle went on. By October, sensing that Signor Ingrao was threatening their bureaucratic hold over the party machine,

Signor Longo and his associates joined hands with Signor Amendola. The Center and the Right were united; the Left was isolated.

Thus Signor Ingrao and his colleagues were confronted with the classical dilemma of a Communist opposition which does not quite dare to act as such. They did not produce counter-theses and they did not go to the country with a platform of their own. But the leadership did not have things all its own way. In some smaller places, such as Bergamo, it was actually routed in the local party arguments that preceded the congress. Even in big towns like Rome and Florence it had quite a fight. Ultimately, however, the inevitable happened and the organized majority defeated the improvised opposition. By the time the congress met the leadership could rely on enough delegates to be sure of success.

Three interconnected points stood at the heart of the debate: international strategy, the Italian way to socialism and inner-party democracy. The first issue got muffled during the congress. The Chinese were critcized by Signor Longo in the name of the "anti-imperialist struggle," which requires Communist unity. But the issue did not figure prominently. As the congress met, the Italian leadership seemed less reluctant than in the past to attend an international conference in Moscow. But to everybody's surprise the Russian delegate, Mr. Suslov, did not say a single word against China. The Italians therefore decided to postpone this argument.

The differences over the party's domestic strategy were more easily noticeable. First, there was disagreement over the assessment of the Center-Left government. For Signor Longo and his friends it was a tottering failure and the fall of the government just when the congress met seemed to add weight to this argument. The followers of Signore Ingrao replied that the Center-Left coalition had been successful, by its lights, in absorbing the Socialists into the system and thus isolating the Communists. Second, there was the question of acceptable partners in the search for a united workers' party. The minority insisted on having only left-wing partners—that is, the PSIUP (the splinter group which has broken away from the Nenni Socialists), the Lombardi opposition within the Socialist Party, and left-wing Catholics. The majority refused to be bound by any such limitations. This may explain the third divergence, with the majority pleading for day-to-day tactics and no long-term strategy, and the minority arguing in favor of a long-term program for a "socialist alternative" for Italy. Yet the Ingraoists, though clearly more aware of the problems of modern Italy, have not really evolved their own Socialist model, and partly because they were too much on the defensive to feel able to suggest that the present leaders were leading the party astray.

And so the conflict was concentrated on the right of dissent and the publicity that should be given to disagreements. But, here again, it was an unequal battle. Since he is still the prisoner of a monolithic conception to the party, Signor Ingrao was forced to condemn the very idea of fractions, trends, or groups. His only chance lay in sticking to the issue of public debate. But the divisions within the leadership played a big part in stimulating the pre-congressional debate among the rank and file. If the conflicts at the top continue to be given publicity, the debate within the party will go on, and will presumably lead to divisions.

By refusing either to recant or to attack, Signor Ingrao became an easy target. He was attacked violently, first by the temperamental Giancarlo Pajetta, and then, more systematically, by the ambitious editor of *Unita*, Mario Alicata. It was not difficult to point out that the debate had been exceptionally free and then to urge the dissenter to state clearly his objections. It was left to Signor Longo and his lieutenant, the rising Enrico Berlinguer, to make the same criticisms more moderately. But there was no concession to the opposition in Signor Longo's summing up. Indeed, to an outsider used to more anti-clerical Communists, the only surprising thing in his performance was the emphasis that he put on the dialogue with the Roman Catholic church. As Signor Longo, an old party functionary who now looks like a French Radical politician, went on and on praising the Vatican, your correspondent could not help seeing cardinals lining up on the platform against the background of the hammer and sickle. But this was just a surrealist mirage.

Was moderation the price the opposition had to pay for staying within the party? It is more likely that it owes its survival to the mood of the rank and file that was revealed by the big debate. In the circumstances it was thought safer to use salami tactics rather than to run the risk of a split. There are still some twenty representatives of the opposition in the new central committee of 151 members. The reorganization of the top bodies, which took place on Tuesday, made it possible to eliminate Signor Ingrao from the secretariat, which is filled with followers of Signor Longo and Signor Amendola. The job of the newcomers will be to check the spread of "heresy." The first setback is likely to occur in the cultural field because those who used to be in charge had started a bold and pioneering dialogue with outsiders.

Historically, the Communist parties of Western Europe are only just emerging from their subservience to Moscow. Will they go reformist? Will they keep their monolithic structure, which is allegedly justified by their revolutionary aims, and yet try to play the parliamentary game? Will they split? The answers to these questions, vital for the politics of Italy, France, and possibly Spain, will depend on what happens outside as well as within the parties. The Italian debate, mild by the standards of the nineteen-twenties and yet unprecedented in the last quarter of a century, has shown that Communists have a great thirst for discussion once they are given the opportunity. The tactics of the defeated Pietro Ingrao can make sense only on the assumption that the seeds that have been sown cannot be uprooted. If his calculation is wrong, he will have given future oppositions a lesson on how not to fight.

Italy After the "Miracle"

SEPTEMBER 17 AND 24, 1971
New Statesman

CONDITIONED REFLEXES DIE hard. It required big fascist gains in local elections, last June, and therefore the ghost of Mussolini, to revive temporarily some interest in Italian affairs. What, they're at it again? True, in the intervening years, the Western public was occasionally reminded of the Italian "miracle," the country's second industrial revolution. Italy was from time to time quoted as the success story of the Common Market—its most backward member becoming the pace-setter in economic growth. Yet these stories do not seem to have made much impact. In the Western subconscious Italy is still strangely lumped together with Portugal or Greece.

Whatever the chances of a Fascist revival in Italy, it is absurd to think in terms of Greece and its colonels. The economic miracle has at least altered the social structure sufficiently to dismiss such analogies. The Italy of Fiat, Pirelli, and the big state corporations presents different problems and requires other solutions. Admittedly, the northern industrial triangle is only a part of the picture, even if the decisive part. The classical "southern question," far from vanishing with the general development of the country, is more acute than ever: Today the relative backwardness of the Mezzogiorno simply increases social tensions. Indeed, it can be argued that both the northern expansion and the withering of the south are part of the same process, of the same pattern of development. Yet, taken as a whole, Italy must be looked at as one of Europe's "advanced" countries.

Naturally, even a miracle can be interpreted in various ways. The story of Italy's postwar development can be described in glowing terms, stressing for example, the trebling of the national income in the last twenty years. But the same statistics can be translated into symptoms of social stress, of peasants uprooted by the million (even in Italy farming now accounts for less than 19 percent of the total labor force), of mass migration from south to north. And these shifts have been coupled with their traditional companions—overcrowding, slums, the inadequate expansion of such social services as health or education. The accumulation of these discontents explains the explosive nature of Italian society despite the impressive glitter of production records.

The temptation to speak of the "miracle" in the past tense is strong. One reason is that the most dynamic sectors of the economy—steel, the car industry, and its ancillaries as well as other consumer durables—have probably lost some of their momentum. More closely integrated into the European Community and more open to world competition, Italy will now have to rely increasingly on the more advanced and sophisticated sectors requiring greater capital outlay, investment in research, the infrastructure, and so on. The untapped resources, including the reserve army of labor, may be yielding diminishing returns at the very time when popular pressure pushes the social cost up.

But the main pointer to the end of one period and the beginning of a new one is the profound change on the labor front. The wave of strikes which swept the country and reached a climax in the "hot autumn" of 1969 marks in fact a new era of class struggle. Not only did the strikes spread on an unprecedented scale and the wage increases beat all previous records—and after all, Italian capitalism could absorb such a redistribution—but the Labor movement, starting spontaneously from below, set itself new objectives. Attacking the hierarchical order of the factory, the very principle of incentives, the link between reward and productivity, it clashed with the logic of the capitalist system. The wave is still not spent. The new questions raised are still unanswered and the resulting uncertainty dominates Italy's political equation.

The employers must make up their mind whether to pin their hopes on trade unions as potential mediators capable of channeling the movement of protest or whether to opt for an open clash. In other words, they must decide between a form of planning, involving some kind of an incomes policy, and a trial of strength. The answer varies with the size of the firm. The big corporations still seem to favor the *programmazione*. The same problems face the ruling coalition. The Centro-Sinistra, or Center-Left, is an alliance dominated by the Christian Democrats but including since the end of 1963 the Nenni Socialists (Partite Socialiste Italiano). Its purpose can be summed up as an attempt to carry out the inevitable reforms without endangering the nature of the system. Now, however, it is divided over the question whether the "opening to the Left" should be extended so as to absorb the Communists, if not yet into the government at least into its potential majority, or whether the coalition should swing to the Right. It must opt for the search for consensus or for conflict. Finally, the PCI, the biggest Communist Party in the west, must determine the risks it is ready to run for the sake of its political integration.

To render a complex equation still more complicated, fascist success in local polls has driven the Christian Democrats to revise their electoral calculations. But the Fascist revival, in turn, must be put in its proper context. It is a reflection of a regime reformist enough to squeeze or threaten marginal or economically obsolete groups, but not radical enough to provide valid solutions. It is also a reflection of the failure of the Italian Left to offer an attractive alternative. It is in the South that this failure is most obvious and it is there that the Fascists have been able to exploit genuine discontent.

Conflicts of yesteryear, with their roots in the industrial revolution, are coupled here with conflicts of today and tomorrow over control in the factory, the nature of education, the content of everyday life. Italy is now a society both in transition and in crisis, the two aspects feeding one another. Its crisis is ours, because it tackles the problems of advanced capitalism, but it takes a more explosive, more dramatic form, because of the scope and sweep of its social upheaval. This is why, though curiously neglected by the outside world, Italy has been, at least for the last three years, the most fascinating battleground of social struggle in Western Europe.

In 1969, 300 million hours of work were lost through strikes in Italy. The following year there were fewer national contracts to be renegotiated, but the number of hours lost still amounted to nearly 150 million. This was twice as much as in Britain during the same year, a year breaking all previous British records since the general strike of 1926. The gains in terms of money are no less impressive. In 1970 average wages in Italian industry were 23 percent higher than in the previous year. In engineering the annual increment was over 27 percent and in the chemical industry it was more than a third. These indeed are figures to give Anthony Barber a nightmare and Hugh Scanlon food for thought. And yet for the Italian Labor movement the real significance does not lie in those figures.

In May 1968 France surprised the world with its sudden, concentrated, explosion, raising at once the question of political power in the country. Italy followed with its *Maggio strisciante,* its "creeping May," stretched over a longer period, but possibly even more damaging to the established social fabric. In Italy, too, the upheaval was heralded by the student movement of protest violently attacking the very nature of education, its social function, the role ascribed to its products. Unlike the experience in France, however, the contact between the young revolutionaries and the workers was fairly smooth. What is more important, as their struggle gathered momentum, the workers invented new methods of organization and worked out fundamentally new demands.

The innovations in organization may strike the British public as not particularly original. It must be remembered that Italy, like France, does not have a single TUC. It possesses three main confederations of labor (CGIL, CISL, UIL), divided on political lines. It, therefore, knows no closed shop. Unity of action was imposed on this occasion from below.

The slogan launched in many factories by the rank and file, "We are the trade union," was an open challenge to the labor bureaucracy. The strikes were often controlled by general assemblies, including union- ists and nonmembers. In the process the movement produced its new organs, the shop and factory councils with delegates often elected directly by the rank and file. For all its novelty in the Italian context, this search for a kind of direct democracy can be minimized as a Conti- nental equivalent of the British shop stewards movement.

Italian Labor's new platform cannot be so dismissed. The new mood was well illustrated by the slogan "more money for less work," a slogan which made no pretense about higher productivity and what the system can bear. Money, inevitably, figured prominently in their demands, though even here there were striking innovations. In most cases, the workers were asking for an equal raise for all, not a percentage increase, thus consciously narrowing differentials. They were fighting against job valuation, the incentive system, the barrier between wages and salaries. In some places they asked for a thirty-six-hour week, in others they rejected the principle of monetary compensation for unhealthy condi- tions. All over the place, they challenged the pace of assembly lines and, by the same token, the employer's authority in the factory. The move- ment differed radically from its predecessors in the way in which it seemed to follow its own logic without apparently bothering whether it clashed with the basic rationality of capitalist enterprise.

One reason for the new mood is to be found in the changing make- up of the industrial labor force. Until quite recently skilled workers were the most articulate and influential element within the trade unions. The conflicts of the late sixties felt the impact of the semi-skilled, the south- ern peasants turned northern workers during the "miraculous" years. Italy is thus witnessing the double emergence of a "new working class," both in the metaphorical sense fashionable in other countries (the numerical growth of technicians, researchers, scientific and manage- rial staffs etc), and in the literal sense of millions of migrant workers now manning the assembly lines. Unlike those in other European countries, Italy's "new proletarians" are not foreign workers. It is their growing weight which may account for the echo of the levelers in the labor conflicts of Turin or for the natural extension of the struggle beyond the factory gates in campaigns over housing and health.

Employers were not the only ones to be shaken by the new strains in the class struggle. So to some extent were the union leaders because the unions, whatever their ideological posture, tend to cope with conflicts within the existing framework. Suddenly they were faced not just with a slight redistribution of shares in the national cake or small alterations in the recipe. What seemed at stake was the very nature and purpose of the cake itself. The unions, headed by the biggest, the Communist-Socialist CGIL, decided to swim with the tide so as to keep the trend within tolerable bounds. They succeeded, on the whole, though they often had to change their habits and make concessions to do so.

It is still too early to say how deep and how lasting the recent strike wave will be on the structure of Italian trade unions. Institutions, after all, are merely means. Even the most "subversive" among them, like the shop and factory councils with their delegates, can be absorbed by the system unless they are sustained by a genuine impetus. But the movement cannot preserve the same intensity for very long. The employers' reaction to the onslaught was to cut down investment. Industrial production in the first half of this year was lower than in the corresponding period of 1970, with inevitable consequences for employment.

What impact all this will have on the fighting spirit of the workers remains to be seen. Besides, the new features of the movement, clashing most with the rationality of modern capitalism—stressed in this survey because of their importance and novelty—remained spontaneous and sporadic. They have not yet been able to develop to the full in the absence of a broader strategy, of an organization on a national scale. And yet enough has happened in the last three years to sow seeds of future conflicts: This is why the ghost of revolutionary change is haunting the boardrooms of Turin and Milan.

Struggle for the South

Arguing in the abstract, one could construct a perfect explanation of the fascist revival in Italy. Threatened in its vital interests, Italian capitalism has resorted to the classical Fascist remedy. It is ready to welcome thugs establishing law and order in the streets for the sake of preserving its law and order in the factories. The snag with this classical thesis is that it simply does not fit the facts in Italy today.

This should not be taken as a general certificate of good conduct for Italian big business. Italian employers, should they find it practicable, will use Fascist exploits to redress the balance in the factories. Their spokesmen will seize on the threat to prevent the political balance from shifting too far to the Left, and leader-writers, here as elsewhere, will wax lyrical about democracy fighting on two fronts. The state itself is not beyond suspicion. Preventive arrests of young protesters or the antics of the riot squads show that the Italian government needs no lessons in repression. But nothing that the leaders of private industry or the big state corporations have said or done seem to suggest that they are resigned to fascism. On the contrary, they still seem to be pinning their hopes for profits on a "conflictual cooperation" with the unions. Another ingredient of the past is missing—jingoism with its imperial dreams.

What then are the mainsprings of the new phenomenon? Allowing for national differences and traditions, the fascist revival is rather akin, for the time being, to the French Poujadism of the 1950s, a reaction against the speeding up of economic concentration. After the recession of 1963–64, the tightening squeeze affected marginal farmers and shopkeepers, the craftsmen and small industrialists. But, work productivity rising faster than wages, the government had some room for maneuver. Now that the wage bill has gone spectacularly up, the scope for softening the effects of concentration has narrowed and even some of the middle- and upper-class beneficiaries of the boom may begin to feel the pinch. Nobody likes to be eliminated in the name of "economic progress." The mighty and privileged among those who now feel threatened can rely on the genuine discontent of millions, frightened by the economic forces and rebelling rather incoherently against the state. It is in the Mezzogiorno, the south, that the roots of that discontent are strongest.

Advocates of the Common Market can claim that the most backward member has grown fastest, not that it has solved in any way the problem of the backward areas. The failure to solve the "southern question" is admitted by Italian spokesmen themselves, who now proclaim the opening of a third phase in which, to quote the socialist minister Signor Giolitti, the South will be treated as "the fundamental problem of national economic development." There is no reason why this third phase should prove more successful than its predecessors, centered around public works and then around industrial projects. It is no accident that big modern plants built in the South are like "cathedrals in the desert," that local small-scale industry goes on crumbling. The new investments, whether sponsored by the state or by big business, are northern bridgeheads in quasi-colonial territory. The process has been described as really dual: The North naturally absorbs southern resources (men, orders, profits), while the state artificially pumps money into the south. It cannot do much more without clashing with the workings of the profit mechanism.

Unsolved does not mean unchanged. The social and political structure of the south has altered greatly. Land reform after the war weakened the power of the block dominated by the big landlords. It did not prevent the mass exodus of small peasants and farm laborers. They account for the bulk of the more than three million who, within twenty years, had to seek a living abroad or in the booming north. Migration from country to town, however, was also local, which explains the growth of the sprawling, parasitical southern towns, with their pockets of speculation, and large areas of underemployment and misery.

The partial vacuum left in the power structure has been filled by the distributors of public patronage. Jobs for the boys on Tammany Hall lines are a joke by comparison. When a public investment can spell the life or death of a district, when in entire regions more people live on assistance than on their earnings, when thousands including the educated young cannot find stable employment, the political potentate who can turn on the tap or provide jobs wields tremendous power. Next to the "'black barons" of land rent have grown "pink barons" of the Center-Left.

It would be absurdly alarmist to speak of a fascist wave threatening to engulf Italy. Neo-Fascism is still a weapon of reserve and its function, for the time being at least, is to act as a pressure group, as an insurance against governmental temptations to move too far to the Left. As such it has already made an impact.

The previous big turning point in Italian politics took place in December 1963, when the Nenni socialists (the PSI) broke with the Communists and their own left wing to join the government. The resulting coalition, the Centro-Sinistra, cannot be described as either a success or a failure. It has managed to survive. It has failed to carry out the social reforms which were to be its justification. The outburst of 1968 was partly the penalty for this failure. But Italian industrialists still need some guarantees on the Labor front to plan their development and the most influential among them still think they can best get them through trade union mediation. Only, after the storm, this implies a closer collaboration with the CGIL and, indirectly, with the Communist Party.

Collaboration with the Communists—the very suggestion still sounds dramatic. But some cooperation is already on. Deputies are elected in Italy by proportional representation and the PCI gets roughly 27 percent of the votes cast. In a parliamentary assembly in which governmental whips are pretty powerless its weight is often decisive. The special economic decree or the recent housing bill are two examples of legislation which could not have been passed without open or tacit Communist support. On the other hand, there is no question of the Communists joining the coalition, no vision of a Popular Front. What is at stake is something different, the prospect of a modus vivendi between a bourgeois government and a Communist opposition, of a deal in which one side would promise a relative peace on the Labor front and the other would pledge reforms likely to make this peace-keeping easier. The Socialists, who sit with the Christian Democrats in the government and with the Communists in the CGIL, could play a crucial role as intermediaries in such an arrangement.

For the mighty Communist Party, with its 1.5 million members, this is naturally a momentous choice. The nature of its choice is not only illustrated by votes in Parliament. It has been made plain in speeches of party leaders who, in the midst of the labor conflict, picked a "productivist" line, urging the workers to get on with the job.

This option for reforms within the system involved a price. Like all other Communist parties, the PCI now has to reckon with several small revolutionary groups on its Left (Potere Operaio, Lotta Continua, Avanguardia Operaia, etc.). It has also suffered a split in its own ranks. In 1969 a group of influential activists, including three members of the party's central committee, founded a review, *Il Manifesto*, and dared to question both the Socialist nature of Soviet society and the overall strategy of their own party. This was too much. The dissenters were excluded. Their assumption is that the crisis just begun puts a revolutionary solution on the agenda, that revolution is possible in an advanced capitalist country.

The PCI has drawn the opposite conclusion and taken a calculated risk. Yet barely has it embarked on the long road toward integration than its potential partners are having second thoughts. This is where the fascist revival comes in. The Christian Democrats, who have ruled Italian politics since the war, are themselves a sprawling coalition. Fascist success has enabled the right wing in the party to argue that the time has come to bother about one's own conservative supporters rather than to indulge in reforms and concessions. With the forthcoming presidential election preoccupying party strategists and next year's parliamentary poll at the back of the deputies' minds, the political equation is in a state of suspense. The Centro-Sinistra goes on, but nobody is sure whether it will swing to the Right or to the Left.

And what if one looks beyond the immediate electoral horizon? At the end of a long journey and of many discussions, two broad theses seem to emerge. The first can be described as a continuation of past trends. A mini-recession will further weaken the momentum of the Labor movement and allow the resumption of a slow advance towards "conflictual cooperation" between the leaders of dynamic capitalism and the official party of the proletariat. The snag with this projection is that it seems to underestimate the limitations imposed on the regime's freedom of action by the new mood of the workers and by increased international competition. The second version, on the contrary, assumes that to deal both with the Labor front and with resistance to modernization in its own ranks, the regime will be driven towards a more authoritarian—i.e. toward the Gaullist—solution. Here the objection is not that Italy has no General. History, after all, seems to provide "saviors" when needed and throw them overboard when they have served their time. The objection is that Gaullism has failed in this very technocratic function.

It would be foolish to see a new Duce just round the Italian corner or to suggest that revolutionary power is soon to be generated in the streets. The prospect is one of a deepening, of a creeping crisis, opening up all sorts of possibilities. Neither revolution nor Fascism tomorrow; yet it is probably in Italy that the struggle for Europe's future will first be fought.

The Bloody Cul-de-Sac

OCTOBER 24, 1994
The Nation

ON MARCH 16, 1978, Aldo Moro—a key figure of Italy's ruling Christian Democracy—was captured in Rome in broad daylight by the Red Brigades (Brigate Rosse, hence the initials B.R.). Fifty-five days later, the government having refused any negotiation with the kidnappers, he was executed. Mario Moretti, the mastermind of this operation and one of the historic leaders of the B.R., is now forty-seven and serving the thirteenth year of a life sentence. He is the author of a recent Italian bestseller, *Mario Moretti: Brigate Rosse. Una storia italiana* (Anabasi). Or, to be more accurate, this book is a lengthy interview with Moretti by Carla Mosca, a journalist on Italy's public radio, and—last but not least—by Rossana Rossanda, who also wrote the preface.

Rossanda, once in charge of culture for the Italian Communist Party, was kicked out of that organization as one of the founders of the *Il Manifesto* group, which criticized the Soviet Union at the time of the invasion of Czechoslovakia. *Il Manifesto* still exists as a daily paper, and Rossanda is viewed by many as the voice of conscience of the Italian Left. Neither she nor her journal had any sympathy for the vanguard violence preached and practiced by the B.R. On the other hand, she is aware that their story is a political, not a criminal, one and, in a tragic way, a part of the history of the Left as a whole. Thus, Moretti's interviewers show a great deal of understanding but no indulgence, and this inner tension contributes to the value of this document.

The Moro episode takes up less than a third of the book. Moretti describes in detail the preparations, the action, the talks with Moro while they were waiting for the official response. He takes full responsibility for everything, including the execution. He hotly denies that the Red Brigades were terrorists: They never bombed blindly and always attacked specific targets. The death of Moro's guards was part of "the war with the state"; the guards took the same risks as he and his comrades. The striking feature in this description of the drama is the astonishment of the protagonists: Moretti's strange surprise on discovering that the C.P. is backing the government to the hilt and Moro's terrible realization that his closest colleagues are unwilling to make a gesture—the liberation of a few prisoners—to save his life. There is also the horrible admission, hinted at by Moretti, that killing a stranger is one thing, but killing a man with whom you have lived and talked for fifty-five days is something quite different.

Was it absolutely necessary to kill the former prime minister? The interviewers admit that the kidnapping—which showed the underground movement's ability to challenge the state—was popular in some quarters, but insist that the execution was not. Releasing Moro, they argue, would have gained much approval for the B.R. and raised real problems for the establishment. Moretti rejects such analysis with passion. "For an organization of guerrillas which had carried out such an extraordinary operation . . . to have let Moro go without an exchange," he maintains, would have been to admit that "the revolutionary policy is on the defensive and the state is invincible. This was unacceptable." This strange view was apparently almost unanimous among his comrades, which suggests that a guerrilla movement driven underground develops a logic of its own.

Italy's Red Brigades were unique. They were unlike the Sandinistas, the Tupamaros or, to stick to Europe, the IRA, all movements of national liberation, whereas the Brigades described themselves as "the armed instrument of class struggle." And, unlike the Weather Underground or Germany's Red Army Faction, the B.R. had genuine roots inside factories. Actually, they were born in the big enterprises of Milan, such as Pirelli (where Moretti had been a technician) and Siemens, then spread to Turin, Italy's other industrial center, and only afterward to Rome. They were also the by-product of a vast social upheaval, the "hot autumn" of 1969, which revealed the militancy of the Italian Labor movement.

Their early actions—seizing and then releasing bosses in various factories to show that authority could be challenged on the shop floor—generated a lot of sympathy and support. The hard core of the B.R. was always rather small; there were only ten to fifteen real illegals in each factory brigade. Even counting all sorts of auxiliaries, the B.R. never numbered a thousand people. But because of that backing they were nevertheless able to defy the Italian state and its mighty machine of repression for a dozen years. Does this mean that the B.R. were in the factories like fish in water? Reading this book makes me realize that one of the mistakes of the Brigades was working under this assumption.

Moretti is right in arguing that their ultimate defeat coincided with the economic crisis, the restructuring of industry, and the collapse of militancy in the Labor movement. But their decline began earlier. When the B.R. changed their targets and began attacking lawyers and journalists, they lost part of their support. Moretti confuses workers' reluctance to denounce buddies to the police with approval of the B.R.'s policies. Indeed, the move from factory to society at large and to an attack on the state, of which the Moro episode was a climax, was in itself a signal that the movement was losing its bearings. By 1981, when Moretti was arrested, popular support was dropping and repression rising, and the Brigades had lost any hope of victory. But the logic of the underground guerrilla faction seems to be that it cannot come to a stop even when it has lost its momentum.

And so this is a very sad story, and not just because it is partly written in blood. There are the lives lost, on both sides, but also the lives wasted. When so many activists, often the most devoted and militant, go astray, it is usually not only their fault. As a rule, the official leadership of the Labor movement is also to blame. The Italian case cannot be understood without grasping the contradiction between the dynamism of the social upheaval at the time and the cautiousness of the Communist Party, its determination to drive the movement into electoral channels. That is one of the messages of this book.

The other one is a condemnation of violence waged by a self-appointed vanguard, which starts with the idea of spurring the movement and actually sets it back. It does so because, whatever its intentions, it substitutes itself for the people instead of developing their political awareness and activity. The search for a historical shortcut, gun in hand, usually leads to a dead end, and often a bloody one at that. Though the tragedy is highly Italian, it has meaning for us all.

PCI—
What's in a New Name?

APRIL 16, 1990
The Nation

I THOUGHT I was going to the opulent city of Bologna, with its ancient red-brick palaces, for the funeral of the Italian Communist Party. The city's modern *palazzetto dello sport,* where the confrontations usually involve basketball, did witness four days of theater and tension, of drama and passion. But the PCI's Nineteenth Party Congress was never a duel to the death: It was shadowboxing or, more accurately, a fight in which the punches were pulled.

It was the third evening of the congress, March 9, that brought its undoubted climax, with a standing ovation for Pietro Ingrao, leader of the party's opposition. Next morning, as Ingrao publicly embraced PCI first secretary Achille Occhetto amid cries of "Unity! Unity!" it was possible to conclude that the party stood together and that its future was rosy. But, in fact, my original instincts were probably correct. Bologna may not exactly have been a funeral for the party but it was probably the beginning of the end.

However ambiguous the debate may have been, the issue addressed by the largest Communist party in the West was crucial: Now that the Communist world is collapsing in Eastern Europe, what is the role of the Western parties that were once connected to that myth? Indeed, what is the function of any progressive party? Occhetto unwittingly raised this question back in November when he proposed to change the party's name and structure to make it better able to win elected office—if not to take power. But he did not bargain for the resistance he encountered. This came not only from the left wing of the party but from the centrist majority that Occhetto heads. After a three-month fight, the *Sì* vote for his proposed changes carried the day by two to one, not a very impressive victory if one considers the clout of functionaries within the party, the habit of deference to the leadership, and the news media's overwhelming backing of Occhetto.

WHAT'S IN A NAME?

Clearly there was more at stake than a change of name. The reasons for dropping the word "Communist" were somewhat symbolic: If the word implied a party prepared to seize power in revolutionary fashion, the PCI—inventor of the *compromesso storico,* or "historic compromise"—had long ago lost any such reputation. Nor was the aim to avoid guilt by association. Admittedly, it is absurd to claim that the Italian party was never Stalinist: All the parties of the Third International were. It is also worth recalling that twenty years ago, the party expelled the editors of *Il Manifesto*—then a budding monthly, now an independent Communist daily—for refusing to accept that the Soviet invasion of Czechoslovakia could be explained as "an error" and insisting that the crime said something about the very nature of Soviet society.

On the other hand, perhaps because the PCI had to work underground during the Fascist period, Moscow's direct influence was less than elsewhere; the subtle ideas of Antonio Gramsci, one of the party's founders, survived to some extent. Then, after the war, Palmiro Togliatti proved a more sophisticated leader than Maurice Thorez in France by elaborating the concept of polycentrism (the forerunner of Euro-Communism) before his death in 1964. By 1981, the divorce with Moscow was complete, with PCI secretary general Enrico Berlinguer arguing publicly that "the impetus of October [1917] is by now exhausted." The Italian party, then, is less damaged than its French or Portuguese counterparts by the collapse of regimes in Eastern Europe that it had openly condemned.

The real reasons for the proposed change in name and structure are essentially domestic. Under Berlinguer, the party appeared to do well at first, propelled by the labor offensive that began in the "hot autumn" of 1969. Yet the historic compromise that Berlinguer offered to the dynamic wing of Italian big business after the fall of Allende in Chile and the onset of the deep economic crisis of the seventies was never taken up in earnest. After a time, the tide moved in the other direction. In Italy, as elsewhere, the restructuring of the economy led to a series of defeats for Labor, notably at Fiat's Turin factory in 1980. Besides, while incomparably more flexible than the French Communist Party, the PCI never really came to terms with the three successive social movements of students, women, and ecologists. To make matters worse, the general swing to the Right has been exploited to some extent by Bettino Craxi—the ambitious new leader of the Italian Socialist Party—whose connection with Socialism is purely nominal.

The party that Occhetto took over in 1988 is still, in some senses, a powerful force. Commanding the support of roughly a quarter of the Italian electorate, it is the dominant force on the Italian Left, nearly twice as strong as Craxi's PSI. But it is losing ground, with no electoral prospects and, at this point, no other vision. The apparent purpose of reorganizing the party into a looser body is to make it easier for new-comers to join, although one fails to see why women, students, greens, or intellectuals should be any more attracted to a movement that offers an even less radical alternative.

The change of name makes more sense in the context of a search for an alliance with Craxi, or perhaps even a formal alliance with his Socialists. The PCI, claiming 1.5 million members, remains a mass party with the vague reputation of intending somehow to transform society. By dropping the name "Communist," it proclaims (or confirms) that it is in the same business as Craxi—the management of capitalism.

Sì for Schizophrenia?

It was necessary to recall all this history as Achille Occhetto ascended the rostrum to recite his marathon report, his image projected, larger than life, on eight giant video screens. Occhetto spoke slowly and distinctly, and what he said sounded like sweet and reasonable music to leftist ears. He talked about the end of Yalta and the decline of the nation-state, the need for the entire European Left to adapt to the new situation and the impossibility of the PCI doing so alone. He spoke of liberty and equality, of the crucial contribution of women's liberation, of the search for a "nondominant, nonviolent relationship with nature."

And yet, as he went on, I felt a certain unease, which I understood only later as I reread the text of his speech. The reverend Occhetto was trying to be all things to all people; he preached everything and its opposite. But it is impossible to express solidarity with Daniel Ortega and at the same time accept NATO bases on Italian soil, even on newly negotiated terms. One cannot say that the workers must determine "the type, the rhythm, the finality, and the organization" of their labor and also extol the "positive function" of private enterprise; or talk of a society "freed from all forms of exploitation and domination" while dismissing the conflict between the Communist movement and capitalism as old hat. Or, if one does, one should expect to be dismissed with an Italian song popular a few years ago: "*Parole, Parole, Parole.*"

This gap between rhetorical proclamations and concrete proposals was a feature of all the pleas for the *Sì*—though less so in the case of the "colonels," Occhetto's younger assistants, than in that of orators with a leftist background. The epitome was the intervention of Bruno Trentin, leader of Italy's biggest union, the General Confederation of Italian Labor, and a quarter of a century ago one of the most original thinkers of Europe's New Left. The tall, elegant Trentin sounded true to his past as he spoke intelligently of "the conquest of the new spaces of freedom by the subordinated workers, by the citizens, by all free subjects." The snag was that his speech had no apparent connection with the battles being fought at the congress, the realignment of the party, or the prospective alliance with Craxi.

I gained a better grasp of the need for duality when I talked that evening to a young college lecturer, a woman from a solidly Communist family who now finds herself on the fringes of the party. "My mother feels really let down," she said. All that we got, her mother thought, we got from capitalism; our own dreams are shattered. It was easy to tell her mother that capitalism gave only what it had to; it was much harder to deny the collapse of many of her ideals. The desire of many party members to see the PCI play an active role in reforming Italian society is what gives Occhetto his chance. Their thirst for a project, for an alternative vision, explains why the pragmatic spokespeople for the *Si* must also sound as if they have loftier ambitions.

INGRAO FOR CATHARSIS

While the advocates of the *Si* had to waffle to conceal the contradictions in their arguments, their opponents refrained from pushing them to the point of provoking an open clash. Aldo Tortorella, who delivered a sort of counterreport on behalf of a *No* vote, did tell Occhetto that he could not remove "democratic centralism" through the door and then bring it back through the window: If the majority had the right to rule, the minority had the right to organize in order to reverse the party line. But he did not go so far as to say, You must choose, you can't have it both ways. Both Tortorella and Alessandro Natta, a former first secretary who made a similarly passionate speech, gave the impression of deliberately steering away from a collision course.

Tortorella and Natta were former members of the party establishment who refused to follow Occhetto. But the most eagerly awaited spokesman for the *No* was Pietro Ingrao, the veteran leader of the party's left wing. Presenting the closing argument for his side, Ingrao spoke in a gritty voice, visibly containing his emotion. That the world has changed and that the party has to do likewise is obvious. But the divergences begin with the question of what is to be done. Ingrao attacked the timidity of the party line in foreign affairs, especially on Germany. Why talk vaguely of the future dissolution of blocs instead of putting the issues of demilitarization and neutrality on the agenda?

He then moved on to the changes in contemporary society, the commercialization of the world of science and information, the altered nature of work since the days of Henry Ford and of Chaplin's *Modern Times*. The old struggle had to be resumed at a new level in order "to reassert the worker's new capacity for control and self-determination." Without a new strategy and a revived movement, the PCI risks falling into a "subordinate collaboration" with Craxi's Socialists. Then, the intellectual taking over from the political fighter, Ingrao mused that, while the computer may be faster than the mind, the riches of the human spirit "cannot be measured by any yardstick of the market." He ended cryptically: "It's true there are the guardians. But it is difficult to put the world in a straitjacket. And, on reflection, these keepers, however strong and ferocious, are in the end rather stupid." The audience paused for a moment, either puzzling his meaning or thinking he had not yet finished, then burst into an extraordinary ovation. For some ten minutes people clapped, cried, chanted, hugged one another, sang *"Bandièra Rossa"* with its praise—strange under the circumstances—of *communismo e libertà*.

Why should a hall two-thirds filled with the followers of the leadership react in this way to the spokesman for the opposition? The answer is complex, and may give us an idea of the mood of this congress and the state of the party. There was clearly an element of personal admiration for the man himself, a respect for the prophet rather than the commissar. There was also a feeling of gratitude that he had preserved unity: Ingrao urged people to join the PCI, not to leave it (which makes sense, for the leaders of the *No* fear that their followers will now quit the party). And there was affection for the past, a note of nostalgia. Funeral rites may not have been entirely absent from this celebration, but there was something else at work: the half-conscious wish to be an agent of history, the desire among most of Occhetto's followers to believe in the more radical part of his contradictory pronouncements.

The next morning, Occhetto had the last word in the debate. He made some concessions—on Germany, on the right of organized dissent— and was rewarded with a standing ovation of his own. But his was more organized, more rhythmic, more routine. It matched the spontaneity of the previous night only when he embraced Ingrao. Thus, the congress closed with an ambiguous image.

Divided They Stand

Before the congress, there were rumors that Occhetto, having made an alliance with the right wing of the party, would need the backing of the Left to redress the balance. But such theories can now be discounted. Occhetto has made a strategic decision to seek an alliance with Craxi and is strong enough to carry the party with him. Whether the PCI will be split in the process is harder to answer. The party now has a full agenda. It is supposed to open negotiations rapidly with intellectuals and anybody else who wants to talk. It is also due to hold a special convention to define its new program, and then to stage a new congress to approve its reincarnation—in principle, before the end of the year. Will Occhetto and his colonels take advantage of their position to ram the whole process through? Will the now-organized opposition accept the line, resist, or choose to split rather than yield?

The so-called Pintor affair, which created a stir during the congress, provides some clues. The morning after Occhetto's first report, Luigi Pintor, co-editor of *Il Manifesto*, wrote a scathing attack accusing the party leader of doing nothing to attract his political opponents. Twenty years ago, Pintor went on, we were three (an allusion to Pintor himself, Aldo Natoli, and Rossana Rossanda, Central Committee members who were kicked out of the party because of their link with *Il Manifesto*); now it is a third of the party, and if Occhetto proceeds in this way, he will be responsible for a deep division. Next day, the party paper, *L'Unità,* and a number of PCI leaders and sympathizers launched a violent attack on Pintor for being divisive, reminding him that his election as an "Independent Left" deputy had depended on Communist support. The proud Pintor promptly resigned as deputy and the whole affair hit the headlines. The episode was a reminder that the party apparatus has not entirely abandoned its old habits: Moving to the Right does not necessarily mean becoming more liberal and democratic.

There are other historical echoes in the Pintor case. If so few people followed the *Manifesto* group twenty years ago, it was largely because their mentor, Pietro Ingrao, opted for unity. Does his embrace of Occhetto suggest that he will do so once again when it comes to the crunch? Or is he now, as people close to him say, determined to stick to his line, whatever the consequences? My own guess is that Communism as an idea may yet have a future in Italy, but that the days of the PCI as an instrument of the radical transformation of society are over. In beautiful Bologna, with its walls mellowed by the centuries, a world was coming ambiguously to an end.

Fiddling While Rome Smolders

JULY 29, 1991
The Nation

Rome

IS ITALY ON the eve of a major political crisis? Is a change of regime, or perhaps even the birth of a new republic, imminent? President Francesco Cossiga, who has been quiet for years, is suddenly performing strange antics; Socialist leader Bettino Craxi waits in the wings, hoping for a change from the parliamentary to the presidential system; the Mafia, octopuslike, spreads its tentacles, while the northern *leghe*, or leagues, reveal both regional jingoism and mainly middle-class discontent; and everybody is fed up with *partitocrazia*, the paralyzing and permanent rule by the parties. No wonder that Rome is rife with rumors of an impending institutional upheaval.

On the other hand, there seems no imperative need for such a drastic solution. Admittedly, the two historic items on the national agenda—a unified European market by the end of 1992 and a common currency before the end of the millennium—are likely to prove a strain on the Italian economy, with its huge budget deficit and hefty public debt. But the capitalist establishment need not fear any dangerous resistance from the Left. Why bother, then, to install authoritarian rule? As a preemptive strike to take advantage of the opposition's present weakness? France now seems to have been "normalized," along American lines.

Will it be Italy's turn next? These were some of the puzzling problems I traveled to Italy to discuss with colleagues and political friends.

MEZZOGIORNO AND MAFIA

The first time I went to Rome was as a student; I hitchhiked from London. As we approached the Italian capital, my Milanese truck driver pointed south and proclaimed with emphatic contempt, "We are entering Africa!" He was exaggerating, of course. The dividing line lay much farther south, and even beyond Naples it was not quite Africa. But he drew my attention to Italy's "southern question," to the existence of two countries within one nation, to the gap that still yawns after years of dizzy economic transformation.

Northern Italy is very much part of prosperous Western Europe. It shows in conspicuous consumption—and not only in the big cities. On a recent visit to such smaller towns such as Verona and Vigevano, a shoe-making center south of Milan, I was struck by the number of luxurious boutiques reminiscent of Bond Street, the Faubourg St. Honoré, or the poshest stretch of Fifth Avenue. Helped no doubt by tax evasion, the local upper classes must have plenty of money to spend. Admittedly, there is no shortage of money in the South either: State subsidies poured down the Southern drain were not lost for everybody, and the Mafia offers its own rewards. But the difference remains striking. The South's per capita product is barely more than half the North's, while the unemployment rate, at 21 percent, is more than three times as high. (This, incidentally, is a topical lesson the East Germans—and Eastern Europeans in general—should ponder before they swallow the message of the Harvard hustlers.) In Italy, the gap is, in fact, even worse than the figures suggest because of the damage wrought by the secret societies.

An Italian TV clip shows a luxurious hotel with liveried flunkies. Then comes the terror—a hand trampled by a heel against broken glass. On the soundtrack, the aria *"Nessun dorma"* from Puccini's *Turandot* and whispered voices: "Don't ask me, I have three children. . . ." Finally, the message ("Mafia. Whoever keeps silent, consents") and a telephone number. Altogether sixty seconds that can now be seen on one commercial and one public channel, with more to come, in an attempt to break the law of *omertà*.

"You can't mention the Mafia as one of the major causes of the current tension," a prominent Sicilian-born journalist objects, "since we have lived with it for years." Others disagree. The Mafia has changed, they argue, since the early seventies, when it became heavily involved in drugs. It now kills wholesale, sparing neither women nor children. If one includes not only the Sicilian Mafia but the Camorra as well, secret societies now poison political life in Sicily, Calabria, and the Naples region. The infection has reached into Apulia, and drug money is making its mark on Milan's financial market. The killers' impunity strengthens the impression not so much of bad government, *malgoverno*, as of its absence, the abdication of central authority.

That TV clip is a sign of impotence rather than determination—and not surprisingly. It is hard to smash the Mafia when it has such strong links with the ruling coalition, particularly the dominant Christian Democrats (D.C.). Indeed, one of the reasons it may be difficult to grasp Italy's prospects is the prevailing confusion between censors and sinners. Cossiga, who now lectures almost daily on the vices of the system, is a pure product of the D.C. Craxi, the Socialists' would-be presidential savior, is the clever leader of a party that has received a much larger share of the spoils during his tenure than that of any previous leader. The snag is that such men get a hearing because of the degree of public discontent.

IN FRANCE'S FOOTSTEPS?

This time, arriving in Rome by train, I was struck by the contrast between the glorious sunshine and the darkness of the political climate. Indeed, the mood was reminiscent of France in the winter of 1957–58, when the question was not if but when the tottering Fourth Republic would collapse. In Italy, the prophets of doom even had a timetable. After the June 16 local elections in Sicily, which promised to be disastrous for the former Communists (and turned out just so, with their share of the vote dropping from 19.3 to 11.4 percent), the Socialists would precipitate a government crisis. A general election would follow in the autumn, with Sunday, October 6, being tipped as the likely date. Later scenarios varied: a constituent assembly, a referendum to demand the election of the president through universal suffrage, or even more dramatic pressures to alter the Constitution.

The French establishment chose to alter the Constitution and opt for Gaullism in 1958 because it assumed that traditional parliamentary democracy would not be able to cope with both the Algerian War and France's entry into the Common Market. Italy has only to deal with the further integration of the European Community. Angelo Ciampi, governor of the Bank of Italy, recently proclaimed that "time is running short" for Italy to catch the European train. He outlined the necessary steps: halve inflation (currently close to 7 percent), bringing it into line with the levels in France and Germany; cut the public-sector borrowing requirement, which still exceeds 10 percent of gross domestic product; and drastically reduce the public debt, which is now slightly larger than that annual product.

That is a tall order, but it does not necessarily require a new system of rule, especially given the weakness of political opposition. The Italian Communist Party, now rechristened the Party of the Democratic Left (PDS), appears bent on its own downfall. Bruno Trentin, the ex-Communist leader of the biggest labor union, the CGIL, expresses the hope that Fiat strongman Cesare Romiti will take over the leadership of the Employers Association (the Confindustria), while the latter stresses the need for strong unions. This is not class struggle but a contest in courtesy. Obviously, other reasons are needed to explain the rumors of crisis.

The *leghe*, of which the Lombard League is so far the strongest, provide some clues. The movement is often wrongly compared to *poujadisme*, the revolt of small shopkeepers in the poorer parts of France against commercial concentration. Rather, the leagues are a rebellion of richer regions unwilling to subsidize poorer ones. In a country that has been unified for only 120 years, there is apparently still scope for regional jingoism. League members dislike not only the newcomers from Africa but Italian migrants from the South as well. Predictably, they are against high taxation and in favor of strong government. The various leagues are expected to get about 10 percent of the national vote, much more in their Northern strongholds. So far they are merely unpleasant, but they could turn nasty.

In an effort to cut the budget deficit, Italy has increased its tax burden, but it is still spread very unevenly and aggravated by fraud. Recently published statistics show that in almost every branch of the economy, the employers, on average, declare a lower income than the employees. A friend, as we dine, gives an immediate example: The restaurant's owner cheats the state of taxes by fraudulently minimizing his profits, then lends the state that money at a high interest rate by buying bonds.

Italians are not against Social Security, or the unemployment insurance that made economic restructuring bearable, or even against subsidies for the South. What galls them is the unfair fashion in which the money is raised, the wasteful way it is used and, above all, the political channels through which it transits. Italy is now the only country in Western Europe in which the same party has been in power since World War II. As Parliament is elected through proportional representation and the D.C. gets only about a third of the vote, it has to govern with three or four allies; it even granted Craxi the premiership for more than three years—enough to whet his appetite. But the D.C. has never lost control.

This government by coalition has given birth to a complicated system of sharing the spoils. It affects not only the top *nomenklatura,* the control of TV channels, and key jobs in the vast public sector. It also determines patronage down to the lowest level, the distribution of manna in the South or the misappropriation of funds after an earthquake. It is *clientelismo* developed into a fine art. It is not parliamentary democracy that the Italians are fed up with but the usurpation of power by the party machines. A successful film that should soon be seen in the United States—*Il Portaborse (The Briefcase Carrier)*—will give you an idea of what drives them mad.

THE SCRIBBLER AND THE COMMISSAR

Nanni Moretti is a leading member of the new wave of neorealists in the Italian cinema. Moretti is the producer of *Il Portaborse* and its leading actor, playing the *onorevole* Botero, an unscrupulous Socialist minister. The other protagonist is the *portaborse* of the title, which could have been "the ghostwriter." He is a provincial high school *professore* whose gift for clever phrases wins him a post on the ministerial staff. With the job come the perks: His woman friend, also a teacher, is transferred to Rome; his family house, in need of repair, is declared a historic monument; he gets a trendy sports car. Yet after a brief spell in the job, he quits in a rage.

Admittedly, his minister is almost too bad to be true. Elected with the help of fraud, he makes money on the privatization of public property. He has never read a book, only introductions and conclusions. He cheats in the name of modernity and dismisses qualms of conscience as old hat. In his angry letter of resignation, the professor claims that the minister and his peers, far from being champions of modernity, are like feudal lords.

Yet, such is Moretti's talent that Botero appears almost attractive or, rather, irresistible with his ability to turn everything to his advantage. At the end, after being reelected, Botero does a TV interview at home, surrounded by his wife and children. And what does he say in his moment of triumph? He proclaims with great conviction, "Our task is still unfinished, we must now turn our attention to the entrenched feudal lords."

Nowhere in the film is it specified that the minister is a Socialist, but everyone took it for granted, including the party itself, which dismissed Botero as a caricature. Undoubtedly, the director, Daniele Luchetti, was not striving for subtlety, and the film has elements of farce. But many people see Craxi's party—"modern," Americanized, and unscrupulous—as destroying, almost inexorably, the rich heritage of the Italian Left.

Bettino Is No General

The most sober description of the situation I heard came from a sophisticated observer of Italian affairs, a former labor leader who is now an independent senator elected with Communist backing. President Cossiga, he argued, can describe "gladiators"—that is, CIA agents—as Italian patriots; he can vituperate against magistrates and attack the Constitution he is supposed to protect. But when he preaches for a presidential system, he is backed neither by his party nor by crucial members of the business establishment, such as Fiat owner Gianni Agnelli. Cossiga's criticism of the parliamentary system may help Craxi's presidential ambitions, but without D.C. support, the latter cannot go very far.

My veteran analyst proceeds, as is now the fashion, by analogy with the recent French past. Craxi cannot do a de Gaulle: He has neither the general's charisma nor his track record. Nor can he rely on colonels from Algeria to bully Parliament. The Italian Constitution can be altered only by a two-thirds majority of the two houses combined in two successive votes. Support for his own party hovers between 15 and 20 percent, so even with the backing of the leagues and Italy's small Fascist Party (which also favors a stronger regime), he cannot even dream of such a figure.

In theory, Craxi should be able to do a Mitterrand—that is, win as the leader of a left-wing coalition. There is every indication that Achille Occhetto's PDS would agree, however reluctantly, to be the junior partner in such an alliance. But the time factor makes this solution purely hypothetical. Mitterrand bided his time twenty-three years for his ultimate victory. Craxi's party, I am told, cannot afford to stay six months out of government; it is too dependent on patronage.

Granted that pressure can be exercised in other ways, notably through a referendum, one may hope to split the sprawling Christian Democracy. The European context, however, works against an antiparliamentary coup. Italy is now closely tied to the Common Market, and the European establishment would not put up with such an authoritarian nationalist outcome, my veteran expert concluded.

No Weimar, but . . .

Other friends disagree, notably those from *Il Manifesto,* a newspaper run by a group that was expelled from the C.P. because it refused to dismiss the 1968 Soviet invasion of Czechoslovakia as merely an "error." They believe that such an optimistic reading of the future underestimates the degree to which Italian politics has been thrown out of balance by the decline and probable fall of the ex-Communist Party. While they obviously do not see renewed Fascism on the horizon, they do think that the European establishment will be delighted if Italy, in turn, is normalized, with the power of Parliament greatly reduced.

A recent Italian newspaper headline declared that this would be "the first post-Yalta election." Indeed, domestic politics in Italy used to be viewed as a sort of "peaceful coexistence" between the D.C. and its allies and the Communists. True, the latter had long ceased to be a revolutionary force. Nevertheless, the party did still preserve a distinct culture, a memory of resistance, a vague belief in a radically different society. It is this capital that Occhetto and Craxi are now squandering with such indecent haste.

Faced with the slow but steady erosion of his party's electoral strength, Occhetto had a vision: If you can't beat them, join them. By changing the party's name and nature, he would win on the swings without losing on the roundabouts. But the opposite proved to be true. The party gained nothing on its right, while the breakaway Left group, the Rifondazione Comunista, is much stronger than anyone predicted. Official figures tell the story. A year ago the C.P. still had more than 1.3 million members; the PDS now claims 827,534. Even if one adds the 150,000 members of Rifondazione, the loss is considerable, and everything suggests it will be greater still at election time. There are efforts to preserve links between the Rifondazione and those leftists who stayed in the PDS through clubs bearing the name of Berlinguer,

Gramsci, or Luxemburg. Optimists might argue that the PDS's slide will stop one day or that the Rifondazione will grow to become an alternative. But all this, at best, will be a long process. In the meantime, for the right, this is the moment to strike.

Craxi's scenario suffered a setback on June 9–10, when Italians were asked in a referendum to restrict the number of their "preferences" from four to one. Under proportional representation one votes for lists, and the system of preferences—candidates the voter marks as favorites—was originally designed to give him or her greater power. But it turned out that the mechanism helped only the party machines, the Mafia, and fraud in general. In the South, it favored the D.C. and the Socialists. In the referendum campaign, the party lines were not clearly drawn. Nevertheless, the main Christian Democratic leaders pooh-poohed the event, while Craxi advised the voters to go to the beach rather than the polling stations. His hope was that the turnout would not reach the quorum of 50 percent of the electorate. As it turned out, 63 percent voted, and 96 percent of them said *Sì* to the reduction of preferences. Clearly Italians want more, not less, democracy. The problem is that this discontent, in the absence of a clear alternative, can easily be misdirected.

A Parting Shot

Termini is Rome's modern railway station, built just after the war. Outside, on a sunny Sunday, there is an impressive jam of buses and a host of foreigners—migrants from the Third World rather than European tourists. Inside, narrow-hipped men and women with wistful eyes, turbans, and colorful robes add an exuberant African touch to the scene. I ask an Italian where they are from; his answer suggests that they are not welcomed by everyone.

How time flies. Twenty-five years ago, I reported from Switzerland, which was then proportionately the heaviest importer of foreign labor. There, too, the immigrants tended to gather on Sunday at train stations. Only they were Italians. This change symbolizes the tremendous transformation of Italy within a quarter century. Now the birthplace of so many, emigrants must learn to live with immigrant workers, and the process is far from smooth. As the progressive movement loses strength, racism raises its ugly head. Unless the Left awakens soon from its current lethargy, the prospect for sunny Italy may be quite dark. That is the conclusion that runs through my head as the night train, the Palatino, takes me back to Paris.

Forza's Destiny in Italy

APRIL 11, 1994
The Nation

AN EARTHQUAKE FOR nothing? As I was crossing Italy, trying to sense the mood on the eve of the crucial parliamentary elections of March 27–28, a line from Lampedusa's *The Leopard* kept coming to mind: "If we want things to stay as they are, things will have to change."

I had come to witness the collapse of a discredited regime, an expression of the people's revulsion against the corruption of politics by money. Though the now-despised system had been dominated for nearly half a century by the Christian Democrats, in the past decade its most symbolic figure was probably the party's "Socialist" ally, Bettino Craxi, yesterday's prime minister, today one of the many politicians awaiting trial in the corruption scandal that's rocked Italian politics for two years. Now, Craxi is a man of the past. Judging by the campaign thus far, the man of the future is none other than Craxi's favorite television tycoon, *Sua Emittenza* (his broadcasting highness) Silvio Berlusconi, the Citizen Kane of the electronic age, who, like Kane, turned to politics. What we have seen in this campaign has been the marketing of a would-be prime minister—Berlusconi—and a new political movement, Forza Italia.

And yet it would be wrong to conclude that the election was much ado about little. A victory by Berlusconi and his allies—Umberto Bossi and his Northern League, Gianfranco Fini and his neo-Fascists in the

South—would mean a big change in Italy, and for the worse. The corrupt but rather tame moderate Right that had been running Italy would be replaced by the hard Right.

The most striking phenomenon I encountered on my Italian journey was general bewilderment. The experts were at a loss and the people puzzled. They were asked to elect a new Senate and a new lower chamber but they did not know whom to elect or how.

For one thing, they are voting under a new set of rules. In choosing members of the crucial Chamber of Deputies, with its 630 seats, the voter must cast two separate ballots. With the first, for one-quarter of the seats, she has no major problems, since the procedure is like that under the old system of proportional representation. She votes for her party and hopes it will get the 4 percent of the national vote necessary to qualify for the allocation of seats. The 155 deputies are then chosen from party lists in proportion to the votes obtained in twenty-five regional constituencies.

The trouble starts with the ballot for the remaining three-quarters of the members, who are to be elected from 475 single-member constituencies by a simple majority, as in Britain or the United States. This principle of "first past the post" has polarized politics, forcing the parties of the Left into a reluctant alliance and those of the Right into a shotgun wedding. Will the Italians, who are given daily voting lessons on television, learn and accept the rules? Will they be able to make their choice among the "recycled" parties and politicians? (The word "recycled" is used for the postscandal practice of candidates changing parties and parties changing their names.) Will they accept the idea of voting for the lesser evil or, feeling deprived of true choice, will they stay away from the polls?

At any rate, by the time you read this the results will be known. You will be able to see whether the Right, for whom the rather unreliable public opinion polls predicted more than 40 percent of the vote, captured the 316 seats needed to form a government. And whether the Left, whose vote pollsters estimated to be over a third of the electorate, made gains in the two weeks before the election, when the publication of polls was prohibited. Or whether the Christian Democratic Center, depleted and discredited, nevertheless retained a voice. I can only set the scene—which should be done even for a tragicomedy.

THE JUDGES TAKE OVER

The political corruption scandals caused a stupendous upheaval in Italian politics. The Milan prosecutors uncovered a fantastic web of complicity between the ruling parties and big business based on kickbacks for state or municipal contracts. The system provided parties and politicians with millions, while insuring the suppliers a monopoly. Ministers, party leaders, and about a third of all parliamentarians are under investigation. The catch was as impressive in the business community.

The first victims of the purge were, naturally, the five parties that made up the ruling coalition. Craxi's Socialist Party was wiped out altogether and the once-mighty Christian Democratic Party has been reduced to a shadow of its former self. The immediate beneficiaries were two parties outside this establishment that had no occasion to be bribed: the Northern League and the neo-Fascists. The Democratic Party of the Left (PDS) also profited. In its earlier incarnation as the Communist Party, it did not get seriously involved in the corruption, although in its search for "historic compromise" it did not effectively attack the corrupt system. Not only was the PDS the only big party to emerge unscathed, it also gained in another sense. Previously squeezed between its splinter movement, Rifondazione Comunista (Communist Refounding), made up of die-hard Communists, and Craxi's party on the Right, it gained room for maneuver when the Socialists collapsed.

Even before the national election, the political upheaval had electoral consequences. The first was the conquest of Milan's town hall by Umberto Bossi's Northern League. Then, in the municipal elections last November, the Fascists made a spectacular leap in Rome and Naples. Yet the real winner was the PDS, which emerged as the leader of a broad alliance of the Left, comprising Rifondazione; the Greens, who never quite took off in Italy; La Rete (The Network), the anti-Mafia movement headed by Leoluca Orlando, mayor of Palermo; and a number of moderate democrats. This coalition, under the Progressive banner, swept all the key municipal elections, and experts began touting PDS leader Achille Occhetto as the new prime minister of Italy. They did not allow, however, for the polarizing effect of the majority-wins system. Thus they were surprised when, in January, with an impressive number of television spots, a new product was launched in the political marketplace: Citizen Silvio Berlusconi and his Forza Italia.

FARSA ITALIA

When you telephone Forza Italia's headquarters in Rome, while waiting you hear the party song and then the slogan from which it takes its name: *"Forza Italia!"* This exhortation (best translated as "Go! Go! Italy!") is used by Italian sports fans when cheering one of their national teams. It resounded at the winter Olympic games in Norway, giving Berlusconi's party some free publicity, which was badly needed since the party salespeople were supposed to build an electoral machine almost overnight, one that is not organized as a party, but rather as a network of social clubs.

To see how these clubs functioned, I went to EUR, the suburb named after Mussolini's universal exhibition of Rome, staged there in the thirties. The meeting was held in an apartment rented for the purpose atop a block of flats. About twenty people were present: three trendily dressed young women, three more conservatively attired women, a couple of yuppies, a few lower-middle-class social climbers, and some pensioners. As Berlusconi had recently been attacked as a Robin Hood in reverse, because his tax proposals penalized the poor, the group spent much of the time discussing how to counter this criticism. Under my prodding, it was revealed that one of the two candidates the club was backing was a recycled Christian Democrat. Otherwise, the talk centered on a musical show and various cultural outings. On the face of it, they did not seem a very dangerous bunch—nor a very efficient one. In fact, the group seemed to be putty in the hands of Berlusconi's plastic men at party headquarters in Rome.

The headquarters is located in an old palace, close to Via Corso, filled with striking modern furniture and computerized to the hilt. While some of the junior staff members may have been hired, the key positions are held by people from Fininvest, the Berlusconi consortium, and particularly from its advertising subsidiary, Publitalia. They are sales types in double-breasted jackets and gray trousers, the kind of corporate go-getters who get invited to the company do in Monte Carlo as a reward for their achievements. These are the ruthless hollow men of the Center waiting obediently for the orders of the supersalesman himself.

Smooth and slick, dark, and rather handsome, Berlusconi was born in Milan in 1936. The son of a bank clerk, he made his first fortune during the building boom of the sixties with shady funds transiting through Switzerland (the origin of his money is often beyond proof but seldom above suspicion). He went into television at the end of the seventies and made another fortune. An admitted member of the P2, the Masonic lodge whose members plotted the death of the republic, he plausibly explained that he was never deeply involved. After all, the political establishment treated him very well. His links with prominent Christian Democrats and, above all, his close connection with Craxi resulted in broadcasting laws being bent to serve his interests. Today, Italian television is divided roughly in two: three networks run by the state and three run by Berlusconi. He also owns pay-TV channels, film companies and, through the publishing house of Mondadori, a host of publications, including *Panorama*, a weekly paper. In short, he sits atop a media empire so large as to pose a threat to democracy. Add to it insurance companies, a chain of stores and, last but not least, A.C. Milano, the soccer champion of Italy and Europe.

Admirers point out that Berlusconi's conglomerate is the second largest privately owned business in Italy. Critics stress the dubious origins of his fortune and his sizable debts, estimated to be at least $2.2 billion. If the Left were to win this election, his house of cards could come tumbling down. If he lost one of his television channels,

Publitalia might not keep its dominant position in advertising, the banks might start calling in his loans, etc. etc. Berlusconi is no Ross Perot, rich enough to dabble in the political game. For him, politics is a matter of economic survival.

It is no easy task to unite the Right. Berlusconi has two partners who are not on speaking terms with each other. Bossi, the leader of the Northern League, has only insults for the neo-Fascists. He does not speak kindly of Berlusconi either, and it appears that he already regrets their pact because it could mean that he will lose some of his supporters, who are shocked by his deal with a man of the old regime. On the other hand, some of his backers among the Northern bourgeoisie may regard Berlusconi as a more respectable candidate.

Berlusconi has a much better relationship with his Southern partner, Gianfranco Fini. Youthful, intelligent, and well-mannered, Fini is the new marvel of Italian politics, a neo-Fascist with a human face. Indeed, it was unsettling to watch his television debate with Occhetto; the expected duel turned out to be a competition in moderation. For this election, Fini changed the name of his party to National Alliance, and he is trying to bring it into mainstream politics.

To see how presentable his party looks (What's in a new name?), I went to Naples, where at the regional parliamentary assembly I met the leader of the local neo-Fascist group, a big, jovial-looking man with a stentorian voice. My purpose was to get his true view of Fini's strategy, which implies that just as the PDS condemned Stalinism, his party should disown Fascism. For twenty minutes or so, he resisted, then, under pressure, erupted with praise for Mussolini and boasted that his father had been jailed as a Fascist after liberation. The candidates I watched that evening confirmed the impression that Fini has a long way to go in shedding the Fascist past.

In beautiful Naples, where contrasts between rich and poor bludgeon the eye, where the press recently reported a link between the Camorra (the local Mafia) and the judiciary; in the South, where the unemployment rate is more than double than in the North and where welfare funds may be shrinking—the likely progress of neo-Fascists under whatever name is a worrisome prospect, And, yet, at this stage, the most dangerous man of the Right is probably Berlusconi, the demagogue who promises lower taxes and one million jobs. Why would the Italians massively vote for such a man and thus perpetuate the Craxi connection? Because he is a businessman, not a politician. Because he is a champion, like A.C. Milano. Because he has made pots of money and nothing succeeds like success: Such explanations imply that he is moving into an ideological vacuum vacated by the once-powerful Left.

ALTERNANZA AND ALTERNATIVA

In a big exhibition hall just outside Rome, in front of several thousand people, Achille Occhetto, with a graying mustache and a twinkle in his eye, was launching the campaign of the Progressives. Youth groups waved red, white, and green flags, but the mood was not delirious and the speaker made no attempt to whip up enthusiasm. He had just returned from London, where he got the blessing of the City, and was going to Brussels, to get the approval of NATO. He shared the platform with Luigi Spaventa, the stern budget minister, whom nobody would suspect of Socialist leanings but who is the Left's candidate against Berlusconi in the heart of Rome.

But then I did not see much enthusiasm at a rally in Rome where Lucio Magri, the sophisticated theoretician, told his Rifondazione comrades that the gravity of the crisis and the electoral law made it impossible to contract out of the Left alliance; his speech was an appeal to reason rather than to emotion.

The mood on the Left, at least among its leaders, is best illustrated by the violent attacks against the new secretary of Rifondazione, the former labor leader Fausto Bertinotti, when he dared to propose the taxing of interest on treasury bills. Italy's public debt is larger than its annual gross national product, and servicing it is a tremendous burden. Besides, the tax exemptions on treasury bills have made renting out money more attractive than putting it into productive enterprises.

Thus, Bertinotti had good economic reasons, as well as considerations of equity, for raising the question. The subsequent outcry on the Left against his proposal can only be explained by the shift of Occhetto's party, which, with the fall of its potential allies, has been driven to the Center. It was thus forced to accept the deflationary economic policy of the last couple of years—with its slashing of social services and its attack on wages—and adopt the author of this policy, the governor of the Bank of Italy turned Prime Minister Carlo Azeglio Ciampi, as its model.

This election is fascinating because Italy is both lagging and leading. Its course of "normalization" is reminiscent of France after the fall of the Fourth Republic in 1958, only in speeded-up form. De Gaulle reshaped the nation's political institutions. Italy has begun this process and will soon be urged to move toward a more presidential system. In France, Mitterrand brought the Left into consensus politics by abandoning the dream of a different society. In Italy, the fashionable word is *alternanza,* meaning a system in which two similar parties alternate in power. A Left that no longer represents a radical alternative will thus be allowed to take office.

But Italy points also to the future. Throughout Western Europe the capitalist establishment must determine how it will cope with the deepening structural economic crisis: by class collaboration or by other means? For left-wing candidates the snag is that there is no longer any scope for historic compromise. What they will be asked to do is to attack the welfare state, the protection of wages, all the postwar victories of the Labor movement. What is pathetic about the Left's performance in this election is that on key issues—unemployment, privatization, the market—its main party does not seek alternatives. For example, how to invent new forms of social ownership? How to entrust the working people with some power over their fate? Almost twenty years ago, Chris Marker made a documentary film with a title both eloquent and difficult to translate: *Le Fond de l'air est rouge.* The underlying weather is no longer red or even pink. It is Tory blue and threatening to turn black. If the Left wants to survive, it must begin to redress the ideological imbalance.

The Silvio Show

JULY 3, 1995
The Nation

ORWELL HAD IT right. It is not enough to obey Big Brother. You must love him, too. On June 11, rejecting proposals for reform put to them in a referendum, the Italians allowed TV tycoon Silvio Berlusconi to keep his Fininvest empire, with its three television networks— watched by about half the national audience. In a fit of masochism, they also authorized Berlusconi to interrupt TV films or plays with an unlimited number of commercials. Finally, they voted for the partial privatization of Italy's public television, the RAI.

Paradoxically, the way the verdict was reached showed how badly the proposed controls were needed. With the RAI—whose top leadership had been changed during Berlusconi's stint in office—remaining neutral, Fininvest could mobilize all its resources into a fantastic propaganda campaign, running numerous spots and showcasing its top performers. The object was to persuade the Italians that, should the reforms be carried out, they would be deprived of their favorite soap operas, game shows, or sporting events. The real issue was the desirability of one media mogul wielding so much political power. The campaign confirmed the danger.

To describe the situation as Orwellian may be overdramatic. The Italians did not respond as one to the call. Normally very heavy voters, on this occasion they approached U.S. levels of abstention. Only 57 percent of those eligible went to the polls and roughly the same proportion voted in favor of Berlusconi. Considering the extraordinary propaganda effort, that showing is not too impressive. Besides, the referendum is not the end of the matter. The Italian Constitutional Court decided that no individual is entitled to own three networks at the same time, and Berlusconi is apparently negotiating some change in ownership. The day after his win, he claimed that for the sake of "clarity" he would divest the bulk of his shares. Rumor has it that a consortium headed by the Saudi Prince al-Walid bin Talal and including a German group and Time Warner as junior partners will purchase Fininvest, but no one seriously believes that Berlusconi will give up the controlling interest in the firm on which his political power rests.

In any event, the referendum has altered the situation. The parliamentary commission dealing with the monopolistic aspects of television is bound to be affected by the popular verdict. Above all, the political climate has changed. In mid-May, the regional elections having shown a clear swing to the Left, Berlusconi's position was threatened. He had lost the premiership the previous December, when he was deserted by Umberto Bossi, leader of the Northern League. And his leadership was being questioned by closer allies, including neo-Fascist Gianfranco Fini, who were pondering the wisdom of his tactics of virulent "anti-Communism," so obviously at odds with its target, the very moderate ex-Communist Democratic Party of the Left. Today, having demonstrated once again the power of his propaganda machine, he is back in charge, and is readying his coalition for a general election this fall.

For the Left, it is a defeat self-inflicted. Its leading party, the PDS, did not fight this battle on the principle that so much power in the hands of one man is undemocratic. It could not because it was seeking a deal with Berlusconi almost to the very end. Thus, while one side was not fully mobilized, the other was in a perfect position to demonstrate the political power of television in our society. Yet the matter cannot be reduced to one of mistaken tactics. Berlusconi's electoral victory last year was the outcome of some fifteen years of intellectual retreat by the

Left, during which the Italians were taught that private is beautiful, profit virtuous, and money the only real criterion of achievement. To put it differently, it was the result of the ideological domination—*hegemony*, to use the right word in Gramsci's country—of the Right. Unless the Left learns how to tackle the unlimited power of money and the commercialization of culture, even if it gains office it will merely make its contribution to our Orwellian future. Although it takes a specific form in Italy because of Berlusconi's control of the media, the problem is not limited to that country, or indeed to that side of the Atlantic.

Italy's Olive Tree

MAY 13, 1996
The Nation

WHO WOULD HAVE guessed a few years ago that Italy's Communists, converted or otherwise, would win control of their country's government with the blessing of the U.S. president, provoking a boom on the Milan stock exchange amid visible signs of approval from the international money markets? All this happened with the April 21 vote, showing how much the former Communists (renamed the Democratic Party of the Left, or PDS), and also the world, have altered. It also suggested that, so far rebuffed in efforts to follow the U.S. example by cutting the cost of the welfare state, the Western European establishment may be toying with new ideas.

There are real reasons for rejoicing over the results of the general election, and the main one is that the worst has not happened. Silvio Berlusconi, the TV tycoon turned triumphantly into a prime minister two years ago, did not stage a comeback on this occasion, and his chief partner, the smooth neo-Fascist with a human face, forty-four-year-old Gianfranco Fini, suffered a serious setback in his rise, the 15.7 percent of the vote gained by his National Alliance falling very short of expectations. Their combined failure insured the success of the Olive Tree, or Ulivo, the Center-Left coalition nominally headed by Romano Prodi, an earnest and uncharismatic professor of economics, but actually dominated by the PDS, which opted for total conversion to capitalism and is now led by Massima D'Alema. On its own, Ulivo cannot govern, but it commands an absolute majority in both chambers together with its rival and ally, the other splinter from the C.P., the hard-line Rifondazione Comunista. Its leader, Fausto Bertinotti, has made it plain that his party will give the government full backing—and submit it to popular pressure.

While symbolically significant, the victory of the Left is hardly overwhelming. There was no "landslide." Only Rifondazione—whose share of the vote climbed to nearly 9 percent—made substantial progress. The Left won because of defections from the opposite camp. Two years ago, Berlusconi could rely on an alliance with the narrow, nationalist Northern League of Umberto Bossi. This time Bossi stood on his own and, appealing to the selfish patriotism of the rich northern regions, did better than anybody thought he would, capturing 10 percent of the national vote with candidates in only one-third of the country.

The other thing to keep in mind is that the victorious Left is far from radical. Its prospective Prime Minister Prodi, a former Christian Democrat, is no more than a mild reformer. To see how far the coalition has moved to the Right, one need only mention the new member recruited just before the election; outgoing Prime Minister Lambert Dini. His career speaks for itself: For years a high-level official of the International Monetary Fund, this former deputy governor of the Bank of Italy was the finance minister of Sr. Berlusconi. And, judging by their first pronouncements since victory, the leaders of Ulivo seem closer to the banker Dini than to the Communist Bertinotti.

That such a key figure of the financial establishment as Dini should have chosen to join the Left, that its victory was hailed by a 5 percent rise in the share index and a climb of the lira, hints at the import of this experiment whose significance spreads beyond Italy's frontiers. For several years now, the governments of Western Europe have been told by international advisers that their countries can no longer afford the social "luxuries" to which they have grown accustomed in the period of postwar prosperity. But attempts to attack the welfare state—by Berlusconi in 1994 and the French government last winter—have so far met with a passionate response.

The question is whether the new Italian government, with a parliamentary majority, the good will reserved for a newcomer, and the sympathy of the labor unions, can reform the system and preserve its support—or whether, bound to financial orthodoxy by a determination to stick to the rules of European integration, the country will be led to bitter disappointment. It may seem churlish at this point, when the Left finally enters the corridors of power and its supporters celebrate in the piazzas of Rome and Bologna, to see also the seeds of defeat. Alas, there are precedents, and the consequences of another left-wing bankruptcy could be disastrous in a country where even today a neo-Fascist gets 15 percent of the vote and a xenophobe another 10 percent. The new period of transition and movement in Western Europe bears serious risks along with great opportunities.

On Intellectuals

::

Party Line

A Review of Louis Aragon: *Les Communistes*

MAY 19, 1950
Times Literary Supplement

M. LOUIS ARAGON, once a surrealist and now the high priest of French Communist literature, could have avoided many pitfalls had he set the beginning of his long fiction-cum-propaganda war history of Communism in France a couple of years later—at any rate after 1941. But he apparently intended to take the bull by the horns and to face squarely as a French Communist the problem of the Russo-German pact. His book is the first installment of what is likely to be a long series of novels; it covers the period between the fall of Republican Spain in February 1939, and the outbreak of the Second World War.

It might be argued that, whatever the propagandist drawbacks of M. Aragon's decision to begin his story so early, it might have been of considerable literary advantage. The conflict between the Communist's conscience and the new party line was, in fact, more dramatic than his latter struggle within the resistance movement. The Communist erring in the wilderness is more interesting than a Right-thinking determinist. Such an argument, however, would imply that the Communist writer should place his artistic integrity above the party line; in other words that M. Aragon should claim for himself the same freedom enjoyed by M. Picasso and M. Eluard.

All the ingredients of a drama are present. The problem of Felzer, for instance, the Communist teacher in a secondary school and a Jew, faced with the party's new attitude toward Hitler, was implicitly tragic. M. Aragon succeeds in transforming it into farce. When the "renegade" *Humanité* journalist Orillat expresses the fear that the party will find itself in the position of an isolated minority like the Trotskyists, Felzer replies, unperturbed, "We are not becoming Trotskyists. Trotskyists are cops, that's all. They do not present a philosophical problem." This is not an unfair sample of the philosophical and psychological profundity of the book.

There is a famous tale about Dumas's two drawers; in one he kept the living characters of his novels, in the other those who had already died. His chambermaid, while cleaning the desk, unwittingly resurrected some of the corpses; and soon ghosts began to appear in the serial. M. Aragon is suffering from the opposite trouble. Some efficient and orthodox party maid seems to be watching to see that none of his puppets escape from the respective black-and-white pigeonholes. The result is that *Les Communistes,* instead of providing vivid drama, is empty and stereotyped *histoire de pantins.* The puppets come on and off the stage, but never attain to life. Mayakovsky wrote in 1925, "I want . . . Stalin, on behalf of the Politbureau, while reporting on iron and steel production, to also give a report on the output of verses," and it appears likely that M. Aragon's future output, for all the talent he has shown in the past, must be measured exclusively in quantitative terms. This story, for which he has mobilized some of the characters from *Aurélien, Les Cloches de Bâle,* and *Les voyageurs de l'impériale,* is not even good propaganda.

Old Men Forget

OCTOBER 21, 1967
The Economist

M. ANDRÉ MALRAUX has returned to writing (the unkind would say to fiction) to the accompaniment of full orchestration by television, radio, and the press. Everyone seems to be writing or talking about him—and buying his book. His *Antimémoires* (Gallimard) is long, tough going, but a bestseller.

At sixty-six, M. Malraux is France's minister of culture, the intellectual feather in the Gaullist cap, the man who has cleaned up Paris. But this is not what all the fuss is about. The Malraux legend is embedded in the past: It concerns the man of action who in the 1930s translated his experiences into one or two great novels. It is thirty years since he wrote a major work. So there was natural interest to see whether these "selected" memoirs would provide the key to the metamorphosis in Malraux's own character and beliefs.

M. Malraux's years of action were spent in Indochina, China, Spain, the French Resistance. The theme of his novels was always basically the same: man's destiny, his search for meaning, for dignity, his revolt against the absurdity of life and against death. His heroes gradually advanced from adventurers to rebels, from rebels to revolutionaries. The quintessence came with his masterpiece *Man's Fate* (*La condition humaine*), set in Canton against the background of Chiang Kai-shek's massacre of the Communists. The characters portrayed in this novel show how Malraux thought it possible for man to reach out beyond his condition: Tchen, the terrorist; Kyo, the revolutionary; Ferral, the aspiring superman; Clappique, the clearsighted clown.

After serving with the republican air force in the Spanish Civil War, M. Malraux wrote *Man's Hope*. The apocalyptic tone of this novel foreshadowed the end of the author's revolutionary journey. His next book, *Walnuts of Altenburg*, marked this resignation as rebel. It also showed that M. Malraux was ready to attach himself to someone else's orbit. This did not happen for some time; it was not until 1945 (after he had led a brigade in the French Resistance) that M. Malraux met his great man, General de Gaulle.

He was the general's minister of information in the postwar period, attacking from the Gaullist platform his old comrades in the Communist Party. During the years when General de Gaulle was in the wilderness, he tried to find a solution to the problems of mankind and himself in the world of art. But when, in 1958, General de Gaulle returned to power, M. Malraux returned with him.

In his account of his first meeting with General de Gaulle, M. Malraux attempts to explain his position, but neither here nor anywhere in his *Antimémoires* does he really explain his conversion from internationalism to nationalism, from Communist fellow-traveler to anti-Communist professional. His encounter with Nehru, for example, is the occasion for a Malraux monologue on India and Hinduism, with Nehru providing the cues. His conversation with Mao Tse-tung, however, has greater interest (though hindsight of the Cultural Revolution may have helped). He quotes Mao as stressing the unfinished nature of the revolution: "Khruschev seemed to think that a revolution is accomplished when a Communist Party has seized power—as if it were a case of national liberation."

His memoirs show M. Malraux to be still a great writer—in flashes. He is a master of incisive imagery (he describes the compromises leading to the phony war: "They put half a soldier into half a tank to fight half a war"). But there is all too much romantic nineteenth-century prose, purple patches and, particularly difficult for the reader, huge unexpected jumps in the author's reasoning. And for readers who have not read Malraux's earlier books, there are passages that must mean nothing at all. A large chunk of the book, for instance, is devoted to a laborious joke about an alleged meeting in Singapore between Malraux and Baron Clappique, who, as the initiated know, is that bitter clown from *Man's Fate*.

In *Man's Fate*, Clappique is the contrast, the foil to the men of action. He can reinvent the world, but is too perceptive to trust his own make-believe. One wonders whether he is revived in the *Antimémoires* to suggest that his creator is, after all, not so comfortable sitting on Olympus, playing the part of a minister. It could be a hint that the former man of action, who translated his experiences so forcefully into ideas, is not altogether happy in the role of voyeur, however high and mighty. The proverb for his predicament could be *"On ne peut pas être et avoir été."*

The Rise of the Nouveaux Liberals

NOVEMBER 12, 1983
The Nation

NOTHING IS LOUDER than the silence of intellectuals. This summer, the French government's chief press spokesman, Max Gallo, accused left-wing intellectuals of not speaking out in support of President François Mitterrand. Gallo's charges, which were made in a front-page article in *Le Monde,* unleashed a flood of polemic, for months filling the columns of that paper and overflowing into others. Much ado about nothing? To some extent the affair was an example of literary politics at their most comic, but it also had its serious side.

Since at least 1898, when French intellectuals issued a manifesto petitioning for the reopening of the Dreyfus case, the word "intelligentsia" has usually been associated with the Left. Its silence today, therefore, is eloquent. In the capital of commitment, of engagement, there has been a shift to the Right. The political "mistakes" of Jean-Paul Sartre are being discussed and contrasted to the "wisdom" of his former school friend, the liberal conservative Raymond Aron. The rightward shift is not limited to France, of course, and it raises a series of questions. The French case might help us understand the changed climate throughout the world.

Let us begin on the lighter side, in Paris. Every literary circus has its clowns. Among the mourners and critics of the French Left is, inevitably, Jean-Edern Hallier, former editor of the *Idiot International,* who, for the sake of a headline, could bury his grandmother and not just Socialism. Or, take a writer who is perhaps better known in the United States: Philippe Sollers, former editor of *Tel Quel*, who is living proof, in political terms, of the proposition that weather vanes never change, only the wind. During the revolt of May 1968, he cursed the rebellious students because they did not toe the line of the great party of the working class. Next he condemned the French Communist Party and almost everyone else on the Left in the name of Chairman Mao and his "little red book." Now he is a convert to Reaganism and religion. If there is something peculiarly French in all this jumping from bandwagon to bandwagon, it is the speed and arrogance with which the act is performed. Yesterday's errors justify today's wisdom: You are considered wise because you were stupid, a *voyant* (seer) because you were blind.

Which brings us to more eminent figures, like historian Emmanuel LeRoy Ladurie, who preaches that "totalitarian Communism" is the root of all evil and the Soviet Union the greatest threat confronting humankind. He was, and presumably still is, a serious scholar. He became a television personality in 1975, when his book *Montaillou: The Occitan Village* became a surprise bestseller. Since then he has been a familiar name in the media, lecturing on Communism and the Soviet bloc. Apparently, if one is an authority on medieval peasants in the Languedoc, one is considered an expert on collective farmers in the Crimea. Ladurie has another reason for sermonizing: Like many people of the generation that grew up during World War II, he joined the Communist Party after the war and left it when he became disillusioned with Stalinism.

Stalin having died thirty years ago, however, the number of former Communists who are still trying to atone publicly for their Stalinist sins is dwindling. Hence, to understand the changed mood in France one must look at another acrobatics act, the somersault of the so-called *nouveaux philosophes*. In Britain and America, where the Communist Party was weak, the public recantation coincided with the advent of the cold war in the late forties. Its essence was captured in the title of the 1949 book *The God That Failed*, which contained the apologies of prominent ex-Communists, like Arthur Koestler, Stephen Spender, and Richard Wright. In France, the public soul-searching came a quarter of a century later and at a much lower level. The "children of Marx and Coca-Cola," the Maoist offspring of the revolts of 1968, "discovered" the existence of Russian concentration camps in Solzhenitsyn's books and concluded that Marx was the great begetter of barbed wire. Some of these *nouveaux philosophes* were duly celebrated in a *Time* cover story.

The new philosophers no longer make the headlines. The most clever among them, André Glucksmann, now criticizes Mitterrand for being too soft on Qaddafi in Chad. The career of the prettiest and the best self-promoter, Bernard-Henri Levy, belies the truth of the French saying "Ridicule kills." In a devastating review of his *Barbarism with a Human Face*, historian P. Vidal-Naquet demonstrated that Levy had got his facts all wrong, but the intellectual dandy survived that execution and is still a power in publishing. If the *nouveaux philosophes* are no longer as prominent as they were in the seventies, it is because they have fulfilled their function—by which I don't mean the minor role they played in the 1978 elections, when they were allowed on television to warn viewers that if they voted for the Socialists they would end up in the gulags.

No, these born-again freedom fighters have played a larger role in French intellectual life. The pillars of the establishment were shaken in the sixties, when a new generation questioned alienating work, economic and social injustice, and the absurdities of the consumer society. In France and in Italy, students and young workers outlined terms of a possible alliance. Women and ecologists added their concerns to the Left's agenda. In the seventies, the world economic crisis could have provided the movement with what it needed most—unity of purpose.

The powers that be realized that such a unification had to be prevented. They had to discredit not just the Russian experiment but the idea of revolution itself. This dirty job had to be carried out by young ex-leftists whose ideological wounds were still bleeding. A Raymond Aron lecturing on the Soviet hell and defending capitalism as a lesser evil wouldn't do in the mid-seventies. He would have drawn yawns. But the political mood does change in seven years. When Aron's memoirs were published a few weeks ago, they were praised to the skies by his critics, and on his death in October, the funeral orations were so unanimously laudatory that it seemed the divide between Left and Right had vanished.

The collapse of the Soviet model as a radical alternative and the concomitant decline in the influence of Western Communist parties have certainly contributed to the resurgence of conservatism. As a result, it is often argued (even, occasionally, in the pages of the *Nation*) that it is a mistake for the Left to criticize the Soviet Union. With our enemies busy slandering the Soviet bloc, the argument runs, the Left should husband its scarce resources and limit its criticism to domestic or capitalist targets. I think that attitude is both wrong and politically shortsighted.

In contrasting Aron's "wisdom" on the Soviet Union to Sartre's "foolishness," conservative manipulators ignore the historical context of the debate. The cold war and the Korean conflict are forgotten. American imperialism did not exist. It is conveniently forgotten that organs of "cultural freedom," like *Encounter* or *Preuves,* and the "free" labor unions, like Force Ouvrière, were financed by the CIA. The Right's distortion of the past is facilitated by the fact that for a number of years not only faithful Stalinists but agnostics, like Sartre, chose to keep silent on the Soviet Union's crimes so as "not to bring despair to Boulogne Billancourt," the Paris suburb where the Renault auto works is located, regarded as the fortress of the French working class. The cover-up inevitably boomeranged. When the truth came out, the establishment's spokesmen had an easy time lumping together Communism and the concentration camp.

But should the Left play fair with an opponent who is permanently cheating? The answer is, Yes: Our morals and our aims are very different. The Right, whose purpose is to preserve the rule of a privileged minority, can do so only by fooling most of the people some of the time. The Left can win only through the political education of the majority. If Socialism is conceived not as a gift from above but as a gradual

acquisition of power by politically conscious working people, then success through deceit is by its very nature self-defeating. This does not
mean that the Left is disarmed facing its domestic adversary—quite the
contrary. Having clearly specified its own reasons for attacking
Andropov or Jaruzelski, the Left can expose the hypocrisy of the Right.

In particular, it can expose the latest bunch of turncoats as they follow the familiar road from heretic to renegade, to borrow a phrase from
the title of one of Isaac Deutscher's books. Their odyssey began during
the Algerian War when they accused the French C.P. of not being sufficiently anti-colonialist; now they urge Mitterrand to act as the gendarme
of Africa. The same people who in 1968 accused the Communists of
betraying the anticapitalist revolution are now the staunchest defenders and panegyrists of capitalist society. The truth of their early charges
does not render their present posture any prettier. Far from it.

France's great accusers of Stalinism have borrowed its methods.
They use innuendo, libel, and guilt by association to discredit opponents. We have no proof that pacifists are in the pay of the KGB, they
say, but "objectively" . . . Recalling Zhdanov at the height of the cold
war, they insist on the idea of the "principal enemy"—in their case the
Soviet Union—which allows them to turn a blind eye to crimes perpetrated in Chile and El Salvador. Describing local Communists as
"Red Fascists," they have even managed to revive, in a new guise,
Stalin's blundering characterization of Nazism and social democracy
as "twin evils," in the early thirties.

In Paris, this "antitotalitarian" campaign is approaching its second
climax. The first came around 1979. The new philosophers had laid the
groundwork for the return of what once was called the "respectful
Left"—respectful of capitalism, that is, though the derisive nickname
was inspired by Sartre's play *The Respectful Prostitute*. At the turn of the
decade, these "moderates" wanted the Socialist Party to choose a new
leader, Michel Rocard, and break off its alliance with the Communists.
Mitterrand was regarded as an obstacle to victory and rudely told to get
out of the way. He refused to oblige. Not only did he win the battle for
the leadership of the party; he won the battle for the presidency as well.

On the morning after the election, it was rather enjoyable to see his groveling ex-critics eat their words. But they didn't change their minds. They merely shut up for a year or so, until the post-victory euphoria wore off. Then, as the Socialist government got bogged down and resigned itself to adapting to its capitalist environment, they gradually recovered their voices. This time, they raised them in praise: Mitterrand stands up to the Russians, they cried; hence, his foreign policy is marvelous. He has become more realistic in economics and he recently dropped the very idea of class struggle. Now he need only draw the logical conclusion and kick the Communists out of the government.

The French Communist Party is prone to hand its opponents sticks to beat it with: Its attacks on Lech Walesa and Solidarity are only the most recent examples of that proclivity. The party's critics naturally take advantage of those opportunities, though they often use them merely as a pretext for slamming the party—not for its very real faults but because of its past image as a revolutionary force and a defender of the interests of the working class. The present campaign of the renegade intellectuals is aimed at reviving the idea of a "third force"—though not in the international sense of making France, and ultimately Europe, a neutral party between the superpowers. The campaigners are pro-NATO and violently hostile to the pacifist movement. Neutralism has lost a great deal of ground in France. Le Monde used to be painful prose for the U.S. State Department because of its nonaligned positions; now it makes pleasant reading. Whether it rains in Lithuania or shines in Alabama, its editorials continually draw the same conclusion: Europe needs the Pershing-2s and the cruises.

What the French cold warriors have in mind is a domestic third force, an alliance of the Center against "both extremes." This would involve no change in foreign policy, but at home it would mean a deal between moderate Left and moderate Right, between social democrats and liberal conservatives. In other words, the subordination of labor to capital. There is a precedent for such a realignment, though not one that sponsors of the policy care to mention. Nearly thirty years ago, a similar coalition was formed under the notorious Guy Mollet. Mollet was the

"Socialist" Prime Minister who presided over the Algerian War and the Anglo-French invasion of Egypt after Nasser nationalized the Suez Canal in 1956. The principal gravedigger of the Fourth Republic, he was also responsible for the slow death of the SFIO, as the Socialist Party was known before its resurrection under Mitterrand's auspices.

Pressures on the Left to move toward the Center are not strictly a French phenomenon. In Britain, the Social Democratic Party was founded with a similar goal. Such an idea makes sense from the point of view of the establishment. The economic crisis leads to polarization in politics. The Right grasped this fact at once and immediately dropped the mask of consensus. The Left's logical counter to that move would be greater radicalization, and the establishment is trying to prevent this by hook or by crook. In Britain, the Social Democratic Party was founded to counteract the leftward shift of the Labor Party. The campaign in France has the same objective. This similarity suggests that the collapse of the Soviet model is not the main cause of the present disarray of the Left. It might have played a crucial role in France or Italy, which have large Communist parties, but not in Germany, Britain, or the United States, where the Left is also faltering. The Left is bewildered because it has no coherent and credible answer to the economic crisis.

In his call for leftist intellectuals to speak in support of the government, Max Gallo was both foolish and wise. Foolish because if they do raise their voices it will be to condemn the government, to contrast yesterday's promises with today's practices, which differ so little from those of previous governments. The traditional gap between dream and reality? No, the traditional betrayal of Socialist principles for the sake of subservience to the logic of the capitalist system. On the other hand, Gallo was wise because a left-wing government stands no chance of success without offering solutions that are reached through an open debate. Mitterrand is threatened not only by the silence of the intellectuals but by the mass desertion of his supporters.

The Socialists, having rapidly reverted to the management of capitalist society, and the Communists being still tied to the Soviet model, a great deal of the blame for the present plight belongs to those who call themselves members of the New Left. While the economy was still booming, they raised the right questions about the reorganization of the workplace, about new patterns of consumption and about attacking state power at its roots in social inequality. Yet when the economic crisis placed those issues on the political agenda, these people vanished from the scene. It will be argued that new ideas and projects can't arise without foment from below, without a social movement demanding them. But there can also be no progressive social movement without ideas, without a project.

Time is running out. Amid increased social tensions, the Right is revealing its ugly Fascist face. The Left, if it wants to avoid total defeat, must begin, however belatedly, to find its own way out instead of accepting borrowed ideas. It should ignore the turncoats who are exploiting conditions in Eastern Europe for their own ends, crying, "Gulag, Gulag" to conceal vested interests. Our former companions on both sides of the ocean who yesterday claimed they wanted to change society radically and today are, nakedly or in disguise, the stooges of the establishment can be dismissed with the celebrated words of Shelley to Wordsworth:

> *In honoured poverty thy voice did weave*
> *Songs consecrate to truth and liberty.*
> *Deserting these, thou leavest me to grieve*
> *Thus, having been, that thou shouldst cease to be.*

*

P.S. As a singer and actor, Yves Montand is a great craftsman. He is much less skilled in politics, and therefore openly says things that his colleagues would prefer to utter privately. As such, he is a good illustration of how far an honest man who has genuine regrets over his association with Stalinism can travel. One hopes he can still awaken and realize where this journey is taking him.

Born Yvo Livi sixty-two years ago in Tuscany, Montand was brought to France by his Communist father. He was launched in his career immediately after World War II by Edith Piaf, and his tall figure onstage came to personify the jolly prole confident of his future. He and his wife, Simone Signoret—the striking *Casque d'Or* who became a great actress—were a prominent left-wing couple. She occasionally performed in progressve plays; he sometimes sang at the annual jamboree of *L'Humanité*. Many assumed, wrongly, that they were members of the Communist Party.

Montand was booked to sing in Moscow at the time of the Hungarian insurrection in 1956, and he kept the engagement. In her moving autobiography, *Nostalgia Isn't What It Used to Be,* Signoret describes his soul-searching at the time. That was the beginning of the end of their affair with the Soviet Union. Yet, while trying to make up for past mistakes, the couple retained their leftist convictions. They both played in *The Confession,* a Costa-Gavras film about the 1952 Slansky trial in Prague. They gave their signatures, money, and time to various causes—relief for the victims of Franco in Spain, the Chartists in Czechoslovakia, the mothers of the "disappeared" in Argentina, imprisoned members of Solidarity in Poland. In recent months, however, one got the impression that the arguments of the *nouveaux philosophes* had gone to Montand's head. He began talking as if fighting the "Red peril" were his top priority. Then came the municipal election in Dreux.

Dreux is a town some sixty miles west of Paris with a population of about thirty-five thousand, one-fifth of whom are immigrants. The racist National Front chose this place to play on the xenophobic instincts of the French voters. The election put Dreux on the political map. Not because the Right conquered the town hall; the swing away from the Left is at this stage widespread. Not even because the National Front polled nearly 17 percent of the votes cast. It was a historic occasion because the respectable Right gave its blessing to the Fascists. In France you don't vote directly for a mayor; you vote for a list of municipal councilors who then elect the ballot. If no list wins an absolute majority on the first ballot, there is a second one. In this vote, candidates of one party are often merged on lists with those of other parties. That is what happened in Dreux, where the honorable liberal conservatives, followers of Giscard d'Estaing and Jacques Chirac, added four racists from the National Front to their list. The Right was thus true to its pre-war self, when in the hour of crisis it proclaimed, "*Plutôt Hitler que le Front Populaire* ("Rather Hitler than the Popular Front").

Now, as then, there are exceptions, the most prominent being Simone Veil, former president of the European Parliament and a former inmate of Nazi concentration camps. Though she is a conservative, Veil said she would abstain from voting in Dreux because of the presence of the National Front candidates on the conservatives' list. Her stand, which revealed, by contrast, the true nature of the "honorable men" presiding over the French Right, created quite a stir. One morning, I was awakened by a man yelling over the radio that he too would abstain in Dreux. Another conservative with a conscience? No. The man was shouting that he could not vote together with the supporters of those who overran Afghanistan and Poland. "But those are the arguments of the Right," objected the interviewer. To which the man responded, "They always throw it at you: 'Be careful, you'll play into the hands of Reagan.' Fuck them. . . . The principal enemy is not there, he is in the gulag . . . one doesn't say it because Reagan . . . shit!" It sounded like the yelling and swearing of somebody trying to convince himself. But there were no second thoughts.

Montand was the man I heard shouting that morning, and he spoke in the same vein on TV shortly afterward, adding, among other gems, "Why didn't the intellectuals, the pacifists stage demos when the Russians were deploying their SS-20s?" Apparently, he just couldn't omit any songs from his repertory.

When Simone Veil preached abstention in Dreux, she voted against racism. When Montand preached abstention, he backed the National Front. In doing so, he accepted the premise of the unscrupulous right—that four "nationalist" councilors in Dreux are less harmful than "four Red Fascists." If he can swallow that absurd proposition, he should in the future rely on his accompanist for political advice. The difference is so simple, it could be played with one finger on the piano.

Dancing on the Grave of Revolution

FEBRUARY 6, 1989
The Nation

LONG LIVE THE revolution—as long as it is dead and buried with no prospect of resurrection. That thought springs to mind as the French begin to celebrate the bicentennial of their Great Revolution. The program is most impressive. Books and documents published or reissued for the occasion run into the hundreds. In Paris alone, fifty-six conferences devoted to the subject are scheduled for this year, not counting the massive exhibition on Europe and the French Revolution, various smaller exhibits and innumerable plays, operas, concerts, and other shows (including *1789*, a Maurice Béjart ballet based on Beethoven's symphonies). Provincials and Parisians alike are already flocking to *La Liberté ou la Mort*, a spectacular play that reconstructs the most famous scenes from the Revolution. But the climax will come, naturally, on July 14, when French President François Mitterrand will be accompanied by such iconoclastic sansculottes as George Bush, Maggie Thatcher, and Helmut Kohl—a party that appears more suited to honor Marie Antoinette than commemorate the storming of the Bastille.

This is not the only irony of history. The paradox begins with the very patron of this revolutionary jamboree. Mitterrand's new claim to fame is to have "normalized" his country and brought it into the realm of compromise and consensus—in other words, to have deprived it of its revolutionary heritage, the belief in the possibility of radical change through political action. No wonder, then, that the media should have promoted the historian François Furet as the oracle for this year's ceremonies. His book *La Révolution* is a sort of funeral oration: Its subtitle might well be "And the Worthy as Well as Difficult Means of Bringing It to an End." His 1989 is the French Revolution as celebrated by the Thermidorians, the gravediggers of the Revolution who took over after the fall of Robespierre and his companions on July 27, 1794—the ninth of Thermidor.

Furet's commercial success is in a sense puzzling. His is not a moving description of the great upheaval, a lyrical narrative like that of Jules Michelet, which carries the reader along in spite of its errors and omissions. Furet's *Révolution* is really an essay, a commentary on French history from 1770 to 1880 that requires from the reader a fairly good knowledge of events. Such books do not, as a rule, do well. Furet's has been on the best-seller list for ten weeks now, and there are two possible explanations. One is that the French, like anyone else, buy their coffee-table books to look at, not to read, and Furet's *Révolution,* a most handsome book that costs a most handsome $70, is sumptuously illustrated. The other reason is that the media do, in fact, have real influence, and Furet provided just the message they were looking for.

Furet's main thesis is that the age of revolution is over. From the very start, his sympathies are with those, beginning with Mirabeau, who try to arrest the course of events. Yet, it still takes ninety years in Furet's version for the revolutionary process to come to an end. It takes the massacre of the Communards in 1871, exorcising for a time the ghost of revolution, as well as a deal between their murderer, Adolphe Thiers, and moderate Republicans, for a Royalist assembly to proclaim the Third Republic and for July 14 to become France's national holiday— as it did in 1880. "The French Revolution," the author concludes, "had come into harbor." Or, to put it another way, the bourgeois republic was firmly established at last (although to maintain his thesis of a completely finished process, Furet has to drop the adjective "bourgeois").

Some historians, influenced by rather primitive Marxism, may well have tended to analyze the Revolution in too crudely economic terms. Furet and his friends, however, are all political. In his other

contribution to the occasion, a critical dictionary of the Revolution coedited with Mona Ozouf, there is no entry for Robespierre's young
companion, Saint-Just (famed, *inter alia,* for his contention that "happiness is a new idea in Europe"). This is quite evidently a question of
judgment and political bias. The absence of an entry for the "bourgeoisie," however, is a matter of fundamental conception. For Furet's
version to stand, democracy as a concept must be stripped of any economic and social context. The purely political treatment of events in
his *Révolution* is therefore not accidental. Toward the end of the book,
he cites Léon Gambetta as expressing "quite a different idea: not of a
social conflict rooted in the economy, of which 1789 would be only the
preface and that a new revolution must inevitably settle. But, on
the contrary, of democracy as an irresistible force of integration on the
march." Attributed to Gambetta, this is in fact the author's own credo.

But Furet himself seems hardly convinced that the revolutionary
journey was over by 1880. The Paris Commune of 1870–71, despite its
tragic ending, acts as a link between the sansculottes of 1793 and the
Bolsheviks of 1917. Throughout Europe it proved impossible to limit the
idea of equality to a purely legal fiction. The bourgeois order, whether
republican or monarchical, was threatened from within and from without by Socialist subversion. Dropping any pretenses to the detachment
of the historian, the prolific Furet has also joined with two companions
in a book eloquently titled *La République du Centre,* in which he
announces the second death of the French Revolution. In this version,
it takes another century, the dissolution of Stalinist mythology, the
exposure of the gulag, the collapse of the French Communist Party, and
the end of the great conflict over religious versus lay schools for France
to join the European mainstream. Thank God, Furet sighs, it is no
longer the odd one out among the "Western democracies."

The French, probably more than any other people, tend to view the
past through the prism of current confrontations. Attitudes to the
Great Revolution once marked the dividing line between Republicans
and Royalists, between Left and Right, though that line rapidly became
blurred. After that, views on the Revolution became a litmus test for
divisions within the Left. Sympathy for Danton, for Robespierre, or for

the *enragés* was a fairly safe guide to a person's place on the political spectrum. In Stalin's time, a defense of Robespierre was quite often read as an indirect plea for the Moscow trials. Furet, himself a zealous practitioner of Stalinist history in his youth, subsequently attacked his former fellows for their political contortions. Yet he and his new companions are equally guilty of projecting their present prejudices onto the past.

As head of the Raymond Aron Institute and co-chair of the Saint-Simon Foundation, François Furet is a high priest of the cult of "Rocbar" or, if you prefer, "Baroc"—terms coined by coupling the name of Michel Rocard, the most moderate of French Social Democrats and the present prime minister, with that of Raymond Barre, a moderate Conservative and former prime minister. It is the French equivalent of Britain's Butskellism of the fifties and sixties—the middle-of-the-road philosophy identified with R.A. (Rab) Butler, the liberal Conservative, and Hugh Gaitskell, the right-wing Labor Party leader. Rocbar/Baroc, like Butskellism an expression of the golden mean, is quite naturally favored by the media.

In France, as far as the Revolution is concerned, the Rocbar crowd really did have to shift back to the Center, having moved too far to the right at one stage. Influenced by the *nouveaux philosophes*, they had tried for a time to discredit the whole idea of revolution, attributing to it an innate tendency toward terror. They were quickly overtaken on this terrain by such truly rabid reactionaries as the group of historians around Pierre Chaunu, who exploited this breach to publicize books about, say, the revolutionary "genocide" in the Vendée. Furet and his friends then had to retreat. When he talks about his dictionary of the Revolution, for instance, Furet takes pains to note that the list of contributors, while containing no Marxists, also excludes any "anti-moderns." Politically, too, Rocbar adherents would like to occupy the vast territory between the Communists and the National Front. But what is really striking is the extent to which these French thinkers, like their Anglo-Saxon counterparts who preach the "end of ideology," positively ooze their own brand of it. Read, for example, Michel Winock's rather lively *1789: Une Année Sans Pareil.* The author gives the game away in his concluding section when he argues that "the abolition of private property is but a preamble to the suppression of liberties." This is familiar stuff in the flimsiest of disguises, offered up by latter-day evangelists preaching the same old gospel of capitalism from here to eternity.

If the idea of revolution is unpopular for the time being—at least outside some parts of the Third World—this is due to more than just the clever tactics of its opponents and their servants. In 1917, when Russians demonstrated that workers could seize power, the revolutionary idea made a leap forward. But then, as the Revolution failed to spread westward, Marxism began to pay the price for its vagaries in a backward country for which it had not originally been designed, and for the continued identification of Socialism with the crimes committed in its name. That price is being paid outside the West as well, as I was reminded last October in Barcelona at a conference attended by Soviet intellectuals. The well-known novelist Fazil Iskander spoke movingly, with a peasant's earthiness, of the rhythms of nature and the seasons and the terrible danger of artificially speeding the pace of events. Throughout the Soviet bloc, a vast proportion of the intelligentsia, once bitten and twice shy, is now fearful of taking shortcuts, of accelerating history—gun in hand—of vast upheavals and mass movements from below.

It is our duty, when the occasion arises, to remind them that revolutions are not just the handiwork of active minorities but the combined result of accumulated discontent and the inability of a system to offer solutions. To remind them, too, borrowing the words of Bertolt Brecht, about the violence not just of the current but of "the riverbanks that squeeze the current between them." Yet, in the present Western context, the danger is not remotely of shortcuts or premature action. As higher productivity in the West produces great unemployment, revealing the contrast between our technological genius and the absurdity of our social and political organization, the image that springs to mind is not one of premature birth but of the monsters that result from an overextended, unending pregnancy.

"Pregnancy" leads to "midwife," which opens up a potentially dangerous metaphor: Marx's reference to revolutionary violence as the midwife of history has sometimes been taken too literally, reducing the historical process to its most spectacular outbursts. In practice, 1789 and 1917 were very different in nature. Whereas the French bourgeoisie gained its ascendancy within the feudal order, the Russian proletariat did nothing of the sort. Yet can one envisage a Socialist revolution that would gain power at all levels before it seized power at the top—that is to say, winning cultural hegemony in the Gramscian sense as part of its conquest of power?

In any case, the historians who dismiss revolution as the curse of the Third World or merely a historical feature are not maintaining that the next social upheaval will inevitably be different from the storming of the Bastille or the seizure of the Winter Palace. They are really arguing that there will be no such upheaval at all. Clearly, they are too clever, and too keen on their profession, to proclaim openly the end of history. Yet like all faithful servants of an established order, they treat that order as something filled in perpetuity. By denying its class nature, by dismissing the possibility of radically altering property and other social relations, they allow for quantitative but not qualitative change. Precluding an alternative, they limit their own vision, and that of their readers, to the capitalist horizon.

Twenty years after 1968, with the ghost of revolution no longer haunting Europe, its leaders think they can afford to take certain risks. While I have put the accent on Furet and his friends, because they are fashionable and because that fashion is significant, they are not the only ones to be appearing in print this year. One should also mention the work of Michel Vovelle and his colleagues from the Institute of the History of the French Revolution, as well as the documents and the old classics that are being reissued for the occasion. Besides, the public is not forced to accept the tame messages or the bowdlerized versions of history being peddled by these quasi-official voices. The example of people trying to change their life by political action is by its very nature contagious, and the revival of revolutionary history—whatever the efforts of its Thermidorian chroniclers—inevitably contains an element of subversion.

For instance, in the conclusion to his classic book *The French Revolution*, Georges Lefebvre stresses that, in addition to the bourgeois interpretation of the revolution as a question of the equality of rights, it was open to two other interpretations—the Social Democratic and the Communist. Supposedly buried by Napoleon Bonaparte, both were revived in the nineteenth century and have remained vigorous. For friends and foes alike, Lefebvre wrote, "it is the Revolution of Equality and, as such, though the passing of time drags it slowly into the past, its name will not be silenced soon on the lips of men." In today's Europe, with its millions of unemployed, its welfare state threatened, and inequality once again raised to the status of a new gospel, this message sounds more topical than ever.

Europe's deep freeze may be drawing to an end. The first cracks are already visible in Moscow and its dominions. Who knows when a new climate will take hold in Paris, London, or Berlin? The champions of the established order—François and George, Maggie and Helmut—who will flock to the French capital in July for the farcical celebration of a revolutionary anniversary, as well as their prophets, employed to recite the funeral oration for the second and final death of the revolutionary spirit, would do well to pay attention. If they stand by the ornate column that now graces the vast square where the symbolic prison fortress of the Bastille once stood and listen carefully, they may hear the rising echo of Rosa Luxemburg's parting words, "You stupid lackeys, your order is built on sand. Tomorrow the Revolution will raise its head again and proclaim to your sorrow amid a brass of trumpets: I was, I am, I shall always be. . . ."

Rev Readings

François Furet's *La Révolution, de Turgot à Jules Ferry* 1770–1880 is published by Hachette; the *Dictionnaire Critique de la Révolution Francaise*, which he coedited with Mona Ozouf, is published by Flammarion.

Michel Vovelle's latest, *La Révolution contre l'Eglise: De la Raison à l'Être Suprême*, is published by Editions Complexe. He has also written a new preface to Jean-Paul Marat's *Les Chaînes de l'Esclavage* (same publisher). Another classic just reissued, by Armand Colin as a single-volume compilation, is Georges Lefebvre's *La Grande Peur de 1789* and *Les Foules Révolutionnaires.*

For those particularly interested in the debates over the rights of man there are two new books: Christine Faur's *Les Déclarations des Droits de l'Homme de 1789* (Payot) and de Bacque, Schmale, and Vovelle's *L'An I des Droits de l'Homme* (Presses du C.N.R.S.).

The new biographies, significantly, do not deal with the radical heroes of the Revolution. There are three books on Condorcet, of which the best known is Elisabeth and Robert Badinter's *Condorcet: Un Intellectuel en Politique, 1743–1794* (Fayard). Also in print is a new biography of the author of the famous essay "What Is the Third Estate?", Jean-Denis Bredin's *Sieyès* (Editions de Fallois). For a good, easy read with lots of illustrations, try Georges Soria's three-volume *La Révolution Française* (Bordas).

Not surprisingly, books by Edmund Burke, Benjamin Constant, and Madame de Stael are being reissued. Most classics on the Revolution are available. Two years ago, Editions Messidor completed a new edition of Jean Jaurè's *Histoire Socialiste de la Révolution Française. La Grande Révolution,* by Pierre Alexandre Kropotkine, is hard to find, but Daniel Guérin's *La Lutte de Classes sous la Seconde République,* though not reissued, is still in print.

Exploiting a Tragedy, or *Le Rouge en Noir*

DECEMBER 13, 1999
The Nation

A review of *The Sword and the Shield: The Mitrokhin Archive and the Secret History of the KGB* by Christopher Andrew and Vasili Mitrokhin; *The Black Book of Communism: Crimes, Terror, Repression* by Stephane Courtois et al.; *The Passing of an Illusion: The Idea of Communism in the Twentieth Century* by Francois Furet

THE AUTHOR OF this review is the son of a *zek*: My father barely survived his deportation to a Siberian camp in Vorkuta. This, incidentally, adds nothing to the wisdom, or stupidity, of my views on the subject. At most, it suggests that I am not one of those latter-day Columbuses who discovered the gulag in Solzhenitsyn. I mention this fact merely to avoid misunderstandings and superfluous accusations. If you oppose the new orthodoxy, in which the Red is painted in black or brown, you are branded as shamefully oblivious to Stalinist—or, to be really in tune, "Bolshevik"—crimes.

"Only that historian will have the gift of fanning the spark of hope in the past who is firmly convinced that even the dead will not be safe from the enemy if he wins," wrote Walter Benjamin; a Polish wit added that we don't know yet what our past is going to be. The recent past is now being rewritten at a fast pace. In the revised version, Lenin equals Stalin, Communism equals Nazism, and Marx is responsible for the concentration camps. All this is needed to prop up the doctrine, erected on the ruins of the Berlin Wall, that Socialism is dead and buried while capitalism will live forever. My objection to the corpse-counting historians is not that they tell a horrible story. It is that they are reducing a major tragedy—a revolution in a backward country failing to spread and the terrible result then presented to the world as a model—to a *Grand Guignol*. And these historians are not doing it to prevent the repetition of horrors in future transformations. They are doing it to destroy the very idea of radical change. They are painting the East in black to whitewash the West.

The opening, still incomplete, of the Soviet archives will not alter our vision fundamentally. We know too much for that. But it should allow us to fill some very important gaps and make it possible to add shading to this dark picture. While serious historians are already busy at it, the books that have hit the headlines are of a different nature. They are either potboilers, spy stories naming names of alleged Soviet agents, or propaganda pieces describing the evil of our former enemy to boost both our past and present positions. *The Sword and the Shield* belongs to the first category. For professor Christopher Andrew of Cambridge, England, this is not the first collaboration with a Soviet defector, but this time his partner is particularly strange. We are told that Vasili Mitrokhin, an officer in the external services of the KGB, drew the conclusion from the Soviet invasion of Czechoslovakia that his country was unreformable. He therefore took advantage of his position as caretaker of the archives and, between 1972 and his retirement a dozen years later, took notes on the innumerable documents at his disposal, smuggled the notes out and concealed them in his *dacha*. But it was only in 1992, after the dreaded regime had collapsed, that he contacted the British and then joined them with his treasure.

Thus this book is based not on original documents but on second-hand notes. True, Andrew gives his sources in the footnotes; and so we learn, incidentally, that there is nothing in the "Mitrokhin archive" directly connected with the big stories—the Rosenbergs, Alger Hiss, or the attempt to assassinate the Pope. But, as Andrew writes about everything, drawing on his own books and indiscriminately from anti-Communist literature, it is all rather confusing. In addition, Andrew uses code names rather than real ones (prudent, given that Oleg Gordievsky, a onetime collaborator, cost publishers damages in an unrelated project for asserting that British Labor leader Michael Foot was a Soviet agent). Even the careful reader, consulting the many footnotes, will have difficulty distinguishing truth from half-truth or innuendo, fact from fiction.

The other drawback is that the really interesting period of the Soviet secret services is the early, heroic one, when foreigners thought they were helping world revolution. Strange as it may seem, this feeling persisted in Stalin's time. But Professor Andrew has little new to tell us about Richard Sorge, who gave Stalin the unheeded message about the German invasion, or about Britain's well-known famous Cambridge Five, "traitors to class and country." Thereafter, when the motives were mercenary, the KGB was not very different from its Western counterparts (naturally, we are talking here about its external, not its domestic, role).

For all its tales, details, and secrets, and despite the fact that spying is increasingly economic, *The Sword and the Shield* leaves one with the impression that cloak-and-dagger stories are splendid stuff for thriller writers but only a marginal tool for the historian. It strengthened my conviction that our writing on the cold war remains terribly slanted. Thus, we learn in passing that in the 1948 Italian election, the CIA helped the Christian Democrats against the Communists by "laundering over ten million dollars from captured Axis funds for use in the campaign." The authors do not find this shocking: Only Russian gold stinks, the American dollar being Chanel No. 5. The Italian journalists working for a leftish evening paper are supposed to feel ashamed because their publication is alleged to have received some Russian money, whereas the contributors to *Encounter, Monat,* and *Preuves,* whose checks were cut by the CIA, can proudly parade as champions of cultural freedom. This is consistent with most writing on the cold war, which does not declare a plague on both their houses but poses the struggle as one between Good and Evil.

While *The Sword and the Shield* simply makes use of that ideology, *The Black Book of Communism* and *The Passing of an Illusion* are helping to produce it, and it is not entirely surprising that they should be French. The establishment everywhere has the art of getting the ideological services it requires, but these were needed more in France, which had a strong Communist Party and which in 1968 was shaken by a student rising and a big general strike. When, in the mid-seventies, a structural economic crisis came on top of ideological questioning, the system called to the rescue the so-called "new philosophers." Having primitively chanted "Marx, Engels, Lenin, Stalin, Mao, and Lin Piao," they simply reversed the slogan and blamed Marx for the concentration camps. They provided no more than seasoning for a mixture of von Hayek, Karl Popper, and Solzhenitsyn. But as a theme of sustained propaganda, their warning—you may rebel individually, but if you act collectively to alter society you will end in the gulag—was very effective. Still, its effects did wear off.

With discontent growing again in the nineties and the collapse of the Soviet empire offering an opportunity, a new campaign has been launched to convince people that to move beyond the confines of existing society is terribly dangerous. Here you have two illustrations of this drive, one very vulgar, the other more sophisticated.

It may at first glance seem difficult to pass judgment on *The Black Book of Communism*, because this collection of essays is very uneven. Nicolas Werth, the author of the longest piece, on the Soviet Union, is a creditable historian. He is aware of the passions and discontent unleashed in war-ravaged Russia and is even ready to recognize that the "Judeo-Bolsheviks," as their enemies called them, were sometimes also the victims of that violence. His biases, however, are striking. His portrait of Lenin as a fanatic is caricature, and he manages to write a chapter on the civil war without once mentioning foreign intervention. On the other hand, though it does not suit his thesis of "continuity," he does admit that there is a qualitative difference in repression between

Lenin's and Stalin's times. It is unfortunate that he agreed to take part in the exercise of propaganda staged by the chief editor of this book.

The main snag with Stéphane Courtois is not the mediocre scholarship of his contributions, of which the chapter on the "Comintern in Action" he cowrites is a good example. Instead of a serious analysis of how the instrument of world revolution became a tool of Soviet policy and how parties with a real following were turned into Moscow's puppets, we get a potted history in which, say, the Hungarian revolution of 1919 becomes a sinister story about the action of bullies called "Lenin's Boys." It is not even that Courtois tries to equate the elimination of the kulaks as a class with the racial extermination of the Jews or, ignoring time and population factors, insists that the Communists killed more people than the Nazis and, therefore, must be equated with them. (This revisionism, incidentally, leads logically to an entirely new vision of World War II; there are already signs of it in this book, notably in the authors' greater sympathy, in the chapter dealing with Yugoslavia, for the Chetnik Colonel Draza Mihailovic, who collaborated with the German occupiers of his land, rather than Tito, who didn't.) The real trouble is that the whole purpose of this book is, only too obviously, to pile up corpses—victims of bullets, the camps, or starvation—to reach the total of one hundred million dead (the Chinese provide two-thirds of that total, the bulk accounted for by the famine of 1959–61). Our preachers will use this magic figure to frighten the younger generation with the fate that awaits them should they not play according to the established rules.

We shall return to this one hundred million mark, but even in polemics it is better to deal with an opponent of some stature. Stéphane Courtois is known as the "poor man's Furet"; indeed, if François Furet had not died in 1997, he would have presided over this whole operation. Since Furet's *Passing of an Illusion*, a bestseller in France, has just been published in this country, one might as well tackle the master rather than his epigones. Furet was an original, if controversial, historian of the French Revolution. A member of the C.P. in his younger days and then a left-wing Socialist for years, he ended his career as a pillar of the establishment, a member of the Academy in France, an "immortal," and in this country holder of a chair financed by the very unprogressive Olin Foundation. He was also busy preaching that the age of revolution was over. Whereas his more radical colleagues maintained that the French Revolution, bourgeois by nature, was unfinished by definition, he argued that it ended in 1880, when Bastille Day became a national holiday, or otherwise in the eighties, when François Mitterrand brought France into consensus politics. In writing this book about the Soviet Union and Communism, for which he had no academic credentials, Furet probably wanted to show rival historians, who view 1917 as a continuation of 1789, how their dream turned into a nightmare. He apparently also wanted to understand his own earlier infatuation.

Central to Furet's argument is the belief that in a Europe shaken by World War I, Communism and Fascism were propping each other up. While the totalitarian nature of Stalin's Russia is undeniable, I find the thesis of "totalitarian twins" both wrong and unproductive. To sustain it, Furet is bound to twist facts. Though he recognizes that Mussolini reached power through a compromise with traditional elites and that Hitler had the backing of big business, the author hotly denies that Fascism and Nazism could be rotten products of capitalism. The Nazi-Soviet Pact is for him perfect proof of complicity between the two systems, but the Munich Agreement—for which he has all sorts of justifications—is nothing of the sort. Such double standards prevail throughout his book. Notably, in dealing with Spain, Furet is harsh on Soviet action but full of indulgence, nay, understanding, for the British conservatives and their strategy of nonintervention, which insured the victory of Franco.

The basic weakness of both *The Black Book of Communism* and *The Passing of an Illusion* is their incapacity to explain anything. If you look at Communism as merely the story of crimes, terror, and repression, to borrow the subtitle of the *Black Book,* you are missing the point. The Soviet Union did not rest on the gulag alone. There was also enthusiasm, construction, the spread of education, and social advancement for millions; when this momentum was lost in the Brezhnev years, the system was close to the end of its tether. Similarly, it is impossible to grasp the fascination of outsiders for the Soviet myth and their reluctance to see the reality if you don't view them in their own environment. If you ignore the Great Depression, the strikes and other struggles against exploitation, the colonial oppression and deadly poverty, the wars in Algeria or Indochina—in short, if, like these authors, you idealize the Western world—you cannot comprehend why millions of the best and brightest rallied behind the Red flag or why a good section of the Western Left turned a blind eye to the crimes committed in its name. History is understanding, not just propaganda.

Which brings us back to the Hundred Million. Propaganda ought to be countered, though not by yet more comparisons with Nazism. If we were to produce another *Black Book,* one to name misdeeds perpetrated under capitalist regimes, there would be no need to go back to the Industrial Revolution. Sticking just to our cruel century, there are two world wars and numerous massacres, ranging from Armenia in 1915 through Indonesia, with its slaughter of more than half a million, to the genocide of the Tutsis in Rwanda. And since, in this comparison, the accounts are not limited to murder and executions, each annual UN Human Development Report brings us stories of lives lost or shortened through disease, lack of clean water, starvation—in short, through poverty in our increasingly unequal world. Contrary to the tale told by the establishment, young people must be shown that what is immoral and dangerous—because of the ecological limits of our planet—is not the attempt to change our society radically but the willingness to preserve it precisely as it is.

Yet a balancing of corpses is no solution: Even if the victims were a small fraction of the Hundred Million, the wound would be unforgivable and unforgettable. While the criminality of capitalism may be no discovery to us, Socialism was supposed to open a new era, and these crimes were committed in its name. It can be objected that Socialism could not have died in Eastern Europe because, if we define it as mastery of the working people over their work and their fate, it never lived there. That is right but not sufficient. Nor is it enough to emphasize, again rightly, Russia's backwardness, its isolation, the resulting task of primitive accumulation. We must proceed much further in our exploration, look critically at the Leninist conception of the party and move beyond it. There should be no taboos whatsoever, and it would be most un-Marxist if Marx himself were not questioned in this reexamination. The whole exercise, however, is worthwhile only on two conditions: First, the judgment, however stern and ruthless, must be made not in the void, in the abstract, but in historical context, taking into account real conditions and the available alternatives. Second, it must serve a practical purpose, so that when the people next take power, it will be to exercise it themselves. In other words, democracy must be not the crowning of the revolutionary process but its central element from the very beginning of the transformation.

For our aim—let us not be ashamed to say so—is to revive the belief in collective action and in the possibility of radical transformation of our lives. On the other hand, the ambition of many is to take advantage of the circumstances, of the terrible heritage, to destroy the Promethean spirit of humankind. You feel it while reading their prose. In his foreword to the *Black Book,* Martin Malia actually proclaims that "any realistic accounting of Communist crime would effectively shut the door on Utopia." Furet the historian is too wise to accept Francis Fukuyama's nonsense about the end of history. One day, he concludes, humankind will resume its search. But, he qualifies, not in our time: "Here we are, condemned to live in the world as it is." This, let us hope, is their illusion.

What should we name the Parisian providers of this "French flu" and others who spread it on this side of the ocean? To call them scavengers of death would be too Stalinist in style. But it seems fair to describe them as keepers of the cult of TINA—the mindset that There Is No Alternative—preachers of human resignation. Parading as champions of freedom and questers after truth, they are, in fact, the obedient servants of the established order.

Sartre's Roads to Freedom

JUNE 5, 2000
The Nation

ASKED WHERE HE was coming from, my friend's son replied, "From the demo against the death of Sartre." It was April 19, 1980, and the definition fitted perfectly, for Sartre's funeral, attended by some fifty thousand, could be described as the last demo of the New Left. It was posthumous in another sense. The engagement associated with Sartre—the intellectual's or writer's social and political commitment—had been cast aside five years earlier by the self-appointed "new philosophers," crude in thought but skilled in propaganda—who loudly proclaimed that any attempt to alter society radically was bound to end with the gulag. Indeed, the cliché fashionable well into the eighties was that Sartre's fellow at the highly competitive École Normale, Raymond Aron—an intelligent pillar of the Western establishment, a sort of superior Daniel Bell—had always been right, whereas *son petit camarade* Jean-Paul had always been wrong. But such was the pressure of propaganda that the other side merely snapped back that it was better to be wrong with Sartre than to be right with Aron.

Has the mood changed twenty years on? Six books devoted to Sartre have just been published here for the anniversary. Newspapers have been full of portraits, weeklies, and monthlies replete with extracts, comments, and assessments. Are these not signs, as many titles suggested, of a comeback, a resurrection? On the international scale, judging by the conferences held and books printed, Sartre has never quite been forgotten. Yet even in the narrow Parisian and political sense, one can talk only of a partial revival. Sartre is feted not because of his engagement but in spite of it. Of the books mentioned, only the smallest, that of Benoit Denis, which is devoted to literary commitment from Pascal to Sartre, does justice to the latter's contribution to the struggles of the intellectuals. Philippe Petit, who seems sympathetic to *la cause de Sartre*, writes essentially about that extraordinary monument of literary criticism, *The Family Idiot*, Sartre's 2,988-page unfinished analytical portrait of Flaubert. And Olivier Wickers elegantly muses on various aspects of this literary figure. But three others start from the premise that Aron was always right. Indeed, since they describe Sartre as Stalin's stooge and a servant of totalitarianism, we shall have to return to the heart of the matter. But first, why so much talk about the man at all?

Younger people cannot remember the impact, the extraordinary charisma, of this far from handsome little man with a lazy eye. I am not referring here to the postwar craze, when tourists invaded the *caves* and cafes of Saint-Germain-des-Prés in search of existentialists and innumerable youngsters took as their model the "free couple" of Jean-Paul and Simone (known as *le castor*, French for "beaver," of which her name de Beauvoir was apparently a reminder). No, I am talking about the crucial part performed by Sartre for at least three decades after the war in the cultural and political battles on the international stage, about his role as the chief critic of the Western world (in retrospect, and considering the importance of *The Second Sex*, one should probably talk of the influence of the couple).

Prolific and *many-sided* are ridiculous euphemisms when applied to Sartre. We know from *The Words* that he acquired in childhood the habit of writing for six to seven hours a day, and much more (with the help of all sorts of drugs) when the issue fascinated him or the timetable required it. He wrote some philosophy with literary elegance and put philosophical ideas into his novels. But he was also a playwright, a major literary critic, a screenwriter, and a cultural and political essayist, not to mention the innumerable petitions he wrote or signed whenever he thought injustice was involved. He turned down all the honors bestowed by the establishment, including the Nobel Prize for Literature. Herbert Marcuse once called him "the conscience of the world."

Fame and political involvement came rather late. Sartre was almost forty when World War II ended. A teacher by training, he had already published an important novel (*Nausea*), a collection of short stories (*The Wall*), had had two plays staged (*The Flies* and *No Exit*), and had finished his major philosophical work (*Being and Nothingness*). Though he was vaguely leftish, he was not very involved in politics. More serious was his hatred for his own milieu, the bourgeoisie, which cannot be explained in purely psychoanalytic terms (his father died when he was one, and his happy life with his widowed mother was interrupted eleven years later by his bourgeois manager stepfather). Sartre's Resistance record, while not heroic, was honorable. Yet it was only after the war that he began to preach the imperative of political commitment.

Most commentators attribute the change to his brief stay in a German camp for French prisoners of war. Sartre the individualist found himself for the first time in a popular collectivity and enjoyed it. This certainly helped, but the reasons were much deeper: It was the war, the Resistance, and the situation after the conflict. Like Mathieu, one of the heroes of his *Roads to Freedom*, Sartre the libertarian individualist had finally to answer the question: Freedom for what purpose? The subject of literature, he now said, has always been man in the world. The writer "must show the reader his power to make, or to unmake, in short to act—for man is to be reinvented every day." He even suggested that the task of the writer was "to struggle in favor of the freedom of the person and of Socialist revolution."

This activist message accounts for Sartre's tremendous popularity as well as for the hatred he aroused as "the corrupter of youth" (right-wingers actually paraded with the slogan "Shoot Sartre"). This attitude corresponded to the mood of the times. France was torn, radicalized by war and occupation. The movement of colonial liberation was spreading. And the world was soon to be split in two by the cold war. It is interesting to note that at war's end, though he was unquestionably a leftist, Sartre took several years to choose his side. While now interested in Marxism and the class struggle, Sartre was very often the target of attacks by Communists, both French and foreign. He was among the writers about whom the Soviet hack A. Fadeyev said, at an intellectual congress in 1948, that "if hyenas could use fountain pens and jackals could use typewriters" they would be writing like them. But it was give and take. Sartre wrote that "the politics of Stalinist Communism are incompatible with the honest exercise of the literary profession." He argued that Stalinism had rendered Marxism sterile, because you cannot turn "dialectics into formulae for catechism." His monthly magazine, *Les Temps modernes*, did admit that "there is no Socialism when one citizen out of twenty is in a camp." Indeed, for a time Sartre and other leftists tried to create their own movement, for a Socialist Europe separate from the Soviet Union as well as the United States. It was only in 1951–52 that he chose sides.

The last days of Stalin's reign, with ghastly trials in Eastern Europe, may not have been the best period for conversion, but with the Korean War, the witch hunts, and the hardening of lines on both sides, this was a time when choice was thrust upon people. Sartre reacted to the demonstration against NATO commander General Matthew Ridgway, smashed in Paris by the police, with his famous "an anti-Communist is a dog." His basic premise at the time was that the Communist Party was the only revolutionary representative of the French working class and that the Soviet Union was a Socialist state in need of repair (*en panne*). He then wrote a pamphlet in honor of a French Communist sailor resisting the French invasion of Indochina; he spoke at the peace congress in Vienna in 1952; he also traveled to Russia and wrote things that he should not have: for instance, that "freedom of criticism there was complete." Yet, even then, collaboration between Sartre and the Communists was mutually suspicious, and it broke off in 1956, when Soviet tanks entered Budapest. Sartre then proclaimed that he would sever links with Soviet writers who did not condemn this massacre; "as to the men who at this time direct the French C.P., it is not, and it would never be, possible to resume relations."

Never say never. Circumstances altered. There was some hope of a thaw in the Soviet Union and Eastern Europe and the putsch that brought de Gaulle to power in 1958. Add the anticolonial struggle (Sartre discovered Castro's Cuba and wrote the violent preface to Frantz Fanon's *The Wretched of the Earth*), especially the war in Algeria, during which, incidentally, Sartre's Paris flat was blown up by rightist OAS thugs. And, so, he reappeared on common platforms with Communists and resumed his fairly frequent journeys to the Soviet Union. (We now know that these visits also had a sentimental reason: his beautiful translator and guide, Lena Zonina.) But the collaboration was always strained, since Sartre was no man to march to a party line. For instance, he signed and published in his journal the famous "Manifesto of the 121," approving the desertion of French soldiers in the Algerian War, whereas the C.P. was against it. But the final break came in 1968: In May, the student demonstrations and the strikes ultimately convinced Sartre that the French C.P. was not a revolutionary force. In August, the tanks entering Prague persuaded him that the Soviet Union and its bloc needed much, much more than repairs. He ceased to believe in its progressive function.

Sartre was thrilled by the radical spirit of French students and young workers, and this prompted his Maoist phase. He didn't quite share all the mad ideas of his protégés; ideologically, he was closer to the *Il Manifesto* group, the left-wing dissidents from the Italian C.P. But he duly protected his French favorites, taking up the title of editor of a paper whenever his predecessor was indicted or imprisoned (and de Gaulle had the wit to tell his subordinates that "one does not jail Voltaire") or selling the Maoist weekly *La Cause du Peuple* in the street. But when his comrades advised him to write populist novels, he stuck to his "bourgeois" task—the unfinished Flaubert. Then in 1975 came the terrible tragedy—full blindness. Sartre could still sign petitions and give interviews, but real creation was over.

After this thumbnail sketch, we can face the three political prosecutors. The first two can be dismissed quickly. Denis Bertholet is the author of a biography full of facts; since his purpose is not pamphleteering, one wonders why he picked Sartre as a subject, so obvious is his allergy to his hero's political philosophy (when he gets interested in Marxism, "he gets down on his knees"; and the mood of the Russell tribunal, presided over by Sartre, which investigated U.S. war crimes in Vietnam, is described as quasi-Fascist in its treatment of the "American scapegoat"). Michel-Antoine Burnier is a former groupie (to walk with Sartre to the newsstand, he recalls, was like going up the Champs-Elysées with Brigitte Bardot) who, now repentant, insists on Sartre's one-sidedness and repeats the hackneyed catalogue of things Sartre should have said and didn't, or vice versa.

It is best to tackle Bernard-Henri Lévy, known for publicity's sake as "BHL." As one of the inventors of the "new philosophy," he was the enemy of engagement, but now he describes this century as belonging to Sartre. He is visibly fond of the man and, inevitably, impressed by the extraordinary fame achieved before the full reign of television.

This time BHL has done his homework. He shows us how Sartre picked from Kierkegaard, Husserl, or Heidegger whatever he found useful for his own phenomenology. BHL actually portrays two Sartres. One is the good man—the author of *Nausea* and *Being and Nothingness*—who cares about freedom and does not give a damn about the world. The second, the villain, wants to improve mankind and, in so doing, becomes the servant of the totalitarians. Naturally, the story has shades and even a happy ending. You may remember that the blind Sartre had as his reader and companion Pierre Victor, *aka* Benny Levy. This former Maoist leader was in the process of conversion from the Little Red Book to the Talmud. They even produced a joint text just before Sartre's death. BHL sees in it the makings of a Jewish Sartre, following in the footsteps of Emmanuel Lévinas.

There is another Parisian paradox in the book. Whatever his politics now, BHL still claims as his great master Louis Althusser, the best-known French Communist philosopher. He even argues that Sartre went wrong when he abandoned the Althusserian "anti-humanism." Be that as it may, Althusser was a party cardholder throughout his political life, whereas Sartre was never a member of the C.P. and, as seen, could not even be described as a real fellow-traveler. Why, then, is the master spared, while Sartre is described as "a fanatic," "a preacher of voluntary servitude," suffering from "totalitarian delirium"? The trouble is, all these indictments are written outside historical context. *Vae victis*: This is the story as written by the victors. What happened had to happen. One does not even contemplate, for instance, whether—with a different policy from above and pressure from below—the course of events might have been different in the Soviet area.

And the victors are also morally right. When the knights of cultural freedom meet in Berlin at the time of the Korean War, they are splendid, and it in no way disturbs our authors that they were financed by the CIA. They cannot even understand why Sartre was always worried that his action might help the "other side." There is no other side. When BHL proclaims that Marxism is dead and the evil spirit of revolution buried forever, he does not mean that Stalinist theology is in the historical dustbin where it properly belongs or that the radical transformation of society will now have to take a different form from the storming of the Winter Palace. He means that we must be content with small changes and that the reign of capital is eternal. Our new literary dandies do shed tears for victims in one place or another. Unkind critics suggest that they do so only if TV cameras are nearby and if it does not disturb the establishment. But even if we assume that they are genuinely grieved by the millions of children who die through sickness or starvation, it will never cross their minds to question the system that produces such results. No wonder they cannot understand Sartre's struggle and his hatred for his own class.

One quality BHL cannot be denied is his sense of the coming fashion. He claims that he started this book five years ago, that is to say, immediately after the strikes and demonstrations that shook France in 1995. By then, the "new philosophy" was old hat, and clearly something more than the gulag was needed to persuade the French people to resign themselves to their fate. But he wrote it before Seattle, which suggests that sooner or later there may be an international search for an alternative society. Only when this happens shall we see books doing justice to Sartre. I don't mean hagiographies—there will be full portraits, with warts and all. Thus, from documents published we now know that the famous couple was not quite as ideal as it was painted. There will be questions about the identification of Socialism with the Soviet Union and about Sartre's coolness toward left-wing critics of Stalinism. One will have to reexamine the many quarrels, including the most famous break, with Albert Camus in 1952. Retrospectively, there is no doubt that Camus had more sensitivity, more sympathy for the victims of Soviet repression; yet when it came closer to home, during the Algerian War, it was not Sartre "the politician" but the moralist Camus who claimed—when getting his Nobel in Stockholm—"I believe in justice, but I will put my mother before justice."

Above all, there will be the inner contradictions between Sartre's original philosophy and its further development, illustrated by the fact that he never published *Morale,* which was to follow *Being and Nothingness,* or the promised second volume of his *Critique of Dialectical Reason.* But out of all these contradictions will emerge the picture of a small man of tremendous vitality, extraordinary generosity, and real grandeur. It will also show the tragic dilemma, in the second half of the twentieth century, of a leftist who wanted to change things at home, where the bulk of the working class voted Communist, and in the world, where for all its ambiguity the Soviet Union was the only brake on U.S. imperialism. To be active while saying a plague on both their houses was not easy at the time.

Yet this, however interesting, is history. The Soviet Union, with its subordinate Communist parties, is gone. But we still have plenty to learn from Sartre the freedom fighter, Sartre the activist, who told writers that "to keep quiet is not to be mute; it is to refuse to speak and hence to speak in a way." In the years after the "demo against his death," intellectuals abandoned politics, particularly progressive politics, and not only in France. Now there are some hopeful signs of a move in the opposite direction. Sartre the champion of commitment still has plenty to teach us as we resume our advance along the Roads (plural on purpose) to Freedom, *Les Chemins de la liberté.*

Letters from Europe

::

The Politics and the Pity

MAY 12, 1979
The Nation

"WE ARE ALL German Jews" chanted fifty thousand Frenchmen at the gates of the Bastille in 1968; I was recently reminded of this episode, which has become revolutionary lore, when *Holocaust* was shown here. Seven out of ten French viewers followed the saga of the Weiss family on their television screens, even though here as everywhere, progressive critics tore the show to pieces. But the questionable mixture of commercial TV serial and inhuman atrocity, of family life and horror, gripped millions, provoking polemics in French newspapers, magazines, and private homes. The exceedingly passionate nature of the stir was predictable and that is why the French government, jealous master of its TV, was very reluctant to broadcast *Holocaust* and did so only under strong pressure.

And why was the French government so worried by a serial describing only German atrocities? Because it does not want the country to awaken from the collective amnesia affecting a dark period of its recent past, the five years of Vichy and collaboration. Or, to be more accurate, it wants to preserve the legend that France, with a few exceptions, was on the side of the angels. This myth was constructed immediately after the war on the basis of a simple syllogism: de Gaulle was a resister; de Gaulle is France; hence, France was a nation of resistance. And everybody, for different reasons, played a part in this mystification.

The Gaullists did so not only because it enhanced the stature of their legendary hero. As resisters they were, in a sense, both traitors to and saviors of their class. The bulk of the French bourgeoisie had backed Vichy wholeheartedly. Some businessmen collaborated actively with the Germans in keeping with the slogan of the thirties: *"Plutôt Hitler que le front populaire"* ("Rather Hitler than the Popular Front"). Others merely welcomed Marshal Pétain as the current symbol of law and order. Naturally, there were many exceptions and these temporary outcasts rallied around de Gaulle. After the war, and facing strong pressures from the underground for a radical overhaul, the Gaullists were only too glad to purge individuals while preserving the system.

The Left acquiesced for more pedestrian reasons, because it had its own black sheep and its own skeletons in the cupboard. The Socialists preferred to forget that many of their deputies had voted the full powers for Pétain. The Communists did not wish to remember that they became the main force within the Resistance movement only after 1941, i.e., *after* the German invasion of Russia. Some people argue that this mythmaking was an inevitable contribution to national unity. National unity, however, is often achieved at the expense of political consciousness. The Left, having then forgotten its motto about truth being always revolutionary, has been paying the price for its complicity ever since.

Conservative France required the myth and the mystification to reforge its unity just as it needs them now to preserve it. When General de Gaulle was brought back to power by the Algerian colonels in 1958, most former supporters of Vichy climbed on his bandwagon. I remember a French friend protesting indignantly at the time that his in-laws, who had a portrait of Pétain over their mantelpiece during the war, put a picture of General de Gaulle in its place; in his indignation, my friend overlooked their consistency. Ten years later, in May 1968, as society was threatened by the students' rebellion and the workers' strike, conservative France rallied, once again, around the general. In their big procession up the Champs-Elysées, former Resistance leaders marched in front, while neo-Nazis in the back chanted: "Cohn-Bendit to Dachau."

(For those who may have forgotten: Daniel Cohn-Bendit was a colorful student leader, Jewish and German by accident, whose expulsion from France prompted thousands of young Frenchmen to proclaim themselves German Jews.) I am not suggesting that none of the pro-Gaullist marchers was shocked by the ghastly slogan, yet, when it was reported in the press, none of them uttered publicly a word of protest. In the hour of danger, the Right could not afford the luxury of morality at the risk of dissension, and today, still under pressure, it tries to complete its reconciliation. Giscard d'Estaing is the open champion of such reconciliation even if, for the time being, he cannot crown it spectacularly by burying Pétain at Verdun, the site of his World War I exploits. The country is still too deeply divided and the memories too fresh for that.

Everything is being done, meanwhile, to let bygones be bygones. For a projected BBC program on how World War II is being taught in the schools of various countries, I had to look over several French textbooks the other day. In five out of six, you get quite a good account of the twists and turnings of that conflict, but only the haziest picture of Vichy France, with its misguided old man (Pétain), its villain (Laval), its hero (de Gaulle), and its united nation which, after some early misgivings, rallied massively around the hero of the Resistance. No wonder that *The Sorrow and the Pity*, the Marcel Ophuls film reviving through documents and interviews the real atmosphere of that period, produced such a shock when it was shown in a Paris cinema; children stunned by their discovery began asking their parents questions about the past and their past. No wonder either that this brilliant documentary, produced for TV back in 1970, has not been shown on French television. The television in France is state-owned and is very much its master's voice. The government had no wish to show to a mass audience such an iconoclastic performance.

With *Holocaust* the authorities were rather lucky. The TV program in which it was shown, *Les Dossiers de l'écran*, usually combines a film with a live debate. At the time, however, a television strike was on and nothing could be filmed live. The debate was thus limited to the last episode and it was properly stage-managed. Though twenty persons were invited to take part, the limelight was clearly focused on Simone Veil, the minister of health. Madame Veil is undoubtedly the most popular member of the ruling coalition and had just been chosen by Giscard d'Estaing to head the list bearing his colors in the forthcoming elections. She is elegant, has charm and personality. She also has tragically valid credentials to participate in the discussion. In 1944, at the age of sixteen, she was deported with her whole family and lost her parents and a brother in the death camps. As expected, she dominated the debate with dignity, understanding, and tact. Everything thus worked well until almost the last moment when a youth, invited to represent the rising generation, asked her point-blank: "Why does your government tolerate that a man who had aided and abetted the Nazis should be the major press lord in France?" Mme. Veil then lost her temper and her poise and accused the youngster of asking irrelevant questions, and the young in general of "confusing issues."

A word of explanation is needed here. The man at issue is Robert Hersant. During the war, he was a leader of a small but rabidly pro-Nazi group. He vituperated against the Jews at a time when words were deadly weapons and, after the war, was sentenced to "national indignity." But a great deal of water has flowed under the bridges of Paris since then: Today, Hersant (*Le Canard Enchaîné*, the satirical weekly, always spells his name Herr Sant, so as not to forget his political origins) has a controlling interest in three major national dailies: the popular *France-Soir*, the once respectable *Le Figaro*, and the middle-class *L'Aurore*. He also owns a host of provincial papers and knows on which side his bread is buttered. He was a friend of Jacques Chirac. He and his papers are now wholeheartedly for Giscard d'Estaing. Mme. Veil found it awkward to condemn publicly such a powerful ally.

Whatever she may say, past and present are deeply intertwined. Indeed, *Holocaust* would probably not have been shown in France but for the uproar provoked by a scandal at the close of last year. The Paris weekly *L'Express* chose then, presumably for commercial reasons, to splash an interview with a certain Darquier de Pellepoix. That honorable gentleman was Vichy's commissioner for Jewish affairs. Sheltered all this time in Franco's Spain, he had learned nothing and forgotten nothing. Whereas in France today, except in the gutter Fascist press, racists must take precautions, proceed by allusions and innuendoes, the unrepentant criminal spoke with the xenophobic venom of the good old days of collaboration. Too much was too much. M. Hersant's papers joined in the chorus of indignation over his indecency. If they thought that stirring up old memories would create trouble, they were right. Former resisters, victims of concentration camps, and plain liberals raised their voices asking for truth, the full horrible truth.

In the pandemonium it was discovered that other men who had presided over the deportation of Jews from France were still at large. It turned out that a M. Jean Leguay, head of police in occupied France, was living in Paris on a pension as a retired civil servant and apparently adding to his income by working for American companies. In the private proceedings started since then by the families of some Jewish victims, it is being alleged that M. Leguay not only negotiated the deportation of Jews with the Nazis but also showed zeal in his collaboration. Where the Germans asked for the adults, the French offered them the children as an additional gift, at a time when death was the only possible destination. It was also discovered that his former superior in the Vichy hierarchy, a M. René Bousquet, was now the honorable adviser to an important merchant bank (*was* because after the outcry he had to resign under threat from the labor unions) and had been on the board of the internal French airlines, a state company headed by Antoine Veil, the husband of the lady minister. Indeed, gossip has it that he occasionally attended the smart dinner parties given by the Veils. Here one's mind boggles: What sort of striped ghosts hovered over their banquets?

History has these cruel ironies as well as lessons that are seldom learned. At the anti-racist meetings I have attended here since the airing of *Holocaust*, the young were most firmly opposed to commemoration for its own sake. They want memory to be used as a weapon. In their passion, they may occasionally forget the specificity of the genocide of the Jews. Yet, fundamentally, they are right in their emphasis on the universality and the permanence of the disease. Anti-Jewish scribblings on the walls, occasional attacks against a synagogue, the fact that the dean of a faculty of medicine in Paris has just dared to proclaim himself a racist and a Nazi (even though he had to resign immediately)—all these are disquieting signs. But anti-Semitism is not, or not yet, the main symptom in France. The same newspapers, the same interests, the same people, or their successors, have for the moment picked foreign workers as their main target. A burglary, a rape, a mugging is for them a good occasion to conjure up the shadowy figure of a "dark-skinned foreigner." They put the blame for unemployment, for the overcrowding in schools and hospitals, on the "foreign invasion." They stir up hatred, appealing to man's most irrational fears and his basest instincts. Racism is a many-headed hydra.

As the crisis deepens in Europe and unemployment rises, we must be lucid and vigilant if we don't want the middle classes first, and then entire nations, to run amok once again. Whatever her ladyship may preach from her ministerial pulpit, the young are right in "confusing issues." It can happen here, it can happen anywhere, and it is not just a question of German Jews. Come to think of it, when the thousands of young Frenchmen proclaimed their German Jewishness I stood in the crowd next to Aimé Césaire, the great poet from Martinique, who, made this caustic comment, "I am willing to shout, but nobody will believe me." Aimé Césaire is black.

Imagination Has Not Yet Taken Power

JANUARY 29, 1983
The Nation

"WHAT HAS HAPPENED to your 'Socialist' France? Is it going the way of all social-democratic flesh?"

Because I live in Paris I am asked such questions frequently by sympathetic American friends and by skeptical Brits who remember their own experiences under a Socialist government. I could easily avoid this debate by pointing out that I was among the doubters in the heady days following François Mitterrand's victory in May 1981, but I think these questions should be tackled for a number of reasons.

France, with its tradition of upheaval, is different from Harold Wilson's Britain. Mitterrand's experiment, far from finished, has not yet reached the point of no return. Most important, the international economic climate is not at all what it was in the sixties. As a result of the Right's failure to cope with the current European economic crisis, the Socialists have been given a chance in Athens and Madrid as well as in Paris: If the reformist Left, in turn, proves unable to cope, the consequences could be grave.

In fairness, it must be stressed from the first that the French Socialists' record is not entirely negative. They began by abolishing the death penalty, granting residence and labor permits to illegal immigrants, and clearing the air of the pollution left from years of "law and order" rhetoric. Also, at a time when the welfare state is increasingly under attack, they raised the legal minimum wage, boosted substantially the family allowance, and augmented other social benefits. They outlined plans for a gradual transition to a thirty-five-hour workweek and for retirement with a full pension at age sixty. They also passed legislation providing for an additional week of vacation. Yes, it must be repeated to incredulous Americans, all working people in France are entitled by law to five weeks of holiday with pay. (This, incidentally, was a Popular Front invention. Two weeks of paid holiday for all was granted by the Léon Blum government in 1936.)

Domestic critics, members of the previous government, who are partially responsible for the present mess, and monetarists the world over can be silenced fairly easily. These champions of economic stagnation and mass unemployment have no lessons to offer. Besides, the disasters that the Right predicted would ensue upon the admission of four Communists into the French government haven't happened. In Paris, natives and tourists are still sipping drinks at Fouquet's, and sales of Rolls-Royces in France, according to Le Monde, went from fifty-two in 1981 to eighty-one in the first nine months of 1982. Civilization is safe.

More seriously, Mitterrand's France does not compare unfavorably economically with its neighbors. The gross national product has grown slightly less slowly (0.3 percent in 1981 and 1 percent in 1982) than those of most of its Common Market partners and unemployment has grown less rapidly. With 8 percent of the labor force jobless, France's unemployment rate is well below Britain's and no longer higher than West Germany's. Finally, the rate of inflation has been brought down, admittedly with the aid of a price and wage freeze, to just under two figures.

These facts are good for scoring debater's points, but they tell only half the story. The prospects for rising employment and expansion are now bleak. Particularly since the second devaluation of the franc, last June, there has been a clear shift in the Mitterrand government's emphasis from social justice to price stability, from equality to profitability. Taking its supporters for granted, the government has been trying, with predictable lack of success, to woo investors, domestic and foreign.

How did it all happen so quickly? The Socialists, on taking office, hoped to revive the economy by putting more money in consumers' pockets. The rise in wages, the expansion of social benefits, and the budget deficit were all designed to boost consumption, which, in turn, would spur production and stimulate investment. But as the government had not altered the rules of the game in any fundamental way and had left trade barriers down, the main result of its policies was to increase imports. The trade deficit rose spectacularly. The gnomes of Zürich and other financial capitals, distrustful of a Socialist government, however moderate, had good reasons to speculate against the franc. After little resistance, the French government was driven toward economic orthodoxy and policies more acceptable to the international financial establishment.

Mitterrand's managers of the economy were a trifle unlucky. They had been banking on a general economic recovery throughout the West in vain. Instead, they discovered the difficulty of a situation in which "everyone is out of step but our Johnny." The high international interest rates did not help, and the dramatic rise of the dollar added a lot to the French import bill.

Yet, the basic reason for France's troubles was to be found elsewhere. The Socialists were seeking to cure the mild disease of yesterday. They did not recognize that the extraordinary quarter of a century of relative stability and prosperity of the capitalist system—based on the spread of durable consumer goods, on increased state intervention, and on military expenditures—was over. Faced with this new crisis, capitalists in Britain and the United States dropped all pretense of consensus and launched an all-out attack on the Labor movement. Mitterrand's economic advisers, in the same circumstances, chose to revive Keynesianism. Their failure is not the failure of Socialism, which has not even been tried. It is simply proof that Keynesian methods are inadequate when the capitalist crisis becomes really serious.

It might be objected that the French experiment, involving an enlargement of the public sector and the spread of new rights to the workers, cannot be described as pure Keynesianism, and, in a sense, that is true. In keeping with his campaign pledges, Mitterrand's government has duly nationalized seven major industrial groups in electronics, engineering, petrochemicals, and military equipment. It has taken over the ailing steel industry, the joint-stock banks that were still in private hands, and the two big *banques d'affaires*, the Paribas and the Suez. It is too early to say what impact the expanded public sector will have on the French economy. But it can already be asserted that the whole operation is not designed to strike at the heart of capitalism—to alter fundamentally the traditional relations between owners and workers. On the contrary, nationalization is conceived of as a sanction: The state intervenes in areas where private enterprise has proved unwilling to invest or incapable of competing in international markets. It is in this sense that French nationalization follows an essentially Keynesian strategy.

The measures taken to increase the power of the workers have been similarly limited. The provisions of the so-called Auroux bill, which bears the name of the Socialist minister of labor, have reduced the power of the bosses in the factories by granting employees the right to be informed about and consulted on certain matters. But so far they have not radically altered labor relations or made them qualitatively different from those in neighboring countries. Indeed, critics have suggested that the Auroux bill did more to antagonize employers than it did to please the workers or significantly shift the balance of power in the factories. It must be added, however, that the government never seriously claimed that the legislation would bring about a democratic revolution on the shop floor. A left-wing government coming into office after twenty-three years of conservative rule could have acted quite differently. It might have addressed its supporters as follows: "Though the years ahead will be tough and we will have little to parcel out, we do have our common vision and we should at least begin to implement this joint project. We can raise the wages only of those on the bottom of the scale, while lowering the highest salaries. Otherwise, from a slowly growing national economic pie, there will be little surplus to distribute. But we can start a gradual transfer of power to the workers in factories and offices. Our ultimate objective is a free association of producers, a society in which working people are the masters of their own destiny. Meanwhile, during the transitional period, let us determine together how to change our work and our lives. We also need your wholehearted support to stand up to the inevitable counteroffensive of capital."

This would have been the language of a leadership dedicated to forging a unified political coalition capable of long-term action. But such language would have provoked a strong reaction, and it is not surprising that Mitterrand chose instead the classless message of national unity.

When leftist governments feel compelled to take a conservative line, reporters rush to write about the clash between dream and reality. In France, the cliché is even more inappropriate than usual. Dreaming is conspicuously absent from the current French experiment. Indeed, it is difficult to recall that less than fifteen years ago, during the May uprising, Paris was in ferment with ideas on new ways of producing and consuming. The rebels acted as though they had reinvented life and love. Actually, there may be a link between the not-so-Utopian dreaming of yesterday and the apparent realism of today. After the unexpected uprising of students and workers in May 1968, the task of the French Left, Communists and Socialists alike, was to persuade its supporters that although a radical break with the past was impossible, steady improvements in living standards under a left-wing government would greatly alter their condition. But by the time the Left was able to guide the revolutionary fervor into electoral channels, a generation of rising prosperity had come to an end throughout the Western world.

Strange as it may seem, the Left has never pondered publicly the political consequences of this economic downturn. When the Socialists and Communists elaborated their "common program" in 1972 or, two years later, when Giscard d'Estaing defeated Mitterrand narrowly for the presidency, the economic crisis was not a major issue. In 1977 and 1978, when the Left appeared to have victory within its grasp, it staged something that sounded like a parody of a debate on the subject. The Communists painted the future in terms of a Japanese-style growth rate, thus evading the problem. Michel Roccard, today's minister of planning, hinted that as the means had diminished, one should scale down the ends, while Mitterrand, like all astute politicians, preferred to postpone decisions till after the elections. After the Communists chose to split with the Socialists rather than join them as junior partners, the Left managed to snatch defeat from the jaws of victory. Its supporters were stunned, and since there was no longer any search for a joint program, there was no need to discuss the crisis. Victory came in 1981 as a "divine surprise," a gift from heaven.

A huge electoral victory that was unrelated to any important social movement—this may be the historians' verdict on the latest Socialist success in France. When the Popular Front was swept into office in 1936, its triumph was hailed by workers occupying factories. On the night of Mitterrand's victory, young people stormed the Place de la Bastille to dance and lightheartedly berate the *ci-devant* Elkabbach and Mougeotte, the now-forgotten TV personalities of the ancient regime. Absence of support by an open social movement gives a left-wing government room to maneuver, as it can generally rely on the sympathy of the labor unions. The disadvantages, however, are much greater. Lack of pressure also means lack of passionate support, which is indispensable for intimidating the opposition. In 1936, big business pleaded with Blum to make a deal with the workers, whatever the price; all that mattered was to salvage the system. Following Mitterrand's election, business, big and small, has remained unfrightened.

The Socialists were well aware how great an asset a social movement could be. Yet they did nothing to encourage its development because of their reluctance to antagonize business. One recent incident will serve to illustrate the point. Addressing a rally of business leaders, Jacques Delors, the minister of finance, made a surprise announcement that the real minimum wage would not be raised by 4 percent in 1983, as had been promised, but only by 3 percent. The change, though not big enough to alter the government's economic planning, did anger its supporters, particularly those who had been justifying austerity measures on egalitarian grounds. But the timing of Delors's announcement had a symbolic purpose. It was intended to show that this government is orthodox, reasonable, and ready to defy its own supporters.

Since this letter seems to have become an indictment, I had better add some qualifications. The situation in France is not a repetition of the Harold Wilson story in Britain, with its surrenders and betrayals. Mitterrand did not promise any revolutionary change and has, so far, kept most of his campaign pledges. The story, rather, is one of anachronistic platforms and obsolete remedies. Capitalism was so successful for a quarter of a century that most of the Left, including Western Communists, were converted to some version of reformism. But the Socialists in France were voted into office at a time when capitalism had plunged into a crisis that, by its very nature, was a crisis of reformism as well. Today, it would be more realistic to tackle the problems raised by the May "utopians" fifteen years ago—what growth, for what purpose, in whose interest?—than to follow the "realists," who are unable to imagine anything beyond the confines of existing society, with its prospects of greater exploitation and higher unemployment.

Naturally, the search for a radical alternative would be merely a beginning. There are a host of questions to be answered about the nature of a different society and how to construct it. How would the people express their deep aspirations and shape them into a policy? How would a measure of planning, necessary to coordinate change, be combined with power at the grass roots—centralism with genuine democracy? Could a country like France start the experiment on its own? How long could French Socialism last without a European contagion, and to what extent could it afford to forgo some of the advantages of the international division of labor? With the Soviet model derailed and the Western model, once praised for its "permanent motion," running obviously out of steam, the Left must embark on an uncharted road and show an extraordinary capacity for invention. I am not condemning the French for not providing all the answers, merely suggesting that they are not asking any of the right questions. With the Socialists paralyzed by the prerogatives of power ("office" might be the more accurate word), the Communists dizzied by a series of volte-faces, and the New Left totally absent, as if the May Movement had no children at all, one may put it nostalgically: Imagination has not seized power in Paris so far.

Paris, Athens, Madrid today, and possibly Lisbon tomorrow—everywhere the bankruptcy of the Right paves the way for Socialists, for reformers who will be faced with the same dilemma as the French. Admittedly, in a Spain just emerging from the Franco nightmare or a Greece run previously by all sorts of colonels, the Socialists must also liberalize the country, perform the task of the bourgeois revolution. Yet, fundamentally, their problem is the same as in other Socialist countries. When the Left advances boldly on the economic front, reshaping society, it can be brilliantly libertarian. When it retreats, it can be reduced to cheap electioneering and mean concessions. On law and order, on immigrant workers, on the rights of women, the official mood in Paris is no longer what it used to be.

But the pendulum has not swung completely the other way either. The worst is never a certainty. If the government forgets the class struggle, the employers do not. The unions backing the government will begin losing votes in factory elections. The goodwill of the workers will not be eternal. And there is François Mitterrand, too, determined to leave his mark on history, and he knows he cannot do so by following in Harold Wilson's footsteps. In this rather lengthy and gloomy letter, I have tried to paint the whole canvas and stress the dilemma. In future letters, I shall fill in the gaps with more specific and, possibly, more hopeful messages. The only thing I promise is to attempt, then as now, not to present my dreams as French or European reality.

The Resistible Rise of Jean-Marie Le Pen

SEPTEMBER 7, 1985
The Nation

Paris

HISTORY, *PACE* HEGEL and Marx, need not repeat itself as farce. When the French Right blames bloody immigrants and the Reds in the Mitterrand government for growing unemployment, memories of the thirties send shivers down the spine. Admittedly, the jobless are not as numerous today as they were then and their fate is not quite the same. There are also some encouraging signs of reaction on the Left—for example, the Woodstock-like rally in the heart of Paris on June 15 which drew some three hundred thousand youngsters to the Place de la Concorde to listen to rock groups and comedians under the anti-racist banner of the "Hands Off My Pal" campaign. But before assessing the possibilities of a reversal, one must look at the grim tide itself, and especially at Jean-Marie Le Pen, the man whose name is synonymous with the recent revival of overt racism in French politics and society.

He no longer wears a black patch over his left eye, which he lost in a political brawl. It made him look less like a pirate than like the thug he has been throughout his adult life. Smiling, smartly dressed, he now seems—particularly on television, where he is on his best behavior—a frank and reasonable fellow saying aloud "what everybody really believes," telling people "what they already know," a man who merely echoes the basic precept of that great American Ronald Reagan:

namely, that Communism is the root of all evil. A red-faced, rather fat man who warns the "silent majority" against muggers, drug addicts, gays, and crypto-pinkos, Le Pen might be described as a sort of French Spiro Agnew preaching law and order, except that he is not of Greek or any other foreign extraction. That is an important difference, because the man and the movement he leads, the National Front, trumpet the slogan "Frenchmen First" and spread the fairy tale that everything would be fine in the streets and hospitals, in the schools and even the factories were it not for the foreign hordes invading France, particularly those crossing the Mediterranean. France would be just marvelous without Marxists, Arabs, and other aliens.

Jean-Marie Le Pen was born fifty-seven years ago in Brittany. The orphaned son of a fisherman, he came to Paris to study law and rapidly became notorious in the Latin Quarter as a Red-baiter and an active participant in drunken or political brawls. He completed his education as a soldier, going to Indochina with the paratroopers of the Foreign Legion after the French defeat at Dien Bien Phu. At the age of twenty-six and back in Paris, he was elected to Parliament as a member of a political movement whose rise helps us understand the current success of the National Front.

The fifties in France saw the beginning of mass migration from the countryside and of industrial as well as commercial concentration in the cities. Since nobody likes to be eliminated, even in the name of economic progress, the traders, craftsmen, and other victims of the squeeze rebelled. Their discontent was exploited by a shopkeeper from southern France who cleverly put the blame for their misfortunes on eggheads, tax collectors, and Jewish-owned big business. His name was Pierre Poujade. To everybody's surprise, his movement, a seven-day wonder, gained nearly 11 percent of the vote in the 1956 elections and more than two score deputies. Le Pen, an unscrupulous but efficient demagogue, was for a while Poujade's lieutenant, and in the Parliament he expressed his distaste for racial impurity with this oft-quoted apostrophe to Prime Minister Pierre Mendès-France, a Jew: "You crystallize in your person a certain number of patriotic and almost physical repulsions."

In 1957, a year after the elections, Le Pen split with Poujade and turned his attention to the colonial war in Algeria, volunteering for service as a paratrooper. Herein lies another clue to his present support: He has the backing of European settlers who fled to France when Algeria won its independence. Recently a skeleton was taken out of his closet: *Le Canard Enchâné* provided chapter and verse showing that, among other exploits, Le Pen had been an active performer in the torture chamber at the notorious Villa Susini, in Algeria, where instruments ranged from old-fashioned whips to modern electrical gadgets. A story in *Libération*, drawing on Algerian witnesses, accused him of acting as an executioner. Le Pen sued both publications for libel, but they won. The judge reasoned that you couldn't defend the principle of the use of torture in Algeria, as Le Pen had done, and be libeled when accused of putting the principle into practice. Le Pen had argued not that the facts were wrong but that his honor had been impugned.

For the extreme Right, the war in Algeria was a high-water mark. The chief beneficiary of their struggle, however, was General Charles de Gaulle, who took advantage of the 1958 political crisis to bring down the tottering Fourth Republic. When he sought to extricate himself from the colonial mess, the European settlers in Algeria and the military barons who had made him king felt betrayed. They formed the Secret Army Organization (OAS) and succeeded in spreading terror in Algeria and even in exporting it to France. The tide of popular opinion was flowing against the OAS, however, and Le Pen was clever enough not to tie himself too closely to a loser. But there was no doubt about his feelings. In 1965, three years after Algeria won independence, he served as campaign manager for Jean-Louis Tixier-Vignacourt, a presidential candidate who sought to unite the mourners of *Algérie Française* with older fragments of French reaction. Tixier-Vignacourt, who had been the chief attorney for the OAS leaders and a former junior minister in Marshal Pétain's Vichy government during World War II, symbolized the union of colonialism and collaboration. This mixture brought him no more than 5 percent of the votes cast, the high point of the Far Right's support for several years to come.

For Le Pen, those were lean years. Having lost his seat in the National Assembly, he had to earn a living. With some colleagues, he set up a company specializing in historical phonograph records, mainly of military songs. They were sued and fined under France's anti-racist laws because the liner notes on an album of Nazi songs described Hitler's movement as "on the whole popular and democratic." Politically, things were hardly better. Fascist thugs were swept out of their favorite Latin Quarter haunts by the mass student movement in 1968. Four years later, the various extremist sects of the Right merged to form the National Front. Le Pen, the least disreputable of the lot, was chosen to be their leader, but their electoral strength was still measured in fractions of a percentage point.

Then came a stroke of good fortune. A degenerate, or shall we say worthy, heir of an industrial empire (the Lambert cement company) died young, leaving his fortune to the leader of the National Front. Part of the family wanted to fight the will on the ground that its author was of unsound mind, but an out-of-court settlement in 1977 gave Le Pen a mansion on the outskirts of Paris and enough money not to have to worry about financial matters. In fairness, it should be said that prosperity did not weaken his political appetite, though the fat years were still to come. In the 1974 presidential poll, won narrowly by Valéry Giscard d'Estaing, Le Pen obtained 0.75 percent of the vote. Seven years later, when François Mitterrand triumphed, Le Pen could not even find the number of elected officials required in France to sponsor a presidential candidacy. The economic crisis of the seventies helped spread xenophobia, preparing the ground for the National Front. But the victory of the left in the 1981 elections and its subsequent failure to cope with the crisis was necessary before Le Pen could take off.

The French Right, deprived of the spoils after twenty-three years in office, was desperate to return to power. When the euphoria of the Socialist victory dissipated after a year, the Right hit back without scruple, pandering to fears and prejudices. After a quarter-century of heedless urban development, the cities were coming apart at the seams. Growing unemployment had, predictably, fostered petty crime and a general feeling of insecurity. These were attributed to the Left and its "lax" Minister of Justice Robert Badinter, in particular. Although during the previous two decades the Right had presided over the mass importation of cheap foreign labor, it placed blame for the immigrants "grabbing your jobs" squarely on the shoulders of France's "Marxist" rulers. It is well known, after all, that the "Reds," like the Labor Party in Britain, liberals in the United States, and Socialists in France, are nigger, Jew, and Arab lovers.

Orthodox conservatives, however unscrupulous, are not champions at this game. The National Front always stoops lower than they do. While conservatives criticize the minister of justice, the newspaper of the Front writes that he is "always for the marginal and against a society that had for a long time rejected the Badinters," and the reader translates: bloody foreign Jews. While the right talks of unemployment, the Front invents the absurd but eloquent equation "two million immigrant workers equals two million unemployed Frenchmen." And Le Pen speaks of invaders "who want to sleep in my bed, with my wife."

In the local elections of March 1983, the main theme was law and order. The National Front was probably the chief beneficiary of this issue, scoring well for the first time in many urban areas. Le Pen himself was elected to one of the twenty Town Halls of Paris. The turning point, however, came six months later, in the battle of Dreux, a small town northwest of Paris. The original vote was so close that another poll was ordered, and the National Front, with an openly racist platform, managed to capture 16.7 percent of the first-round vote. That was bad enough, but there was worse to come. As no side had gained an absolute majority, a second round was required, and between ballots the "respectable" Right welcomed members of the Front on its own list. Klan candidates on its ticket. Racism rewarded.

It must be granted that not all conservative politicians approved of this squalid arrangement. Simone Veil, a former president of the European Parliament and a survivor of a Nazi concentration camp, said that had she been a voter in Dreux, she would have abstained. Yet she did not resign from her party or from the right-wing coalition whose main leaders—the very distinguished Raymond Barre, Jacques Chirac, and Valéry Giscard d'Estaing—did not share her distaste. The late Raymond Aron, the famous sociologist who is now being hailed as a paragon of democratic conservatism, sided at the time with those who argued that to have four "quasi-Fascist" councilors in Dreux was nothing compared with having four "Red Fascists"—read Communist ministers—in the government. As Mark Antony would have put it, these are "honorable men"; indeed, one of them is certain to be the next conservative candidate for the presidency.

The label of respectability bestowed on the front had its obvious consequences. Its rating in opinion polls rose sharply. Le Pen became a popular guest on the talk shows and proved to be a clever performer. He knows how to hold back on television and then let loose at rallies of his own supporters. The reward came in June of last year. In the elections for the European Parliament the Front obtained nearly 11 percent of the vote (like Poujade in his time): that is to say, almost as much as the Communist Party. Ten National Front deputies now sit in the European assembly, next to their Italian comrades from Giorgio Almirante's neo-Fascist Italian Social Movement.

Nor was it a flash in the pan, as some had hoped, on the assumption that voters do not much care who sits in the European Parliament. In regional elections held earlier this year, the Front roughly equaled its June score, considering it did not put up candidates throughout the country. Indeed, it polled 20 to 30 percent of the vote in some towns on the French Riviera, in Marseilles, and in Montpellier. It did exceptionally well in regions where most of the French refugees from Algeria have settled. Now that the voting system for parliamentary elections has been switched to proportional representation, Le Pen and his gang are bound to win seats in the National Assembly next March. Indeed, some Socialists are relying on the threat of this to prevent a clear-cut verdict for the "respectable" Right.

The entry of avowed racists into the French Parliament is not in itself the worst prospect. As the old saying goes, "You don't bring the temperature down by breaking the thermometer." I am not even most shocked that in France today one person out of ten, one out of five in many places, votes for a party whose leader is an open defender of apartheid and an admirer of General Augusto Pinochet. More worrisome is the underlying ideological shift to the Right, the radical metamorphosis of the substance and form of political debate, of which this plague is only a symptom.

It will be objected that this is merely a revival, that anti-Semitism in France goes back to the last century, to the Dreyfus case and beyond, that in the thirties, Fascism paraded openly and racism was incomparably more virulent. True, but that was before the Holocaust. After that, for some thirty-five years, people didn't dare speak, or even think, in quite the same terms. Now they do again. Yesterday, they had to say, I am not a racist but . . . . Today they no longer take the precaution. And apparently decent people echo Le Pen almost unawares. To paraphrase Brecht, the "filthy beast" was not killed off in Nazi Germany. If we don't keep a watchful eye, it will pounce back on the political stage wherever it gets an opportunity.

In the Heart of
Le Pen Country

JUNE 18, 1988
The Nation

Marseilles, France

"IT CRIES IN my heart as it rains on the town," wrote Verlaine, and it was pouring over Marseilles as I arrived just before the Whitsun holiday. Then the mistral cleared the sky and the sun shone on all the celebrated landmarks: the vast avenue of the Canebière descending to the Old Harbor, the View Port itself, with its armada of small boats in white or blue, and the bigger ones taking the tourists to the Château d'If of Monte Cristo fame. But for all the fine weather, the time was for tears rather than smiles in Marcel Pagnol's country. With 102,541 of its 361,804 voters picking Jean-Marie Le Pen in the first presidential round in April, Marseilles, the old melting pot, the gateway to Africa and the Orient, has become the racist capital of Europe.

As last week's national elections approached, all the main leaders of Le Pen's xenophobic National Front swooped over the region, the department of Bouches-du-Rhône, like vultures in search of parliamentary seats. Le Pen himself picked the eighth district of Marseilles (where in April he had polled nearly 30 percent). But attention is already being focused beyond the current election, toward the Ides of March, the likely date of next year's poll for the Town Hall. Can a neo-Fascist become the mayor of France's second city? The very fact that the question can be raised requires a lot of explanation.

The Thug and the Politician

If you want to see a folkloric image of the danger, take the left side of the Old Harbor, move beyond the restaurants whose enterprising own-ers solicit you to taste their bouillabaisse, to the Bar des Yachts. You can't miss it: Posters of the leader are plastered all over with the now-obsolete stickers "Le Pen—President." On the left-hand side there is a symptomatic kitsch painting: a priest with a holy cross is exorcising a devil painted in red. So that the point should not be missed, the devil has 1789—the date of the French Revolution—scribbled on his back. The bar's owner, Dédé (short for Andrew), a man well known for his exploits with fists or gun, is well in line with the painting: "It's the Alamo here. Only instead of being on the defensive, we shall attack." Then, changing periods and metaphors: "Charles Martel [who stopped the Arabs near Poitiers in the seventh century]—that's kid stuff. It's from here that the great anti-Islamic crusade will start . . . " The cus-tomers, who look like a bunch of aggressive salesmen, nod approvingly. If the National Front attracted only such reactionaries, nostalgic for the King, Pétain, and French Algeria, the threat would not be too great.

To measure its seriousness, I have to go to the other side of the Old Harbor, beyond the seventeenth-century Town Hall, where the Social-ists are still the masters, to a warehouse that had been turned into offices and plastered with portraits of Le Pen with or without a tie. There I meet the local leader of the National Front. Sixtyish and paunchy, Pas-cal Arrighi is one of the reactionary notables who rallied to Le Pen. A former high-level public servant, he is a clever politician and a smooth talker. Why does his party do well in this area? In addition to economic circumstances, there are two basic reasons—immigration and "its daughter, insecurity." Marseilles, he claims, is a hospitable city, but the Arabs are just too much. When I venture that the arguments used to explain their otherness—different race, different religion, they don't mix or intermarry—had been advanced to oppose Jews before the war, he weighs me up suspiciously then decides to play it safe: No, the Jews had "the gift of adaptation and the will to integrate," whereas the Arabs are unbearable. He takes me into his confidence: "A cousin of mine, a doctor, her name was not in the telephone book, but they found it to shout obscenities because she had refused to sign phony certificates for social security. They just get on everybody's nerves."

When he talks of local politics, the man can be quite witty. I asked him why he was so sure that candidates of the respectable Right, the followers of Jacques Chirac and Raymond Barre, would stand down for National Front men and vice versa, whatever the official orders from Paris. "Because they don't want to commit political suicide," he replied.

"On the fourth floor, faced with the choice between the window and the staircase, you obviously can jump, but . . ." Dedé is there for Arab-bashing and Arrighi for vote-catching—the Front, after all, is doing well here in both posh and popular districts—but when it comes to fundamentals their message is the same. It panders to the lowest prejudices and plays on the deepest fears, seeking the ultimate root of all evil in the outsider, the alien; in this case, the Arab.

MOHAMMED THE SCAPEGOAT

Next to the names of National Front candidates on the billboards there are small posters with a minaret in the background and a quotation: "In twenty years' time, it is sure, France will be an Islamic republic." It is not worth checking whether the Hezbollah leader to whom this is attributed really did make such an absurd forecast. All foreigners combined account for less than 7 percent of the French population, a proportion that has remained roughly stable for the past dozen years, and immigrants from North Africa represent 2.6 percent. Besides, it is estimated that only some 5 percent of the potentially Islamic population are practicing Muslims. But to give credence to such forecasts is no more irrational than the often-heard suggestion that if you want a job, a subsidized flat, or a place in a kindergarten, you had better be called "Ben-something" than Dupont. This kind of whispering campaign is universal; only here it is unusually successful. Is it because foreigners are so much more numerous here in Marseilles? Not really, since according to the 1982 census, they number 80,752—or 9.3 percent of the population; immigrants from North Africa, estimated at 56,784, account for 6.5 percent of the total. Admittedly, they are more visible, since the immigrant ghetto lies in the center of the city. The district stretching between the Canebière and the railway station with its monumental staircase, full of narrow streets and shady hotels, has always been a shelter for the poor of the planet. By now it has expanded and looks like a North African casbah. Arabs are thus to be found not only on the outskirts in the most overcrowded and derelict housing projects but also in the very hem of the town. On top of it all, there is the population afloat. The port of a Marseilles is the main transit place and provisional stop for North Africans entering or leaving France.

Yet one cannot attribute the political explosion of racism to some optical illusion. Having once gone to school here, I can testify that Marseilles is an ethnic patchwork, the nearest thing to the United States with its successive waves of immigrants. The Arabs come after the Spaniards, Armenians, and Greeks on the solid foundations laid by the Corsicans and, above all, the Italians. In 1931 foreigners accounted for a quarter of the town's population, so to talk now of a "threshold of tolerance" is nonsense. Besides, the proportion of foreigners has not grown perceptibly in the past seven years, during which the National Front has climbed from marginality to political pride of place in this city. To understand this rise, racism alone is not sufficient explanation; it is necessary to glance at the deeper crisis of this town, of its living conditions, its economy and its system of power.

La Rose in Concrete

The eighth electoral district of Marseilles, picked by Le Pen to test his strength, is a mixture of popular and middle-class sections. You can reach it by the new modern subway, getting off at La Rose station, the end of the line. Outside you have blocks and blocks of flats. Indeed, as you reach the suburbs of Marseilles you are struck by a series of high-rise, cheap housing projects, which have grown like mushrooms during the building boom. Those at La Rose are not among the worst and therefore not packed with immigrants. Yet, here, as elsewhere, there are no cultural amenities, and community spirit has vanished. The blue- and, increasingly, white-collar workers feel insecure, worried about travel in the evenings, about their jobs, about the future. Marseilles seems to be surrounded by a concrete wall of crumbling expectations.

Experts on the spot confirm what is written in the few studies on the subject, namely that Marseilles has mismanaged its economic modernization. It is not just that the harbor was affected by the end of the French Empire; this was partly compensated for by the development of oil traffic. Marseilles failed to build an industrial hinterland, to diversify beyond its traditional activities connected with the harbor, or with the soap, oil, and food manufacturing industries. The failure was concealed for a time by the building boom, linked with the jump in population—from 660,000 in 1954 to 882,000 in 1968—spurred partly by the return of French settlers from North Africa. But beneath this bustle, the local bourgeoisie, satisfied with petty speculation, missed its opportunity during the postwar transformation of the French economy to more capital-intensive methods of production. Or, to be more accurate, the chance of regional expansion conceived of in the late sixties through the Fos complex (i.e., petrochemicals and a steel industry based on imported ore) came too late. The "miracle" was over and the vast plan got bogged down in the international crisis.

As a result, Marseilles is a town whose population is dwindling and where industrial jobs are declining—a very partial explanation of the collapse of the local Communist Party, whose electoral strength declined in seven years from 25.8 to 10.9 percent. White-collar employment has not expanded sufficiently to compensate and is, on the whole, on the lower end of the pay and status scale. Marseilles, lagging behind the national average in higher or technical education, is well above it in unemployment. The North Africans, brought over during the boom years, particularly for work in the construction industry, provide their contingent of the jobless. The economic deterioration goes a long way to explain the melancholy mood of this town and coincides with the end of one man's political reign.

In Search of a Godfather

On arrival in Marseilles, everybody tells you that this month's parliamentary elections are merely skirmishes for next year's big municipal battle, which will determine the choice of the new godfather. This mafia analogy is disrespectful—if not entirely unfair—to the Socialist Gaston Defferre, a well-off Protestant lawyer from neighboring Hérault who dominated local politics throughout the postwar period. He was mayor of Marseilles for thirty-three years until his death in 1986, but his system lasted for thirty; it was set up in 1953, when, fearing a Communist takeover, the Right—except for the Gaullists—made an alliance with the Socialists. The pact was based on the assumption that the bourgeoisie would get the profits and the Socialists the patronage. Thus, town planning, for example, was entrusted to the Right, which explains the social segregation that has seen the poorer people driven from the city center to the new high-rises of the periphery. The Socialists were in charge of the allocation of lower-rent flats and also controlled jobs provided by the municipality and the harbor. Indeed, they turned the network of power and patronage into a fine art; hence the passion in the present struggle for the Town Hall.

Strained by the economic and social crisis, the pact collapsed under the impact of national politics. Defferre could not sit in government in Paris (where he was minister of the interior) together with the Communists and at the same time rule in Marseilles in alliance with the Right. In 1983, he chose to fight the municipal election with a popular front. the two big parties of the respectable Right, determined to defeat him, based their campaign on law and order. To their surprise, a completely unknown list called Marseilles-Security captured more than 5 percent of the poll. The way in which not only the Right but the Socialists too wooed this jingoist electorate between ballots was one of the most shameful pages in the S.P.'s history.

While Defferre survived by the skin of his teeth, his system was in ruins. In the European elections a year later the National Front made a triumphant entry with 21.4 percent of the votes cast, grabbing support from all sides. In the parliamentary elections of 1986, which unlike this year's were run through proportional representation, it climbed to 24.4 percent, while the Left, once an overwhelming power in the town, was reduced to about 40 percent. Le Pen's score in this April's presidential poll thus marks a steady rather than a spectacular advance. The swing is no longer from the classical Left to the extreme Right. The loser is Jean-Claude Gaudin, the conservative bloc's crafty leader, rather than its strongman. He thought it clever to be elected president of the regional council with the support of the National Front, then to take neo-Fascists as his assistants. He simply rendered the Front more respectable. With 28.3 percent of the poll, Le Pen won more votes in Marseilles than Chirac and Barre combined.

It was this showing that induced Le Pen to seek his fortune here. Yet, he was taking quite a gamble. To get a parliamentary seat, let alone the Town Hall, Le Pen, who got 33 percent of the poll in the first ballot, on June 5, required the backing not just of some but of all the supporters of the respectable Right to stand a chance of winning. Had we reached that stage, the situation would be desperate, which it is not. With Le Pen faltering, the Socialists will now present as their candidate for mayor Michel Pezet, the man who won the skin game for Defferre's succession. But they were playing it safe.

Le Pen was not the only "parachutist," as carpetbaggers are called in France, in this area. Bernard Tapie, the handsome tycoon and media personality, landed in Marseilles with the Socialists' blessing, promising to cure unemployment. That this capitalist champion of "restructuring" should be one of the few cases of *ouverture* is symptomatic. Come to think of it, Mitterrand's "opening" is really the Defferre system writ large on a national scale, a Socialist alliance with the bourgeoisie, with the respectable Right renamed the "center" for the purpose. This will be the test in next year's municipal elections. In the polarized world of French politics, it will not be an easy one, either in Marseilles or the rest of the country.

The Thermometer and the Epidemic

I have written so far as if Marseilles were an island. Admittedly, this volatile port has some unhappy precedents: Simon Sabiani and his gangsters controlled the city in the early thirties, and the Gaullist Rally at its worst conquered the Town Hall in 1947. But today, Marseilles has ceased to be so distinctive. It has the same disease only in stronger or more advanced forms. It is not even very much ahead of the trend in the Midi. The electoral map of southern France now looks pretty ghastly. Le Pen got a quarter of the vote in the regions around Marseilles, Nice, and Toulon; a fifth in the Avignon, Nîmes and, further west, Perpignan areas. The greater success of the National Front in the southern regions is partly due to the presence there of French settlers from North Africa—adding to French racism their own anti-Arab brand—and possibly to a greater fear of European integration. But nobody likes to be squeezed in the name of economic progress, or to call "modernization" what is perceived as unemployment. Le Pen has reached close to 10 percent support in Brittany, for instance, where there are no foreign workers. The disease has become national.

What Marseilles does reveal is how the National Front has grown, and the timing of its growth. The economic crisis and a good number of immigrants were not sufficient on their own. The Left had first to get into office—on the one hand to madden the Right, and then, on the other, having failed to keep its promises, to disappoint its own supporters. It was in 1983–84, with those two preconditions fulfilled, that the National Front took off. Then, in the past two years, the respectable Right had to get back into office and confirm its own inability to cope, giving a new boost to the Front.

Historians will probably describe this period as the end of an era for two major movements: the Gaullist Party, which had managed to harness the authoritarian trend of the French Right, and the Communist Party, which had furnished hope and the semblance of a solution to left-wing protesters. Consensus politics will not exorcise the Front. If the crisis and unemployment continue, as they are likely to, and no section of the Left provides a radical alternative, Le Pen has quite a future ahead of him.

Is this forecast not too gloomy now that the share of the National Front in the total vote has gone down from over 14 percent to less than 10 percent, and the party has been virtually deprived of deputies? No. A movement whose growth is so recent and which lacks well-known figures was bound to lose some ground in an election where local personalities matter, while the disappearance of deputies is purely the effect of a change in the electoral law from proportional representation to a winner-take-all system. The danger now is that those who have altered the way one reads the thermometer may convince themselves that the disease is cured. Yves Montand, the brilliant performer who now seldom misses the chance to say something politically silly, argued the other day that one cannot describe as Fascists the people with whom he plays *pétanque* on the Riviera. Jackboots somehow do not fit into Pagnol's country.

But serious trouble does not begin when the men with jackboots or with cloven hoofs opt for Fascism. It begins when the tinker and tailor, your neighbor and your cousin, are driven sufficiently mad by circumstances to vote for an admirer of Pinochet, a preacher of apartheid, a man for whom the gas chambers are a mere "detail." As I looked down from the steps of the station, on departing this outwardly still-warm and attractive town, I could not help feeling that moral pollution is not so easily perceived. All the more reason to probe below the surface, to sound the alarm and, above all, to seek a cure—unless we want to wake up one day, too late, in a fully contaminated city or country.

The Ghosts of Nationalism

MARCH 23, 1992
The Nation

THE SPECTER HAUNTING Europe today, as it approaches the twenty-first century, is the ghost of nineteenth-century nationalism. It sends shivers down spines everywhere on the no-longer-formally-split-but-still-deeply-divided continent. In Eastern Europe, the collapse of the Stalinist empire, followed by the fragmentation of the Soviet Union itself, has provided scope for the resurrection of local nationalisms. Since the alleged purpose of the whole operation is to reverse the course of recent history, this revival of nation-states is logical, even if it does not make much sense. In Western Europe, where history has developed more in line with what was expected and the boundaries of the nation-state are being blurred, rejection of the alien, of the other, is spreading from Brussels to Vienna; the racist Jean-Marie Le Pen is no longer the odd man out. Is there some link between these two dangerous trends?

Recent developments in Central and Eastern Europe are probably easiest to understand. The Stalinist regime had been thrust upon these countries, even if it was imposed by the Red Army liberating them from the Nazis. The discarding of "Communism" in 1989 was at the same time a rejection of Russian domination. Since then, the new regimes, while enjoying their newly found independence, have been fast discovering its economic limitations. But, as discontent is rising and the governments do not dare to rebel against the iron rule of the International Monetary Fund, they must seek scapegoats. Putting the blame on the "Commies" can work for a while, and attacks against "aliens," within or without national frontiers, are a classical substitute for solutions.

On the face of it, the evolution of the former Soviet Union is more difficult to grasp, since nationalism was supposed to have been uprooted there by seventy years of Socialism and equality of national groups. The plain answer is that there was no more equality than there was Socialism. The Russification of the outlying republics was no more acceptable because it was practiced by a Georgian tyrant and the ruthless dictation from Moscow no more bearable because it was disguised in Marxist mumbo jumbo. Nationalism was never uprooted in the Soviet Union. In Russia itself it was at times extolled and at other times suppressed. In the other republics it was always driven underground. There it festered. When *perestroika* unleashed pent-up discontents and *glasnost* allowed their expression, nationalism came back with a vengeance.

By the time Mikhail Gorbachev perceived that the union could be saved only through some form of federation of independent states, it was too late. In fairness, it must be added that he was not helped by Russia's so-called democrats. In his relentless struggle for power, Boris Yeltsin played the nationalist card to the hilt, and he must now pay the price for his victory. Why should the Bashkirs, Tatars, or Komi in Russia treat Russia as "one and indivisible" when the Kazakhs, Uzbeks, and the Russians themselves refused to grant that definition to the Soviet Union? Why should the Ukrainians or the Belarussians permit Yeltsin in Moscow to set their economic and military policy now that they are allegedly sovereign members of a commonwealth? After all, they refused such dictation by Gorbachev while they were still full members of the Soviet Union.

In principle, devolution—the transfer of power from a monolithic center to republics—is progressive. In practice, a nationalism based on common blood, ethnicity, and historical tradition is seldom conducive to democracy. Besides, the disruption it will cause is likely to be tremendous. In human terms, the Soviet Union was a melting pot. Seventy-five million people, a quarter of the total population, live outside their native republics. Non-natives account for more than 60 percent of the population of Kazakhstan, nearly half the population of Latvia and Kyrgyzstan, and more than 27 percent of Ukraine, which gives an idea of possible migrations should there be ethnic conflict in these republics. In economic terms, because of central planning under Communism, the integration is very high. The trade among the Soviet republics, as a percentage of the national product, has been nearly twice as high as that among the member states of the Common Market. The emergence of different currencies and tariff walls is bound to have a paralyzing effect on the economy.

Why did the leaders of the republics opt for such a harmful solution? Partly because, like sorcerers' apprentices, they set in motion forces they have not been able to control. Partly because, within their narrower frontiers, they and their friends expect they will be better able to dominate the process of privatization and thus consolidate their power and privileges. They also hope to carve for themselves a bigger slice of foreign investment. In the case of Russia, which has half the population of the former union but more than 60 percent of its production and the bulk of such resources as crude oil and natural gas, the new leaders may hope to bully their way back to an imperial position. All these conflicting expectations, however, point to a dangerous future.

Naturally, Stalin cannot be blamed for it all. The tragic situation in Yugoslavia, where under Tito the nationalities policy was less repressive, shows not only the explosive potential of the post-Soviet equation. It is also a reminder that the uprooting of antagonistic nationalism (though obviously not of cultural identity) is a more complex problem than Marxist textbooks tended to suggest. Yet, when all this has been said, the simultaneous revival of primitive capitalism and the nation-state in Eastern Europe fits into an established pattern and points to the past (nationalism there was described as an "infantile disorder," to use Lenin's expression in another context, of the transition to capitalism).

On the other hand, the revival of xenophobia and racism in a Western Europe of vanishing frontiers does not fit that pattern and is a pointer to the future.

Admittedly, the nation-state has not disappeared in Western Europe. Indeed, General de Gaulle showed how effective an instrument it could be in the hands of a determined ruler. Nevertheless, the deal struck last month with IBM by the French company Groupe Bull, the state-owned company picked by the general himself to counter the American computer invasion, confirmed how difficult it is for a medium-sized state to resist economic encroachment on its own. The road from Maastricht, the Netherlands (site of the recent conference on unification), however tortuous and full of pitfalls, will lead Western Europe to some form of federation. Why is this gradual lifting of frontiers accompanied by a big boost for xenophobic parties in recent elections in Austria, Belgium, Italy, and Switzerland; by violent attacks against immigrants throughout Germany; by (if things go as expected) another advance for Le Pen's National Front in France's regional elections this month?

The one answer that can be dismissed at once is the prevailing one that the foreign population in Western Europe has exceeded the so-called "threshold of tolerance," beyond which the host country rejects any newcomers. France, where this new wave of xenophobia reached a political level, is an old country of immigration, and the share of foreigners in its population, and in its labor force, is exactly the same today as it was before the last war. Indeed, the proportion of immigrants in Western Europe was roughly the same twenty years ago as it is today, and it was perfectly bearable. It was only after 1975 and the rise of unemployment that it began to be described as intolerable. The phenomenon is thus not due to any population "threshold" but to an economic crisis.

Immigrant labor massively entered the European economy in the sixties and early seventies, that is to say, in the second phase of the unprecedented expansion that changed the face of Western Europe. Indeed, manning the assembly lines and filling jobs that were dirty, difficult, monotonous, or dangerous, the immigrant workers were a key element in that economic miracle. By standing on the backs of these people, the natives could climb the ladder to the higher-skilled, white-collar jobs. Everything was fine until the mid-seventies, when the deep structural crisis altered the mode of production and lowered the demand for unskilled immigrant labor. Then it was discovered that the provisional had become permanent, that the "guests," as the Germans euphemistically called them, had come to stay.

Not that it was possible to get rid of them rapidly in any case. The natives were not rushing to fill their unrewarding jobs. But the foreigner could now, once again, be painted as the culprit, responsible not only for rising unemployment but also for overcrowding, insecurity, the decline in social services—in short, for all the social evils concealed during the period of rapid growth and now revealed by the economic crisis. That aliens are scapegoats is illustrated all the time. In the recent epidemic of immigrant-bashing in Germany, there were many more cases in the East, where foreigners are few, than in the West, where they are more numerous. And the argument is carried ad absurdum by Poland's anti-Semitism without Jews. Jingoism is not a reflection of the number of immigrants. It is a symptom of a deeper sickness in society.

August Bebel, one of the founders of German social democracy, described anti-Semitism as the "Socialism of fools," and there is a great temptation to extend this formula to all forms of xenophobia. The snag is that the recent waves of jingoism are not very "National Socialist" in the propaganda. Nearly all the movements have had anti-Semitic undertones and quite often a weak spot for the Nazis, but they do not echo the allegedly anti-capitalist slogans of their predecessors from the thirties. A Le Pen can vituperate against the Brussels bureaucracy, but he cannot attack the Nazis' *bête noire*, the "Jewish-American plutocracy," and at the same time describe himself, as he does, as a sort of French Ronald Reagan.

This significant shift cannot be explained simply by the fact that Socialism today is unfashionable. It is largely due to a difference in the economic context. Although unemployment in Western Europe is now roughly three times higher than it was twenty years ago, it has not reached the proportions of the prewar Depression, nor is the fate of its victims comparable. Although discontent is high, workers are not flock-ing en masse to Le Pen and his equivalents. The danger for Western Europe is not an immediate takeover by various National Fronts. The threat lies in the gradual extension of the disease: the spread of racism and the weakening of class solidarity, sapping society's capacity for resistance should a really catastrophic slump bring back another bout of the deadly epidemic.

What connection is there between this creeping xenophobia in the west and the potentially more explosive jingoism of Eastern Europe, where economic tensions are already reaching the breaking point? The first link is obvious now that Europe's great divide has been formally abolished. Until the last war Eastern Europe was a great provider of immigrants for Western Europe, as well as for the United States. Deprived of this source, the advanced countries of Northwestern Europe had to look to the south for labor, first to Italy, Spain, and Por-tugal, then to Turkey or, across the Mediterranean, Africa.

Now that Western Europe is no longer mobilizing its army of labor, it is faced with two waves of recruits, one coming from the south, the other from the east. In Poland, the pioneer on the road to capitalism, the percentage of jobless has already reached double figures and keeps on rising. As Russia follows its "shock therapy," the figure one will have to play with will approach not three million but thirty million unem-ployed. No wonder that the countries of the Common Market are now trying to formulate a joint immigration policy. With the Berlin Wall dis-mantled, can they erect a new economic iron curtain along the Oder-Neisse line?

There is a deeper link between the revival of nationalism in the two halves of Europe. It is the simultaneous disappearance of a Socialist alternative. Oversimplifying, one may say that nineteenth-century nationalism had two versions. The first, stemming from the American and French revolutions, was rationalist and universalist, trying to carry its values to the world at large. Socialism, promising not only to lift fron-tiers but also to give social content to the otherwise empty slogans of lib-erty and equality, was, in a sense, its heir. The other version, sponsored by German thinkers, was based on blood, kith, and kin, and a historic tradition played to the tune of the *Nibelungen*. Now that the heritage of the former has been temporarily discredited through Communist crimes and social democratic surrender, the latter, darker side of nationalism is now dominant.

The error of those who proclaim the "end of history" is to assume that the collapse of the neo-Stalinist empire, and with it, however unfairly, the Socialist dream, heralds the smooth advance of classical capitalism. It is true that capital now supplies the only universal model, with its McDonald's, its television serials and, more important, its system of management and exploitation. Yet, as it spreads across the planet, it squeezes, marginalizes, and antagonizes growing numbers. Unless a new Socialism that is cured of the disease of centralism and its overemphasis on growth provides those millions with democratic solutions—control over their economic as well as their political life—they will inevitably turn to the dangerous mixture of race, religion, and ethnicity, a mixture that, incidentally, is not only for Muslim consumption. Which brings us back to the beginning: Until a resurrected, reinvented Socialism inspires the people with hope and vision, and their rulers with genuine fear, the specter that is haunting Europe from Paris to Moscow will be the specter of nationalism.

Hate in a Warm Climate

APRIL 20, 1992
The Nation

HE CAME, HE threatened, but he didn't conquer. The French Riviera will not be the first important region in Europe to be ruled by neo-Fascists. The growing shadow of Jean-Marie Le Pen prompted people throughout France to go to the polls on March 22. Half of them were expected to stay home, but at the last minute some 69 percent cast their ballots, thus reducing the share of the xenophobic National Front. Since Le Pen had boasted in advance that he represented a wave submerging the country, France sighed with exaggerated relief.

Actually, the disease is getting more serious. Garnering 14 percent of the vote, the Front managed to do as well in a regional election as its charismatic leader had done in a more favorable presidential poll. One person out of seven throughout the country, and one out of four in large sections of southern France, was willing to vote for a party that admired apartheid, praised Pinochet, and intends to kick Arabs across the Mediterranean.

The last-minute democratic surge was no boost for the establishment. Indeed, consensus politics, barely introduced into France, is already threatened with extinction. François Mitterrand, who did the introducing by destroying the Left as a radical alternative, discovered that his countrymen are not fond of the politics of Tweedledum and Tweedledee. The Socialists, who promised to "change life" and then nicely fitted into the prevailing pattern, are now paying the price. For a ruling party to win less than one-fifth of the vote, as the Socialists did, is plainly disastrous. Yet their principal rival—and partner in the establishment—the conservative coalition headed by Jacques Chirac and Valéry Giscard d'Estaing, did not take advantage of this fall. Receiving barely one-third of the vote, it too suffered a setback. The only winners were the outsiders: the National Front and the environmentalists, who, in their two incarnations, the Green Party and the Ecological Generation, also took 14 percent of the vote. One has the feeling that, in a society shaken by crisis, citizens are groping toward new forms of political expression. The March elections conveyed a double message: The spectacular climb of the ecologists is a potentially optimistic portent for the future; the continued rise of the National Front is a sinister reminder of a ghastly past.

But is this not reading too much into a local election? The results in France were confusing because of the combination of two polls and the complexity of local government. France is divided into ninety-six departments, including Corsica. These are split into cantons, but in 1982 they were also merged into twenty-two regions. On March 22, half of France chose councilors for the departmental assemblies from the cantons, each of which is represented by a single member. At the same time, voters elected members of the regional assemblies by a system of proportional representation. It was this nationwide poll that offered scope for political interpretation.

Let me focus on the region that was most in the limelight, the so-called PACA, which stands for Provence, Alpes, Côte d'Azur. It is a region containing six departments, the three biggest centered around the cities of Marseilles, Nice, and Toulon. Each department is entitled to a number of councilors based on its population, and each party puts up a full slate, which has a local head and which proclaims whom it would support for president of the regional assembly. The PACA was in the limelight because in addition to the incumbent, the conservative Jean-Claude Gaudin, it had as candidates for the presidency of the region two stars of the media, the tycoon Bernard Tapie, running as a

Socialist, and Le Pen himself. To find out how real the Le Pen danger is, I followed the leader down south to Nice.

GODFATHER'S SUCCESSION

With the mountains to its back and the superb Bay of Angels before it, Nice is a unique city. The British upper classes appreciated it in the eighteenth century. The *promenade des Anglais,* which recalls their memory, stretches for more than three miles along the bay. It is now lined with big blocks of flats for tourists or well-off pensioners. The monotony is broken from time to time by an odd construction like the baroque Hotel Negresco with its pink dome. As you drive westward along the coast toward Antibes and Cannes, you have the impression that the town never ends. Yachts, golf courses, gambling casinos—it's filthy rich and terribly commercialized.

If Nice itself is relatively prosperous, why did Le Pen choose it as the best place to run? The presence of immigrants cannot be the real explanation, since foreigners made up only 8.7 percent of the population in the 1990 census, not much above the national average. Indeed, xenophobia in this area seems rather strange. As you walk around the old town with its ocher houses, you have the illusion of being in Italy. That is not surprising, since the city once belonged to the House of Savoy and became French only in 1860. Generations of Italian immigrants came to find work in the ensuing years. Nationalists often have short memories.

There are other reasons, however, for the success of the National Front in Nice. Unemployment, at 12.4 percent of the labor force, is above the national level. The *pieds noirs,* the French repatriated from North Africa, who have no love for Arabs, are particularly numerous; the climate suited them and they were politically welcome. Finally, this is the paradise of French old-age pensioners, who, like pensioners elsewhere, are very receptive to the right wing's propaganda about law and order.

Yet there is a deeper reason for Le Pen's choice, which has to do with heritage and a system of rule. Nice is the only big city in France that was governed for more than sixty years by the same family. Jean Medecin was its mayor from 1928 to 1965 except for a brief spell after the war when he was ineligible because as a deputy he had voted Marshal Petain, the Nazi collaborator, into office. He presided over a system normally associated with southern Italy, with fixed bribes for offices to be gained or for services rendered, and a network of district committees, which could be described as social clubs—or as organized corruption. But the machine worked, and he bequeathed it intact to his son Jacques, who ruled for another quarter-century.

During that time, Nice, the fifth-largest city in France, with a population close to half a million, became a different place. The entire area changed: A scientific city was set up at Sophia-Antipolis and high-tech firms like IBM moved in. Petro-dollars flowed in from the Middle East and Mafia money, for laundering, from Italy. Control over the gambling became important, and the battle for the casinos was Chicago-like. When a widow owning an important gambling place refused takeover bids, her daughter was somehow forced to sell her shares and then mysteriously vanished. The bidder in that case was J.D. Fratoni, a bosom friend of the mayor.

Medecin had actually brought in a new team, graduates of Nice University and former members of the Fascist student caucus. But he grew careless. Remarried to an American, he often traveled to California, where he was introduced as "Count de Medicis." He was also caught by the U.S. customs services trying to smuggle jewelry. At home, his use of public money for private purposes became too blatant. In September 1990, when the noose tightened and he faced a trial, the professional anti-Communist "chose freedom" in Uruguay. Between Medecin, who twinned Nice with Cape Town, and Le Pen there was very little political difference. It was only a question of each one wanting his turf. With the godfather out of the way, Le Pen could begin his bid for the succession.

The Challenger at Work

The Greenery Theater is a tentlike structure in the heart of Nice. Its two thousand seats are filled. The loudspeakers blare out Wagner. Images on a giant video screen proclaim "The National Front—It's You," "Oppose Exclusion of Frenchmen," "For the Death Penalty." The candidates are introduced, and the woman sitting next to me explains that *pieds noirs* are numerous, both on the National Front slate and in the hall. Now the music rises—the "Hymn of the Slaves" from Verdi's *Nabucco*—and the people chant, "Le Pen! Le Pen!" It's time for the star.

He looks like a retired prize-fighter. His face is bloated and his stylish suit does not conceal that he is overweight. Yet he is still quite a performer, a ham actor who will revel in the limelight for the next two and a half hours. Before this audience, he can get away with anything. He does not have to present a policy or a program. He can claim that the German Greens were founded by the Stasi and were linked with terrorists. He can describe Socialist politicians as "a band of thieves, gangsters, and racketeers," after proudly proclaiming that his candidacy has the blessing of Jacques Medecin, presumably a symbol of moral rectitude. He is here to thrill and to amuse. He impresses his audience with Latin quotations. He makes them laugh with music-hall jokes: "When you're in muck up to your ears, you must be careful to keep your mouth shut."

Le Pen has been told that to win votes he must keep his tongue in check, so he's on his best behavior. He makes no openly racist or anti-Semitic remarks. Yet, listening carefully, you can still judge the man. His reference to Jean-Claude Gaudin as "the bearded woman"—a not so gentle hint about the incumbent's alleged homosexuality—gives an idea of his moral tone. The contempt he puts into the words "of every race and religion," describing demonstrators he saw in London, is also revealing. So is his scorn for those who stir up unpleasant memories of World War II: "They only want to talk about Petain and Touvier" (a wartime torturer, hidden for years by the clergy and only recently arrested). "Whatever the subject, it reminds them of Hitler and Vichy."

Toward the end, he becomes more dramatic. He reminds his listeners of the four plagues: immigration, insecurity, unemployment, and economic degradation. He speaks in apocalyptic terms about the nomads storming the sedentary people, reciting, in a rather strange sequence, "the Huns, the Magyars, the Turks, and the Persians." In Algeria, he intones, the choice was between the suitcase and the coffin—fleeing or dying. Now there is no suitcase. But we must survive for the survival of France.

Outside, the militants are pleased but complain that their hero had to pull his punches. Should one be reassured by his more "moderate" tone? Recalling the expressions of hatred on the faces of the audience when Le Pen referred to "the privileges for foreigners to the detriment of the French," the two middle-aged women hysterically chanting "Le Pen! Le Pen!", the tough-looking guards whom nobody would want to meet in a dark alley, I cannot pretend I really feel reassured.

THE DOCTOR AND THE SUPERSALESMAN

The disease in Nice got so serious that they had to call the cancer specialist, said a wit. He was referring to Professor Leon Schwartzenberg, a famous authority on cancer, who volunteered to lead the Socialist slate against Le Pen. Gray-haired, small and thin, the professor looks frail. He is speaking in a modern hall in the expensive and luxurious Acropolis building, erected recently under Jacques Medecin. This is the last big meeting for his slate. It's attended by government ministers running in neighboring departments and by the head of the regional Socialist slate, Bernard Tapie. The professor speaks movingly about how the French people were promised a change of life by the Socialists. At first there were advances, such as the abolition of the death penalty and five weeks of holiday with pay. But now is a time of gloom and fear. Unemployment and insecurity are linked and unemployment is spreading in capitalist countries. The time of revolutionary certitudes is over, and some of those certitudes were foolish to begin with, for instance, the belief in unlimited economic growth. We must communicate with our planet as a gardener does with the plants. Dr. Schwartzenberg does not hesitate to quote Marx or to include early Communists among his political ancestors. He closes with a famous quotation of Saint-Just: "Happiness is a new idea in Europe."

All this was fine, yet what connection did it have with the technocratic pronouncements the ministers made, or the colorful personality of Tapie? Tapie deserves a separate piece. Here let me just say that he is a self-made man. Born of a modest family in the "Red Belt" of Paris, he is, at forty-nine, a millionaire. He makes money buying companies in trouble, improving their balance sheets—notably through a cut in the labor force—and then selling them at a profit. He is more a salesman than an industrial tycoon, and he has a great flair for publicity. His ownership of the best soccer club in France, Marseilles, is also an instrument for self-advertising.

Having had a brief career as a pop singer in his youth, he is very much the showman, exuding charm and wit. He is quite funny on this occasion, giving a French version of the anti-David Duke propaganda heard in New Orleans. Tell your well-off friends about the conventions that will not be held in Nice, he says, and the investments that will go elsewhere if Le Pen is elected. Since they love themselves more than their neighbors, tell them at least to be kind to their bank accounts. But it is with managers, not the workers, that he intends to discuss his economic program. Clearly, the "associated producers" are not part of his, or the ministers' for that matter, version of "Socialism."

When I interviewed Dr. Schwartzenberg a few days later at his modest headquarters, he showed no illusions. He had waited three months for a Socialist leader to take on Le Pen and volunteered only when nobody came forward. He has not been helped much by party headquarters in Paris, and the local Socialist Party is almost nonexistent. The only anti-Le Pen initiatives have come from intellectuals, who sponsored a petition, an exhibition of cartoons, and a demonstration. Led by a band, several thousand people marched, carrying signs with slogans like, "We are all children of immigrants, first, second, or third generation," or, borrowing from Tacitus, "Willing slaves make tyrants." But that was at best a beginning. When the Socialist Party chooses a Tapie as leader in Marseilles, which used to be its stronghold, it is clear how far it has sunk. As for the Communists, under Georges Marchais they have achieved their own self-destruction.

BAY OF SCOUNDRELS

It takes a couple of hours to go from Nice to Marseilles by train; I went there for the sake of comparison. In Marseilles, the reasons for the rise of the Front seem more obvious. The casbah, the poor man's ghetto, still lies in the very heart of the city. Unemployment has risen sharply, and the National Front has moved its headquarters to a more impressive building. Its campaign this time was headed by Bruno Megret, a small, thin-lipped product of France's top engineering school and a former public servant who is now Le Pen's second-in-command.

On reflection, each area has its peculiar reasons. Nice has a right-wing tradition, while Marseilles used to be dominated by the Left. The south, with its many reactionary repatriates, has merely proved a pioneer. Now the Front captures about a fifth of the vote in Alsace and in the industrial belt surrounding Paris. For Le Pen's movement, the immigration issue is merely a pretext. Discontent is mainly inspired by unemployment, insecurity, fear of the future, the absence of hope. And, one is tempted to add, by the bankruptcy of the Left.

During the campaign, Tapie caused an uproar with his statement that if Le Pen is a dirty bastard, then people who vote for him knowing what he stands for are also dirty bastards. The leftish comedian Guy Bedos, addressing a pro-Schwartzenberg rally, provoked his audience by saying, "No, they are not all bastards," and then won it over by adding, "Some of them are bloody fools."

But the matter is much more complicated because the very same people can be good or bad, angels or scoundrels, depending on circumstances. As long as a Le Pen is followed by certified thugs and Fascists of old vintage, the danger is small. It is only when apparently ordinary people, driven by discontent, fear, and lack of perspective, are ready to follow dangerous prophets that the situation threatens to get out of hand, as it now has.

Even if he failed to reach his goals, Le Pen did much better than some people realize. In Nice, the Front came first with just over 30 percent of the poll. In the department of Alpes-Maritimes, it came in second with 27 percent of the vote, and in the regional assembly it won thirty-four out of 123 seats, a good base for launching new offensives. Unless a resurrected left rapidly opens new horizons, Le Pen may prove more successful next time, and the beautiful Baie des Anges may yet become the bay of scoundrels.

Death of a Collaborator

JULY 19, 1993
The Nation

EARLY ON THE morning of June 8, a messenger arrived at an apartment in one of the poshest districts of Paris bearing documents to be signed by a former high-level government official and prominent banker. Once ushered in, the messenger pulled out a gun and shot the host four times at point-blank range. The old man who was killed was René Bousquet.

Fifty years ago, Bousquet was head of the police at the height of the mass deportation of French Jews, so the initial guess was that the killing must have been the work of a descendant of one of his victims, unable to bear the idea that such a scoundrel should be living so comfortably, untormented by conscience. As it turned out, the "avenger" was a frustrated scrivener who craved celebrity rather than justice. The media gave him the limelight he was seeking, but in killing Bousquet he deprived France of a trial that would have thrown light on the complicity of high-level officials in Nazi crimes.

Bousquet was one of three elderly Frenchmen facing trial for crimes against humanity committed during the Nazi occupation in World War II. He was, however, the crucial one. Paul Touvier, for so long protected by the Catholic clergy, is a sort of junior Klaus Barbie, a bloody torturer who operated on a local scale in the Lyons area. Maurice Papon, who became an influential politician after the war, was also a local figure, whose atrocities were confined to Bordeaux. Bousquet was much more than a provincial, anti-Semitic thug. He was a brilliant member of the establishment, and as head of the French police in 1942–43 he was responsible for repression and deportations throughout France. His example shows how far *raison d'état* combined with ruthless ambition can lead. His case is worth examining because it tells us a great deal about the ambiguous relationship between postwar French politics and wartime collaboration.

Murderer in White Gloves

René Bousquet, born in 1909, seemed destined for a high post in government. He picked the prefectural service, which is most subservient to the powers that be. (The prefect is not so much the servant of the state as the instrument of the government in power, its direct representative in one of the ninety-five departments into which France is now divided.) The young civil servant garnered laurels and medals, showing personal courage in a rescue operation during a flood.

Bousquet cannot be described as the product of the French anti-Semitic right. He hails from the Toulouse region in southwestern France. During the interwar period Toulouse was dominated by the Radical Party, which, despite its name, was the mouthpiece of the moderate Left. (It was said to be like a radish: red on the outside, white on the inside, and always on the side the bread is buttered on.) With good connections in such quarters, Bousquet found that his rise was not interrupted when the Popular Front government of Léon Blum came to power in 1936—quite the contrary. But it did not slow down after Blum was thrown out of office, because Bousquet linked his fate with that of another prominent politician, Pierre Laval. Indeed, his climb continued as the Third Republic collapsed, and the Vichy regime of Marshal Philippe Pétain was set up under German auspices. At the age of thirty-one, Bousquet was the youngest prefect in France. Yet the real jump in his career came in April 1942, when Laval returned as prime minister in the Vichy government, which collaborated with Nazi Germany.

Laval brought Bousquet to Vichy as secretary general of the police with ministerial rank. The ambitious newcomer was determined to preserve as far as possible the sovereignty of the French police—or so he would say later in his own defense. To prevent the Germans from acting, he explained, one had to do the dirty jobs for them. One had to collaborate in the ruthless repression of the Resistance, which was inspired, as one of the joint agreements between the French and the Nazis put it, "by Jews, Bolsheviks, and Anglo-Saxons." One had to provide French policemen to round up Jews in Paris and later to raid Jewish homes throughout so-called unoccupied France—rather than let the Germans do it. One had to prove one's zeal by adding small children to the lists. One had to supply thousands and thousands of Jews for the Nazi gas chambers. The distinguished young minister, a darling of the Vichy *haut monde,* was too elegant and too smart to stoop personally to torture like a vulgar Vichy militia thug. But he had more blood on his hands.

By the end of 1943, as a result of factional struggles within the Vichy government, Laval was pushed out and so was Bousquet. The latter was subsequently ordered into forced residence in Germany. Back in France after the war, Bousquet stayed in jail until 1947. He was tried two years later for collaboration, when passions were spent and society almost back to normal. With the influence of southwestern Radicals, the jury somehow failed to probe into his role in the deportation of the Jews, and he was sentenced to only five years of "national indignity." And even this was lifted almost at once because of "services rendered to the Resistance Movement." (It is striking how many pro-Nazis like Bousquet took the precaution of rendering such services.)

Even so, Bousquet could not resume his career in public administration. He could, however, build a new one in business. With the help of former associates, he went into merchant banking and rose to second in command of the important Bank of Indochina, which later merged with the Bank of Suez. He was also on the board of umpteen companies, including a government-owned airline and the influential Toulouse daily, *Dépêche du Midi.* Having recovered his Legion of Honor (first awarded in 1930), he lived for the next thirty years as a prosperous and respectable pillar of French high society. It was only in the late seventies that the past began to catch up with him again. A team of researchers, headed by lawyer Serge Klarsfeld, acting on behalf of children of the victims, produced incriminating documents from the German archives. Touvier, Papon, and Bousquet's right-hand man in Paris, Jean Leguay, came under investigation, and since France had accepted the principle that there was no statute of limitations on "crimes against humanity," they all could be prosecuted. To understand why matters dragged on for so long, why none of them were ever tried (Leguay died), one must consider the French establishment's failure to settle accounts with its Vichy past.

WHITEWASHING VICHY

The French did put the Vichy traitors on trial. Those who were caught and tried early enough paid the price. Laval and the pro-Nazi editor and writer Robert Brasillach were judged and executed in 1945. Many lesser figures were shot or jailed. All over France, women had their heads shaved because of their horizontal collaboration. What never took place, however, not even during the trial of Pétain, was a fundamental indictment of the prewar regime, an examination of why key institutions had served the Nazi occupier, why the bulk of the bourgeoisie collaborated, in keeping with the prewar slogan, "Better Hitler than the Popular Front." Since, betraying the hopes of the Resistance, liberation did not usher in a new society, the old one, when restored, needed judges and jailers, police and upper classes. A veil was discreetly spread over the awkward past.

This conspiracy of silence was facilitated by a clever syllogism. Because General de Gaulle had led the Resistance and de Gaulle *was* France, ergo, France was a nation of resisters. This myth suited almost everybody. The Communists, who were a key element in the Resistance, could boast of their record without anyone bringing up the less glorious period between the Nazi-Soviet Pact and the German invasion of Russia. The Gaullists were, naturally, the main beneficiaries of the legend. They also required a degree of obfuscation to prevent a split within the Right between the majority who had followed Marshal Pétain and the minority who had rallied round de Gaulle. When Georges Pompidou granted Touvier a presidential pardon in 1971, it was not just to please the church. It was also to unite the conservative forces at a time of social stress. To achieve that purpose, however, one had to be discreet about wartime history. In French schoolbooks at the time, you could learn more about the Battle of Britain or Pearl Harbor than about Pétain, Vichy, and collaboration.

That silence provoked Marcel Ophüls to make his splendid documentary, *The Sorrow and the Pity* (1971), which revived the Vichy era, warts and all. French television banned his film for years, but it was shown in theaters and French young people began asking their parents, "And what were *you* doing during the war?" Since then there have been two conflicting trends in France. One is revisionist, featuring a small number of people trying to deny or minimize the Holocaust and a larger number treating collaboration not as a sin but as political wisdom. On the other side, we have writers, historians, and filmmakers determined to tell the general public, and particularly the younger generation, the full, unvarnished story of that period. The trials of Touvier, Papon, and Bousquet have been conceived as highlights in this campaign of collective education.

The attitude of successive governments in this affair has been, to say the least, ambiguous. To stage the trial of Klaus Barbie was fine, since it simply confirmed the criminality of the Germans. To bring a Bousquet to court was quite a different matter. A trial would adduce evidence of French complicity in those crimes at the highest level. It was likely to lead to a real debate about the state, its institutions, its function, and its morality. The French authorities were clearly not enthusiastic about proceeding. The reluctance of the government and of the establishment, including the legal one, dragged out the procedure over a long period of time on the tacit assumption that the defendants would die, depriving the trials of their *raison d'être*.

The delays were countenanced by governments of all political complexions. François Mitterrand provides an example of this double-think. Although Mitterrand was a member of the Resistance, every year until last he laid a wreath on Pétain's tomb to celebrate the anniversary of Verdun—as if one could neatly separate the "hero" of World War I from the "villain" who, during World War II, led the French into one of the most shameful episodes of their history. In the case of Mitterrand this duality may also reflect his enthusiastic discovery of consensus politics, which, by definition, is opposed to splitting society and undermining its ruling class.

REMEMBRANCE OF THINGS PAST

But why bother at all to bring to justice a few guilty men who are on the brink of the grave? The obvious answer—because amnesia is a collective as well as an individual disease and a society that cannot come to terms with its past is handicapped in facing renewed dangers—is more relevant than ever at a time when racism once more raises its ugly head throughout Europe. When Turkish homes are torched in Germany, when "ethnic cleansing" in the former Yugoslavia reminds us where prejudice can lead, the battle against racial and ethnic discrimination must again be waged, and memory is an important weapon in this struggle.

The two contradictory trends mentioned earlier are both gaining strength. Today in Paris, for instance, you can see two films, one fictional and not very good but purporting to show Pétain and Laval as villains, another a documentary, a selection of wartime newsreels compiled by Claude Chabrol to show Vichy propaganda in its ridiculous vulgarity and hypocritical repulsiveness. After Bousquet's murder, French public television showed a different documentary, in which four Jewish survivors tell how as toddlers they were deported by the French police.

Against this you must set the trend, not limited to France, of what is best described as sneaking or creeping revisionism. You start, say, by bluntly proclaiming that Jean-Paul Sartre was wrong because he was pro-Soviet, and his schoolmate Raymond Aron was right because he chose the American side, a case you can make more easily by removing the argument from its historical context. You then publish a book in Paris suggesting, without proving, that Jean Moulin, head of Resistance on French soil, executed by the Nazis, was a Soviet agent (of course, you can't claim that helping the Russians during the war was treason, but wait . . .). From there, using the fashionable equation of "twin evils," you can maintain, like the German revisionist historians, that those who, like Heidegger, picked the lesser of two totalitarian evils, the Nazi rather than the Bolshevik one, were right. We are not at that point yet, but if we don't react strongly against the poison, it will continue to spread.

A trial of Bousquet would have had another benefit. It would have reminded criminals against humanity, not limited to Serbia or Croatia, that their turn may one day come. It would have warned those bastards all over the world that to claim "superior orders" or obedient service of state and country is no defense. It would have made it plain that the thugs doing the dirty work may not be the worst criminals, that distinguished gentlemen sitting behind their desks in the capital can do more harm with their pens (or, today, with their computers).

Yet the most crucial contribution of the trial would have been to advance the campaign against growing jingoism, against the mounting intolerance of the foreigner, the alien, the other. It does not always take spectacular forms like the burning of the Turks. In Germany, you have hundreds of thousands of people born on German soil who are not second-class citizens but not citizens at all, and the government is still resisting widespread demands that it bestow nationality on people of a "different ethnic background." In France, politicians pandering to Jean-Marie Le Pen's ultra-Right constituency take all sorts of measures to render the lives of immigrants miserable. The first breaches have even been made in the *jus soli*, the principle that those born on French soil are entitled to French nationality. Kith and kin, blood brothers, that is the fashionable vocabulary. Start with *jus sanguini*, the law of the blood, and you end up with ethnic cleansing and buckets of blood spilled from Bosnia to Tajikistan.

The punishment meted out to old men like Bousquet has been irrelevant for some time. But the description and analysis of their crimes, thanks to a trial or by other methods, was and remains important. It is the crucial link between past and present, the indispensable connection. Although the Holocaust was, in a sense, unique, and although today the first victims would be not the Jews but the Turks in Germany and the Arabs in France, it is the same struggle. Rendered urgent again by growing mass unemployment and the resulting social strains, it is a struggle against the barbarian future, a battle against all the Bousquets of this world.

The Euroleft, or,
Who's Afraid of TINA?

JANUARY 11, 1999
The Nation

EUROPE, YOU ARE rightly told, is swinging to the Left. In thirteen of the fifteen countries making up the European Union, the Social Democrats are now in office. And on the eve of the historic moment when eleven of the union members will inaugurate their common currency, the euro, these leftist governments were reportedly putting pressure on the central bankers to relax their deflationary policy, to lower interest rates in order to spur production. With only Spain and Ireland still having openly conservative administrations, the European electorate has clearly rejected right-wing rule.

But does this herald a Socialist revival or, less ambitiously, the resurrection of social democracy? And if the prospect is even less exciting, can a new New Left, buoyed by a movement from below, put pressure on these governments and push them in a more radical direction? As the certitudes of the ruling religion of the market are being shaken by the world economic crisis, the change of chancellors in Germany—the replacement of the Christian Democrat Helmut Kohl by the Social Democrat Gerhard Schröder—has put such unorthodox questions on the European agenda.

To answer the questions requires defining the shifting terms and, hence, a bit of history. Social democracy once stood for the parties trying to bring the reign of capital to an end; Lenin and Rosa Luxemburg were Social Democrats. The sense of the word, however, was reversed after World War II. It has since meant the reformist management of the existing society; indeed, the quarter-century after the war, the so-called golden age of capitalism—years in Western Europe of exceptionally rapid growth, rising living standards, and the extension of the welfare state—was a period particularly favorable for this new interpretation. The climate in Western Europe was "social democratic" even when left-wing parties were not in office.

The irony is that by the early seventies, when almost everybody—including the Communists deprived of their Stalinist model—was converted to the idea that the aim was no longer to change society but to make changes within its framework, the era of unprecedented prosperity was over. The last quarter-century has seen a reversal of policy, an attempt to take back the concessions granted in the years of expansion and a growing tendency to follow the American example. The past fifteen years have also witnessed a complete change in the ideological climate. Keynesian reformism went out of fashion as the system returned to the law of the capitalist jungle. Those who protested were silenced with the magic formula "TINA"—there is no alternative—the nickname given Maggie Thatcher, who had General Pinochet for tea and who used to proclaim louder and more often than anybody that there is no exit from our society. The snag is that TINA then became the dominant feature of political debate, accepted, nay, absorbed by the Left, whose moderate leaders were offered the unenviable task of acting as the counterreforming managers of existing society.

Are they now rebelling against this difficult duty? It must be remembered that whatever the readiness of Britain's Tony Blair, France's Lionel Jospin, Germany's Gerhard Schröder, or Italy's converted Communist Massimo D'Alema to follow the U.S. model, it was always tempered by popular resistance to attacks on the welfare state, resistance that was strongest in France and weakest in Britain. Besides, now that they are all in office together, they are well aware that they will be judged essentially on their handling of unemployment. With the gospel of globalization weakened by the economic crisis, they now have more room to maneuver. In any case, their audacity should not be exaggerated. Federal Reserve Chairman Alan Greenspan has cut interest rates three times; paradoxically, for once the U.S. financial establishment is not on the side of Europe's keepers of financial orthodoxy. Washington wants Western Europe to play an active role in fighting the threat of world depression.

The problem facing Europe's Social Democrats is not only monetary. It is whether they are ready to challenge financial orthodoxy with a project designed to fight unemployment and, more broadly, to defend the interests of working people. Much will depend on the performance of the newcomers. In Germany, the mood of the rank and file and the stand of IG Metall and other labor unions will determine whether Oskar Lafontaine, the country's new economic overlord, will challenge the financial establishment and its protégé, the Dutchman Wim Duisenberg, the president of the new European Central Bank, who cares more about a strong currency than about low unemployment. In the months after the reign of the euro starts on January 1, Germany may be the place to watch. Meanwhile, to understand the dilemmas of the European Left, one must look at Britain, with its Clintonian Tony Blair; at France, where something is stirring on the fringes of the Left; and at Italy, which has dramatically raised the question of the relations between radicals and moderates within the European movement.

THATCHERISM WITH A HUMAN FACE

If you want to know the philosophy inspiring Tony Blair, read the opuscule of his purported guru, Anthony Giddens, *The Third Way*—or, because seldom have so many platitudes been packed into so little space, I shall spare you the effort by summing up its essence. The gist of his argument is based on the assumption that we are living in a world in which there are no alternatives to capitalism, that Socialism is dead and that even the reformist objectives of social democracy are obsolete. There is still a difference between Left and Right, concedes Giddens, but fortunately it has been so reduced that "it permits exchange across political fences." With such a diagnosis it is easy to imagine the remedies. The state has an essential role to play in providing "the infrastructure needed to develop an entrepreneurial culture." The welfare state must be "reconstructed," with social benefits kept not too high so as to avoid "moral hazard." (Read: The lazy blighters won't work.) The author is, naturally, against "an obsession with inequality" and against "limits to the working week fixed by government."

How does Tony the performer get away with playing such a script? Charisma, spin doctors, and efficient publicity? No, there is a deeper reason: In Britain, Europe's Labor movement suffered its most serious defeat back in 1984, when Thatcher took on the miners. Because other trade-union leaders did not rally behind the strikers, she defeated them after an epic one-year struggle that altered the balance of forces in the country. It takes time to recover from such a major setback. Blair now has more latitude to ignore popular discontent because he did nothing, on coming to power, to restore the balance in favor of working people. Naturally, such situations are not eternal. There are already some signs of discontent within the Labor Party. At the last party conference, held in Blackpool at the end of September, in the elections to the National Executive Committee from the constituency branches— the only direct vote reflecting the mood of the militants, of the rank and file—the Left, critical of the current line, won four of the six available seats.

The leadership, however, need not worry. With its control of the party machinery and with the rules tightened still further in undemocratic fashion, the critics will be gagged. What is more important, most of the places in both parliamentary and local elections will be duly reserved for the faithful. Blair is safe, especially as long as he rides high in the ratings, though these could slump next year if the economy falters. In any case, for the time being, the leader of the Labor Party is the only one in Europe who can drive his party and his country in the American direction. Britain, to borrow the language of Giddens, "could be a sparking point for creative interaction between the U.S. and continental Europe." If Tony's social democratic colleagues try to change their economic course, you can count on him to apply the brakes. With speeches full of references to dynamism and enterprise, he will be there defending the interests of the employers.

"LA GAUCHE DE LA GAUCHE"

Lionel Jospin is at the other end of the social democratic spectrum. Not that he looks beyond the capitalist horizon. Far from it. He was an influential member of François Mitterrand's team, which converted the French Left to consensus politics and obedience to the rules of the international market. Indeed, during his nineteen months as prime minister he has privatized more than his conservative predecessor. But Jospin is also the by-product of the strikes and demonstrations that shook France in the winter of 1995. He is sensitive to pressure from below. To preserve his leftish reputation, he has decreed that a thirty-five-hour workweek will be legally binding in two years, and he's urged his European partners to put the struggle against unemployment at the top of their agenda. Unlike Blair, he does dream of a reformist management of the existing society, though he does not mobilize the mass movement that would be necessary for this purpose.

What did that French winter of discontent change? Nothing fundamental in the structure of the country, but something subtle in its mood. It precipitated President Chirac's decision to hold a snap parliamentary election, which brought the victorious Jospin to the prime minister's office. It probably drove Jospin to form a coalition with the Communists and the Greens as junior partners in his government. The existence of this "plural Left," as it is called, created a void on *its* Left. In the local elections held last March, the Trotskyists captured nearly 5 percent of the vote. This was not a sudden French conversion to the ideas of the prophet of permanent revolution but a warning by the radical electorate accusing the rulers of excessive moderation, a warning that was particularly worrying for the Communists but perturbing for all members of the coalition. The government must take into account the fact that it can lose votes on its Left.

The change in the general atmosphere is at once difficult to define and undeniable. The idea of TINA is no longer supreme. Articles and essays are being published questioning the reign of the market, domestic and foreign, as well as the domination of our life by money. The monthly *Le Monde Diplomatique*, a nonconformist journal, has gained in influence. A series of little books, not necessarily red in color but critical in substance, edited by the well-known sociologist Pierre Bourdieu and called "Reasons to Act," is selling like hotcakes. (Serge Halimi's indictment of the media servants of the system holds the record so far, with two hundred thousand copies). The virulence of attacks against Bourdieu since he has become more directly involved in politics is symptomatic. He is accused of using his prestige and his position at the top of the French academic establishment—he is a professor in the holy of holies, the Collège de France—to undermine the established order. The anger of his many accusers is a sign that the priests of the ruling religion have lost their supreme self-confidence.

But they are not on the run. Indeed, the protesters have failed so far in their greatest ambition. At the height of the strike in 1995, labor activists and intellectuals decided to work together in search of alternative solutions. And they did for quite a time, both in Paris and the provinces. The contacts thus established have certainly proved useful, but these General Estates of the Social Movement did not produce concrete counterproposals, let alone the outlines of an alternative project. They did not crown their efforts, as was originally projected, with a vast national conference. But the search for different solutions, for another future, has not been abandoned. Actually, a new body, the Copernic Foundation, has just been set up by unionists and intellectuals to encourage such work.

It is clear, however, that it will take quite a lot of time, and a great deal of pushing by a genuine movement from below, before the vision of an alternative society emerges. Yet one has the impression that France is already ripe for the rebirth of a new New Left. It could be centered around radical labor activists and the militants in what the French call *le mouvement des sans* ("movement of the withouts"—people without shelter, workers without jobs, immigrants without documents). If they can combine their activity with a broader project, they would exercise a great attraction not only for many Communists but also for the Left ranks of the Greens and the Socialists, thus changing substantially the political balance in the country.

Divided They Fall?

How should this budding radical Left—numerically inferior, to begin with—deal with the mainstream Left, more respectful of the established order? The problem has become salient in Italy since October 9, when, amid a chorus of condemnation, Fausto Bertinotti, leader of Rifondazione Comunista, or Communist Refounding, chose to bring down a Center-Left government headed by Romano Prodi. Was he right in principle? And if so, were his timing and manner appropriate?

Italy's Communist Party changed its name and policies after 1989 to move out of opposition. Now, as the Left Democrats (DS), they sit on the conservative side within the Socialist International, and since October their leader, Massimo D'Alema, has been Italy's prime minister. Meanwhile, many militants left the party and set up Rifondazione, which was joined by fragments of Italy's New Left. By 1994, the new party had a two-headed leadership: The traditionalists were represented by the president, Armando Cossutta; the radicals by the secretary, Bertinotti, a newcomer who had built his reputation as a progressive labor leader.

In April 1996, the Left won the parliamentary election. D'Alema's party, though the strongest within the ruling Olive Tree coalition, which included the Left Democrats, leftish Christian Democrats and technocrats, did not demand the prime minister's job, which was given to Prodi, a moderate Catholic economist. The task of the government was to tighten the country's belt, to reduce the deficit so that Italy could join the euro from the start. Rifondazione stayed outside the government, but its thirty-four votes were needed for a parliamentary majority.

There were strains. In October 1997, a break was avoided only at the last minute when Prodi promised a law ordaining a thirty-five-hour workweek as a reward. But it was clear that once Italy was admitted into the monetary club, matters would come to a head. Bertinotti expressed it in a metaphor: You are made to walk in the desert because you must reach the oasis on the horizon. Once there, you are told: Sorry, it was a mirage, keep on going. His party was not moving. Unless it was shown a concrete shift in policy in favor of the working people, it would not vote for the budget. Cossutta protested that to precipitate the crisis now was to open the door for the tycoon Silvio Berlusconi and the neo-Fascist Gianfranco Fini. Although Bertinotti carried the party, Cossutta held the parliamentary group. Twenty-one Rifondazione deputies voted for the budget, but thirteen followed Bertinotti and voted against it. That was enough. Prodi was defeated 313 to 312.

Now we can move on to the heart of the matter. I think Bertinotti was right on the principle at stake. All the precedents in the left-wing movement, notably in the British Labor Party, show that if you turn the defense of the bad against the worse into a categorical imperative, you carry no weight. You let the Clintons, Blairs, and Prodis get away with murder. They take you for granted. The only way you count is if they know that beyond a certain point, you will not hesitate to veto their action. The timing? The result did not prove as dramatic as predicted. D'Alema, the real master, replaced Prodi as prime minister. Admittedly, to get this result, the votes of the Christian Democratic supporters of the reactionary former president, Francesco Cossiga, were required. You now have a government with a follower of Cossutta sitting together with supporters of Cossiga. This should worry his comrades, and the Left Democrats should be perturbed to discover how far their party is ready to move to the Right. But these are confirmations of the state of things rather than new departures.

The ideal way in which the radical Left should proceed is by sketching the vision of a different society, by presenting an alternative project and mobilizing a mass movement behind it. It can win in Parliament only if it wins the minds of the people in the country. Bertinotti would probably not disagree, though he can plead that

Rifondazione is not the only party that is still in the early stages of its search for an alternative.

This, then, is the state of the European Left at the fascinating stage when things are beginning to move once again. Historians may well conclude that the French winter of discontent was the ideological turning point. TINA was badly shaken when the protesters proclaimed, "If that is the future we are offered, to hell with it, alternative or no alternative!" But to get rid of TINA altogether, we must build on this foundation. Democratically, from below, we must start elaborating an alternative project, outlining the vision of a different future. This task, however, is not specifically Italian, French, or European. It is our urgent and common task.

Days of Hope
::

Reports from Portugal 1974

For Pacifica Radio

JULY 18

PORTUGAL TODAY HAS merely a provisional government. Palma Carlos, the prime minister, and several of his colleagues have handed in their resignation.

It may seem curious to bother about a government in crisis in a country which less than three months ago changed regimes, a country where a Fascist regime nearly half a century old was overthrown on April 25. But the government crisis is important because it is an inherent part of the struggle for the succession, of the battle over the nature of the system which is to be built on the ruins of the Fascist regime. Will Portugal have a kind of a Gaullist reign; will General Spinola playing the part of a local de Gaulle; or will the 25th of April mark the beginning of a radical transformation of the country?

Professor Palma Carlos and his colleagues prefer the first solution: no radical change. This is why they have suggested that a constitutional referendum be held rapidly, followed by a presidential election. Its result would be inevitable. General Spinola would be elected. The General hasn't got the resistance record of a de Gaulle; quite the contrary. But he has a name, prestige, and popularity due to the fact that he rallied the revolutionary movement. At the same time, President Spinola could be relied upon to preserve bourgeois rule in Portugal.

But the proposal to stage a presidential election rapidly was blocked. Who has the power to block such a swing to the Right? The "Armed Forces" as they are called here, the young officers—lieutenants, captains, colonels who had stayed the April coup and overthrown Fascism. And, so, for the moment, it is a stalemate in history and anything can happen.

What impression does one hear on the spot seventy-five days after the historic overthrow was greeted by popular joy and huge mass demonstrations?

In one sense, life has changed altogether. You can read freely Socialist books, Communist newspapers, leaflets of the New Revolution Left without fear of the once-dreaded PIDE, the political police.

In another sense, nothing has changed. The factories, the banks, the big estates are run by exactly the same people.

Or to be more accurate, something has changed. Walking in Lisbon, you see a small crowd gather around a poster, in which the employees of a bank denounce their boss. Two days ago civil servants, public employees, demonstrated demanding more equal wages. Yesterday, it was the turn of young radicals protesting against the arrest of two young officers who refused to be strikebreakers. And you heard of local strikes in a factory, in an office, even of successful strikes by farm workers.

Obviously, it's but a beginning. The question is whether the process will be allowed to spread, will be given time to develop. This is the real, serious question behind the apparently futile governmental crisis. The future of Portugal is really at stake.

*

PORTUGAL HAS A new government, its second government since the overthrow of the Fascist regime on April 25. The week's crisis is over. The new government is again a coalition, including the Communist leader Cunhal, the Socialist Soares, and representatives of the

Popular Democratic party. But the new government is headed by a military colonel, Vasco Gonçalves, and it contains several officers in key roles as the ministry of the interior or that of labor.

Usually the replacement of civilians by soldiers marks a swing to the Right. This is not the case today in Lisbon. To understand why, I must repeat something about the current crisis I have already told you and say a word about the so-called Movement of the Armed Forces which holds effective power in Portugal since April.

Last week I told you that the government crisis had been precipitated by the prime minister's attempt to have a constitutional referendum, a presidential poll, and to put off parliamentary elections till doomsday. The idea was to boost the provisional president, General Spinola, to introduce a presidential regime, but also to prevent any radical developments. This swing to the Right was foiled by the opposition of the Movement of the Armed Forces.

The Movement of the Armed Forces, or MAF, is the name given to the large group of lieutenants, captains, and majors fed up with the colonial war, disgusted with the unequal and corrupt society they live in—the group which struck in April and overthrew the Fascist regime. But the young officers themselves can be described as a coalition. The movement has its left wing favoring radical reforms; its right wing which, like the General Spinola, would like to stabilize things without attacking bourgeois rule and a big wavering center.

Having prevented a swing to the Right, the young officers can no monger just pull strings from the background. They have been forced to enter the government.

But what they are trying to maintain above all is their own cohesion. This is why they cling to their program, which claims that their role is to restore democracy, return the power to the people, and that, once the elections have been held—in principle, next March—decisions will then be taken about the future of the regime.

But can one wait on such a way? Key social and economic decisions have to be taken at once. Not to take them is to allow the bourgeoisie, a bit frightened at present, to recover its poise and reestablish its rule.

Not to act is also a form of action and the young officers will soon have to make up their mind in which direction they are heading—a capitalist or Socialist one. The proof of the pudding is in the eating.

Portugal, recovering its freedom, is in a way an exhilarating place to be at the moment. But political freedom has to be consolidated and given a social content. The young officers—the Movement of the Armed Forces—are now openly in power. It remains to be seen what they are going to do with it and what the Portuguese people are going to do with their spring.

PORTUGAL: THE REBIRTH OF A NATION
AUGUST 1974

WHAT HAPPENS TO a country which reawakens after nearly half a century of Fascist dictatorship?

To find, out I went to Portugal in July. Because the Portuguese had lived for forty-eight years under Fascist rule. Back in 1926, the military seized power in Lisbon. Two years later they handed it over to a professor of economics, Antonio Salazar, who stayed in power until his death in 1968. The dictatorial regime then continued under Marcello Gaetano. Last March, the song you've just heard, "Villa Grandola Morena," was the signal of the first abortive military coup. A month later, on April 25, the young officers of the Movement of the Armed Forces overthrew the hated regime and millions of Portuguese invaded the streets to chant and rejoice over its fall. That the regime was doomed could be guessed. Portugal. Nine million people. One of Europe's poorest countries clinging to its African possessions: Guinea Bissau, Mozambique, Angola. Thirteen years of a hopeless colonial war, with no glimpse of a solution. A stagnating economy and thousands of Portuguese emigrating every year to find a job in France or in Germany. Even the brighter members of big business had grasped that the time had come for a change, for a shift from old colonialism to the new, from Africa to Europe, and from Fascism to more sophisticated bourgeois rule.

The symbol of such an orderly change is the provisional head of the republic, General Antonio de Spinola, the would-be de Gaulle of Portugal. But don't confuse him with France's legendary hero. In the original anti-Fascist struggle they stood on opposite sides. Antonio de Spinola fought on Franco's side in Spain and also volunteered to fight against the Russians in the Second World War. He then gained fame and rank as a colonial commander. But he was clever enough to understand that the colonial war was leading nowhere, except toward an explosion at home. And, so, he wrote a book last year, preaching a compromise in Africa. The book was attacked. Its writer became a hero. And the junior officers promoted Spinola to president when they took over in April.

A change from Salazar to Spinola, on its own, would not be an earth-shaking event. But Antonio de Spinola, while not just a figurehead, is not really the master. Power lies in the hands of the junior officers, who seized it last April. Their control is no longer a secret. In July, one of the leading members of the small coordinating committee of the Movement of the Armed Forces, Vasco Gonçalves, officially became the prime minister and three of his colleagues took over key governmental jobs.

Since the MAF (Movimento das Forças Armadas Portuguesas), the Movement of the Armed Forces, will figure prominently in this program, let me tell you briefly something about these lieutenants, captains, and occasionally colonels who are the artisans of the Portuguese spring. First, they do not include all the officers, but they represent the bulk of the officers' corps and certainly its more progressive elements.

Second, they come from different social backgrounds. In the last dozen years or so of a colonial war, the children of the bourgeoisie were not particularly keen on a military career. But in a poor country, with expensive education, the army offered an outlet to bright young men from the lower-middle class or even for sons of peasants. Besides, since many jobs had to be filled, the government was compelled to call up reservists, the *Milicianos,* to mobilize graduates coming from universities, the hotbed of resistance to the regime. The ferment began to spread. It took ten years to reach explosive proportions.

The young officers are a motley crowd. They range from moderate bourgeois reformers, admirers of Spinola, to genuine Socialists. They cling together by sticking to their joint program. But the program, in turn, reflects their contradictions. On the one hand, it proclaims the need for equality and social justice, for an attack on the power of the monopolists, for a rapid improvement in the condition of the working people. On the other hand, it gives its pledge not to carry out any radical reforms, leaving the decision to the electorate which, in principle, should express itself in the spring. But in the meantime, with inflation, unemployment, and a country dreaming of a new deal, time will not allow a stop. Nor will big business, shaken for a moment, waste this respite.

The second and crucial reason why the Portuguese spring is not merely a shift from Salazar to Spinola is the entry of the masses on the political stage. On May Day more than half a million people paraded in Lisbon. It's like if five million people paraded through New York. And it wasn't limited to Lisbon. The same thing happened in Oporto, Coïmbra, Setubal, Evora, and so on. Nor was it limited to May Day parades. The workers, discovering their new freedom, proceeded to strike, fighting for better wages, improved living conditions, for a new dignity. And it wasn't just industrial workers, public or private, but also employees; even farm laborers began to ask for a better deal.

It is this awakening of a nation that is most difficult to convey. The mike can't always record it and ordinary Portuguese people don't speak English. The best I can do is to mention some of the things that happened during my stay in Portugal. There were two mass demonstrations of the Left in support of the Armed Forces Movement and three smaller demos of the extreme Left against colonialism and in support of two officers who refused to be strikebreakers. Public employees went on a brief strike because the proposed wage increase was not sufficiently egalitarian. In a fishing town I visited, the fishermen had just won better wages and their first holiday with pay. In a small carpet factory near Evora, when the boss declared he couldn't afford to pay higher wages, the working women threatened to run the factory on their own.

And I could go on and on, giving examples without conveying to you the essential, the extraordinary popular thirst for reading, learning, doing. . . . Elsewhere, when you distribute leaflets, a good portion is left scattered on the ground. In Portugal today, they are neatly folded and put into the pocket, to be read again, studied, and discussed. . . .

Isn't such a political awakening of the masses the beginning of a revolutionary process? Not really or, rather, not necessarily. To keep the movement from below in check, within tolerable bounds, you have the armed forces, but also the political parties. After half a century of a corporate state, political parties are growing like mushrooms. An expert listed for me more than fifty. But for the moment only three really matter. There is the PPD, the Popular Democratic Party, a party which claims to hold the Center, but which will be driven more and more to the Right. There is the Socialist Party, headed by foreign secretary Mario Soares, trying to strike real roots in the country. Last but not least, there is the Communist Party, led by Álvaro Cunhal, emerging proudly from the underground as the main victim of the old regime, but also the main force of resistance; a C.P. that is an important pillar of the new order, disciplined, responsible, preaching discipline and patience to the impatient masses.

I've talked to several Communists in Portugal. (We didn't talk in English and that's one reason why the conversations are not recorded.) Portuguese Communists differ in sense from their French or Italian colleagues. They haven't gone through years of relative comfort in a bourgeois democracy. They come straight from the underground. The young leader who, in Oporto, in a friendly argument, defended the party line, was still in his mid-thirties. He had twelve years of jail behind him.

If their immediate background is different, the party is the same as in France or in Italy. It's the Popular Front, the historical compromise; it's very much the nation and democracy. The struggle is against monopolies and Fascism, not against bourgeois rule. There is no question of Socialism, of revolution, not even of the conquest of commanding heights. The leftists, spreading strikes, are playing into the hands of the enemy.

I tried to find out how one could at one and the same time preach patience to the workers and do nothing about the fundamental power of big business. But though my sympathy for this genuine fighter was obvious and though we spoke the same language, we talked at cross purposes. I was talking of state and revolution and he of what's to be done. I mentioned the masses in motion. He replied about recruiting members and organizing unions. I talked of the power of the bourgeoisie, he of the danger of Fascism. I—of unique opportunities for action from below; he—of the situation not being ripe. Listening to this nice young man—whose courage and devotion required no additional proof—I wondered whether for his party, as it now is, the situation would ever be ripe for revolution.

But this is an other matter, stretching well beyond Portugal. The part played in Portugal by the Communist Party was my first question to Jorge Sampaio,[*] an ex-student leader, now a prominent civil rights lawyer and member of the MES (Movimiento de Esquerda) . . .

(Break in transcript for taped interview)

The first hundred days are over. The new Portuguese government, the new regime have plenty on their plate. They have to tackle inflation, fight against unemployment, get rid as quickly as possible of their colonial empire. The young captains must also lay the foundation of democratic rule in a country just emerging from half a century of dictatorship. Will they remember that the rule of the people is not just a question of elections?

By car I went back from Portugal to Paris through Spain. This was an excuse, a pretext for setting foot in Franco's Spain with an easy conscience. But my Spanish refugee friends had given me their blessing anyway, with the assurance: Portugal today, Spain tomorrow. "Next year in Madrid" is the new hopeful greeting.

* Sampaio is now the president of Portugal.

With Portugal liberated, Greece getting rid of its military rulers, and the Franco regime apparently doomed, I could not help asking whether big business hadn't decided to get rid of most dictatorial form of bourgeois rule before they are smashed by a popular explosion. I wonder about the role Communist parties are playing in Portugal and may play in Greece tomorrow, and Spain after tomorrow, as the potential pillars of the new regime, as the crucial helpers in the transition. But won't the same issue have to be faced pretty soon in Italy and then in France? To put it differently: What is the nature of the gathering storm, of the economic and social crisis facing Western Europe? Does it leave scope for reform rather than revolution? And, in that case, can the Communist parties perform the function once performed by their social democratic ancestors?

These are the awkward questions for tomorrow. Today, at the end of my Portuguese journey, I cannot help having a feeling of confidence in the action of the people themselves, strengthened by this demonstration of their capacity to awaken even after a half-century of political slavery. Thinking of the Lisbon strikers fighting for more equal wages, of the women trying to take over their small factory, of the young Portuguese so eager to learn to do, to change—I can't help hoping that sooner or later, here or elsewhere, a regime will change, a revolution will take place, not just allegedly for the people, but genuinely, really, through the people . . .

Only a Beginning . . .

France 1981

MAY 23, 1981
The Nation

Paris

NOTHING IS OVER but the counting and not even that. In the last two Sundays of June, Frenchmen will return to the polls, and François Mitterrand will invite them to confirm their verdict by electing a new, Socialist-dominated National Assembly. In the electoral campaign, the new president will have to reveal more clearly his program and his alliances. His government will also measure the resistance of big business, domestic and foreign.

On the historic night of May 10, such thoughts for the future were absent from the minds of the huge crowd flocking spontaneously to the Place de la Bastille. They had come to celebrate the end of conservative rule. It cannot be said that all had waited eagerly for this moment for twenty-three years, since many were barely that old.

It was a night to savor as the men who had treated the state as their private property started to pack while their wealthy backers began to worry about their basic interests. One man, traveling that night from Château-Chinon to his small house in the heart of Paris, had a special reason for rejoicing. At sixty-four, François Mitterrand had finally reached his goal. Whatever one thinks of his maneuvers as a politician, he has been consistent on how the Socialists should regain power.

Ever since French settlers and paratroopers from Algeria destroyed the Fourth Republic and brought General Charles de Gaulle back to power in May 1958, Mitterrand has guided his party on the assumption that the Left needs Communist support to win but will accept it only if the Communists are the junior partners in the coalition. In 1977, when victory was within his grasp, the Communists suddenly turned down the role they had accepted. Defeated a year later and written off by most commentators, Mitterrand bounced back. In the April 26 first-round elections, the Communists paid a price for having shattered the alliance, and their setback ruined Valéry Giscard d'Estaing's campaign by depriving him of the indispensable Red bogy. On May 10, the left rallied more wholeheartedly behind Mitterrand than the Right behind Giscard d'Estaing. A swing of about 2.5 percent was enough to ensure a comfortable victory of 15.7 million to 14.6 million votes for the first Socialist president of the Fifth Republic.

Mitterrand will keep his campaign pledges in two stages. When he assumes the presidency, probably on May 25, he will at once form a government and dissolve the National Assembly. Without a Parliament, his government can only proceed by decree. It can, however, raise the minimum wage, or set up a commission to prepare for the reduction of the workweek to thirty-five hours.

Meanwhile, from their new position of strength, the Socialists will be negotiating with their potential partners—mainly the Communists—trying to reach an agreement providing both for an electoral pact and for some Communists participating in the government. The Socialists hope to improve the economy by boosting consumption. Their platform also contains a limited program of nationalization, including the remainder of the banking system, nine big industrial groups, steel, and sections of the nuclear, space, and armament industries already financed by the state.

By normal capitalist standards this is quite a lot, but the change cannot be described as revolutionary. Mitterrand was right when he denied the charges of Giscard d'Estaing that his election would mean the conversion of France to Socialism and "a change of society." He is clearly trying to carry out reforms within the framework of existing society, and the trade unions will give him, at least for some time, the benefit of the doubt. Nevertheless, any statements about Mitterrand's reformism must be qualified in two ways.

First, because of the world economic crisis, the climate is hardly favorable for reform. With the French economy stagnant, or growing very slowly, drastic measures are required to bring about relatively small improvements. The second qualification applies to all left-wing governments. Whenever they are elected, capital—domestic or foreign—plays it safe for a while, waiting to see whether the newcomer respects the rules of the game. It stops investing, and sends its money abroad. Thus, the economic equation is rapidly altered and the left-wing government is forced either to surrender or to become more radical than it originally intended. In Paris, the Bourse and the foreign exchanges have responded to the Socialist accession in typical fashion, but it is still too early to say whether the capitalist establishment will face François Mitterrand with the usual challenge. Nor can we know what his response will be, if it does.

Let us rather return to the historic night. The festivities were not limited to Paris or to pedestrians. Throughout France, joyriding drivers were honking their horns rhythmically to the phrase *"Ce n'est qu'un debut."* ("This is only a beginning.") It may seem strange that so revolutionary a slogan was revived on an electoral occasion. But the slogan is literally true. Mitterrand's victory is only a beginning, a turning point. For France alone?

City of Fight

MARCH 24, 1997
The Nation

Paris

IT WAS A splendid demonstration. On that sunny Saturday, February 22, there were more than one hundred thousand people in the streets, starting symbolically at the Gare de l'Est, from which the Jews were deported during the war, and marching through Paris to proclaim that immigration was not a central problem but a phony issue designed to divide and disturb; that the racist Jean-Marie Le Pen, as one poster put it, is himself "alien" to France's democratic tradition and that politicians pander too much to his constituency. Considering that political parties and labor unions played a minor role in organizing it, the demo was a tremendous success, as had been the petition and the mass collection of signatures that prompted this unprecedented episode. The pretext was the umpteenth bill to tighten regulations governing the entry and stay of (poor) foreigners, including a new provision requiring French hosts to report the departure of their foreign guests—in other words, to act as informers. (Danielle Mitterrand, the president's widow, said she would not comply, following the example of her father, a headmaster who, during the war, refused to report who among his teachers was Jewish.)

But the indignation had deeper roots: the electoral conquest by the xenophobic National Front of a fourth town in southern France (this time by an absolute majority, and not the result of a triangular fight); reports from the three other cities of the Front gradually extending its control over cultural life; the gut feeling that if nothing is done to fight back, the cancer will spread. And, so, when a group of young film-makers published a pledge to disobey the new law, it opened the flood-gates: Thousands and thousands wanted to sign. For the first time in years, the intellectuals had awakened the community.

Legally, they achieved little. The government dropped the informer clause and got the rest of the bill easily through the House. According to opinion polls, most people here favor stricter controls on immigration; this may explain the strangely moderate posture of left-wing leaders and particularly of the Socialist Lionel Jospin during the whole confrontation. Admittedly, industrial workers were not legion in that Saturday demo, and to carry out one's policy it is necessary to win a majority. But how? By putting one's head in the sand, avoiding awkward subjects, and allowing Le Pen to dictate the political agenda? Or by tackling the central problem of unemployment, offering solutions instead of scapegoats, and attacking racism head on, wherever it is to be found, including within the working class?

In the winter of 1995, through a series of strikes and mass demonstrations, the French people rejected the downsizing model and its dismantling of the welfare state. This refusal to accept the blackmail that there is no alternative marks a date. It is now up to the French Left to reconcile that movement of social protest with the new one of moral indignation, linking the two through concrete economic proposals and the vision of a radically different society. When and if it does so, Paris will really be the pioneer, showing the way to the Western world.

Why We Need a New Manifesto

MAY 1988
Monthly Review

WE NEED A new manifesto. Not a blueprint, not a detailed program. But a project, the vision of a different society, the proof that history has not come to an end, that there is a future beyond capitalism. We need it badly because its absence is the main weapon of our enemies. The nickname of Maggie Thatcher, TINA (There Is No Alternative), is the foundation on which their mighty propaganda machine rests. I shall illustrate this by an analogy.

Thirty years ago, 1968 was the year of youth rebellion from Berkeley to Tokyo, highlighted by the French students and workers rising in the merry month of May (a reminder, incidentally, that everything was far from perfect in the so-called "golden age of capitalism"). Still, the system did survive, and it is amusing to remember that, at the time, it was not defended on the ground that there is no alternative. Capitalism, it was argued, had found the secret of eternal growth. Why abolish a society which has managed to get rid of its worst calamities, in which the harsh laws of the market have been replaced by Keynesian fine-tuning and the long lines of the jobless by the social protection of the state? How strange it all sounds. Today nobody is trying to talk about "capitalism with a human face." We are plainly back to the laws of the jungle, which we must just accept because, allegedly, there is no way out. And this is why it is crucial to resurrect a project, a vision, an alternative.

I will not have the cheek, the chutzpah, to pretend to produce the solutions. But I will dare to venture, inevitably in shorthand, the issues that, in my opinion, the Western Left must tackle and solve if it wants to be, once again, historically relevant.

First, we must deal with the problem of the allegedly vanishing work. We are living in a society in which our technological genius, translated into higher productivity, means either bigger unemployment or greater polarization with the so-called working poor. Marx's suggestion that "the theft of somebody else's labor time" is a miserable foundation to calculate our wealth—which we should measure by disposable time not by labor time—is so much truer today than it was 150 years ago. We have the technological means to live differently. If output were determined not by exchange value, or the weight of your purse, but by social need democratically decided by the people, we could keep growth within ecologically tolerable limits, eliminate unemployment, and reduce the working week. Indeed, in the advanced capitalist countries, we could start reducing heavy, dangerous, and dreary work, thus gradually removing the frontier between labor and leisure.

Globalization is the second item and here we have a double task. On one side, globalization is being used as a substitute for TINA to convince people of the vanity of their struggle. We must therefore remind them that the nation-state is still the terrain on which the struggle for the radical transformation of society must begin. Or, if you prefer to put it in the terms of the Manifesto, "the proletariat of each country must, of course, first of all settle matters with its own bourgeoisie." But this is only half the story. Socialism, like capitalism, tends to be universal, and internationalism is the only genuine reply to globalization. It is an immediate categorical imperative for the labor movements of the different countries of the European Union. But it must be revived all over. The final confrontation will take place throughout the planet, from Paris to Peking and from Seoul to Seattle.

The third issue is equality. We are living in a world in which the wealth of its 447 dollar billionaires exceeded in 1996 the income of half of the world's population. These fantastic discrepancies are not only international. A currency speculator living in New York earned in a few weeks what it would have taken an American in a minimum-wage job one hundred fifty thousand years. And the polarization is increasing. In such a society egalitarianism—not charity, not equity, but a genuine search for equality—must figure at the heart of any progressive project.

Such a search implies a great deal. It implies the end of exploitation. It means that we cannot live at the expense of the so-called Third World. It means that we have to attack the very roots of one of the oldest exploitations—that of woman by man. Egalitarianism is not—as they tell you—leveling, uniformity, but it is an attempt to eliminate the social roots of inequality. As such, it will involve profound changes in property and power relations. Which brings us to the fourth item— democracy.

Last but not least. Democracy is crucial not only because of the crimes committed in the name of Socialism, which make it imperative to prevent any repetition. It is also crucial because, for us, it is not just using your ballot every four years to choose between Tweedledee and Tweedledum. It means people gaining mastery over their work and their fate in the factory and in the office, in the shops, labs, and campuses. It must mean power flowing from below and yet decisions being taken not only at the local level. We must reinvent democracy if we want Socialism to spell the self-management of society.

If the movement goes in that direction, it will be on its way to what I call realistic Utopia. Realistic because it has its roots in the real social and political struggles of today. Utopian, because our enemies call Utopian any effort to move beyond the confines of capitalism and we shall take their insult for a compliment and a challenge. In even shorter shorthand, let me make three final points. First, if we are talking about a fundamentally different society, we are not suggesting that we shall get there overnight. This is not a recipe for instant Socialism. We know that we have a long march ahead, but we can only get going if we have the vision of a radically different society, a vision that will be changed and elaborated as the movement learns, one which becomes more conscious as it advances.

Second, the fact that it will take a long time does not mean that we have plenty of time to start moving. With popular discontent rising, if we don't provide rational, progressive solutions, there are plenty of people waiting in the wings with irrational and reactionary solutions. From France, where I live, and where the xenophobic National Front of Jean-Marie Le Pen has gained another percentage point, I bring you the warning that the ghosts of the past are not buried forever.

Finally, all this is not some particularly Parisian, European preoccupation. Even if we may seem somewhat ahead, this is part of our common struggle. And this is why I shall end with the slogan of the French winter of 1995, that winter of discontent that has given a new impetus to the movement: *Ouais, ouais, tous ensemble, tous ensemble.* All together, all together, let us get going as soon as we can, on both sides of the ocean.

Seattle from the Seine

JANUARY 3, 2000
The Nation

"*LE MONDE N'EST pas une marchandise*" ("The world is not a commodity") proclaimed the large banner in the Parisian demonstration against the WTO. Seen from Paris, what happened in Seattle was striking. It was the revolt of citizens against governments that instead of being their servants are the servants of the multinational corporations. It was a movement from below, across frontiers, against the powers that be.

For years, Western Europeans have been told that they must not only accept the existing system but also endorse its latest version, the American model. Since, in practical terms, that implied the dismantling of their welfare state, it met real resistance. The first blow against TINA—the resigned acceptance that There Is No Alternative—was delivered by the French, in their winter of discontent of 1995, when the protesters said in substance: "If that is the future you are offering us, to hell with your future!" That refusal was momentous, because as long as people believe there is no way out, they will not be looking for one. Yet, so far, the French movement has failed to gather momentum and to outline an alternative, possibly because it lacked a global perspective. Now comes Seattle, with Americans leading the battle against the American model, to provide an international dimension.

For radicals opposing the Maastricht Treaty on one side of the ocean or NAFTA on the other, it was imperative that their stand not be confused with the jingoist opposition of the ultra-Right—of Jean-Marie Le Pen, Pat Buchanan, or even the Tory Euroskeptics. We must not put the blame for the ills of our society on the alien, the stranger. And we must, while we defend our "sovereignty" against the encroachment of big business, make it plain that we are ready to give it up for the sake of collaboration with labor unions and other rank-and-file organizations. In the battle against the WTO, this rhetoric was turned into practice. The community across frontiers was shown when part of the money needed to free José Bové (jailed in France because he took part in the symbolic dismantling of a McDonald's) was raised by the National Family Farm Coalition, and when the same Bové—turned hero overnight because his attack on *malbouffe* (junk food) struck a deep chord—refused to be used by the French government propagandists; he was against export subsidies, because they favored the big farmers, agribusiness, the corporations. The struggle against multinationals and against *malbouffe* knows no frontiers. Viewed from the Seine, the protesters in Seattle—the unionists and the ecologists—seemed united, and kids from "have" nations fought for the damned of the earth against their own multinationals.

Let us not get carried away. The tasks ahead are tremendous. Wages and working conditions in the Third World will not be the only divisive issue. If we allow the profit-driven expansion to continue, we shall soon reach the ecological limits of the planet. The Western nations cannot tell the Chinese or the Indians not to do what we are doing; if we want to survive together we must reshape fundamentally our own patterns of production and consumption. Yet we are intellectually and politically unprepared for such an exercise.

As the events unfolded in Seattle, a small cultural Franco-German television channel broadcasted a recorded dialogue between two of Europe's most famous protesters: Günter Grass, this year's winner of the Nobel Prize for literature, and the sociologist Pierre Bourdieu, who for years has used his prestige to help the expression of dissent. They criticized the extraordinary hold the ruling ideology now has, thanks to the media, on people's minds. They condemned the submission or cowardice of their fellow intellectuals. They deplored the fact that trade unionists cannot organize across frontiers even within the European Union.

It wouldn't be difficult to expand their gloomy perspective. The establishment, clearly taken aback by the sweep and scope of popular discontent, is getting its mighty propaganda machine ready for the counteroffensive. Nor will it be easy to tame the financial Frankenstein unleashed in the recent period. Among the French associations mobilizing against the WTO is an interesting newcomer—ATTAC. Barely two years old, it has 130 local committees and more than 16,000 members. Its primary purpose is to advocate the introduction of a tax on international financial transactions, known as the Tobin tax because it was originally suggested by James Tobin, Nobel laureate in economics. It is no revolutionary measure—merely "some sand into the wheels," in Tobin's words—but it is resisted tooth and nail by the financial establishment as dangerously Utopian. In any case, there is a long way from the Tobin tax to a world that is not a commodity.

And, yet, the protesters in Seattle and beyond have revived the forgotten belief that people can shape things through collective action. Despite the odds, they have set the agenda for the coming millennium by reminding us that there are many people on this planet ready to struggle from below against their own governments and corporations and for a different world—one in which human beings will no longer be merchandise.

Europe: Is There a Fourth Way?

NOVEMBER 6, 2000
The Nation

WONDER BATTERIES, CLAIMS a famous French advertisement, only wear out if they are being used. The opposite is true of democracy. It is now withering away spectacularly in our "advanced" countries, where it has become a money-dominated ritual, thanks to which every four or five years we may abdicate our sovereignty and pick among the candidates of the establishment.

Democracy can only gain ground when people take matters into their own hands—when, at all levels, from the bottom to the very top, they collectively try to gain mastery over their work, their lives and their fate. So why, then, did I feel a certain unease when Europe's protesting truck drivers were using blockades to put pressure on their governments to lower fuel costs? Because to be really genuine, people's power must have a purpose and aim at a more just society.

In the case of the truck drivers, the protest was a reflection of general discontent and the absence of a coherent policy of officialdom. One could imagine a left-wing administration with an ecologically sound energy policy defending the fuel tax as a conservation measure. But that would have meant a government capable of attacking both OPEC and the oil companies, one developing public transport, having a general fiscal policy that penalizes profit and reduces taxes affecting mass consumption, giving working people the feeling that their interests are being defended. The bulk of the population does not feel this. They are told that the West is getting more and more prosperous, yet they perceive that this only applies to a thin layer at the top. A sharp rise in the price of gasoline hit them in their pocketbooks.

In fact, what this crisis showed is that the so-called left-wing governments of Western Europe have no project, no vision, no progressive alternative. We are seeing the final funeral of that nine days' wonder, the fairy tale of the "third way." In Western Europe the period from 1945 to 1975 was one of unprecedented growth (about 5 percent a year of gross national product), and its people probably did better than elsewhere in terms of collective social benefits. This "social democratic" interlude, while not as attractive as it is now being painted in retrospect, did provide advantages worth defending. But, naturally, the miracle of "capitalism with a human face" did not last. After twenty years of defeats of labor around the globe, the United States—with some lessons from Japan—emerged with another potential model, one based on the unquestioned and undiluted dictatorship of capital. It is this model that for several years now has been peddled to Western Europe.

Many voters saw the third way as some sort of combination of America's new ruthless dynamism with the welfare state and social democracy. The leftist label attached to this U.S. model was supposed to convince Europeans, keen on retaining the social gains won in the years of prosperity after the war, that the welfare state would not be dismantled too brutally. The purpose of the third way was to dismantle it, but to carry out the process without promoting a radical response.

Now the leftist governments in Europe may well have fulfilled this task. Last year, eleven out of the fifteen governments on the continent were still run by leftist parties. Since then, Austria has swung to the Right, and the odds are that Italy will follow suit in next year's general election. A triumphant Jörg Haider in Austria, and the formerly open Fascist Gianfranco Fini and jingoistic regionalist Umberto Bossi in Italy, were a lot to swallow. And the extremist Vlaams Blok got a third of the vote in the municipal election in Antwerp, Belgium's second-largest city. But when in quiet, civilized Denmark the xenophobic People's Party of

Pia Kjaersgaard gets 7.4 percent of the vote and now claims double that share in opinion polls, something is rotten in the kingdom of Europe. Fortunately, the most dangerous, Jean-Marie Le Pen's National Front in France, lost momentum through a split. Still, if we don't do our duty, there are plenty of candidates to exploit the growing discontent. But the dividing line between Europe's Left and Right has become so blurred that it requires an expert's eye to draw the political distinction between the conservative José Maria Aznar in Spain and the progressive Tony Blair in Britain or Gerhard Schröder in Germany.

The quickening pace of events in the past few years, however, while a common currency was being set up by eleven members of the European Union, has confirmed the views of the doubters, namely, that a Europe that does not have a different social project, a model of its own, has no chance of standing up to the United States and of really defending its interests. I am not referring here to the fall of the euro, which in twenty months has lost over a quarter of its value. This is merely a symptom. What is more significant is the way in which economic concentration has been proceeding during this period. This process has been speeded up by the disappearance of national frontiers and the use of a joint currency under the EU.

Mergers and acquisitions are multiplying in all sectors. They are no longer limited to the big eating the small. Now giants are swallowing giants, and, increasingly, they are doing it across frontiers. But they are not necessarily, or even predominantly, doing it within the borders of the European Union. When a big Swiss or German bank, having absorbed its neighbors, looks for a target, it is most probably some specialist investment bank, quite likely to be American—for instance, Deutsche Bank has taken over Bankers Trust in New York. With the dollar riding high, Europeans have been pouring their money into the United States, while the Americans are picking plums in Europe. (Incidentally, rumor has it that the rather reluctant U.S. decision to bolster the euro in September was imposed on U.S. Treasury Secretary Larry Summers by U.S. mutual fund holders, worried by the drop in value of their holdings.)

Last year, the United States was the main target of direct foreign investment (276 billion dollars), and the reason is crucial. Why should a European banker or manufacturer disdain a U.S. partner if he thinks the American company is the most profitable? What means has a European government to impose its controls over the free flow of money, the pattern of investment—let alone some form of democratic planning—if at the same time it encourages and praises "globalization," which is to say the spread of the U.S. model? Naturally, there will be conflicts between European and American interests, notably over agriculture. There will be deals and confrontations. But a Europe that does not consciously build a different kind of society, that relies on the U.S. Treasury to back the euro, cannot be taken seriously as a potential equal partner.

There are, to be sure, other domains, like diplomacy and military collaboration, in which Europe may try to assert itself. But here, too, especially after Kosovo, any claims of growing independence are illusory. True, the European Union now has a man in charge of common policy, but he is Javier Solana: In his youth a protester against U.S. weapons in Europe, Solana was Secretary General of NATO in his last job. German Foreign Minister Joschka Fischer, another ex-revolutionary protester turned pillar of the establishment, claims openly that for him the long-term aim remains a "European federation." But the EU for the moment is traveling in the opposite direction, and its very existence may be at stake. Its size, shape, and institutional structure are all uncertain. Started with six members, now with fifteen and expecting to more than double that number with the entry of Eastern European nations and others over the next few years, the EU doesn't even know whether it has a future. If it really aims at a federation, it should build a closely integrated core and a loose periphery. In other words, strengthen the institutions that govern it before admitting new members.

Otherwise, the entry of new members into an organization with weak institutions could kill the very idea of a federal structure. The British are still suspected of being a U.S. Trojan horse bent on turning the whole construction into a vast free-trade area that will be extended beyond the Atlantic Ocean. At the December summit meeting of the ruling European Council in Nice, the fifteen must, in principle, agree on their institutional project so as to be able to proceed with the enlargement of the EU. It would be surprising if the deliberations at Nice, which will mark the end of the six-month French presidency of the EU, closed the year with any significant results. A provisional compromise is much more likely.

But if Western Europe is to try to be truly independent and stand up to the United States, it cannot do it on capitalist lines. It will have to start all over again by defending its welfare state. Because, despite the spread of the working poor, of precariousness and of uncertainty, despite the growing attitude against public pensions, Europe's welfare state is still more attractive than the American, and you can start the struggle only when people have the feeling that they are fighting for their interests. A European New Left would thus have to begin by coming to the rescue of the welfare state, but not fraudulently, as under the third way. It must do so by showing how this welfare state must be broadened, made universal, and rendered really democratic. It must show quickly—almost at once—that you cannot carry out such a progressive strategy and at the same time allow the savage extension of the U.S. model of globalization. That model, by its very inspiration— profit above all—renders any such developments impossible.

Europeans will have to start the battle at once, because it is only in the renewed struggle for higher wages and less precarious working conditions that the labor movement can understand that its demands clash with the very foundations of existing society. The same is true for feminists and radical ecologists. It is through their own experience that they must learn that their aspirations and dreams cannot be fulfilled within the established order. Only then will a genuine New Left be able to seek a "fourth way," one that does not conceal the established disorder but tries to move beyond the confines of capitalist society.

Controls over the movement of capital; the use of state power not to boost big corporations but to combat them; capitalism; Socialism; democratic planning from below—all these have become unused or dirty words. So it would be naive to expect such a policy to be invented, let alone applied, overnight. It is difficult to determine which tendency will prevail, because we are living in a strange period affected by two contradictory trends. On the one hand, the American model is spreading seemingly inexorably, with little effective resistance, and certainly none by European governments. On the other hand, its ideological domination has been shaken and weakened. More and more people, particularly in the younger generation, are now convinced that globalization brings about not prosperity but polarization, social uncertainty, inequality, the strains and stresses of uncertainty about the future.

There is something deeper, a growing feeling that the society it promises has no attraction. The extraordinary success in France of José Bové and his revolt against McDonald's and the *malbouffe*—junk food—that it symbolizes is only one small example. With mad cow disease, with the rushed abuse of genetic modification in the interest of big chemical corporations and agribusiness, there is increasing awareness that a system driven forward by the accumulation of profit cannot take time to study the use to which we should put our extraordinary progress in science and technology; that it is unable to assure the necessary precautions; that, condemned to permanent but uncontrolled growth, it may soon threaten the very future of our planet.

And yet, despite this awareness, especially among the young, the search for an alternative is still very timid. Shall we then wallow in gloom and doom? In some sections of the British former New Left there is now a temptation to retreat into ivory towers and rely on the old Marxist argument that "capitalism contains within itself the seeds of its own destruction." The greatest illusion of all, however, would be to assume that capitalism will accomplish this task of self-destruction on its own, without the help of a vast movement from below, which in its struggle would also be forging the vision of a different society. In 1995, the French "winter of discontent" reminded us that one could resist, at least for a time, even without a clear alternative.

Historically, the lesson of Seattle—if we don't freeze it as a fetish and reduce it to repetitive demonstrations—is even more important. With the Americans taking the lead in the struggle against the world seen as merchandise, we are reminded that globalization is not the only form internationalism can take. What is at stake, it is now clear, is neither the imposition of the U.S. model on Europe nor the defense of Europe's welfare state. It is our common struggle—from below and on a worldwide scale—against a capitalist system both triumphant and in deep crisis. Amid the present confusion, we may actually be watching the early phase of a new historical period.

Remembering Daniel Singer

FEBRUARY 2001
Monthly Review

MY FRIEND DANIEL SINGER, in a piece he wrote for the *Nation* six years ago, said that he often felt like a deserter from the army of the dead because he escaped the Nazi roundup of Jews in Paris by walking across France to Switzerland.

Daniel cheated death again five years ago when he was hit with a life-threatening illness. But this time the Parisian medical profession came to his rescue and he was cured and able to resume his busy life as a journalist, author, radio commentator, and lecturer.

Daniel's luck and the old millennium ran out together; in December 2000 he died after a year-long battle with cancer. We are going to have to find our way in the new millennium without him, although he did leave his last book as a sort of *vade mecum* to help us at least head in the right direction. Fittingly, its title is *Whose Millennium? Theirs or Ours?*

Daniel was born in 1926 in the Warsaw ghetto. His father, Bernard Singer, was a poet, a journalist, and poor. His mother, Esther (affectionately known as Estuchia), was the pride and joy of traditional and wealthy Jewish parents who were dead set against her marriage to Bernard. He was, after all, a dreamer, a scribbler. By what means short of divine intervention would he ever earn enough *zlotys* to support their daughter? But marry they did. Asked years later if Esther had come with a dowry, Bernard laughed. "Dowry? That's what they offered me if I'd go away."

Daniel was born at home, as was the custom. Upstairs in the same apartment house lived another young poet, Isaac Deutscher. Daniel liked to say he'd been close to Deutscher from the day he was born until the day Deutscher died. Indeed, Deutscher was like a father to Daniel and it was Daniel who delivered the eulogy at Deutscher's funeral in London.

Estuchia was the intellectual of the Singer family. She was serious in her convictions, deeply philosophical, and cherished the unforgettable experience of having heard Rosa Luxemburg speak. While still at university, she became a Marxist. Bernard was more of a romantic. Isaac Deutscher has said that Bernard Singer's writing was like a nightingale singing and that Daniel's ability to present complicated ideas with grace and coherence was the combined influence of both parents. It was Estuchia who urged Deutscher to read Marx. He did and went on to become one of the leading Marxist historians and scholars of the twentieth century. So the Marxist triple play was Estuchia to Isaac to Daniel.

In time, Bernard's scribblings defied prediction by bringing in enough money to permit him to move his family out of the ghetto. Estuchia was able to give up teaching to stay home and raise and educate her children who, by this time, numbered three. Daniel was the only Jewish boy in his class at school and, despite the fact that anti-Semitism was a way of life in Poland, he was popular, albeit in the condescending manner of, "We don't like Jews, but you're different." (And, as the joke used to go, especially in the bathroom.)

When he was twelve, Daniel developed a severe form of sinusitis. By now Bernard could afford to send his son to a warm climate for his health. Estuchia packed up Daniel and his sister and headed for Antibes in the south of France. It was the summer of 1939.

The Nazi-Soviet Pact was signed on August 24 of that year. Deutscher, who had left Poland to live in England, traveled to Antibes to tell the Singers war was coming. After Deutscher's visit Daniel and his mother and sister took the train to Paris. Soon after, war broke out. In Paris

Daniel attended the Lycée Montaigne but after some months they relocated to Anger; from Anger they went to St. Jean de Luz where his sister refused to take a boat to go to England, having learned that two ships had been sunk; from there they went to Toulouse, Oloron, and finally to Marseilles. Daniel sold his stamp collection so they'd have money for a place to live. In the summer of 1942 the police came for the Singers. Daniel was not home at the time. Daniel's sister jumped from a window and broke one of her legs. Esther was allowed to take her daughter to a hospital and it was then decided that Daniel should try to escape to Switzerland. With another Polish lad, he traveled some four hundred miles across France, slipped past Swiss border patrols, and made his way to Geneva. Swiss authorities at first put him in a concentration camp but then released him into the custody of the Polish consul in Berne. He enrolled in school. Two years later, he was able to pass the baccalaureate exam in French. He studied philosophy at the university in Geneva where he was eventually joined by his mother and sister.

With the war drawing to a close in 1944, Daniel, his mother, and sister were able to leave for London where they joined Bernard. Arrested in Riga as an undesirable writer in 1940, Bernard had been held for two years in an icy Soviet gulag before being permitted to travel to London. Daniel told me he'd been saved from going through a Stalinist phase in his political development because of the thuggery and *dacoitage* of both the Soviet and Polish Communist parties. The Soviets jailed his father and the Polish party expelled Deutscher for daring to think independently. Daniel had nothing but contempt for the Georgian seminarian and his coterie. I can also add here that Daniel never belonged to any political party. In England he entered the University of London to continue his studies in political science and economics. He graduated with a B.Sc. in politics, economics, and philosophy. Deutscher, too, was in London, building his reputation with articles for the *Economist* and the *Observer*. Daniel started at the *Economist* in 1951 after Deutscher left the journal. He remained on staff for nineteen years.

Jeanne Kérel worked for the National Center of Scientific Research in Paris and was at the London School of Economics writing her doctoral thesis, "The Cost of Living in Paris 1840–1954," when she met a young man who not only had brains and charm but, more to the point, spoke fluent French. She and Daniel married in 1956 with Isaac Deutscher serving as best man. Jeanne received her Ph.D. in economics the following year. In 1958 the young couple settled in Paris where, as Daniel's reputation grew, their home became a haven for visitors from around the world. The Singers were intellectual partners and made a formidable team. She was a critical participant in his work and traveled with him wherever his investigations and speaking engagements took him. At the same time, she continued her own studies in preparation for publication of a major study in economics. They had a marvelous, loving marriage for forty-four years.

While Jeanne continued her work at the National Center, Daniel reported on Gaullist France for the *Economist* and provided radio and television commentary for the national networks in Britain and Canada. When Cable News Network (CNN) tried repeatedly to interview him, he finally told them, "Look, I'm a professional journalist. This is how I make a living." He was saying that if they wanted to hear what he had to say, they had to hire him. It sometimes takes a Socialist to remind the capitalists how the game is played.

It was during this time that he developed a healthy scepticism regarding the objectivity of the British press, as best exemplified by his favorite ditty:

> *There is no way to bribe or twist*
> *Thank God, an honest English journalist*
> *But if you knew what he can do*
> *Unbribed: there's no occasion to.*

A defining moment, perhaps a watershed in Daniel's life, was the French student-worker revolt of May 1968. Daniel covered it as a journalist and was so moved by the experience that he took time off from the *Economist* to write what became the authoritative book on the events of that period. Arthur Wang had offered him an advance and the

Economist gave him six months off without pay to write it; Singer took more, returned briefly in 1969, and resigned for good in 1970, following the book's publication. The book was *Prelude to Revolution: France in May 1968*. The *New Republic* reviewer wrote at the time, "If Marx had been living in Paris during May 1968, he might have written this book." Daniel was now firmly established as a major political writer.

The Road to Gdansk, a book about the Polish uprising in 1980 that produced *Solidarnosc*, was published by Monthly Review Press in 1981. Daniel had a deep attachment to this democratic and exciting moment in the land of his birth and was saddened but not surprised when its revolutionary fervor was undercut and then betrayed. This book also included a prescient analysis of the "seeds of change" in the Soviet Union.

Also in 1981, Daniel was invited to become European correspondent for the *Nation*. He dictated his final column for the magazine from his hospital bed a few days before he died.

Nineteen eighty-eight brought the publication of *Is Socialism Doomed? The Meaning of Mitterand*, once again about the betrayal of a Socialist movement, this time in France.

Daniel's last book, his magnum opus, was *Whose Millennium? Theirs or Ours?*, published by Monthly Review Press in 1999. In it Daniel refutes those who believe that There Is No Alternative to capitalism. (He always referred to this idea by its acronym, TINA.) This masterful work not only proclaims that there is indeed an alternative but raises the development of that alternative to the level of an imperative.

Additionally, Daniel was a standout in the lineup of heavy hitters at the annual Socialist Scholars Conference in New York for many years and during the eighties and nineties, he contributed articles to *Monthly Review* and lectured at colleges and universities throughout the United States.

It is customary when examining the life of a writer to break it into five parts: Childhood and Education; Embarking on a Career; Early Work; In Full Flower as an Established Writer; and, finally, Loss of Illusions. I have described the first four of these segments. As for loss of illusions,

Daniel never had any. He never believed that the Stalinist endeavor was a Socialist paradigm. "More like Paradigm Lost," he quipped, ever the Restoration scholar.

Although Daniel did not think the May 1968 events in France would have any immediate effect, he insisted upon their long-term significance. "Internationalist, egalatarianist, spontaneous, and libertarian," he wrote, "the May Movement suddenly recalled what Socialism once stood for and showed what it could mean again in our times. It accomplished next to nothing, yet it holds a promise for the future." He felt and wrote similarly about the betrayal of *Solidarnosc*.

Daniel further insisted that Socialism hasn't failed, because it has never been tried. He identified himself with the stream of Socialism represented by Rosa Luxemburg. As noted earlier, he was never a member of any political party, but when Staughton Lynd mused at the 1999 Socialist Scholars Conference about starting a Marxist-Luxemburgist party, Daniel swiftly said, "I'll join." That was very likely as close as he ever came to signing up.

My wife Gladys and I spent the last two weeks of November 2000 in Paris in order to visit with Daniel and Jeanne each day during his final hospitalization. Daniel knew his life was ending. He was quite lucid and eager to talk and be talked to. He spoke, for instance, of his regret that some people have an almost mystical belief in inevitability. "It's true," he said, "that capitalism has within it the seeds of its own destruction, but only seeds in the sense of awareness and consciousness. Capitalism will have to be pushed off the stage." He went on to say,

> It will require a revolution. But not a revolution that necessarily requires bloodshed. Rather a revolution in the consciousness of people. And that will take time. And when that time comes, let's hope they get it right. But there is no guarantee. Rosa Luxemburg predicted Socialism or barbarism. I happen to be a Socialist, but if a better idea is produced, so be it. I would not want to foreclose on the future.

And, he added,

There is no certainty about the future. Humanity has the capability of destroying itself, and it may very well do so. The hope is with the younger generation. They will not be able to run away from the problems of the world the way our generation did and the next generation has. But our grandchildren will have to deal with the contradictions.

In *Whose Millennium?*, he wrote, "On the ground littered with broken models and shattered expectations, a new generation will now have to take the lead." And additionally he wrote, "Egalitarianism—not to be enforced with levelling and uniformity—must be at the very heart of any progressive project."

Michael Löwy said at the time of Daniel's death,

Daniel Singer was more than a journalist. He was at the same time a historian, writer, political essayist, and he distinguished himself with his verve, caustic spirit, mordant irony, and an obstinate fidelity to the Socialist dream.

Daniel's close friend István Mészáros summed up Daniel's character and life:

Daniel had a rare gift for relating to people and carrying them with his logic and passion. He was able to live in a world that is basically hostile to his ideas and yet hold strongly on to his beliefs. He could convince not only with the way he wrote, but could convince people also by touching them with the way of his life and the style of his life.

István added,

Daniel had a marvelous sense of proportion which could put even the most disheartening events in historical perspective. That is why, notwithstanding the critical distance which he always maintained from the Stalinist developments in Russia and elsewhere, including his native country, the adversaries of Socialism could never receive even one word of comfort, nor derive one gram of ammunition for their cold war efforts from his books and numerous other writings.

Daniel was an exemplar of the aphorism that the essence of life lies not in the defeat of our dreams, but in the joy that they were ever there at all. With virtually his last breath, he envisaged a Socialist future for humanity.

He loved to end his public lectures with the words spoken by Rosa Luxemburg the day before she was murdered, and I think it fitting to end now with them.

> Your order is built on sand. The revolution will raise its heart again, proclaiming to the sound of trumpets, I was, I am, I shall always be.

Percy Brazil

The Daniel Singer Millennium Foundation Prize

IN KEEPING WITH Daniel Singer's thesis that the promise of Socialism remains the last best hope for humanity, the Daniel Singer Prize Foundation invites submissions for the 2005 prize, to be awarded for an original essay of not more than 5,000 words exploring the following question: In the struggle for Socialism, what should be done to attain and sustain equality and justice? What should we mean by equality and justice?

Essays may be in any language and should be based on fresh, concrete ideas rather than on Utopian dreams. They will be judged by an international panel of distinguished scholars. The winner will be announced in December 2005 and will be invited to deliver a public lecture on the essay. Submissions must be delivered not later than August 31, 2005 to:

The Daniel Singer Millennium Prize Foundation
P.O. Box 334
Sherman, CT 06784

Donations to the foundation can also be sent to the above address.

Index